A YEAR OF GRACE

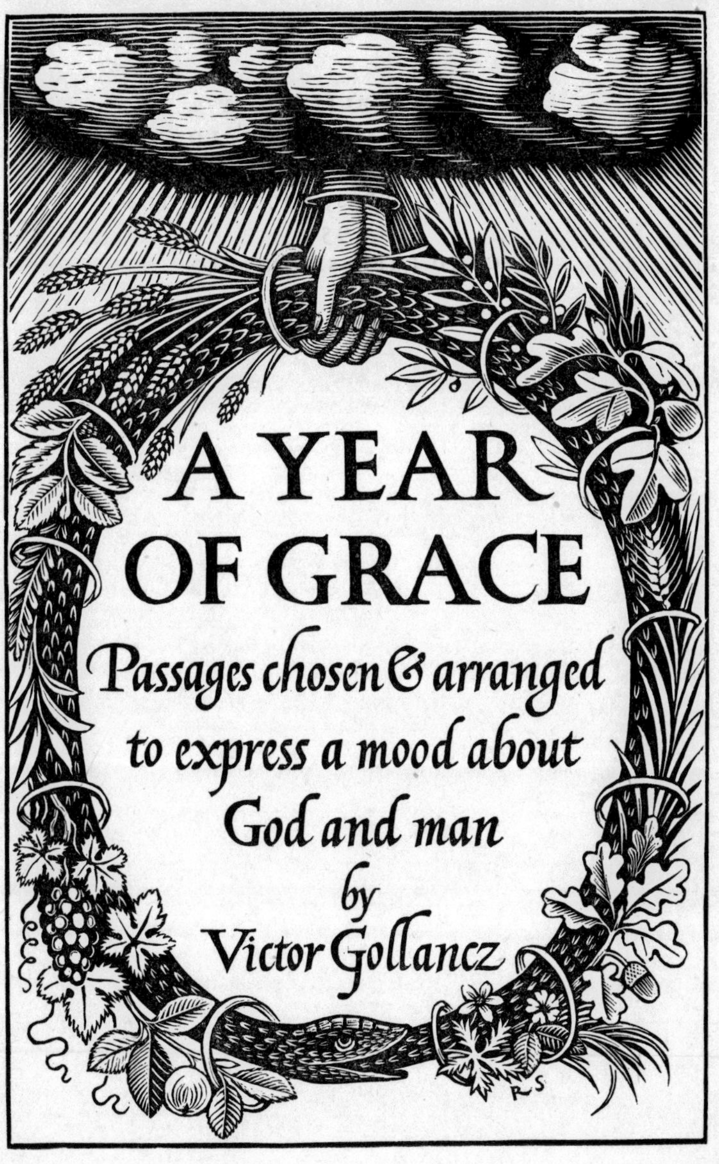
A YEAR
OF GRACE
Passages chosen & arranged
to express a mood about
God and man
by
Victor Gollancz
R.S

FIRST PUBLISHED BY
VICTOR GOLLANCZ LIMITED, LONDON,
AND PRINTED BY
THE CAMELOT PRESS, SOUTHAMPTON,
IN 1950
SECOND IMPRESSION 1950

FOR RUTH

AND TIMOTHY AND PETER VICTOR

AND IN GRATITUDE FOR A SAFE PASSAGE

God loves all existing things.

ST. THOMAS AQUINAS

I believed in God and in Nature, and in the triumph of good over evil.

GOETHE

I believe in the forgiveness of sins.

THE APOSTLES' CREED

* * *

God is the denial of denials.

MEISTER ECKHART

You must love the light so well
That no darkness will seem fell.

GEORGE MEREDITH

The fact of the instability of evil is the moral order of the world.

A. N. WHITEHEAD

* * *

God, having placed good and evil in our power, has given us full freedom of choice; he does not keep back the unwilling, but embraces the willing.

ST. JOHN CHRYSOSTOM

If what is commanded be not in the power of every one, all the numberless exhortations in the Scriptures, and also all the promises, threatenings, expostulations, reproofs, asseverations, benedictions, and maledictions, together with all the forms of precepts, must of necessity stand coldly useless.

ERASMUS

What if Pelagius after all were more right than his detractors?

H. D. LEWIS

* * *

All joys hail from paradise.

RABBI PINHAS OF KORETZ

It requires moral courage to grieve; it requires religious courage to rejoice.

KIERKEGAARD

The evil one is pleased with sadness and melancholy.

ST. FRANCIS DE SALES

* * *

O God, by whom the dignity of human nature was wondrously established.

FROM THE MASS

Man is a sun and a moon, and a heaven filled with stars.

PARACELSUS

Man was created so that he might lift up the Heavens.

RABBI MENDEL OF KOTZK

I say, no creature is so vile but it can boast of being; in proportion to its being is its power of being God, for whatever is being is God.

MEISTER ECKHART

How marvellous that I, a filthy clod,
May yet hold friendly converse with my God!

ANGELUS SILESIUS

Everyone must have two pockets, so that he can reach into the one or the other, according to his needs. In his right pocket are to be the words: "For my sake was the world created," and in his left: "I am earth and ashes."

RABBI BUNAM OF PZHYSHA

Wherever there is lost the consciousness that every man is an object of concern for us just because he is a man, civilisation and morals are shaken, and the advance to fully developed inhumanity is only a question of time.

ALBERT SCHWEITZER (1923)

He who sustains God's creatures is as though he had created them.

TANHUMA

* * *

For God freedom is necessary.

VLADIMIR SOLOVIEV

God has laid upon man the duty of being free, of safeguarding freedom of spirit, no matter how difficult that may be, or how much sacrifice and suffering it may require.

NICHOLAS BERDYAEV

Any morality which is against freedom is a bad morality.

JOHN MACMURRAY

* * *

God will do nothing without Man. If God works a miracle, he does it through Man.

PARACELSUS

Grace cannot do anything without [human] will, nor will anything without grace.

ST. JOHN CHRYSOSTOM

God indeed preserves the ship, but the mariner conducts it into harbour.

ERASMUS

The husbandman gets in the increase, but it was God that gave it.

ERASMUS

It is ours to offer what we can, His to supply what we cannot.

ST. JEROME

* * *

The present state of the world calls for a moral and spiritual revolution, revolution in the name of personality, of man, of every single person. This revolution should restore the hierarchy of values, now quite shattered, and place the value of human personality above the idols of production, technics, the state, the race or nationality, the collective.

NICHOLAS BERDYAEV

The Social Revolution will be moral, or it will not be.

CHARLES PÉGUY

A proneness to think of society as some entity other than its individual members . . . cannot be too severely condemned.

H. D. LEWIS

All our rational investigation and rational planning of the economic and political and social spheres is without meaning unless it is the means to one end—the living of the personal life of community in joy and freedom. To sacrifice life to its own conditions is the ultimate insincerity and the real denial of God.

JOHN MACMURRAY

* * *

The Hebrew form of thought rebels against the very idea of a distinction between the secular and the religious aspects of life.

JOHN MACMURRAY

He [Jesus] is not an idealist—for the same reason that he is not a materialist—because the distinction between the ideal and the material does not arise for him.

JOHN MACMURRAY

Whoever says that the words of the Torah are one thing and the words of the world another, must be regarded as a man who denies God.

RABBI PINHAS OF KORETZ

One should, and one must, truly live with all, but one should live with all in holiness, one should hallow all that one does in one's natural life. No renunciation is commanded. One eats in holiness, tastes the taste of food in holiness, and the table becomes an altar. One works in holiness, and he raises up the sparks which hide themselves in all tools. One walks in holiness across the fields, and the soft songs of all herbs, which they voice to God, enter into the song of our soul. One drinks in holiness to each other with one's companions, and it is as if they read together in the Torah. One dances the roundelay in holiness, and a brightness shines over the gathering. A husband is united with his wife in holiness, and the Shekhina rests over them.

MARTIN BUBER

* * *

There is much less difference between a mystic faith in God and an atheist's rational faith in mankind than between the former's faith and that of a Calvinist whose faith in God is rooted in the conviction of his own powerlessness and in his fear of God's power.

ERICH FROMM

Were the men who have best comprehended God—Sakya-Mouni, Plato, St. Paul, St. Francis d'Assisi, and St. Augustine (at some periods of his fluctuating life)—Deists or Pantheists? Such a question has no meaning. The physical and metaphysical proofs of the existence of God were quite indifferent to them. They felt the Divine within themselves. We must place Jesus in the first rank of this great family of the true sons of God. Jesus had no visions; God did not speak to him as to one outside of himself; God was in him; he felt himself with

God, and he drew from his heart all he said of his Father. He lived in the bosom of God by constant communication with him; he saw him not, but he understood him, without need of the thunder and the burning bush of Moses, of the revealing tempest of Job, of the oracle of the old Greek sages, of the familiar genius of Socrates, or of the angel Gabriel of Mohammed. . . . The highest consciousness of God which has existed in the bosom of humanity was that of Jesus.

ERNEST RENAN

Lastly, although there was no definite religious sentiment mingled with it, there was a continual perception of Sanctity in the whole of nature, from the slightest thing to the vastest; an instinctive awe, mixed with delight; an indefinable thrill, such as we sometimes imagine to indicate the presence of a disembodied spirit. I could only feel this perfectly when I was alone; and then it would often make me shiver from head to foot with the joy and fear of it, when after being some time away from hills I first got to the shore of a mountain river, where the brown water circled among the pebbles, or when I first saw the swell of distant land against the sunset, or the first low broken wall, covered with mountain moss . . . If we had to explain even the sense of bodily hunger to a person who had never felt it, we should be hard put to it for words; and the joy in nature seemed to me to come of a sort of heart-hunger, satisfied with the presence of a Great and Holy Spirit . . . These feelings remained in their full intensity till I was eighteen or twenty, and then, as the reflective and practical power increased, and the "cares of this world" gained upon me, faded gradually away, in the manner described by Wordsworth in his "Intimations of Immortality".

JOHN RUSKIN

* * *

In my State everyone may be saved after his own fashion.

FREDERICK THE GREAT

Some people indulge in quarrels, saying, "One cannot attain anything unless one worships our Krishna," or "Nothing can be gained without the worship of Kali, our Divine Mother," or "One cannot be saved without accepting the Christian religion." This is pure dogmatism. The dogmatist says, "My religion alone is true, and the religions of others are false." This is a bad attitude. God can be reached by different paths.

SRI RAMAKRISHNA

* * *

At this point we are confronted by the argument that such words as "good," "virtue" and the like have no definite meaning, but signify now this, now that, according to the degree of latitude, the colour of the skin, the local mythology. This is, of course, perfectly true. The content of judgments of value is demonstrably variable. Two important points should, however, be noted in this context. The first is that such judgments are passed by all human beings, that the category of value is universally employed. The second is that, as knowledge, sensibility and non-attachment increase, the contents of the judgments of value passed even by men belonging to dissimilar cultures tend to approximate. The ethical doctrines taught in the Tao Te Ching, by Gautama Buddha and his followers on the Lesser and above all the Greater Vehicle, in the Sermon on the Mount and by the best of the Christian saints, are not dissimilar. Among human beings who have reached a certain level of civilisation and of personal freedom from passion and social prejudice there exists a real *consensus gentium* in regard to ethical first principles.

ALDOUS HUXLEY

* * *

No upheaval or crude passion can put out the light of God's revelation of man and of the God-Man: the gates of Hell shall never prevail against it. That is why the source of that light will subsist however dense the surrounding darkness. And we must look upon ourselves not only as the last Romans, faithful to the past, to eternal truth and beauty, but also as the watchers for the dawn, looking towards the yet unseen day when the sun of the new Christian renaissance shall rise.

NICHOLAS BERDYAEV

. . . So when the winter of the world and Man's fresh Fall
When democratic Death feared no more the heart's coldness
Shall be forgotten,
O Love, return to the dying world, as the light
Of morning, shining in all regions, latitudes
And households of high heaven within the heart. . . .

Now falls the night of the world:—O Spirit moving upon the
  waters
Your peace instil
In the animal heat and splendour of the blood—
The hot gold of the sun that flames in the night
And knows not down-going
But moves with the revolutions in the heavens.

The thunders and the fires and acclamations
Of the leaves of spring are stilled, but in the night
The Holy Ghost speaks in the whispering leaves.
O wheat-ear shining like a fire and the bright gold,
O water brought from far to the dying gardens!

Bring peace to the famine of the heart and lips,
And to the Last Man's loneliness
Of those who dream they can bring back sight to the blind!
You are the Night
When the long hunt for Nothing is at rest
In the Blind Man's Street, and in the human breast
The hammer of Chaos is stilled.
                    Be then the sleep
When Judas gives again the childish kiss
That once his mother knew—and wash the stain
From the darkened hands of the universal Cain.

EDITH SITWELL

FOREWORD

I WOULD wish to call attention to the subtitle of this book: "passages chosen and arranged to express a mood about God and man." Every anthology, of course, is compiled with a purpose: the aim may be, for instance, to bring together the most beautiful or the least familiar flowers from a particular field of literature, or merely to print in one volume passages that have given unusual pleasure to the anthologist. But this is an anthology with a purpose in perhaps a peculiar, even rather polemical, sense; and the subtitle indicates what the purpose is.

Anti-religious humanism and anti-humanistic religion are both very prevalent today. The mood expressed in this anthology is therefor an unfashionable one.

While I have not attempted any artificial continuity, by such a device, for instance, as linking passages of my own, the book is nevertheless intended and designed to be read from beginning to end as a consecutive whole: as if, that is to say, it were a continuous piece of writing by one hand, all now appearing for the first time. And I hope that even the most familiar passages may neither be passed over nor be skipped: that, for instance, the fifth chapter of St. Matthew or the extracts from the Prometheus Unbound may be read anew, in their order, as attentively as the Hasidic stories or the Paradise of the Fathers or Erich Fromm. I should of course be pleased if the book might subsequently be found useful for the bedside.

I wish to emphasise the word mood—"to express a mood about God and man." Mood, not doctrine. There is a section, for instance, entitled "Good and Evil." The reader who expects to find in it any intellectually satisfying solution of "the problem of evil" will be disappointed.

The book is full of contradictions, some of them merely apparent (even according to human understanding), some of them real (according to human understanding). But the mood is a consistent one—the contradictions are part of it.

Men have one mood at one time and another at another. The mood of this anthology (with its contradictions) is the mood that has dominantly been mine ever since, as a very small boy, I sniffed the air and sang for joy amid the late autumn leaves in a narrow London garden. Now, when I am fifty seven, "the dust and stones of the street" are still, by God's grace, "as precious as gold" to me; the corn is still "orient and immortal wheat"; and "what my heart first awaking whispered the world was," that and nothing other my heart whispers still. But I would not care to suggest that the mood, though dominant, has been invariable. There have been hours and days (as there will be hours and days again) when, appalled by the evil in myself and others, I could no longer feel that love, with pity and mercy as its chief attributes, was the only reality, and that I, being real, was in communion with it. There was even one whole year, following the year of grace to which my title refers, when I lived second by second in the hell of terror and despair. It is not irrelevant to my theme to mention that only by the greatest effort of will, if even so, can I realise in recollection that terror and that despair, which now appear nothing to me; and that when I live again in those days, as I often do, I live in the love that faithfully cared for me and saw me through to safety.

V. G.

BRIMPTON

New Year's Day, 1950.

CONTENTS

TO BEGIN

SHEMA YISRAEL

Hear, O Israel: the Lord our God, the Lord is One.

And thou shalt love the Lord thy God with all thine heart, and with all thy soul, and with all thy might. And these words, which I command thee this day, shall be upon thine heart: and thou shalt teach them diligently unto thy children, and shalt talk of them when thou sittest in thine house, and when thou walkest by the way, and when thou liest down, and when thou risest up. And thou shalt bind them for a sign upon thine hand, and they shall be for frontlets between thine eyes. And thou shalt write them upon the door posts of thy house, and upon thy gates.

DEUTERONOMY

THE SERMON ON THE MOUNT

And seeing the multitudes, he went up into a mountain: and when he was set, his disciples came unto him:

And he opened his mouth, and taught them, saying,

Blessed are the poor in spirit: for their's is the kingdom of heaven.

Blessed are they that mourn: for they shall be comforted.

Blessed are the meek: for they shall inherit the earth.

Blessed are they which do hunger and thirst after righteousness: for they shall be filled.

Blessed are the merciful: for they shall obtain mercy.

Blessed are the pure in heart: for they shall see God.

Blessed are the peace-makers: for they shall be called the children of God.

Blessed are they which are persecuted for righteousness' sake: for their's is the kingdom of heaven.

Blessed are ye, when men shall revile you, and persecute you, and shall say all manner of evil against you falsely, for my sake.

Rejoice, and be exceeding glad: for great is your reward in heaven: for so persecuted they the prophets which were before you.

Ye are the salt of the earth: but if the salt have lost his savour, wherewith shall it be salted? it is thenceforth good for nothing, but to be cast out, and to be trodden under foot of men.

Ye are the light of the world. A city that is set on an hill cannot be hid.

Neither do men light a candle, and put it under a bushel, but on a candlestick; and it giveth light unto all that are in the house.

Let your light so shine before men, that they may see your good works, and glorify your Father which is in heaven.

Think not that I am come to destroy the law, or the prophets: I am not come to destroy, but to fulfil.

For verily I say unto you, Till heaven and earth pass, one jot or one tittle shall in no wise pass from the law, till all be fulfilled.

Whosoever therefore shall break one of these least commandments, and shall teach men so, he shall be called the least in the kingdom of heaven: but whosoever shall do and teach them, the same shall be called great in the kingdom of heaven.

For I say unto you, That except your righteousness shall exceed the righteousness of the scribes and Pharisees, ye shall in no case enter into the kingdom of heaven.

Ye have heard that it was said by them of old time, Thou shalt not kill; and whosoever shall kill shall be in danger of the judgment:

But I say unto you, That whosoever is angry with his brother without a cause shall be in danger of the judgment: and whosoever shall say to his brother, Raca, shall be in danger of the council: but whosoever shall say, Thou fool, shall be in danger of hell fire.

Therefore if thou bring thy gift to the altar, and there rememberest that thy brother hath ought against thee;

Leave there thy gift before the altar, and go thy way; first be reconciled to thy brother, and then come and offer thy gift.

Agree with thine adversary quickly, whiles thou art in the way with him; lest at any time the adversary deliver thee to the judge, and the judge deliver thee to the officer, and thou be cast into prison.

Verily I say unto thee, Thou shalt by no means come out thence, till thou hast paid the uttermost farthing.

Ye have heard that it was said by them of old time, Thou shalt not commit adultery:

But I say unto you, That whosoever looketh on a woman to lust after her hath committed adultery with her already in his heart.

And if thy right eye offend thee, pluck it out, and cast it from thee: for it is profitable for thee that one of thy members should perish, and not that thy whole body should be cast into hell.

And if thy right hand offend thee, cut it off, and cast it from thee: for it is profitable for thee that one of thy members should perish, and not that thy whole body should be cast into hell.

It hath been said, Whosoever shall put away his wife, let him give her a writing of divorcement:

But I say unto you, That whosoever shall put away his wife, saving for the cause of fornication, causeth her to commit adultery: and whosoever shall marry her that is divorced committeth adultery.

Again, ye have heard that it hath been said by them of old time, Thou shalt not forswear thyself, but shalt perform unto the Lord thine oaths:

But I say unto you, Swear not at all; neither by heaven; for it is God's throne:

Nor by the earth; for it is his footstool: neither by Jerusalem; for it is the city of the great King.

Neither shalt thou swear by thy head, because thou canst not make one hair white or black.

But let your communication be, Yea, yea; Nay, nay: for whatsoever is more than these cometh of evil.

Ye have heard that it hath been said, An eye for an eye, and a tooth for a tooth:

But I say unto you, That ye resist not evil: but whosoever shall smite thee on thy right cheek, turn to him the other also.

And if any man will sue thee at the law, and take away thy coat, let him have thy cloke also.

And whosoever shall compel thee to go a mile, go with him twain.

Give to him that asketh thee, and from him that would borrow of thee turn not thou away.

Ye have heard that it hath been said, Thou shalt love thy neighbour, and hate thine enemy.

But I say unto you, Love your enemies, bless them that curse you, do good to them that hate you, and pray for them which despitefully use you, and persecute you;

That ye may be the children of your Father which is in heaven: for he maketh his sun to rise on the evil and on the good, and sendeth rain on the just and on the unjust.

For if ye love them which love you, what reward have ye? do not even the publicans the same?

And if ye salute your brethren only, what do ye more than others? do not even the publicans so?

Be ye therefore perfect, even as your Father which is in heaven is perfect.

Take heed that ye do not your alms before men, to be seen of them: otherwise ye have no reward of your Father which is in heaven.

Therefore when thou doest thine alms, do not sound a trumpet before thee, as the hypocrites do in the synagogues and in the streets, that they may have glory of men. Verily I say unto you, They have their reward.

But when thou doest alms, let not thy left hand know what thy right hand doeth:

That thine alms may be in secret: and thy Father which seeth in secret himself shall reward thee openly.

And when thou prayest, thou shalt not be as the hypocrites

are: for they love to pray standing in the synagogues and in the corners of the streets, that they may be seen of men. Verily I say unto you, They have their reward.

But thou, when thou prayest, enter into thy closet, and when thou hast shut thy door, pray to thy Father which is in secret; and thy Father which seeth in secret shall reward thee openly.

But when ye pray, use not vain repetitions, as the heathen do: for they think that they shall be heard for their much speaking.

Be not ye therefore like unto them: for your Father knoweth what things ye have need of, before ye ask him.

After this manner therefore pray ye: Our Father which art in heaven, Hallowed be thy name.

Thy kingdom come. Thy will be done in earth, as it is in heaven.

Give us this day our daily bread.

And forgive us our debts, as we forgive our debtors.

And lead us not into temptation, but deliver us from evil: For thine is the kingdom, and the power, and the glory, for ever. Amen.

For if ye forgive men their trespasses, your heavenly Father will also forgive you:

But if ye forgive not men their trespasses, neither will your Father forgive your trespasses.

Moreover when ye fast, be not, as the hypocrites, of a sad countenance: for they disfigure their faces, that they may appear unto men to fast. Verily I say unto you, They have their reward.

But thou, when thou fastest, anoint thine head, and wash thy face;

That thou appear not unto men to fast, but unto thy Father which is in secret: and thy Father, which seeth in secret, shall reward thee openly.

Lay not up for yourselves treasures upon earth, where moth and rust doth corrupt, and where thieves break through and steal:

But lay up for yourselves treasures in heaven, where neither moth nor rust doth corrupt, and where thieves do not break through nor steal:

For where your treasure is, there will your heart be also.

The light of the body is the eye: if therefore thine eye be single, thy whole body shall be full of light.

But if thine eye be evil, thy whole body shall be full of darkness. If therefore the light that is in thee be darkness, how great is that darkness!

No man can serve two masters: for either he will hate the one, and love the other; or else he will hold to the one, and despise the other. Ye cannot serve God and mammon.

Therefore I say unto you, Take no thought for your life, what ye shall eat, or what ye shall drink; nor yet for your body, what ye shall put on. Is not the life more than meat, and the body than raiment?

Behold the fowls of the air: for they sow not, neither do they reap, nor gather into barns; yet your heavenly Father feedeth them. Are ye not much better than they?

Which of you by taking thought can add one cubit unto his stature?

And why take ye thought for raiment? Consider the lilies of the field, how they grow; they toil not, neither do they spin;

And yet I say unto you, That even Solomon in all his glory was not arrayed like one of these.

Wherefore, if God so clothe the grass of the field, which to day is, and to morrow is cast into the oven, shall he not much more clothe you, O ye of little faith?

Therefore take no thought, saying, What shall we eat? or, What shall we drink? or, Wherewithal shall we be clothed?

(For after all these things do the Gentiles seek:) for your heavenly Father knoweth that ye have need of all these things.

But seek ye first the kingdom of God, and his righteousness; and all these things shall be added unto you.

Take therefore no thought for the morrow: for the morrow shall take thought for the things of itself. Sufficient unto the day is the evil thereof.

Judge not, that ye be not judged.

For with what judgment ye judge, ye shall be judged: and with what measure ye mete, it shall be measured to you again.

And why beholdest thou the mote that is in thy brother's eye, but considerest not the beam that is in thine own eye?

Or how wilt thou say to thy brother, Let me pull out the mote out of thine eye; and behold, a beam is in thine own eye?

Thou hypocrite, first cast out the beam out of thine own eye; and then shalt thou see clearly to cast out the mote out of thy brother's eye.

Give not that which is holy unto the dogs, neither cast ye your pearls before swine, lest they trample them under their feet, and turn again and rend you.

Ask, and it shall be given you; seek, and ye shall find; knock, and it shall be opened unto you:

For every one that asketh receiveth; and he that seeketh findeth; and to him that knocketh it shall be opened.

Or what man is there of you, whom if his son ask bread, will he give him a stone?

Or if he ask a fish, will he give him a serpent?

If ye then, being evil, know how to give good gifts unto your children, how much more shall your Father which is in heaven give good things to them that ask him?

Therefore all things whatsoever ye would that men should do to you, do ye even so to them: for this is the law and the prophets.

Enter ye in at the strait gate: for wide is the gate, and broad is the way, that leadeth to destruction, and many there be which go in thereat:

Because strait is the gate, and narrow is the way, which leadeth unto life, and few there be that find it.

Beware of false prophets, which come to you in sheep's clothing, but inwardly they are ravening wolves.

Ye shall know them by their fruits. Do men gather grapes of thorns, or figs of thistles?

Even so every good tree bringeth forth good fruit; but a corrupt tree bringeth forth evil fruit.

A good tree cannot bring forth evil fruit, neither can a corrupt tree bring forth good fruit.

Every tree that bringeth not forth good fruit is hewn down, and cast into the fire.

Wherefore by their fruits ye shall know them.

Not every one that saith unto me, Lord, Lord, shall enter into the kingdom of heaven; but he that doeth the will of my Father which is in heaven.

Many will say to me in that day, Lord, Lord, have we not prophesied in thy name? and in thy name have cast out devils? and in thy name done many wonderful works?

And then will I profess unto them, I never knew you: depart from me, ye that work iniquity.

Therefore whosoever heareth these sayings of mine, and doeth them, I will liken him unto a wise man, which built his house upon a rock:

And the rain descended, and the floods came, and the winds blew, and beat upon that house; and it fell not: for it was founded upon a rock.

And every one that heareth these sayings of mine, and doeth them not, shall be likened unto a foolish man, which built his house upon the sand:

And the rain descended, and the floods came, and the winds blew, and beat upon that house; and it fell: and great was the fall of it.

And it came to pass, when Jesus had ended these sayings, the people were astonished at his doctrine.

For he taught them as one having authority, and not as the scribes.

ST. MATTHEW

FIRST PART

I. GOD'S MERCY AND LOVE

Dolce cresc:
cresc:
cresc:
cresc:
p
p
p
p
dolce

And God remembered Noah, and every living thing, and all the cattle that was with him in the ark: and God made a wind to pass over the earth, and the waters asswaged;

The fountains also of the deep and the windows of heaven were stopped, and the rain from heaven was restrained;

And the waters returned from off the earth continually: and after the end of the hundred and fifty days the waters were abated.

And the ark rested in the seventh month, on the seventeenth day of the month, upon the mountains of Ararat.

And the waters decreased continually until the tenth month: in the tenth month, on the first day of the month, were the tops of the mountains seen.

And it came to pass at the end of forty days, that Noah opened the window of the ark which he had made:

And he sent forth a raven, which went forth to and fro, until the waters were dried up from off the earth.

Also he sent forth a dove from him, to see if the waters were abated from off the face of the ground;

But the dove found no rest for the sole of her foot, and she returned unto him into the ark, for the waters were on the face of the whole earth: then he put forth his hand, and took her, and pulled her in unto him into the ark.

And he stayed yet other seven days; and again he sent forth the dove out of the ark;

And the dove came in to him in the evening; and, lo, in her mouth was an olive leaf pluckt off: so Noah knew that the waters were abated from off the earth.

GENESIS

And Abraham drew near, and said, Wilt thou also destroy the righteous with the wicked?

Peradventure there be fifty righteous within the city: wilt thou also destroy and not spare the place for the fifty righteous that are therein?

That be far from thee to do after this manner, to slay the righteous with the wicked: and that the righteous should be as the wicked, that be far from thee: Shall not the Judge of all the earth do right?

And the Lord said, If I find in Sodom fifty righteous within the city, then I will spare all the place for their sakes.

And Abraham answered and said, Behold now, I have taken upon me to speak unto the Lord, which am but dust and ashes: Peradventure there shall lack five of the fifty righteous: wilt thou destroy all the city for lack of five? And he said, If I find there forty and five, I will not destroy it.

And he spake unto him yet again, and said, Peradventure there shall be forty found there. And he said, I will not do it for forty's sake.

And he said unto him, Oh let not the Lord be angry, and I will speak: Peradventure there shall thirty be found there. And he said, I will not do it, if I find thirty there.

And he said, Behold now, I have taken upon me to speak unto the Lord: Peradventure there shall be twenty found there. And he said, I will not destroy it for twenty's sake.

And he said, Oh let not the Lord be angry, and I will speak yet but this once: Peradventure ten shall be found there. And he said, I will not destroy it for ten's sake.

And the Lord went his way, as soon as he had left communing with Abraham: and Abraham returned unto his place.

GENESIS

Then said the Lord, Doest thou well to be angry?

So Jonah went out of the city, and sat on the east side of the city, and there made him a booth, and sat under it in the shadow, till he might see what would become of the city.

And the Lord God prepared a gourd, and made it to come up over Jonah, that it might be a shadow over his head, to deliver him from his grief. So Jonah was exceeding glad of the gourd.

But God prepared a worm when the morning rose the next day, and it smote the gourd that it withered.

And it came to pass, when the sun did arise, that God prepared a vehement east wind; and the sun beat upon the head of Jonah, that he fainted, and wished in himself to die, and said, It is better for me to die than to live.

And God said to Jonah, Doest thou well to be angry for the gourd? And he said, I do well to be angry, even unto death.

Then said the Lord, Thou hast had pity on the gourd, for the which thou hast not laboured, neither madest it grow; which came up in a night, and perished in a night:

And should not I spare Nineveh, that great city, wherein are more than sixscore thousand persons that cannot discern between their right hand and their left hand; and also much cattle?

JONAH

For to be greatly strong is thine at all times; and the might of thine arm who shall withstand? because the whole world before thee is as a grain in a balance, and as a drop of dew that at the morning cometh down upon the earth. But thou hast mercy on all men, because thou hast power to do all things, and thou overlookest the sins of men to the end they may repent. For thou lovest all things that are, and abhorrest none of the things which thou didst make; for never wouldest thou have formed anything if thou didst hate it. And how would anything have endured, except thou hadst willed it? Or that which was not called by thee, how would it have been preserved? But thou sparest all things, because they are thine, O Sovereign Lord, thou lover of men's lives;

For thine incorruptible spirit is in all things.

THE WISDOM OF SOLOMON

I never give God thanks for loving me, because he cannot help it; whether he would or no it is his nature to.

MEISTER ECKHART

Love ruleth all forever; even They,
The Three in One, are subject to its sway.

ANGELUS SILESIUS

It longeth to the proper goodness of our Lord God courteously to excuse man.

JULIANA OF NORWICH

With Thee 'tis one to behold and to pity. Accordingly, Thy mercy followeth every man so long as he liveth, whithersoever he goeth, even as Thy glance never quitteth any.

NICHOLAS OF CUSA

The ministering angels wanted to sing a hymn at the destruction of the Egyptians, but God said: "My children lie drowned in the sea, and you would sing?"

RABBI JOHANAN

A fire once broke out in Drokeret, but the neighbourhood of Rabbi Huna was spared. The people thought that it was due to the merit of Rabbi Huna, but they were told in a dream that Rabbi Huna's merits were too great, and the sparing of his neighbourhood from fire too small a matter to attribute the marvel to him, and that it was due to the merits of a certain woman who used to heat her oven, and place it at the disposal of her neighbours.

THE TALMUD

Once a poor villager came to the town to earn money for the Passover. After nightfall on his return to the village, laden with purchases, his horse and wagon fell into a pit made swampy by the spring rains. A rich man, passing by, heard his cries, and helped his own driver to extricate the villager. He roped the latter's wagon to his carriage, and accompanied the poor man to his hut. On beholding the abject poverty in which the villager and his family lived, the magnate gave him several hundred thalers.

When the wealthy man died and was brought before the Heavenly Tribunal, it seemed as if his demerits because of certain business dealings would result in his sentence to Purgatory. Suddenly an Angel of Mercy appeared, and asked that the Heavenly Scales be used to determine whether the worth of his good deeds outweighed his sins. When consent was given, the Angel placed on the Scale of Good Deeds the poor villager and his family whom the rich man had saved from misery. But this did not suffice. The horse and the wagon were added, but they did not aid. Then the Angel placed on the Scale the mud and mire out of which the rich man had helped rescue the villager, and lo, the Scale of Good Deeds dipped with its weight, and the magnate was saved from Purgatory.

RABBI ISRAEL OF RIZHYN

From eternity to eternity no spark of wrath ever was or ever will be in the holy triune God. If a wrath of God was anywhere it must be everywhere; if it burned once it must burn to all eternity. For everything that is in God Himself is boundless, incapable of any increase or diminution, without beginning and without end. It is as good sense, as consistent with the divine nature, to say that God, moved by a wrath in and from Himself, began the creation as that a wrath in God ever punished any part of it. Nature and creature is the only source from whence and the seat in which wrath, pain, and vexation can dwell. Nor can they ever break forth either in nature or creature but so far as either this or that has lost its state in God. . . . God, considered in Himself, is as infinitely separate from all possibility of doing hurt or willing pain to any creature as He is from a possibility of suffering pain or hurt from the hand of a man. And this, for this plain reason, because He is in Himself, in His Holy Trinity, nothing else but the boundless abyss of all that is good, and sweet, and amiable, and therefore stands in the utmost contrariety to everything that is not a blessing—in an eternal impossibility of willing and intending a moment's pain or hurt to any creature. For from this unbounded source of goodness and perfection nothing but infinite streams of blessing are perpetually flowing forth upon all nature and creature in a more incessant plenty than rays of light stream from the sun. And as the sun has but one nature and can give forth nothing but the blessings of light, so the holy triune God has but one nature and intent towards all the creation, which is to pour forth the riches and sweetness of His divine perfections upon everything that is capable of them and according to its capacity to receive them.

The goodness of God breaking forth into a desire to communicate good was the cause and the beginning of the creation. Hence it follows that to all eternity God can have no thought or intent towards the creature but to communicate good; because He made the creature for this sole end, to receive good. The first motive towards the creature is unchangeable; it takes its rise from God's desire to communicate good, and it is an eternal impossibility that anything can ever come from God as His will and purpose towards the creature but that same love and goodness which first created it; He must always will that to it which He willed at the creation of it. This is the amiable nature of God. He is the Good, the unchangeable, overflowing fountain of good that sends forth nothing but good to all eternity. He is the Love itself, the unmixed, unmeasurable Love, doing nothing but from love, giving nothing but gifts of love to everything that He has made; requiring nothing of all His creatures but the spirit and fruits of that love which brought them into being. Oh, how sweet is this contemplation of the height and depth of the riches of Divine Love! With what attraction must it draw every thoughtful man to return love for love to this overflowing fountain of boundless goodness!

WILLIAM LAW

What a paltry logic to say, God is righteousness and justice as well as love, and therefore His love cannot help or forgive the sinner till His justice or righteous wrath has satisfaction! Every word here is in full ignorance of the things spoken of. . . .

Let me ask these dividers of the divine nature what different shares or different work had the righteousness and the love of God in the creation of man? Was there then something done by the love of God which ought not to be ascribed to the righteousness of God? Who can be so weak as to say this? But if the love and the righteousness of God is one, as God is one, and had but one work in the creation of man, it must be the highest absurdity to say that in the redemption of man the love and the righteousness of God must have not only different but contrary works, that the love of God cannot act till the righteousness of God, as something different from it, is first satisfied.

All that which we call the attributes of God are only so many human ways of our conceiving that abyssal All which can neither be spoken nor conceived by us. And this way of thinking and speaking of God is suitable to our capacities, has its good use, and helps to express our adoration of Him and His perfections. But to conclude and contend that there must therefore be different qualities in God, answerable to or according to our different ways of thinking and speaking of His perfections, is rather blaspheming than truly glorifying His name and nature. For omnipotent love, inconceivable goodness, is that unity of God which we can neither conceive, as it is in itself, nor divide into this or that.

WILLIAM LAW

The god of Power is not God, but Superman created by man in his own worst image. He is not the God who lives in our hearts when we love and pity and forgive, but Cæsar become absolute. Communion with the God of mercy and love is worship in spirit and in truth, but to bend our knee to the god of Power is blasphemy.

Human "justice" robs men of their liberty, humiliates them, and in some of the more backward countries burns them up with electric current or hangs them by the neck until they are dead. But the god of Power is even crueller: he is the god not merely of punishment and vengeance but of eternal Hell. What has this remote monster to do with the living God, the loving communion of Persons? With the Father who loves all His creatures in the Son, and the Son who, as all humanity, loves the Father?

X

The most evil and sinful social relations between men have been attributed to the relationship between God and man, God and his world.

NICHOLAS BERDYAEV

Sadism is evident even in Christian doctrine, for instance in that of endless punishment in hell.

NICHOLAS BERDYAEV

Hell-fire will ne'er be quenched, you say. Now hear:
Repent, and quench it with a single tear!

ANGELUS SILESIUS

ON ANOTHER'S SORROW

Can I see another's woe,
And not be in sorrow too?
Can I see another's grief,
And not seek for kind relief?

Can I see a falling tear,
And not feel my sorrow's share?
Can a father see his child
Weep, nor be with sorrow filled?

Can a mother sit and hear
An infant groan, an infant fear?
No, no! never can it be!
Never, never can it be!

And can He who smiles on all
Hear the wren with sorrows small,
Hear the small bird's grief and care,
Hear the woes that infants bear—

And not sit beside the nest,
Pouring pity in their breast,
And not sit the cradle near,
Weeping tear on infant's tear?

And not sit both night and day,
Wiping all our tears away?
Oh no! never can it be!
Never, never can it be!

He doth give His joy to all:
He becomes an infant small,
He becomes a man of woe,
He doth feel the sorrow too.

Think not thou canst sigh a sigh,
And thy Maker is not by:
Think not thou canst weep a tear,
And thy Maker is not near.

Oh, He gives to us His joy,
That our grief He may destroy:
Till our grief is fled and gone
He doth sit by us and moan.

BLAKE

FIRST PART

II. A READING OF CHRIST

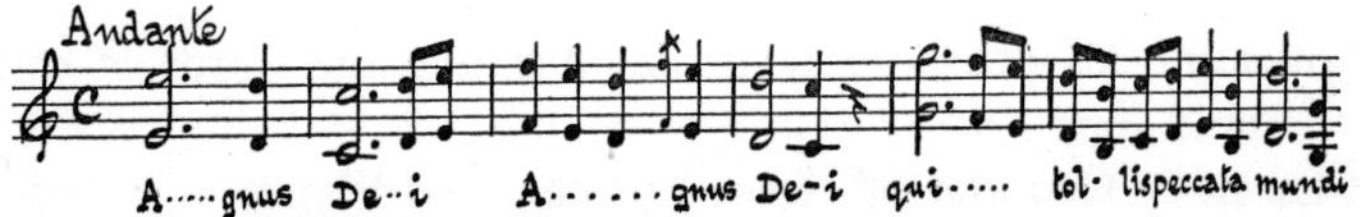
Andante
A·····gnus De··i A······gnus De-i qui····· tol· lispeccata mundi

For in that he himself hath suffered being tempted, he is able to succour them that are tempted.

HEBREWS

Or what was it which he took on
That he might bring Salvation?
A Body subject to be Tempted,
From neither pain nor grief Exempted?
Or such a body as might not feel
The passions that with Sinners deal?
Yes, but they say he never fell.
Ask Caiaphas; for he can tell.

BLAKE (from *The Everlasting Gospel*)

Then I see the Saviour over me,
Spreading his beams of love, and dictating the words of this mild song . . .
I am not a God afar off, I am a brother and friend;
Within your bosoms I reside, and you reside in me;
Lo! we are One; forgiving all Evil; Not seeking recompense. . . .

BLAKE (from *Jerusalem*)

Again, our blessed Saviour says, "Without me ye can do nothing." The question is, when or how a man may be said to be without Christ. Consider again the vine and its branches. A branch can then only be said to be without its vine when the vegetable life of the vine is no longer in it. This is the only sense in which we can be said to be without Christ; when He is no longer in us as a principle of a heavenly life we are then without Him, and so can do nothing; that is, nothing that is good or holy. A Christ not in us is the same thing as a Christ not ours. If we are only so far with Christ as to own and receive the history of His birth, person, and character, if this is all that we have of Him, we are as much without Him, as much left to ourselves, as little helped by Him as those evil spirits which cried out, "We know thee who thou art, the holy one of God." . . .

Consider how was it that the lame and blind, the lunatic and leper, the publican and sinner, found Christ to be their Saviour and to do all that for them which they wanted to be done to them? It was because they had a real desire of having that which they asked for, and therefore in true faith and prayer applied to Christ, that His Spirit and power might enter into them and heal that which they wanted and desired to be healed in them. Every one of these said in faith and desire, "Lord, if you wilt, thou canst make me whole." And the answer was always this, "According to thy faith, so be it done unto thee." This is Christ's answer now, and thus it is done to every one of us at this day, as our faith is, so is it done unto us. And here lies the whole reason of our falling short of the salvation of Christ; it is because we have no will to it.

But you will say, Do not all Christians desire to have Christ to be their Saviour? Yes. But here is the deceit; all would have Christ to be their Saviour in the *next* world and to help them into Heaven when they die by His power and merits with God. But this is not willing Christ to be thy Saviour; for His salvation, if it is had, must be had in *this* world; if He saves thee it must be done in this life, by changing and altering all that is within thee, by helping thee to a new heart, as He helped the blind to see, the lame to walk, and the dumb to speak. For to have salvation from Christ is nothing else but to be made like unto Him; it is to have His humility and meekness, His mortification and self-denial, His renunciation of the spirit, wisdom, and honours of this world, His love of God, His desire of doing God's will and seeking only His honour. To have these tempers formed and begotten in thy heart is to have salvation from Christ. But if thou willest not to have these tempers brought forth in thee, if thy faith and desire does not seek and cry to Christ for them in the same reality as the lame asked to walk and the blind to see, then thou must be said to be unwilling to have Christ to be thy Saviour.

WILLIAM LAW

Should Christ be born a thousand times anew,
Despair, O man, unless he's born in you!

ANGELUS SILESIUS

God is a little lamb, you say. 'Tis true.
How helps you this unless you're his lamb too?

ANGELUS SILESIUS

I think, therefore, that the purpose and cause of the incarnation was that He might illuminate the world by His wisdom and excite it to the love of Himself.

PETER ABÉLARD

How cruel and unjust it appears that anyone should have demanded the blood of the innocent as any kind of ransom, or have been in any way delighted with the death of the innocent, let alone that God should have found the death of His Son so acceptable, that through it He should have been reconciled to the whole world. . . .

It seems to us, however, that we are justified by the blood of Christ and reconciled to God in the following way. His Son took our nature and persevered in instructing us both in words and deed even unto death. This was the singular grace shown us, through which He more abundantly bound us to Himself by love; so that, set on fire as we are by so great a benefit from the Divine grace, true charity should fear nothing at all. . . .

And so our redemption is that supreme love manifested in our case by the passion of Christ, which not only delivers us from the bondage of sin, but also acquires for us the liberty of the sons of God; so that we may fulfil all things from the love rather than from the fear of Him, who, as He Himself bears witness, showed us grace so great that no greater can be found. No man, says He, has greater love than this, that he lay down his life for his friends.

PETER ABÉLARD

The death of Christ justifies us [i.e. makes us just or good by making it easier for us not to sin], inasmuch as through it charity is excited in our hearts.

PETER THE LOMBARD

After all, the fundamental idea both of St. John and of St. Paul is simply that . . . the contemplation of [Christ's] life and death gives other men the power, as nothing else has done, to overcome temptation and to lead lives of love like His.

HASTINGS RASHDALL

The death was an incident in a real human life. . . . The particular mode of death was the outcome and culmination of the mode of life which He had chosen. . . . The death came to Him as the direct and necessary consequence of His faithfulness to His Messianic calling, of a life devoted to the doing of God's will and the service of His fellow-men. . . . His death has been more to Christendom than other martyr-deaths, just because He was so much more than other martyrs, because His life was more than other lives; because His Messianic calling was a unique calling; because, in fact, of all that has led Christendom to see in that life the fullest revelation or incarnation of God. There is nothing in the fact that the necessity for the death did not arise from any objective demand for expiation which can diminish the gratitude and the love which such a death, taken in connexion with such a life, was calculated to awaken towards the Sufferer. And if the character which is revealed by that Sufferer be the character of God Himself, then the love that is awakened towards Christ will also be love of the Father whom in a supreme and unique way Christ reveals. And that love will express itself in repentance and regeneration of life. When the efficacy of Christ's death is attributed . . . to the moral effects which it produces, that . . . does nothing to diminish the love which the contemplation of such a death is calculated to awaken in the mind of him who believes that the whole life and death of Christ was one of love for His fellows, and that in Him who so lived and died the love of God was uniquely and supremely manifested. Such a view of the matter does tend, no doubt, to attribute the saving efficacy of Christ's work not *merely* to the death, but to the teaching, the character, the life of Him who died. It tends, in short, to represent Christ's death as only a part, though a necessary part, of that whole incarnation or self-revelation of God, the object of which was to make known God's nature and His will, to instruct men in the way of salvation, and to excite in them that love which would inspire sorrow for past sin and give the power to avoid sin in the future. . . .

If we can say that in humanity generally there is *some* revelation of God—a growing, developing, progressive revelation, and a higher degree of such revelation in the heroes, the saints, the prophets, the founders and reformers of great religions, then the idea of an incarnation becomes possible. If we can say that God is to some extent revealed in all men, then it becomes possible to think of Him as making a supreme, culminating, unique revelation of Himself in one human character and life. . . . It is only through human love at its highest that we can understand the divine love. Gratitude for ordinary human love —love pushed to the point of self-sacrifice—is the strongest power that exists in this world for attracting to that goodness of which love is the supreme element the soul that has it not, and for producing repentance for that lack of love in which sin essentially consists. In proportion as it is felt that human love reveals the love of God, the answering love which the self-sacrifice awakens will be love to God as well as love to man. The love shown by Christ will have this regenerating effect in a supreme degree in proportion as it is felt that the love of Christ supremely reveals the character of God. . . .

Christ's whole life was a sacrifice which takes away sin in the only way in which sin can really be taken away, and that is by making the sinner actually better. . . . The insistence of popular religious teaching upon the atoning efficacy of Christ's death loses all ethical value in proportion as it isolates and disconnects the atoning efficacy of that death from the saving influence of Christ's life, His teaching, His character. . . .

And here I would particularly insist upon the importance in this connexion of our Lord's *teaching*—that is to say, of the moral ideal which it represents and the corresponding belief as to the character of the God whose nature is revealed by that moral ideal. For many of the earlier fathers, it is not too much to say, it was *primarily* by His teaching that Christ became the Saviour of the world. It was upon the appeal which this teaching made to the reason, the heart, the conscience of mankind that they based their conviction that in Him the Logos was supremely revealed: it was precisely in and through His teaching that His "Divinity" was manifested. . . . The recognition of the supreme importance of Christ's teaching about God and human life, and a profound veneration for the character which that teaching exhibits, are an absolutely essential condition of our being able to discover any permanent meaning in the traditional doctrines of the atonement and the incarnation. It is upon the appeal which that ideal, embodied in the teaching and character of Christ, has made and still makes to the conscience of mankind that any intelligible modern interpretation of the Catholic doctrine of His divinity must depend. . . .

Unless the teaching of Christ does present itself to us as containing the eternally true pith and marrow of the moral ideal, and a true representation of the essential character of God, we have no basis for any theory of Christ's divinity, or even for exalting Him to that central and supreme position among the prophets which would be assigned to Him by most Unitarians. Reverence for Christ as a teacher must be the foundation of any Christology which can find a meaning for the idea of a divine incarnation in Jesus. And it may, with equal truth, be said that it is only in the light of Christ's teaching that we can find any present meaning in a theology which makes much of His death: for it is only in the light of His teaching about the love of God and the supreme place of love in the ethical ideal for man that the cross can be given its true meaning as the symbol of self-sacrifice—not of mere negative self-renunciation or self-denial for self-denial's sake, but of self-sacrifice inspired and directed by love of that moral ideal which is fully realised in God, and by love of the men who are made in the image of God. It is because it is the typical expression of that spirit of self-sacrifice which dominated His life that the death of Christ has played, and will continue to play, a large part in its saving efficacy. When most of the theories about Christ's death have become obsolete and unintelligible the cross will still be the symbol, known and understood by all, of this central feature in Christ's character and in the ideal for which He lived and died. . . .

More and more, I believe, the great spiritual dividing line between men will be the line between those who really accept Christ's ideal of life and those who do not. Those who heartily believe in that ideal will probably in most cases find it possible to accept also Christ's outlook upon the universe as a universe guided and controlled by a conscious Will the nature and purposes of which may best be understood in the light of that same ideal. Those who believe that love is the thing of highest value in human life will generally believe also that "God is love indeed, and love Creation's highest law." But even if through intellectual perplexity they fail to do so, such persons may be placed among those of whom Christ said, "He that is not against us is for us," though they follow not with the great army of Christ's professed disciples. Many, doubtless, are being saved by this ideal who do not call themselves by Christ's name or formally associate themselves with those who do.

HASTINGS RASHDALL

Jesus marks the point in history at which it becomes possible for man to adopt consciously as his own purpose the purpose which is already inherent in his own nature.

JOHN MACMURRAY

Poor creature though I be, I am the hand and foot of Christ. I move my hand and my hand is wholly Christ's hand, for deity is become inseparably one with me. I move my foot, and it is aglow with God.

ST. SYMEON THE NEW THEOLOGIAN

Become as God; then ah! what joy is thine!
Thou drinkest God with every sip of wine.

ANGELUS SILESIUS

The Word of God became man that you also may learn from a man how a man becomes a God.

CLEMENT OF ALEXANDRIA

We are far too apt to limit and mechanise the great doctrine of the Incarnation, which forms the centre of the Christian faith. Whatever it may mean, it means at least this—that in the conditions of human life we have access, as nowhere else, to the inmost nature of the divine.

A. S. PRINGLE-PATTISON

Every Christian must be Christ himself.

ANGELUS SILESIUS

On account of Him there have come to be many Christs in the world, even all who, like Him, loved righteousness and hated iniquity.

ORIGEN

[Christ] does not really teach one anything, but by being brought into his presence one becomes something. And everybody is predestined to his presence. Once at least in his life each man walks with Christ to Emmaus.

OSCAR WILDE

[The Grand Inquisitor speaks to Christ.] Thou didst desire man's free love, that he should follow Thee freely, enticed and taken captive by Thee. In place of the rigid ancient law, man must hereafter with free heart decide for himself what is good and what is evil, having only Thy image before him as his guide. . . . Thou didst not come down from the Cross when they shouted to Thee, mocking and reviling Thee, "Come down from the cross and we will believe that Thou art He." Thou didst not come down, for again Thou wouldst not enslave man by a miracle, and didst crave faith given freely, not based on miracle. Thou didst crave for free love and not the base raptures of the slave before the might that has overawed him for ever.

DOSTOEVSKY

Truth nailed upon the cross compels nobody, oppresses no one; it must be accepted and confessed freely; its appeal is addressed to free spirits. . . . A divine Truth panoplied in power, triumphant over the world and conquering souls, would not be consonant with the freedom of man's spirit, and so the mystery of Golgotha is the mystery of liberty. . . . Every time in history that man has tried to turn crucified Truth into coercive truth he has betrayed the fundamental principle of Christ.

NICHOLAS BERDYAEV

I saw myself, in dream, a youth, almost a boy, in a low-pitched wooden church. The slim wax candles gleamed, spots of red, before the old pictures of the saints.

A ring of coloured light encircled each tiny flame. Dark and dim it was in the church. . . . But there stood before me many people. All fair-haired, peasant heads. From time to time they began swaying, falling, rising again, like the ripe ears of wheat, when the wind of summer passes in slow undulation over them.

All at once some man came up from behind and stood beside me.

I did not turn towards him; but at once I felt that this man was Christ.

Emotion, curiosity, awe overmastered me suddenly. I made an effort . . . and looked at my neighbour.

A face like every one's, a face like all men's faces. The eyes looked a little upwards, quietly and intently. The lips closed, but not compressed; the upper lip, as it were, resting on the lower; a small beard parted in two. The hands folded and still. And the clothes on him like every one's.

"What sort of Christ is this?" I thought. "Such an ordinary, ordinary man! It can't be!"

I turned away. But I had hardly turned my eyes away from this ordinary man when I felt again that it really was none other than Christ standing beside me.

Again I made an effort over myself. . . . And again the same face, like all men's faces, the same everyday though unknown features.

And suddenly my heart sank, and I came to myself. Only then I realised that just such a face—a face like all men's faces—is the face of Christ.

TURGENEV

CHRIST IN THE UNIVERSE

With this ambiguous earth
His dealings have been told us. These abide:
The signal to a maid, the human birth,
The lesson, and the young Man crucified.

But not a star of all
The innumerable host of stars has heard
How He administered this terrestrial ball.
Our race have kept their Lord's entrusted Word.

Of His earth-visiting feet
None knows the secret, cherished, perilous,
The terrible, shamefast, frightened, whispered, sweet,
Heart-shattering secret of His way with us.

No planet knows that this
Our wayside planet, carrying land and wave,
Love and life multiplied, and pain and bliss,
Bears, as chief treasure, one forsaken grave.

Nor, in our little day,
May His devices with the heavens be guessed,
His pilgrimage to thread the Milky Way,
Or His bestowals there be manifest.

But, in the eternities,
Doubtless we shall compare together, hear
A million alien Gospels, in what guise
He trod the Pleiades, the Lyre, the Bear.

O be prepared, my soul!
To read the inconceivable, to scan
The million forms of God those stars unroll
When, in our turn, we show to them a Man.

ALICE MEYNELL

FIRST PART

III. JOY AND PRAISE

Allegretto
p

§ 1

Arise, you little glancing wings, and sing your infant joy!
Arise, and drink your bliss, for every thing that lives is holy!

BLAKE (from *Visions of the Daughters of Albion*)

The Angel who presided at my birth
Said,—"Little Creature, formed for joy and mirth,
Go love, without the help of anything on earth."

BLAKE

Nothing is voiceless in the world: God hears always
In all created things His echo and His praise.

ANGELUS SILESIUS

It is good if man can bring about that God sings within him.

RABBI ELIMELEKH OF LIZHENSK

See, this kingdom of God is now found within us. The grace of the Holy Spirit shines forth and warms us, and, overflowing with many and varied scents into the air around us, regales our senses with heavenly delight, as it fills our hearts with joy inexpressible.

ST. SERAPHIM OF SAROV

There are halls in the heavens above that open but to the voice of song.

THE ZOHAR

The giving of thanks maketh entreaty on behalf of the feeble before God.

THE PARADISE OF THE FATHERS

I will praise thee; for I am fearfully and wonderfully made: marvellous are thy works; and that my soul knoweth right well.

FROM PSALM 139

Bless the Lord, O my soul. O Lord my God, thou art very great; thou art clothed with honour and majesty.

Who coverest thyself with light as with a garment: who stretchest out the heavens like a curtain:

Who layeth the beams of his chambers in the waters: who maketh the clouds his chariot: who walketh upon the wings of the wind:

Who maketh his angels spirits; his ministers a flaming fire. . . .

He sendeth the springs into the valleys, which run among the hills.

They give drink to every beast of the field: the wild asses quench their thirst.

By them shall the fowls of the heaven have their habitation, which sing among the branches.

He watereth the hills from his chambers: the earth is satisfied with the fruit of thy works.

He causeth the grass to grow for the cattle, and herb for the service of man: that he may bring forth food out of the earth;

And wine that maketh glad the heart of man, and oil to make his face to shine, and bread which strengtheneth man's heart.

The trees of the Lord are full of sap; the cedars of Lebanon, which he hath planted;

Where the birds make their nests: as for the stork, the fir trees are her house.

The high hills are a refuge for the wild goats; and the rocks for the conies.

He appointed the moon for seasons: the sun knoweth his going down.

Thou makest darkness, and it is night: wherein all the beasts of the forest do creep forth. . . .

Man goeth forth unto his work and to his labour until the evening.

O Lord, how manifold are thy works! in wisdom hast thou made them all: the earth is full of thy riches.

So is this great and wide sea, wherein are things creeping innumerable, both small and great beasts.

There go the ships: there is that leviathan, whom thou hast made to play therein.

These wait all upon thee; that thou mayest give them their meat in due season.

That thou givest them they gather: thou openest thine hand, they are filled with good. . . .

Thou sendest forth thy spirit, they are created: and thou renewest the face of the earth.

The glory of the Lord shall endure for ever: the Lord shall rejoice in his works. . . .

FROM PSALM 104

Though our mouths were full of song as the sea, and our tongues of exultation as the multitude of its waves, and our lips of praise as the wide-extended firmament; though our eyes shone with light like the sun and the moon, and our hands were spread forth like the eagles of heaven, and our feet were swift as hinds, we should still be unable to thank thee and to bless thy name, O Lord our God and God of our fathers, for one thousandth or one ten thousandth part of the bounties which thou hast bestowed upon our fathers and upon us.

THE HEBREW MORNING SERVICE

A man should utter daily a hundred Benedictions.

RABBI MEIR

BENEDICTIONS FOR VARIOUS OCCASIONS FROM THE HEBREW PRAYER BOOK

Blessed art thou, O Lord our God, King of the universe, who openest the eyes of the blind.

Blessed art thou, O Lord our God, King of the universe, who clothest the naked.

Blessed art thou, O Lord our God, King of the universe, who loosest them that are bound.

Blessed art thou, O Lord our God, King of the universe, who raisest up them that are bowed down.

Blessed art thou, O Lord our God, King of the universe, who givest strength to the weary.

On drinking wine:

Blessed art thou, O Lord our God, King of the universe, who createst the fruit of the vine.

On eating Food, other than Bread, prepared from Grain:

Blessed art thou, O Lord our God, King of the universe, who createst various kinds of food.

On eating Fruit which grows on Trees:

Blessed art thou, O Lord our God, King of the universe, who createst the fruit of the tree.

On eating Fruit which grows on the Ground:

Blessed art thou, O Lord our God, King of the universe, who createst the fruit of the earth.

On eating Flesh, Fish, Eggs, Cheese, etc., or drinking anything except Wine:

Blessed art thou, O Lord our God, King of the universe, by whose word all things exist.

On smelling Fragrant Woods or Barks:

Blessed art thou, O Lord our God, King of the universe, who createst fragrant woods.

On smelling Odorous Plants:

Blessed art thou, O Lord our God, King of the universe, who createst odorous plants.

On smelling Odorous Fruits:

Blessed art thou, O Lord our God, King of the universe, who givest a goodly scent to fruits.

On smelling Fragrant Spices:

Blessed art thou, O Lord our God, King of the universe, who createst divers kinds of spices.

On smelling Fragrant Oils:

Blessed art thou, O Lord our God, King of the universe, who createst fragrant oil.

On seeing Lightning, Falling Stars, Mountains, or Great Deserts:

Blessed art thou, O Lord our God, King of the universe, who hast made the creation.

At the sight of the Sea:

Blessed art thou, O Lord our God, King of the universe, who hast made the great sea.

On seeing Beautiful Trees or Animals:

Blessed art thou, O Lord our God, King of the universe, who hast such as these in thy world.

On seeing Trees blossoming the first time in the Year:

Blessed art thou, O Lord our God, King of the universe, who hast made thy world lacking in nought, but hast produced therein goodly creatures and goodly trees wherewith to give delight unto the children of men.

On seeing a Sage distinguished for his Knowledge of the Law:

Blessed art thou, O Lord our God, King of the universe, who hast imparted of thy wisdom to them that fear thee.

On seeing Wise Men distinguished for other than Sacred Knowledge:

Blessed art thou, O Lord our God, King of the universe, who hast given of thy wisdom to flesh and blood.

On seeing strangely formed Persons, such as Giants or Dwarfs:

Blessed art thou, O Lord our God, King of the universe, who variest the forms of thy creatures.

On tasting any Fruit for the first time in the season; on entering into possession of a new House or Land; or on using new Raiment for the first time:

Blessed art thou, O Lord our God, King of the universe, who hast kept us in life, and hast preserved us, and hast enabled us to reach this season.

On hearing Good Tidings:

Blessed art thou, O Lord our God, King of the universe, who art good, and dispensest good.

Persons who have been in peril of their lives, during journeys by sea or land, in captivity or sickness, upon their deliverance or recovery say the following:

Blessed art thou, O Lord our God, King of the universe, who vouchsafest benefits unto the undeserving, who hast also vouchsafed all good unto me.

At the Wedding Service:

Blessed art thou, O Lord our God, King of the universe, who hath created all things to thy glory.

Blessed art thou, O Lord our God, King of the universe, Creator of man.

Blessed art thou, O Lord our God, King of the universe, who hast made man in thine image, after thy likeness, and hast prepared unto him, out of his very self, a perpetual fabric. Blessed art thou, O Lord, Creator of man.

O make these loved companions greatly to rejoice, even as of old thou didst gladden thy creature in the garden of Eden. Blessed art thou, O Lord, who makest bridegroom and bride to rejoice.

Blessed art thou, O Lord our God, King of the universe, who hast created joy and gladness, bridegroom and bride, mirth and exultation, pleasure and delight, love, brotherhood, peace and fellowship. Soon may there be heard in the cities of Judah, and in the streets of Jerusalem, the voice of joy and gladness, the voice of the bridegroom and the voice of the bride, the jubilant voice of bridegrooms from their canopies, and of youths from their feasts of song. Blessed art thou, O Lord, who makest the bridegroom to rejoice with the bride.

At a Circumcision:

Blessed be he that cometh.

O give thanks unto the Lord; for he is good; for his loving-kindness endureth for ever. This little child, may he become great. Even as he has entered into the covenant, so may he enter into the Law, the nuptial canopy, and into good deeds.

At the Moment before Death:

Blessed be His name, whose glorious kingdom is for ever and ever.

SAINT FRANCIS' PRAISE OF CREATED THINGS

Most High, Omnipotent, Good Lord.
Thine be the praise, the glory, the honour, and all benediction.
To Thee alone, Most High, they are due,
and no man is worthy to mention Thee.

Be Thou praised, my Lord, with all Thy creatures,
above all Brother Sun,
who gives the day and lightens us therewith.

And he is beautiful and radiant with great splendour,
of Thee, Most High, he bears similitude.

Be Thou praised, my Lord, of Sister Moon and the stars,
in the heaven hast Thou formed them, clear and precious and comely.

Be Thou praised, my Lord, of Brother Wind,
and of the air, and the cloud, and of fair and of all weather,
by the which Thou givest to Thy creatures sustenance.

Be Thou praised, my Lord, of Sister Water,
which is much useful and humble and precious and pure.

Be Thou praised, my Lord, of Brother Fire,
by which Thou hast lightened the night,
and he is beautiful and joyful and robust and strong.

Be Thou praised, my Lord, of our Sister Mother Earth,
which sustains and hath us in rule,
and produces divers fruits with coloured flowers and herbs....

Praise ye and bless my Lord, and give Him thanks,
and serve Him with great humility.

THE MIRROR OF PERFECTION

§ 2

Give not over thy soul to sorrow; and afflict not thyself in thine own counsel. Gladness of heart is the life of a man; and the joyfulness of a man is length of days. Love thine own soul, and comfort thy heart: and remove sorrow far from thee; for sorrow hath destroyed many, and there is no profit therein. Envy and wrath shorten a man's days; and care bringeth old age before the time. A cheerful and good heart will have a care of his meat and diet.

ECCLESIASTICUS

Now the Spirit speaketh expressly, that in the latter times some shall depart from the faith, giving heed to seducing spirits, and doctrines of devils;

Speaking lies in hypocrisy; having their conscience seared with a hot iron;

Forbidding to marry, and commanding to abstain from meats, which God hath created to be received with thanksgiving of them which believe and know the truth.

For every creature of God is good, and nothing to be refused, if it be received with thanksgiving. . . .

I TIMOTHY

Man will hereafter be called to account for depriving himself of the good things which the world lawfully allows.

ABBA ARIKA ("RAB")

My deepest and most unshakable conviction—and if it is heretical, so much that the worse for orthodoxy—is that whatever all the thinkers and doctors have said, it is not God's will at all to be loved by us *against* the Creation, but rather glorified *through* the Creation and with the Creation as our starting-point. That is why I find so many devotional books intolerable. The God who is set up against the Creation and who is somehow jealous of his own works is, to my mind, nothing but an idol.

GABRIEL MARCEL

When the Baalshem* was still seeking the proper way to serve the Lord, he found that the observance of the Sabbath according to the injunctions of the later Rabbis practically prohibited any movement, and filled a man with anxiety lest he should transgress some strict regulation. He believed that this contradicted the command of Isaiah to "call the Sabbath a delight." He pondered on this for a long time, and in the night he had a dream:

An Angel took him up to Heaven and showed him two vacant chairs in the highest place in Paradise, brilliantly illumined, as if with vari-coloured gems. "For whom are these intended?" he asked. "For thee," was the answer, "if thou makest use of thy intelligence; and also for a man whose name and residence I am writing down for thee."

He was next taken to Gehenna at its deepest spot, and shown two vacant seats, burning with a hellish flame. "For whom are these intended?" he asked. "For thee," was the answer, "if thou makest no use of thy intelligence; and also for a man whose name and residence I am writing down for thee."

In his dream the Baalshem visited the man who was to be his companion in Paradise. He found him living among non-Jews, ignorant of Judaism, except that on the Sabbath he gave a banquet for his non-Jewish friends, wherein he greatly rejoiced.

"Why do you hold this banquet?" asked the Baalshem. "I know not," replied the man, "but I recall that in my youth my parents prepared admirable meals on Saturday, and sang many songs; hence I do the same." The Baalshem wished to instruct him in Judaism, inasmuch as he had been born a Jew. But the power of speech left him for the moment, since he realised that the man's joy in the Sabbath would be marred if he knew all his shortcomings in the performance of religious duties.

The Baalshem then departed, in his dream, to the place where his companion in Gehenna dwelt. He found the man to be a strict observer of Judaism, always in anxiety lest his conduct was not correct, and passing the entire Sabbath day as if he were sitting on hot coals. The Baalshem wished to rebuke him, but once more the power of speech was taken away from him, since he realised that the man would never understand that he was doing wrong.

Thereupon the Baalshem meditated on the whole matter, and evolved his new system of observance, whereby God is served in joy which comes from the heart.

HASIDIC LEGEND

* See note p. 553.

God Himself dressed Eve's hair, that the first woman might better please the first man.

JEWISH LEGEND

The pleasure of cohabitation is a religious one, giving joy also to the Divine Presence.

THE ZOHAR

The voice of my beloved! behold, he cometh leaping upon the mountains, skipping upon the hills.

My beloved is like a roe or a young hart: behold, he standeth behind our wall, he looketh forth at the windows, shewing himself through the lattice.

My beloved spake, and said unto me, Rise up, my love, my fair one, and come away.

For, lo, the winter is past, the rain is over and gone;

The flowers appear on the earth; the time of the singing of birds is come, and the voice of the turtle is heard in our land;

The fig tree putteth forth her green figs, and the vines with the tender grape give a good smell. Arise, my love, my fair one, and come away.

O my dove, that art in the clefts of the rock, in the secret places of the stairs, let me see thy countenance, let me hear thy voice; for sweet is thy voice, and thy countenance is comely. . . .

How beautiful are thy feet with shoes, O prince's daughter! the joints of thy thighs are like jewels, the work of the hands of a cunning workman.

Thy navel is like a round goblet, which wanteth not liquor: thy belly is like an heap of wheat set about with lilies.

Thy two breasts are like two young roes that are twins.

Thy neck is as a tower of ivory; thine eyes like the fishpools in Heshbon, by the gate of Bath-rabbim; thy nose is as the tower of Lebanon which looketh toward Damascus.

Thine head upon thee is like Carmel, and the hair of thine head like purple; the king is held in the galleries.

How fair and how pleasant art thou, O love, for delights!

This thy stature is like to a palm tree, and thy breasts to clusters of grapes.

I said, I will go up to the palm tree, I will take hold of the boughs thereof: now also thy breasts shall be as clusters of the vine, and the smell of thy nose like apples;

And the roof of thy mouth like the best wine for my beloved, that goeth down sweetly, causing the lips of those that are asleep to speak.

I am my beloved's, and his desire is toward me.

Come, my beloved, let us go forth into the field; let us lodge in the villages.

Let us get up early to the vineyards; let us see if the vine flourish, whether the tender grape appear, and the pomegranates bud forth: there will I give thee my loves.

The mandrakes give a smell, and at our gates are all manner of pleasant fruits, new and old, which I have laid up for thee, O my beloved. . . .

Set me as a seal upon thine heart, as a seal upon thine arm: for love is strong as death; jealousy is cruel as the grave: the coals thereof are coals of fire, which hath a most vehement flame.

Many waters cannot quench love, neither can the floods drown it: if a man would give all the substance of his house for love, it would utterly be contemned. . . .

FROM THE SONG OF SOLOMON

§ 3

I place before my inward eyes myself with all that I am—my body, soul, and all my powers—and I gather round me all the creatures which God ever created in heaven, on earth, and in all the elements, each one severally with its name, whether birds of the air, beasts of the forest, fishes of the water, leaves and grass of the earth, or the innumerable sand of the sea, and to these I add all the little specks of dust which glance in the sunbeams, with all the little drops of water which ever fell or are falling from dew, snow, or rain, and I wish that each of these had a sweetly sounding stringed instrument, fashioned from my heart's inmost blood, striking on which they might each send up to our dear and gentle God a new and lofty strain of praise for ever and ever. And then the loving arms of my soul stretch out and extend themselves towards the innumerable multitude of all creatures, and my intention is, just as a free and blithesome leader of a choir stirs up the singers of his company, even so to turn them all to good account by inciting them to sing joyously, and to offer up their hearts to God. "Sursum corda."

HENRY SUSO

No Business Serious seemd but one; No Work
But one was found; and that did in me lurk.
    D'ye ask me What? It was with Cleerer Eys
To see all Creatures full of Deities;
Especialy Ones self: And to Admire
The Satisfaction of all True Desire:
Twas to be Pleasd with all that God hath done;
Twas to Enjoy *even All* beneath the Sun:
Twas with a Steddy and immediat Sence
To feel and measure all the Excellence
Of Things: Twas to inherit Endless Treasure,
And to be fild with Everlasting Pleasure:

To reign in Silence, and to Sing alone
To see, love, Covet, hav, Enjoy and Prais, in one:
To Prize and to be ravishd: to be true,
Sincere and Single in a Blessed View
To prize and prais.

THOMAS TRAHERNE (from *Dumnesse*)

THE SALUTATION

I

These little Limmes,
These Eys and Hands which here I find,
These rosie Cheeks wherwith my Life begins,
Where have ye been? Behind
What Curtain were ye from me hid so long!
Where was? in what Abyss, my Speaking Tongue?

2

When silent I,
So many thousand thousand yeers,
Beneath the Dust did in a Chaos lie,
How could I Smiles or Tears,
Or Lips or Hands or Eys or Ears perceiv?
Welcom ye Treasures which I now receiv.

3

I that so long
Was Nothing from Eternitie,
Did little think such Joys as Ear or Tongue,
To Celebrat or See:
Such Sounds to hear, such Hands to feel, such Feet,
Beneath the Skies, on such a Ground to meet.

4

New Burnisht Joys!
Which yellow Gold and Pearl excell!
Such Sacred Treasures are the Lims in Boys,
In which a Soul doth Dwell;
Their Organized Joynts, and Azure Veins
More Wealth include, then all the World contains.

5

From Dust I rise,
And out of Nothing now awake,
These Brighter Regions which salute mine Eys,
A Gift from God I take.
The Earth, the Seas, the Light, the Day, the Skies,
The Sun and Stars are mine; if those I prize.

6

Long time before
I in my Mother's Womb was born,
A God preparing did this Glorious Store,
The World for me adorne.
Into this Eden so Divine and fair,
So Wide and Bright, I com his Son and Heir.

7

A Stranger here
Strange Things doth meet, Strange Glories See;
Strange Treasures lodg'd in this fair World appear,
Strange all, and New to me.
But that they mine should be, who nothing was,
That Strangest is of all, yet brought to pass.

THOMAS TRAHERNE

THE ESTATE

I

But shall my Soul no Wealth possess,
No Outward Riches have?
Shall Hands and Eys alone express
Thy Bounty? Which the Grave
Shall strait devour. Shall I becom
With in my self a Living Tomb
Of Useless Wonders? Shall the fair and brave
And great Endowments of my Soul lie Waste,
Which ought to be a fountain, and a Womb
Of Praises unto Thee?
Shall there no Outward Objects be,
For these to see and Taste?
Not so, my God, for Outward Joys and Pleasures
Are even the Things for which my Lims are Treasures.

2

My Palate is a Touch-Stone fit
To taste how Good Thou art:
And other Members second it
Thy Praises to impart.
There's not an Ey that's framd by Thee,
But ought thy Life and Lov, to see.
Nor is there, Lord, upon mine Head an Ear,
But that the Musick of thy Works should hear.
Each Toe, each Finger framed by thy Skill,
Ought Oyntments to Distill.
Ambrosia, Nectar, Wine should flow
From evry Joynt I owe,
Or Things more Rich; while they thy Holy Will
Are Instruments adapted to fulfill.

3

They ought, my God, to be the Pipes,
And Conduits of thy Prais.
Mens Bodies were not made for Stripes,
Nor any thing but Joys.
They were not made to be alone:
But made to be the very Throne
Of Blessedness, to be like Suns, whose Raies,
Dispersed, Scatter many thousand Ways.
They Drink in Nectars, and Disburs again
In Purer Beams, those Streams,
Those Nectars which are causd by Joys.
And as the spacious Main
Doth all the Rivers which it Drinks, return,
Thy Love receivd doth make the Soul to burn.

4

Elixars richer are then Dross,
And Ends are more Divine
Then are the Means: But Dung and Loss
Materials (tho they Shine
Like Gold and Silver) are, compard
To what thy Spirit doth regard,
Thy Will require, thy Lov embrace, thy Mind
Esteem, thy Nature most Illustrious find.
These are the Things wher with we God reward.
Our Love he more doth prize:
Our Gratitude is in his Eys,
Far richer then the Skies.
And those Affections which we do return,
Are like the Lov which in Himself doth burn.

5

We plough the very Skies, as well
As Earth, the Spacious Seas
Are ours; the Stars all Gems excell.
The Air was made to pleas
The Souls of Men: Devouring fire
Doth feed and Quicken Mans Desire.
The Orb of Light in its wide Circuit movs,
Corn for our Food Springs out of very Mire,
Our Fences and Fewel grows in Woods and Groves,
Choice Herbs and Flowers aspire
To Kiss our Feet; Beasts court our Lovs.
How Glorious is Mans Fate
The Laws of God, the Works he did Create,
His Ancient Ways, are His, and my Estate.

THOMAS TRAHERNE

FROM "CENTURIES OF MEDITATION"

Will you see the infancy of this sublime and celestial greatness? Those pure and virgin apprehensions I had in my infancy, and that divine light wherewith I was born, are the best unto this day wherein I can see the universe. By the gift of God they attended me into the world, and by His special favour I remember them till now. Verily they form the greatest gift His wisdom could bestow, for without them all other gifts had been dead and vain. They are unattainable by books, and therefore I will teach them by experience. Pray for them earnestly, for they will make you angelical and wholly celestial. Certainly Adam in Paradise had not more sweet and curious apprehensions of the world than I when I was a child.

All appeared new and strange at first, inexpressibly rare and delightful and beautiful. I was a little stranger which at my entrance into the world was saluted and surrounded with innumerable joys. My knowledge was Divine; I knew by intuition those things which since my apostacy I collected again by the highest reason. My very ignorance was advantageous. I seemed as one brought into the estate of innocence. All things were spotless and pure and glorious; yea, and infinitely mine and joyful and precious. I knew not that there were any sins, or complaints or laws. I dreamed not of poverties, contentions, or vices. All tears and quarrels were hidden from mine eyes. Everything was at rest, free and immortal. I knew nothing of sickness or death or exaction. In the absence of these I was entertained like an angel with the works of God in their splendour and glory; I saw all in the peace of Eden; heaven and earth did sing my Creator's praises, and could not make more melody to Adam than to me. All Time was Eternity, and a perpetual Sabbath. Is it not strange that an infant should be heir of the whole world, and see those mysteries which the books of the learned never unfold?

The corn was orient and immortal wheat which never should be reaped nor was ever sown. I thought it had stood from everlasting to everlasting. The dust and stones of the street were as precious as gold: the gates were at first the end of the world. The green trees when I saw them first through one of the gates transported and ravished me; their sweetness and unusual beauty made my heart to leap, and almost mad with ecstasy, they were such strange and wonderful things. The Men! O what venerable and reverend creatures did the aged seem! Immortal Cherubims! And young men glittering and sparkling angels, and maids strange seraphic pieces of life and beauty! Boys and girls tumbling in the street were moving jewels: I knew not that they were born or should die. But all things abided eternally as they were in their proper places. Eternity was manifest in the Light of the Day, and something infinite behind everything appeared, which talked with my expectation and moved my desire. The City seemed to stand in Eden or to be built in Heaven. The streets were mine, the temple was mine, the people were mine, their clothes and gold and silver were mine, as much as their sparkling eyes, fair skins, and ruddy faces. The skies were mine, and so were the sun and moon and stars, and all the world was mine; and I the only spectator and enjoyer of it. I knew no churlish proprieties, nor bounds nor divisions; but all proprieties and divisions were mine, all treasures and the possessors of them. So that with much ado I was corrupted, and made to learn the dirty devices of this world, which now I unlearn, and become, as it were, a little child again that I may enter into the Kingdom of God.

THOMAS TRAHERNE

If we had never before looked upon the earth, but suddenly came to it man or woman grown, set down in the midst of a summer mead, would it not seem to us a radiant vision? The hues, the shapes, the song and life of birds, above all the sun-light, the breath of heaven, resting on it; the mind would be filled with its glory, unable to grasp it, hardly believing that such things could be mere matter and no more. Like a dream of some spirit-land it would appear, scarce fit to be touched lest it should fall to pieces, too beautiful to be long watched lest it should fade away. So it seemed to me as a boy, sweet and new like this each morning; and even now, after the years that have passed, and the lines they have worn in the forehead, the summer mead shines as bright and fresh as when my foot first touched the grass.

RICHARD JEFFERIES

FROM "THE DAY OF THE DAUGHTER OF HADES"

[*Skiageneia, daughter of Persephone and Pluto, has hidden herself in the chariot bringing her mother to visit Demeter on Enna. She spends her brief "holiday of delight" with Callistes, an islander. Then she hears the muffled roar of Pluto, coming to fetch her back to Hades, and she ascends to the highest point of the island:*]

The island was hers, and the deep,
All heaven, a golden hour.
Then with wonderful voice that rang
Through air as the swan's nigh death,
Of the glory of Light she sang,
She sang of the rapture of Breath.
Nor ever, says he who heard,
Heard Earth in her boundaries broad,
From bosom of singer or bird
A sweetness thus rich of the God
Whose harmonies always are sane.
She sang of furrow and seed,
The burial, birth of the grain,
The growth, and the showers that feed,
And the green blades waxing mature
For the husbandman's armful brown.
O, the song in its burden rang pure,
And burden to song was a crown.
Callistes, a singer, skilled
In the gift he could measure and praise,
By a rival's art was thrilled,
Though she sang but a Song of Days,
Where the husbandman's toil and strife
Little varies to strife and toil:
But the milky kernel of life,
With her numbered: corn, wine, fruit, oil!

The song did give him to eat:
Gave the first rapt vision of Good,
And the fresh young sense of Sweet;
The grace of the battle for food,
With the issue Earth cannot refuse
When men to their labours are sworn.
'Twas a song of the God of the Muse
To the forehead of Morn.

GEORGE MEREDITH

Thou hearest the nightingale begin the song of spring:
The lark, sitting upon his earthy bed, just as the morn
Appears, listens silent; then, springing from the waving corn-field, loud
He leads the choir of day—trill! trill! trill! trill!
Mounting upon the wings of light into the great expanse,
Re-echoing against the lovely blue and shining heavenly shell:
His little throat labours with inspiration; every feather
On throat and breast and wings vibrates with the effluence divine:
All nature listens silent to him, and the awful sun
Stands still upon the mountain, looking on this little bird
With eyes of soft humility and wonder, love and awe.
Then loud from their green covert all the birds begin their song:
The thrush, the linnet, and the goldfinch, robin, and the wren
Awake the sun from his sweet reverie upon the mountain:
The nightingale again assays his song, and thro' the day
And thro' the night warbles luxuriant, every bird of song
Attending his loud harmony with admiration and love.
This is a vision of the lamentation of Beulah over Ololon.

Thou perceivest the flowers put forth their precious odours;
And none can tell how from so small a centre comes such sweet,
Forgetting that within that centre eternity expands
Its ever-during doors that Og and Anak fiercely guard.

First, ere the morning breaks, joy opens in the flowery bosoms,
Joy even to tears, which the sun rising dries: first the wild thyme
And meadow-sweet, downy and soft, waving among the reeds,
Light springing on the air, lead the sweet dance; they wake
The honeysuckle sleeping on the oak; the flaunting beauty
Revels along upon the wind; the white-thorn, lovely may,
Opens her many lovely eyes; listening, the rose still sleeps—
None dare to wake her: soon she bursts her crimson-curtain'd
bed
And comes forth in the majesty of beauty. Every flower,
The pink, the jessamine, the wallflower, the carnation,
The jonquil, the mild lily, opes her heavens; every tree
And flower and herb soon fill the air with an innumerable dance,
Yet all in order sweet and lovely. Men are sick with love!

BLAKE (from *Milton*)

SPRING

Nothing is so beautiful as spring—
When weeds, in wheels, shoot long and lovely and lush;
Thrush's eggs look little low heavens, and thrush
Through the echoing timber does so rinse and wring
The ear, it strikes like lightnings to hear him sing;
The glassy peartree leaves and blooms, they brush
The descending blue; that blue is all in a rush
With richness; the racing lambs too have fair their fling.

What is all this juice and all this joy?
A strain of the earth's sweet being in the beginning
In Eden garden.—Have, get, before it cloy,
Before it cloud, Christ, lord, and sour with sinning,
Innocent mind and Mayday in girl and boy,
Most, O maid's child, thy choice and worthy the winning.

GERARD MANLEY HOPKINS

HURRAHING IN HARVEST

Summer ends now; now, barbarous in beauty, the stooks arise
Around; up above, what wind-walks! what lovely behaviour
Of silk-sack clouds! has wilder, wilful-wavier
Meal-drift moulded ever and melted across skies?

I walk, I lift up, I lift up heart, eyes,
Down all that glory in the heavens to glean our Saviour;
And, éyes, heárt, what looks, what lips yet gave you a
Rapturous love's greeting of realer, of rounder replies?
And the azurous hung hills are his world-wielding shoulder
Majestic—as a stallion stalwart, very-violet-sweet!—
These things, these things were here and but the beholder
Wanting; which two when they once meet,
The heart rears wings bold and bolder
And hurls for him, O half hurls earth for him off under his feet.

GERARD MANLEY HOPKINS

GOD'S GRANDEUR

The world is charged with the grandeur of God.
It will flame out, like shining from shook foil;
It gathers to a greatness, like the ooze of oil
Crushed. Why do men then now not reck his rod?
Generations have trod, have trod, have trod;
And all is seared with trade; bleared, smeared with toil;
And wears man's smudge and shares man's smell: the soil
Is bare now, nor can foot feel, being shod.

And for all this, nature is never spent;
There lives the dearest freshness deep down things;
And though the last lights off the black West went
Oh, morning, at the brown brink eastward, springs—
Because the Holy Ghost over the bent
World broods with warm breast and with ah! bright wings.

GERARD MANLEY HOPKINS

FROM "AMELIA"

And there Amelia stood, for fairness shewn
Like a young apple-tree, in flush'd array
Of white and ruddy flow'r, auroral, gay,
With chilly blue the maiden branch between;
And yet to look on her moved less the mind
To say "How beauteous!" than "How good and kind!"
And so we went alone
By walls o'er which the lilac's numerous plume
Shook down perfume;
Trim plots close blown
With daisies, in conspicuous myriads seen,
Engross'd each one
With single ardour for her spouse, the sun;
Garths in their glad array
Of white and ruddy branch, auroral, gay,
With azure chill the maiden flow'r between;
Meadows of fervid green,
With sometime sudden prospect of untold
Cowslips, like chance-found gold;
And broadcast buttercups at joyful gaze,
Rending the air with praise,
Like the six-hundred-thousand-voiced shout
Of Jacob camp'd in Midian put to rout;
Then through the Park,
Where Spring to livelier gloom
Quicken'd the cedars dark,
And, 'gainst the clear sky cold,
Which shone afar
Crowded with sunny alps oracular,
Great chestnuts raised themselves abroad like cliffs of bloom;
And everywhere,
Amid the ceaseless rapture of the lark,
With wonder new
We caught the solemn voice of single air,

"Cuckoo!"

And when Amelia, 'bolden'd, saw and heard
How bravely sang the bird,
And all things in God's bounty did rejoice,
She who, her Mother by, spake seldom word,
Did her charm'd silence doff,
And, to my happy marvel, her dear voice
Went as a clock does, when the pendulum's off.
Ill Monarch of man's heart the Maiden who
Does not aspire to be High-Pontiff too!
So she repeated soft her Poet's line,
"By grace divine,
Not otherwise, O Nature, are we thine!"
And I, up the bright steep she led me, trod,
And the like thought pursued
With, "What is gladness without gratitude,
And where is gratitude without a God?"

COVENTRY PATMORE

WINTER

I, singularly moved
To love the lovely that are not beloved,
Of all the Seasons, most
Love Winter, and to trace
The sense of the Trophonian pallor on her face.
It is not death, but plenitude of peace;
And the dim cloud that does the world enfold
Hath less the characters of dark and cold
Than warmth and light asleep,
And correspondent breathing seems to keep
With the infant harvest, breathing soft below
Its eider coverlet of snow.
Nor is in field or garden anything
But, duly look'd into, contains serene
The substance of things hoped for, in the Spring,
And evidence of Summer not yet seen.

On every chance-mild day
That visits the moist shaw,
The honeysuckle, 'sdaining to be crost
In urgence of sweet life by sleet or frost,
'Voids the time's law
With still increase
Of leaflet new, and little, wandering spray;
Often, in sheltering brakes,
As one from rest disturb'd in the first hour,
Primrose or violet bewilder'd wakes,
And deems 'tis time to flower;
Though not a whisper of her voice he hear,
The buried bulb does know
The signals of the year,
And hails far Summer with his lifted spear.
The gorse-field lark, by sudden, gold caprice,
Turns, here and there, into a Jason's fleece;
Lilies, that soon in Autumn slipp'd their gowns of green,
And vanish'd into earth,
And came again, ere Autumn died, to birth,
Stand full-array'd, amidst the wavering shower,
And perfect for the Summer, less the flower;
In nook of pale or crevice of crude bark,
Thou canst not miss,
If close thou spy, to mark
The ghostly chrysalis,
That, if thou touch it, stirs in its dream dark;
And the flush'd Robin, in the evenings hoar,
Does of Love's Day, as if he saw it, sing;
But sweeter yet than dream or song of Summer or Spring
Are Winter's sometime smiles, that seem to well
From infancy ineffable;
Her wandering, languorous gaze,
So unfamiliar, so without amaze,
On the elemental, chill adversity,
The uncomprehended rudeness; and her sigh

And solemn, gathering tear,
And look of exile from some great repose, the sphere
Of ether, moved by ether only, or
By something still more tranquil.

COVENTRY PATMORE

I tremble with pleasure when I think that on the very day of my leaving prison both the laburnum and the lilac will be blooming in the gardens. . . . Like Gautier, I have always been one of those "pour qui le monde visible existe."

OSCAR WILDE

There are days now and again when the summer broods in Trafalgar Square; the flood of light from a cloudless sky gathers and grows, thickening the air; the houses enclose the beams as water is enclosed in a cup. . . . Either the light subdues the sound, or perhaps rather it renders the senses slumberous and less sensitive, but the great sunlit square is silent—silent, that is, for the largest city on earth. A slumberous silence of abundant light, of the full summer day, of the high flood of summer hours whose tide can rise no higher. A time to linger and dream under the beautiful breast of heaven, heaven brooding and descending in pure light upon man's handiwork.

RICHARD JEFFERIES

. . . and I think of lank and coaly steamships heaving on the grey rollers of the English Channel and darkling streets wet with rain, I recall as if I were back there the busy exit from Charing Cross, the cross and the money-changers' offices, the splendid grime of giant London and the crowds going perpetually to and fro, the lights by night and the urgency and eventfulness of that great rain-swept heart of the modern world.

H. G. WELLS (from *The New Machiavelli*)

I do not think there is anyone who takes quite such a fierce pleasure in things being themselves as I do. The startling wetness of water excites and intoxicates me: the fieriness of fire, the steeliness of steel, the unutterable muddiness of mud.

G. K. CHESTERTON

TO A LOCOMOTIVE IN WINTER

Thee for my recitative,
Thee in the driving storm even as now, the snow, the winter-
day declining,
Thee in thy panoply, thy measur'd dual throbbing and thy beat
convulsive,
Thy black cylindric body, golden brass and silvery steel,
Thy ponderous side-bars, parallel and connecting rods, gyrating,
shuttling at thy sides,
Thy metrical, now swelling pant and roar, now tapering in the
distance,
Thy great protruding head-light fix'd in front,
Thy long, pale, floating vapour-pennants, tinged with delicate
purple,
The dense and murky clouds out-belching from thy smoke-
stack,
Thy knitted frame, thy springs and valves, the tremulous
twinkle of thy wheels,
Thy train of cars behind, obedient, merrily following,
Through gale or calm, now swift, now slack, yet steadily
careering;
Type of the modern—emblem of motion and power—pulse of
the continent,
For once come serve the Muse and merge in verse, even as
here I see thee,
With storm and buffeting gusts of wind and falling snow,
By day thy warning ringing bell to sound its notes,
By night thy silent signal lamps to swing.

Fierce-throated beauty!
Roll through my chant with all thy lawless music, thy swinging lamps at night,
Thy madly-whistled laughter, echoing, rumbling like an earth-quake, rousing all,
Law of thyself complete, thine own track firmly holding,
(No sweetness debonair of tearful harp or glib piano thine,)
Thy trills of shrieks by rocks and hills return'd,
Launch'd o'er the prairies wide, across the lakes,
To the free skies unpent and glad and strong.

WALT WHITMAN

MIRACLES

Why, who makes much of a miracle?
As to me I know of nothing else but miracles,
Whether I walk the streets of Manhattan,
Or dart my sight over the roofs of houses toward the sky,
Or wade with naked feet along the beach just in the edge of the water,
Or stand under trees in the woods,
Or talk by day with any one I love, or sleep in the bed at night with any one I love,
Or sit at table at dinner with the rest,
Or look at strangers opposite me riding in the car,
Or watch honey-bees busy around the hive of a summer fore-noon,
Or animals feeding in the fields,
Or birds, or the wonderfulness of insects in the air,
Or the wonderfulness of the sundown, or of stars shining so quiet and bright,
Or the exquisite delicate thin curve of the new moon in spring;
These with the rest, one and all, are to me miracles,
The whole referring, yet each distinct and in its place.

To me every hour of the light and dark is a miracle,
Every cubic inch of space is a miracle,
Every square yard of the surface of the earth is spread with
  the same,
Every foot of the interior swarms with the same.

To me the sea is a continual miracle,
The fishes that swim—the rocks—the motion of the waves—
  the ships with men in them,
What stranger miracles are there?

WALT WHITMAN

When I go from hence let this be my parting word, that what I have seen is unsurpassable.

I have tasted of the hidden honey of this lotus that expands on the ocean of light, and thus am I blessed—let this be my parting word.

In this playhouse of infinite forms I have had my play and here have I caught sight of him that is formless.

My whole body and my limbs have thrilled with his touch who is beyond touch; and if the end comes here, let it come—let this be my parting word.

RABINDRANATH TAGORE

Deliverance is not for me in renunciation. I feel the embrace of freedom in a thousand bonds of delight.

Thou ever pourest for me the fresh draught of thy wine of various colours and fragrance, filling this earthen vessel to the brim.

My world will light its hundred different lamps with thy flame and place them before the altar of thy temple.

No, I will never shut the doors of my senses. The delights of sight and hearing and touch will bear thy delight.

Yes, all my illusions will burn into illumination of joy, and all my desires ripen into fruits of love.

RABINDRANATH TAGORE

The same stream of life that runs through my veins night and day runs through the world and dances in rhythmic measures.

It is the same life that shoots in joy through the dust of the earth in numberless blades of grass and breaks into tumultuous waves of leaves and flowers.

It is the same life that is rocked in the ocean-cradle of birth and of death, in ebb and in flow.

I feel my limbs are made glorious by the touch of this world of life. And my pride is from the life-throb of ages dancing in my blood this moment.

RABINDRANATH TAGORE

And joy is everywhere; it is in the earth's green covering of grass; in the blue serenity of the sky; in the reckless exuberance of spring; in the severe abstinence of grey winter; in the living flesh that animates our bodily frame; in the perfect poise of the human figure, noble and upright; in living; in the exercise of all our powers; in the acquisition of knowledge; in fighting evils; in dying for gains we never can share. Joy is there everywhere; it is superfluous, unnecessary; nay, it very often contradicts the most peremptory behests of necessity. It exists to show that the bonds of law can only be explained by love; they are like body and soul. Joy is the realisation of the truth of oneness, the oneness of our soul with the world and of the world-soul with the supreme lover.

RABINDRANATH TAGORE

But do you know, dear Helmuth, what was the most important thing to me?—the fact that I perceived once again that most people take hold of things in order to do something stupid with them (as, for example, to tickle each other with peacocks' feathers), instead of looking at each thing properly and asking it about the beauty it possesses. Thus it comes about that most people simply don't know how beautiful the world is and how much splendour is revealed in the smallest things, in a common flower, in a stone, in the bark of a tree or the leaf of a birch. Grown-up people, who have occupations and cares and who worry themselves about mere trifles, gradually lose the eye for these riches, which children, if they are observant and good, quickly notice and love with their whole heart.

RAINER MARIA RILKE

O, tell us, poet, what you do?—I praise.
But those dark, deadly, devastating ways,
how do you bear them, suffer them?—I praise.
And then the Nameless, beyond guess or gaze,
how can you call it, conjure it?—I praise.
And whence your right, in every kind of maze,
in every mask, to remain true?—I praise.
And that the mildest and the wildest ways
know you like star and storm?—Because I praise.

RAINER MARIA RILKE

THE VACANT DAY

As I walked out in meadows green
  I heard the summer noon resound
With call of myriad things unseen
  That leapt and crept upon the ground.

High overhead the windless air
  Throbbed with the homesick coursing cry
Of swifts that ranging everywhere
  Woke echo in the sky.

Beside me, too, clear waters coursed
  Which willow branches, lapsing low,
Breaking their crystal gliding forced
  To sing as they did flow.

I listened; and my heart was dumb
  With praise no language could express;
Longing in vain for him to come
  Who had breathed such blessedness

On this fair world, wherein we pass
  So chequered and so brief a stay;
And yearned in spirit to learn, alas,
  What kept him still away.

WALTER DE LA MARE

In such access of mind, in such high hour
Of visitation from the living God,
Thought was not: in enjoyment it expired.
No thanks he breathed, he proffered no request.
Rapt into still communion that transcends
The imperfect offices of prayer and praise,
His mind was a thanksgiving to the power
That made him; it was blessedness and love.

WORDSWORTH (from *The Excursion*)

SECOND PART

I. GOOD AND EVIL

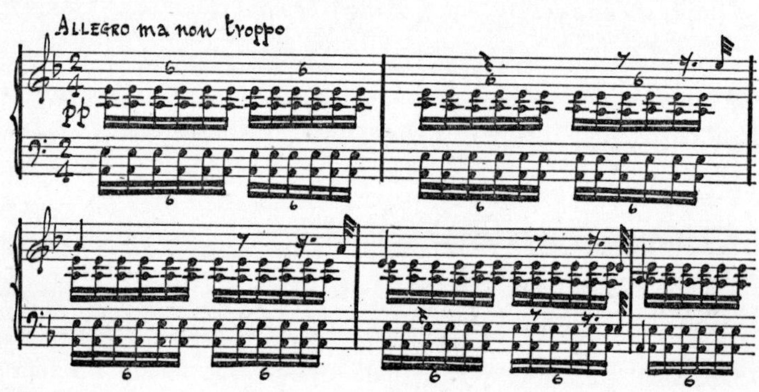
Allegro ma non troppo
pp

Silent and amazed even when a little boy,
I remember I heard the preacher every Sunday put God in
his statements,
As contending against some being or influence.

WALT WHITMAN

Whatever is, is in God, and nothing can exist or be conceived without God.

. . . .

God is the indwelling and not the transient cause of all things.

. . . .

Things could not have been produced by God in any other manner or order than that in which they were produced.

SPINOZA

All that happens is divine.

LÉON BLOY

We shall now briefly say something about devils, whether they exist or do not exist, and it is this:

If the Devil is a thing that is once for all opposed to God, and has absolutely nothing from God, then he is precisely identical with Nothing, which we have already discussed before.

If, with some, we represent him as a thinking thing that neither wills nor does any good, and so sets himself, once for all, in opposition to God, then surely he is very wretched, and, if prayer could help, then one ought to pray for his conversion.

But let us just see whether such a wretched thing could even exist for a single moment. And, if we do so, we shall immediately find out that it cannot; for whatever duration a thing has results entirely from the perfection of the thing, and the more essence and godliness things possess, the more lasting are they: therefore, as the Devil has not the least perfection in him, how should he then, I think to myself, be able to exist? Add to this, that the persistence or duration of a mode of the thinking thing only results from the union in which such a mode is, through love, joined to God. As the precise opposite of this union is supposed in the case of the Devils, they cannot possibly exist.

SPINOZA

Nothingness is immanent in evil.

NICHOLAS BERDYAEV

The depraved sinner, though bereft of the Good by his brutish desires, is in this respect unreal and desires unrealities; but still he hath a share in the Good in so far as there is in him a distorted reflection of true Love and Communion. And anger hath a share in the Good, in so far as it is a movement which seeks to remedy apparent evils, converting them to that which appears to be fair. And even he that desires the basest life, yet in so far as he feels desire at all and feels desire for life, and intends what he thinks the best kind of life, so far participates in the Good.

. . . .

The Good must be the beginning and the end even of all evil things. For the Good is the final Purpose of all things, good and bad alike. For even when we act amiss we do so from a longing for the Good; for no one makes evil his definite object when performing any action. Hence evil hath no substantial being, but only a shadow thereof; since the Good, and not itself, is the ultimate object for which it comes into existence.

. . . .

And if no thing in the world is without a share in the Good, and evil is the deficiency of Good and no thing in the world is utterly destitute of Good, then the Divine Providence is in all things, and nothing that exists can be without It.

DIONYSIUS THE AREOPAGITE

With everything wrong right is always somehow involved. Falsehood gets its glitter from truth. We seek base metal because we think it gold. Our delight in pursuing the bad comes from our belief that it is the good.

JALALU D-DIN RUMI

I have come to the stage of realisation in which I see that God is walking in every human form and manifesting himself alike in the sage and in the sinner.

SRI RAMAKRISHNA

There are people within whom the good traits of Cain's soul have their habitation, and these are very great.

RABBI URI OF STRELISK

For whether they looked upward they saw the Divine Vision,
Or whether they looked downward still they saw the Divine
    Vision,
Surrounding them on all sides beyond sin and death and hell.

BLAKE (from *Vala*)

[God is speaking to Moses.]

Moab is come forth from lust; but Ruth shall come forth from Moab, and David from Ruth, and from David the Messiah.

EDMOND FLEG (from a Midrashic source)

Saul owed his conversion neither to true love, nor to true faith, nor to any other truth. It was solely his hatred of the Christians that set him upon the road to Damascus, and to that decisive experience which was to decide the whole course of his life. He was brought to this experience by following with conviction the course in which he was most completely mistaken.

C. G. JUNG

The roaring of lions, the howling of wolves, the raging of the stormy sea, and the destructive sword, are portions of eternity too great for the eye of man.

BLAKE (from *The Marriage of Heaven and Hell*)

God knows evil under the form of good.

DIONYSIUS THE AREOPAGITE

God's mind perceives all sin and evil in the idea of the corresponding good, not in the form of sin; for instance, he knows lying in the idea of truth.

MEISTER ECKHART

Evil is not therefore wholly evil; it is misplaced good.

SAMUEL ALEXANDER

There is no not-holy, there is only that which has not yet been hallowed, which has not yet been redeemed to its holiness.

MARTIN BUBER (interpreting Hasidism)

Evil has often been likened to a discord which has been resolved. It must be added that both such discord and the passage in which it occurs are alike music. But there is no resolution of the discord which is evil and unmusical on the level on which good and evil both exist. The resolution, so far as it is effected, is effected on the higher level. The evil remains done, but by perishing in its evil form it may subserve deity. The discord remains a discord, but there is no discord in the higher quality, which it subserves but does not enter into as an ingredient.

SAMUEL ALEXANDER

The totality of Divine powers forms an harmonious whole, and as long as each stands in relation to all others, it is sacred and good. This is true also of the quality of strict justice, rigour and judgment in and by God, which is the fundamental cause of evil. The wrath of God is symbolised by His left hand, while the quality of mercy and love, with which it is intimately bound up, is called His right hand. The one cannot manifest itself without involving the other. Thus the quality of stern judgment represents the great fire of wrath which burns in God but is always tempered by His mercy. When it ceases to be tempered, when in its measureless hypertrophical outbreak it tears itself loose from the quality of mercy, then it breaks away from God altogether and is transformed into the radically evil, into Gehenna and the dark world of Satan.

GERSHOM SCHOLEM
(summarising the Zoharic doctrine of evil)

Manifestation, real life, creative activity, is only possible for God through an opposition that is harmonised and reconciled in the very instant of its appearance. Light (whether natural or supernatural) is only itself against a background of darkness. Purposive good-will implies a basis of blind, aimless, infinite desire and want. Spirit needs nature in which to reveal itself. Love and self-giving life cannot exist without the resisting power of egoism. Hence all contraries have been in the Godhead potentially from the "beginning," arising out of the "abyss" (*ungrund*) of indifference—this expression representing the absolute freedom of the Divine will and being. Latent in God is a "centre" or region of potential darkness, wrath, consuming fire, unbounded energy and power; but this dark centre normally remains in perfect harmony and subordination, as a complement and foundation to the higher centre of the Divine nature, the gentleness, the love and light, and the ordered will to all goodness.

When God has formed out of His own nature independent

organs of life and will, those self-conscious spirits whom we call angels and men, the same foundation of darkness and fiery energy is necessary to the perfect functioning of their life of loving activity. . . .

The bitter juice of the acid, unripe fruit is poison to the eater, until these same juices have been tempered and mellowed by the rays of the summer sun. The wholesome essences of every life are poisonous if wrongfully laid bare.

Evil first appears when the created will turns away from its divine origin, seeks its own puny separate good, and so sheds off the harmonising light and love, uncovering the hidden basis of darkness and fire, pain and wrath. Thus evil, whether that of the human soul or as shown in the destructive, degenerative forces of nature, is essentially a *perversion*, a *dislocation* of harmonised elements. It follows that the forces or qualities which appear to cause it are not meant to be eradicated or destroyed, but to be controlled, re-harmonised, "overcome by Heaven" and "again in their place of hiddenness" from which they should never have issued.

STEPHEN HOBHOUSE
(interpreting Boehme's doctrine of evil)

In itself in nature nothing is to be rejected, both [good and evil] must be, else God would not be manifested, and all would be as a still nothing: and the whole Being is together in the eternal God. . . .

JAKOB BOEHME

The anger in the kingdom of God is the great wondrous joy, where nothing of the anger is perceived.

JAKOB BOEHME

The light of the meekness holdeth the darkness captive, and dwelleth in the darkness.

JAKOB BOEHME

And the light shineth in the darkness; and the darkness comprehended it not.

ST. JOHN

[Nicholas Berdyaev accepts, with certain variations, the *ungrund* of Boehme (see p. 97), and finds in what Boehme calls its "indifference"—its indetermination—the origin and explanation both of freedom, the supreme value, and of good and evil.] Anyway, it is certain that there are two freedoms and not only one, the first to choose between good and evil, the last in the heart of good—an irrational freedom and a freedom within reason. Socrates knew only the second of these, and the words of the gospel, "You shall know the truth, and the truth shall make you free," also refer to it, the freedom in Christ. That is the freedom that we have in view when it is said that man ought to free himself from lower influences, to have control of his passions, to throw off enslavement to himself and to his environment, and the highest desire for freedom of spirit aims at it.

The freedom of the first Adam and the freedom in Christ of the second Adam are different. The truth shall make men free, but they must freely accept it and not be brought to it by force. Our Lord gives man the final liberty, but man must first freely have cleaved to him. . . . It is this free choice of Christ that constitutes the Christian's dignity and gives meaning to his act of faith, which is above all a free act. The dignity of man and the dignity of faith require the recognition of two freedoms, freedom to choose the truth and freedom in the truth. Freedom cannot be identified with goodness or truth or perfection: it is by nature autonomous, it is freedom and not goodness. Any identification or confusion of freedom with goodness and perfection involves a negation of freedom and a strengthening of methods of compulsion: obligatory goodness ceases to be goodness by the fact of its constraint. But free goodness, which alone is true, entails the liberty of evil. That is the tragedy that

Dostoevsky saw and studied, and it contains the mystery of Christianity.

Its dialectic works out thus: Free goodness involves the freedom of evil; but freedom of evil leads to the destruction of freedom itself and its degeneration into an evil necessity. On the other hand, the denial of the freedom of evil in favour of an exclusive freedom of good ends equally in a negation of freedom and its degeneration—into a good necessity. But a good necessity is not good, because goodness resides in freedom from necessity. . . .

To be able to understand this world, to keep one's faith in its deep meaning, to reconcile the existence of God with the existence of evil it is absolutely necessary that each one of us should have this irrational freedom in him, for it shows us what is the primary source of evil. The world is full of wickedness and misery precisely because it is based on freedom—yet that freedom constitutes the whole dignity of man and of his world. Doubtless at the price of its repudiation evil and suffering could be abolished, and the world forced to be "good" and "happy"; but man would have lost his likeness to God, which primarily resides in his freedom. . . .

The whole secret of human life and destiny depends on this notion: Freedom is irrational, and therefore it can create both good and evil. To reject freedom on the pretext that it can bring forth evil is to make the evil twice as bad, for if unconstrained good is the only good then compulsion and enforcement so far from being desirable are an aspect of Antichrist. . . .

According to [Dostoevsky] freedom degenerates into arbitrary self-will, this leads to evil, and evil to criminal wrongdoing. . . . Evil is evil: its nature is interior and metaphysical, not exterior and social. Man, as a free being, is responsible for it, but it must be outlawed, hunted down, and destroyed. . . . But evil is also the tragical road that man has to tread, the destiny of his freedom, an experience capable of enriching and raising him. Men are free beings, living as such, and they learn from inner experience the nothingness of evil, how it defeats and destroys itself while it is being experienced, and when they have purged themselves of it they reach the light. . . . Evil is essentially contradictory, and optimistically to conceive it as indispensable to the evolution of good and to try to remove its antinomy in the name of reason is to see only one aspect of it. The good that can be derived from evil is attained only by the way of suffering and repudiation of evil. . . . Freedom has opened the path of evil to man, it is a proof of freedom, and man must pay the price. The price is suffering, and by it the freedom that has been spoiled and turned into its contrary is reborn and given back to man. Therefore is Christ the Saviour freedom itself. . . .

When freedom has degenerated into self-will it recognises nothing as sacred or forbidden, for if there be no god but man then everything is allowable and man can try himself out at will. At the same time he lets himself get obsessed by some fixed idea, and under its tyranny freedom soon begins to disappear. . . . Even if he believes himself a Napoleon, or a god, the man who infringes the limits of that human nature which is made in the divine likeness falls crashing down. . . .

By the way of freedom man comes to evil, and it is in evil that he reaches [the] state of inner division. . . . Unrestrained and objectless freedom, deprived of God and His grace and degenerating into self-will, ceases to be capable of making a choice and is bandied about in opposite directions. Then is the time that two selves appear in a man and his personality is cloven apart. . . To mend that inner cleavage and banish that nightmare of Satan a man must make a definitive choice, and choose Being itself.

NICHOLAS BERDYAEV

All qualities are not only good, but infinitely perfect, as they are in God; and it is absolutely impossible that they should have any evil or defect in them, as they are in the one God, who is the great and universal All. Because where all properties are, there must necessarily be an all possible perfection: and that which must always have All in itself, must by an absolute necessity be always all perfect. But the same qualities, thus infinitely good and perfect in God, may become imperfect and evil in the creature; because in the creature, being limited and finite, they may be divided and separated from one another by the creature itself. Thus strength and fire in the divine nature are nothing else but the strength and flame of love, and never can be anything else; but in the creature strength and fire may be separated from love, and then they are become an evil, they are wrath and darkness and all mischief: and thus that same strength and quality, which in creatures making a right use of their own will or self-motion becomes their goodness and perfection, doth in creatures making a wrong use of their will become their evil and mischievous nature: and it is a truth that deserves well to be considered that there is no goodness in any creature, from the highest to the lowest, but in its continuing to be such a union of qualities and powers as God has brought together in its creation.

In the highest order of created beings this is their standing in their first perfection, this is their fulfilling the whole will or law of God, this is their piety, their song of praise, their eternal adoration of their great Creator. On the other hand, there is no evil, no guilt, no deformity in any creature, but in its dividing and separating itself from something which God had given to be in union with it. This, and this alone, is the whole nature of all good and all evil in the creature, both in the moral and natural world, in spiritual and material things. For instance, dark, fiery wrath in the soul is not only very like, but it is the very self-same thing in the soul which a wrathful poison is in the flesh. Now, the qualities of poison are in themselves all of them good qualities and necessary to every life; but they are become a poisonous evil, because they are separated from some other qualities. Thus also the qualities of fire and strength that constitute an evil wrath in the soul, are in themselves very good qualities and necessary to every good life; but they are become an evil wrath because separated from some other qualities with which they should be united.

The qualities of the devil and all fallen angels are good qualities; they are the very same which they received from their infinitely perfect Creator, the very same which are and must be in all heavenly angels; but they are an hellish, abominable malignity in them now, because they have, by their own self-motion, separated them from the light and love which should have kept them glorious angels.

And here may be seen at once, in the clearest light, the true origin of all evil in the creation, without the least imputation upon the Creator. God could not possibly create a creature to be an infinite All, like Himself: God could not bring any creature into existence, but by deriving into it the self-existent, self-generating, self-moving qualities of His own nature: for the qualities must be in the creature that which they were in the Creator, only in a state of limitation; and therefore every creature must be finite, and must have a self-motion, and so must be capable of moving right and wrong, of uniting or dividing from what it will, or of falling from that state in which it ought to stand: but as every quality in every creature, both within and without itself, is equally good and equally necessary to the perfection of the creature, since there is nothing that is evil in it, nor can become evil to the creature, but from itself, by its separating that from itself, with which it can and ought to be united, it plainly follows that evil can no more be charged upon God than darkness can be charged upon the sun; because every quality is equally good, every quality of fire is as good as every quality of light, and only becomes an evil to that creature who, by his own self-motion, has separated fire from the light in his own nature. . . .

So the angels, when they had turned back into the first forms of their own life, and broken off from the heavenly light and love of God, they became their own hell. No hell was made for them, no new qualities came into them, no vengeance or pains from the God of love fell upon them; they only stood in that state of division and separation from the Son and holy spirit of God, which, by their own motion, they had made for themselves. They had nothing in them but what they had from God, the first forms of an heavenly life, nothing but what the most heavenly beings have, and must have, to all eternity; but they had them in a state of self-torment, because they had separated them from that birth of light and love, which alone could make them glorious sons and blessed images of the Holy Trinity. . . .

That which in a devil is an evil selfishness, a wrathful fire, a stinging motion, is in a holy angel the everlasting kindling of a divine life, the strong birth of a heavenly love, it is a real cause of an ever-springing, ever-triumphing joyfulness, an ever-increasing sensibility of bliss. Take away the working, contending nature of the first qualities, which in a devil are only a serpentine selfishness, wrath, fire, and stinging motion; take away these, I say, from holy angels, and you leave them neither light, nor love, nor heavenly glory, nothing for the birth of the Son and Holy Spirit of God to rise up in.

WILLIAM LAW

Close to God's throne the happy angels play;
Beelzebub's as near, but turns away.

ANGELUS SILESIUS

Be kindled, child; become God's candle light;
The brighter thou, the darker Belial's night.

ANGELUS SILESIUS

[Self-will] is opposition attempted by a finite subject against its proper whole. . . . It is connexion with the central fire which produces in the element this burning sense of selfness. And the collision is resolved within that harmony where centre and circumference are one.

F. H. BRADLEY

Good is that which makes for unity; Evil is that which makes for separateness.

ALDOUS HUXLEY

I have learnt that the place wherein Thou art found unveiled is girt round with the coincidence of contradictories, and this is the wall of Paradise wherein Thou dost abide.

NICHOLAS OF CUSA

Looking back on my own experiences [under the influence of nitrous oxide] they all converge towards a kind of insight to which I cannot help ascribing some metaphysical significance. The keynote of it is invariably a reconciliation. It is as if the opposites of the world, whose contradictoriness and conflict make all our difficulties and troubles, were melted into unity. Not only do they, as contrasted species, belong to one and the same genus, but *one of the species*, the nobler and better one, *is itself the genus, and so soaks up and absorbs its opposite into itself*. This is a dark saying, I know, when thus expressed in terms of common logic, but I cannot wholly escape from its authority.

WILLIAM JAMES

PIED BEAUTY

Glory be to God for dappled things—
For skies of couple-colour as a brinded[1] cow;
For rose-moles all in stipple upon trout that swim;
Fresh-firecoal chestnut-falls; finches' wings;
Landscape plotted and pieced—fold, fallow, and plough;
And áll trádes, their gear and tackle and trim.
All things counter, original, spare, strange;
Whatever is fickle, freckled (who knows how?)
With swift, slow; sweet, sour; adazzle, dim;
He fathers-forth whose beauty is past change:
Praise him.

[1] Streaked.

GERARD MANLEY HOPKINS

[Nature] is a great organ, on which our Lord God plays, and the Devil blows the bellows.

GOETHE

THE LORD [to Mephistopheles]. Here too thou hast the fullest
  liberty.
The like of thee I never hated;
Of all the spirits who deny
The waggish knave least trouble has created.
Man's energy is prone to flag and seek the level,
Unqualified repose too soon he learns to crave;
Hence gladly I to him the comrade gave
Who works, incites, and must create, as Devil.

GOETHE

Even Mme. de Staël was shocked because I had made God the Father so friendly to the Devil.—What will she say if she meets him again in a higher sphere, perhaps even in heaven itself?

GOETHE

Faust reacts and reaches safety, not only in spite of, but actually because of, [Mephistopheles'] influence. For Mephistopheles, though he revolts against the light, is all the same, as he knows himself, a portion of "the Darkness that brought the Light to birth." And that is one reason why, as the drama proceeds and Faust begins to learn, Mephistopheles appears less and less as the tempter and more and more as the instrument of Faust's creative purpose. He bets with God in the Prologue that he will destroy Faust, but from the very beginning it is made clear that he will not win his bet. For by his fundamental nature he cannot help contributing to Faust's progress.

F. MELIAN STAWELL AND G. LOWES DICKINSON

Our Elders tell us that Rabbi Johanan cried out one day: "Alas, alas! Satan hath burned the Temple and massacred the righteous and dispersed Israel among the peoples; and the Holy One, blessed be He, permitteth that the Evil One still danceth in our midst!" From one Sabbath to another the Rabbi fasted, and Satan was delivered up to him. He filled his mouth with lead and shut him up in a cauldron. But all passion ceased in the hearts of men; no child was any more conceived, and images of the Lord were born no more upon earth. Then Rabbi Johanan reopened the cauldron and said: "Let Satan be free, to accomplish God's work."

EDMOND FLEG

Freud [regards] love and hate as wholly independent of each other in their origin, as conflicting in "ambivalence," and as *uniting* in sadism and masochism. I do not take this view, but regard hate as the *frustration aspect of love*, as "tails" is the obverse of "heads" in the same penny. I consider that the most true and *useful* way of regarding the infinitely varied forms of human emotion is as *interconvertible forms of one and the same social feeling*.

. . . .

Hatred, I consider, is just a standing reproach to the hated person, and owes all its meaning to a demand for love.

. . . .

As an example of the difference it makes to assume a primary appetite of aggression I would say that this assumption has led Freud to accept hatred and violence as inevitable, and to suppose that the wisest possible human policy can do no better than find socially harmless targets for this unavoidable hatred. . . . Both Freud and Adler regard the infant as "bad" by nature and as having to be made "good" or "social" by external compulsion, or else allowed outlet for its badness. I consider that the germ of goodness or of love is in the individual (of every species which has evolved a nurtured infancy) from the very beginning, and that our traditional method of upbringing frustrates this spontaneous benevolence and substitutes a "guilt-anxiety" morality for natural goodness.

. . . .

Psychopathy is to be regarded as due to the frustrations, distortions and reactions of the *love* disposition in its first adjustments to family life. I would suggest that the psychoses are to be regarded as the vestiges (and their results) of the child's attempt to find a secure "niche" for itself in the family circle. There is a phase of anxiety, and sometimes of jealousy, which appears in the child's life, as, one by one, the attentions it has enjoyed "from time immemorial" are withdrawn from it. It is not merely forbidden adult gratifications (precocity); it is deprived of infantile sources of comfort and assurance. It has a sense of insecurity—even, perhaps, of loneliness. It becomes self-conscious and self-critical. The rage and anxiety evoked by thwarting is inhibited and goes to build up a sense of guilt. Idealisms are born of its discontent with itself and its rôle. It strives to increase its consequence to other people . . . in so far as it feels it has no one upon whom it can *safely* depend. It wants to be something other than it is, and *what* precisely it *wants to be* depends upon its experience of other people and its conception of their powers and privileges. Its idealism can only be derived from its environment, and its ambitions must be formed by emulation and imitation of some (envied and) outstanding figure within this environment. If this is so we must regard psychopathy as an archaic and (in adult environment) inept attempt to improve love relationships. Correspondingly, Psychotherapy would appear fundamentally as an attempt to assist the patient in his love-quest and to set this upon lines more likely to achieve the desired results.

. . . .

In 1932 I came to the conclusion that the Last Supper dramatised and illustrated *free giving*. Even the body is given as food, as the mother gives it. Further, the whole story of the crucifixion seemed to illustrate free "forgiving" on the understanding that hate and evil *have no independent existence* but are merely the frustration-forms of love itself, distorted as protest, reproach and that kind of aggression which is originally intended to *compel* attention. The last prayer, "forgive them, for they know not what they do," seems to imply that forgiveness is not a condescension to an unworthy object, but a recognition (on somewhat Socratic lines) that evil is merely error, not to be met by retributive error. The whole of this story illustrates non-retaliation—even non-resistance—to the very utmost limit.

IAN SUTTIE

It would seem that the amount of destructiveness to be found in individuals is proportionate to the amount to which expansiveness of life is curtailed. By this we do not refer to individual frustrations of this or that instinctive desire but to the thwarting of the whole of life, the blockage of spontaneity of the growth and expression of man's sensuous, emotional, and intellectual capacities. Life has an inner dynamism of its own; it tends to grow, to be expressed, to be lived. It seems that if this tendency is thwarted the energy directed towards life undergoes a process of decomposition and changes into energies directed towards destruction. In other words: the drive for life and the drive for destruction are not mutually independent factors but are in a reversed interdependence. The more the drive towards life is thwarted, the stronger is the drive towards destruction; the more life is realised, the less is the strength of destructiveness. *Destructiveness is the outcome of unlived life.*

ERICH FROMM

THE PROBLEM OF EVIL

The current of the world has its boundaries, otherwise it could have no existence, but its purpose is not shown in the boundaries which restrain it, but in its movement, which is towards perfection. The wonder is not that there should be obstacles and sufferings in this world, but that there should be law and order, beauty and joy, goodness and love. The idea of God that man has in his being is the wonder of all wonders. He has felt in the depths of his life that what appears as imperfect is the manifestation of the perfect; just as a man who has an ear for music realises the perfection of a song, while in fact he is only listening to a succession of notes. Man has found out the great paradox that what is limited is not imprisoned within its limits; it is ever moving, and therewith shedding its finitude every moment. In fact, imperfection is not a negation of perfectness; finitude is not contradictory to infinity: they are but completeness manifested in parts, infinity revealed within bounds.

Pain, which is the feeling of our finiteness, is not a fixture in our life. It is not an end in itself, as joy is. To meet with it is to know that it has no part in the true permanence of creation. It is what error is in our intellectual life. To go through the history of the development of science is to go through the maze of mistakes it made current at different times. Yet no one really believes that science is the one perfect mode of disseminating mistakes. The progressive ascertainment of truth is the important thing to remember in the history of science, not its innumerable mistakes. Error, by its nature, cannot be stationary; it cannot remain with truth; like a tramp, it must quit its lodging as soon as it fails to pay its score to the full.

As in intellectual error, so in evil of any other form, its essence is impermanence, for it cannot accord with the whole. Every moment it is being corrected by the totality of things and keeps changing its aspect. We exaggerate its importance by imagining it as at a standstill. Could we collect the statistics of the immense amount of death and putrefaction happening every moment in this earth, they would appal us. But evil is ever moving; with all its incalculable immensity it does not effectually clog the current of our life; and we find that the earth, water, and air remain sweet and pure for living beings. All such statistics consist of our attempts to represent statically what is in motion; and in the process things assume a weight in our mind which they have not in reality. For this reason a man, who by his profession is concerned with any particular aspect of life, is apt to magnify its proportions; in laying undue stress upon facts he loses his hold upon truth. A detective may have the opportunity of studying crimes in detail, but he loses his sense of their relative place in the whole social economy. When science collects facts to illustrate the struggle for existence that is going on in the animal kingdom, it raises a picture in our minds of "nature red in tooth and claw." But in these mental pictures we give a fixity to colours and forms which are really evanescent. It is like calculating the weight of the air on each square inch of our body to prove that it must be crushingly heavy for us. With every weight, however, there is an adjustment, and we lightly bear our burden. With the struggle for existence in nature there is reciprocity. There is the love for children and for comrades; there is the sacrifice of self, which springs from love; and this love is the positive element in life.

If we kept the searchlight of our observation turned upon the fact of death, the world would appear to us like a huge charnel-house; but in the world of life the thought of death has, we find, the least possible hold upon our minds. Not because it is the least apparent, but because it is the negative aspect of life; just as, in spite of the fact that we shut our eyelids every second, it is the openings of the eyes that count. Life as a whole never takes death seriously. It laughs, dances and plays, it builds, hoards and loves in death's face. Only when we detach one individual fact of death do we see its blankness and become dismayed. We lose sight of the wholeness of a life of which death is part. It is like looking at a piece of cloth through a microscope. It appears like a net; we gaze at the big holes and shiver in imagination. But the truth is, death is not the ultimate reality. It looks black, as the sky looks blue; but it does not blacken existence, just as the sky does not leave its stain upon the wings of the bird.

When we watch a child trying to walk, we see its countless failures; its successes are but few. If we had to limit our observation within a narrow space of time, the sight would be cruel. But we find that in spite of its repeated failures there is an impetus of joy in the child which sustains it in its seemingly impossible task. We see it does not think of its falls so much as of its power to keep its balance though for only a moment.

Like these accidents in a child's attempts to walk, we meet with sufferings in various forms in our life every day, showing the imperfections in our knowledge and our available power, and in the application of our will. But if these revealed our weakness to us only, we should die of utter depression. When we select for observation a limited area of our activities, our individual failures and miseries loom large in our minds; but our life leads us instinctively to take a wider view. It gives us an ideal of perfection which ever carries us beyond our present limitations. Within us we have a hope which always walks in front of our present narrow experience; it is the undying faith in the infinite in us; it will never accept any of our disabilities as a permanent fact; it sets no limit to its own scope; it dares to assert that man has oneness with God; and its wild dreams become true every day.

We see the truth when we set our mind towards the infinite. The ideal of truth is not in the narrow present, not in our immediate sensations, but in the consciousness of the whole which gives us a taste of what we *should* have in what we *do* have. Consciously or unconsciously we have in our life this feeling of Truth which is ever larger than its appearance; for our life is facing the infinite, and it is in movement. Its aspiration is therefore infinitely more than its achievement, and as it goes on it finds that no realisation of truth ever leaves it stranded on the desert of finality, but carries it to a region beyond. Evil cannot altogether arrest the course of life on the highway and rob it of its possessions. For the evil has to pass on, it has to grow into good; it cannot stand and give battle to the All. If the least evil could stop anywhere indefinitely, it would sink deep and cut into the very roots of existence. As it is, man does not really believe in evil, just as he cannot believe that violin strings have been purposely made to create the exquisite torture of discordant notes, though by the aid of statistics it can be mathematically proved that the probability of discord is far greater than that of harmony, and for one who can play the violin there are thousands who cannot. The potentiality of perfection outweighs actual contradictions. No doubt there have been people who asserted existence to be an absolute evil, but man can never take them seriously. Their pessimism is a mere pose, either intellectual or sentimental; but life itself is optimistic: it wants to go on. Pessimism is a form of mental dipsomania, it disdains healthy nourishment, indulges in the strong drink of denunciation, and creates an artificial dejection which thirsts for a stronger draught. If existence were an evil, it would wait for no philosopher to prove it. It is like convicting a man of suicide, while all the time he stands before you in the flesh. Existence itself is here to prove that it cannot be an evil.

An imperfection which is not all imperfection, but which has perfection for its ideal, must go through a perpetual realisation. Thus, it is the function of our intellect to realise the truth through untruths, and knowledge is nothing but the continually burning up of error to set free the light of truth. Our will, our character, has to attain perfection by continually overcoming evils, either inside or outside us, or both; our physical life is consuming bodily materials every moment to maintain the life fire; and our moral life too has its fuel to burn. This life process is going on—we know it, we have felt it; and we have a faith which no individual instances to the contrary can shake, that the direction of humanity is from evil to good. For we feel that good is the positive element in man's nature, and in every age and every clime what man values most is his ideal of goodness. We have known the good, we have loved it, and we have paid our highest reverence to men who have shown in their lives what goodness is.

The question will be asked, What is goodness; what does our moral nature mean? My answer is, that when a man begins to have an extended vision of his true self, when he realises that he is much more than at present he seems to be, he begins to get conscious of his moral nature. Then he grows aware of that which he is yet to be, and the state not yet experienced by him becomes more real than that under his direct experience. Necessarily, his perspective of life changes, and his will takes the place of his wishes. For will is the supreme wish of the larger life, the life whose greater portion is out of our present reach, whose objects are not for the most part before our sight. Then comes the conflict of our lesser man with our greater man, of our wishes with our will, of the desire for things affecting our senses with the purpose that is within our heart. Then we begin to distinguish between what we immediately desire and what is good. For good is that which is desirable for our greater self. Thus the sense of goodness comes out of a truer view of our life, which is the connected view of the wholeness of the field of life, and which takes into account not only what is present before us but what is not, and perhaps never humanly can be. Man, who is provident, feels for that life of his which is not yet existent, feels much more for that than for the life that is with him; therefore he is ready to sacrifice his present inclination for the unrealised future. In this he becomes great, for he realises truth. Even to be efficiently selfish a man has to recognise this truth, and has to curb his immediate impulses—in other words, has to be moral. For our moral faculty is the faculty by which we know that life is not made up of fragments, purposeless and discontinuous. This moral sense of man not only gives him the power to see that the self has a continuity in time, but it also enables him to see that he is not true when he is only restricted to his own self. He is more in truth than he is in fact. He truly belongs to individuals who are not included in his own individuality, and whom he is never even likely to know. As he has a feeling for his future self which is outside his present consciousness, so he has a feeling for his greater self which is outside the limits of his personality. There is no man who has not this feeling to some extent, who has never sacrificed his selfish desire for the sake of some other person, who has never felt a pleasure in undergoing some loss or trouble because it pleased somebody else. It is a truth that man is not a detached being, that he has a universal aspect; and when he recognises this, he becomes great. Even the most evilly-disposed selfishness has to recognise this when it seeks the power to do evil; for it cannot ignore truth and yet be strong. So in order to claim the aid of truth, selfishness has to be unselfish to some extent. A band of robbers must be moral in order to hold together as a band; they may rob the whole world but not each other. To make an immoral intention successful, some of its weapons must be moral. In fact, very often it is our very moral strength which gives us most effectively the power to do evil, to exploit other individuals for our own benefit, to rob other people of their just rights. The life of an animal is unmoral, for it is aware only of an immediate present; the life of a man can be immoral, but that only means that it must have a moral basis. What is immoral is imperfectly moral, just as what is false is true to a small extent, or it cannot even be false. Not to see is to be blind, but to see wrongly is to see only in an imperfect manner. Man's selfishness is a beginning to see some connection, some purpose in life; and to act in accordance with its dictates requires self-restraint and regulation of conduct. A selfish man willingly undergoes troubles for the sake of the self, he suffers hardship and privation without a murmur, simply because he knows that what is pain and trouble, looked at from the point of view of a short space of time, are just the opposite when seen in a larger perspective. Thus what is a loss to the smaller man is a gain to the greater and *vice versa*.

To the man who lives for an idea, for his country, for the good of humanity, life has an extensive meaning, and to that extent pain becomes less important to him. To live the life of goodness is to live the life of all. Pleasure is for one's own self, but goodness is concerned with the happiness of all humanity and for all time. From the point of view of the good, pleasure and pain appear in a different meaning; so much so, that pleasure may be shunned, and pain be courted in its place, and death itself be made welcome as giving a higher value to life. From these higher standpoints of a man's life, the standpoints of the good, pleasure and pain lose their absolute value. Martyrs prove it in history, and we prove it every day in our life in our little martyrdoms. When we take a pitcherful of water from the sea it has its weight, but when we take a dip into the sea itself a thousand pitchersful of water flow above our head, and we do not feel their weight. We have to carry the pitcher of self with our strength; and so, while on the plane of selfishness pleasure and pain have their full weight, on the moral plane they are so much lightened that the man who has reached it appears to us almost superhuman in his patience under crushing trials, and his forbearance in the face of malignant persecution.

To live in perfect goodness is to realise one's life in the infinite. This is the most comprehensive view of life which we can have by our inherent power of the moral vision of the wholeness of life. And the teaching of Buddha is to cultivate this moral power to the highest extent, to know that our field of activities is not bound to the plane of our narrow self. This is the vision of the heavenly kingdom of Christ. When we attain to that universal life, which is the moral life, we become freed from bonds of pleasure and pain, and the place vacated by our self becomes filled with an unspeakable joy which springs from measureless love. In this state the soul's activity is all the more heightened, only its motive power is not from desires, but in its own joy. This is the *Karma-yoga* of the *Gita*, the way to become one with the infinite activity by the exercise of the activity of disinterested goodness.

When Buddha meditated upon the way of releasing mankind from the grip of misery he came to this truth: that when man attains his highest end by merging the individual in the universal, he becomes free from the thraldom of pain. Let us consider this point more fully.

A student of mine once related to me his adventure in a storm, and complained that all the time he was troubled with the feeling that this great commotion in nature behaved to him as if he were no more than a mere handful of dust. That he was a distinct personality with a will of his own had not the least influence upon what was happening.

I said, "If consideration for our individuality could sway nature from her path, then it would be the individuals who would suffer most."

But he persisted in his doubt, saying that there was this fact which could not be ignored—the feeling that I am. The "I" in us seeks for a relation which is individual to it.

I replied that the relation of the "I" is with something which is "not-I." So we must have a medium which is common to both, and we must be absolutely certain that it is the same to the "I" as it is to the "not-I."

This is what needs repeating here. We have to keep in mind that our individuality by its nature is impelled to seek for the universal. Our body can only die if it tries to eat its own substance, and our eye loses the meaning of its function if it can only see itself.

Just as we find that the stronger the imagination the less is it merely imaginary and the more is it in harmony with truth, so we see the more vigorous our individuality the more does it widen towards the universal. For the greatness of a personality is not in itself but in its content, which is universal, just as the depth of a lake is judged not by the size of its cavity but by the depth of its water.

So, if it is a truth that the yearning of our nature is for reality, and that our personality cannot be happy with a fantastic universe of its own creation, then it is clearly best for it that our will can only deal with things by following their law, and cannot do with them just as it pleases. This unyielding sureness of reality sometimes crosses our will, and very often leads us to disaster, just as the firmness of the earth invariably hurts the falling child who is learning to walk. Nevertheless it is the same firmness that hurts him which makes his walking possible. Once, while passing under a bridge, the mast of my boat got stuck in one of its girders. If only for a moment the mast would have bent an inch or two, or the bridge raised its back like a yawning cat, or the river given in, it would have been all right with me. But they took no notice of my helplessness. That is the very reason why I could make use of the river, and sail upon it with the help of the mast, and that is why, when its current was inconvenient, I could rely upon the bridge. Things are what they are, and we have to know them if we would deal with them, and knowledge of them is possible because our wish is not their law. This knowledge is a joy to us, for the knowledge is one of the channels of our relation with the things outside us; it is making them our own, and thus widening the limit of our self.

At every step we have to take into account others than ourselves. For only in death are we alone. A poet is a true poet when he can make his personal idea joyful to all men, which he could not do if he had not a medium common to all his audience. This common language has its own law which the poet must discover and follow, by doing which he becomes true and attains poetical immortality.

We see then that man's individuality is not his highest truth; there is that in him which is universal. If he were made to live in a world where his own self was the only factor to consider, then that would be the worst prison imaginable to him, for man's deepest joy is in growing greater and greater by more and more union with the all. This, as we have seen, would be an impossibility if there were no law common to all. Only by discovering the law and following it, do we become great, do we realise the universal; while, so long as our individual desires are at conflict with the universal law, we suffer pain and are futile.

There was a time when we prayed for special concessions, we expected that the laws of nature should be held in abeyance for our own convenience. But now we know better. We know that law cannot be set aside, and in this knowledge we have become strong. For this law is not something apart from us; it is our own. The universal power which is manifested in the universal law is one with our own power. It will thwart us where we are small, where we are against the current of things; but it will help us where we are great, where we are in unison with the all. Thus, through the help of science, as we come to know more of the laws of nature, we gain in power; we tend to attain a universal body. Our organ of sight, our organ of locomotion, our physical strength becomes world-wide; steam and electricity become our nerve and muscle. Thus we find that, just as throughout our bodily organisation there is a principle of relation by virtue of which we can call the entire body our own, and can use it as such, so all through the universe there is that principle of uninterrupted relation by virtue of which we can call the whole world our extended body and use it accordingly. And in this age of science it is our endeavour fully to establish our claim to our world-self. We know all our poverty and sufferings are owing to our inability to realise this legitimate claim of ours. Really, there is no limit to our powers, for we are not outside the universal power which is the expression of universal law. We are on our way to overcome disease and death, to conquer pain and poverty; for through scientific knowledge we are ever on our way to realise the universal in its physical aspect. And as we make progress we find that pain, disease, and poverty of power are not absolute, but that it is only the want of adjustment of our individual self to our universal self which gives rise to them.

It is the same with our spiritual life. When the individual man in us chafes against the lawful rule of the universal man we become morally small, and we must suffer. In such a condition our successes are our greatest failures, and the very fulfilment of our desires leaves us poorer. We hanker after special gains for ourselves, we want to enjoy privileges which none else can share with us. But everything that is absolutely special must keep up a perpetual warfare with what is general. In such a state of civil war man always lives behind barricades, and in any civilisation which is selfish our homes are not real homes, but artificial barriers around us. Yet we complain that we are not happy, as if there were something inherent in the nature of things to make us miserable. The universal spirit is waiting to crown us with happiness, but our individual spirit would not accept it. It is our life of the self that causes conflicts and complications everywhere, upsets the normal balance of society and gives rise to miseries of all kinds. It brings things to such a pass that to maintain order we have to create artificial coercions and organised forms of tyranny, and tolerate infernal institutions in our midst, whereby at every moment humanity is humiliated.

We have seen that in order to be powerful we have to submit to the laws of the universal forces, and to realise in practice that they are our own. So, in order to be happy, we have to submit our individual will to the sovereignty of the universal will, and to feel in truth that it is our own will. When we reach that state wherein the adjustment of the finite in us to the infinite is made perfect, then pain itself becomes a valuable asset. It becomes a measuring rod with which to gauge the true value of our joy.

The most important lesson that man can learn from his life is not that there *is* pain in this world, but that it depends upon him to turn it into good account, that it is possible for him to transmute it into joy. That lesson has not been lost altogether to us, and there is no man living who would willingly be deprived of his right to suffer pain, for that is his right to be a man. One day the wife of a poor labourer complained bitterly to me that her eldest boy was going to be sent away to a rich relative's house for part of the year. It was the implied kind intention of trying to relieve her of her trouble that gave her the shock, for a mother's trouble is a mother's own by her inalienable right of love, and she was not going to surrender it to any dictates of expediency. Man's freedom is never in being saved troubles, but it is the freedom to take trouble for his own good, to make the trouble an element in his joy. It can be made so only when we realise that our individual self is not the highest meaning of our being, that in us we have the world-man who is immortal, who is not afraid of death or sufferings, and who looks upon pain as only the other side of joy. He who has realised this knows that it is pain which is our true wealth as imperfect beings, and has made us great and worthy to take our seat with the perfect. He knows that we are not beggars; that it is the hard coin which must be paid for everything valuable in this life, for our power, our wisdom, our love; that in pain is symbolised the infinite possibility of perfection, the eternal unfolding of joy; and the man who loses all pleasure in accepting pain sinks down and down to the lowest depth of penury and degradation. It is only when we invoke the aid of pain for our self-gratification that she becomes evil and takes her vengeance for the insult done to her by hurling us into misery. For she is the vestal virgin consecrated to the service of the immortal perfection, and when she takes her true place before the altar of the infinite she casts off her dark veil and bares her face to the beholder as a revelation of supreme joy.

RABINDRANATH TAGORE

SECOND PART

II. SIN AND REPENTANCE

Molto Tranquillo dolciss. e. espress
p

For thou desirest not sacrifice; else would I give it: thou delightest not in burnt offering.

The sacrifices of God are a broken spirit: a broken and a contrite heart, O God, thou wilt not despise.

FROM PSALM 51

God likes forgiving big sins more than small ones. The bigger they are the gladder he is and the quicker to forgive them.

MEISTER ECKHART

The idolator who learns the Torah is greater than Aaron the High Priest.

ATTRIBUTED TO RABBI MEIR

Though a man be soiled
With the sins of a lifetime,
Let him but love me,
Rightly resolved,
In utter devotion:
I see no sinner,
That man is holy.

THE BHAGAVAD-GITA

How can we tell when a sin we have committed has been pardoned? By the fact that we no longer commit that sin.

RABBI BUNAM OF PZHYSHA

Failure to repent is much worse than sin. A man may have sinned for but a moment, but he may fail to repent of it moments without number.

RABBI BUNAM OF PZHYSHA

We are told by the Psalmist first to leave evil and then to do good. I will add that if you find it difficult to follow this advice, you may first do good, and the evil will automatically depart from you.

RABBI YITZHAK MEIR OF GER

When thou attackest the roots of sin, fix thy thought more upon the God whom thou desirest than upon the sin which thou abhorrest.

WALTER HYLTON

If thou hast broken a vow, tie a knot on it to make it hold together again. It is spiritual thrift, and no misbecoming baseness, to piece and join thy neglected promises with fresh ones. So shall thy vow in effect be not broken when new mended: and remain the same, though not by one entire continuation, yet by a constant successive renovation.

THOMAS FULLER

Man must be lenient with his soul in her weaknesses and imperfections and suffer her failings as he suffers those of others, but he must not become idle, and must encourage himself to better things.

ST. SERAPHIM OF SAROV

We should be in charity with ourselves as with our neighbours

FÉNELON

How shall we expect Charity towards others, when we are uncharitable to our selves?

SIR THOMAS BROWNE

How could man live at all if he did not give absolution every night to himself and all his brothers?

GOETHE

The superstitious, who know better how to reprobate vice than to teach virtue, and who do not endeavour to lead men by reason, but to so inspire them with fear that they avoid evil rather than love virtue, have no other intention than to make the rest as miserable as themselves; and therefore it is not wonderful that for the most part they are a nuisance and hateful to men.

SPINOZA

Noble Natures, and such as are capable of goodness, are railed into vice, that might as easily be admonished into virtue.

SIR THOMAS BROWNE

I can hardly think there was ever any scared into Heaven; they go the fairest way to Heaven that would serve God without a Hell; other Mercenaries, that crouch into him in fear of Hell, though they term themselves the servants, are indeed but the slaves, of the Almighty.

SIR THOMAS BROWNE

Culpable beginnings have found commendable conclusions, and infamous courses pious retractations. Detestable Sinners have proved exemplary Converts on Earth, and may be glorious in the Apartment of Mary Magdalen in Heaven. Men are not the same through all divisions of their Ages. Time, Experience, self-Reflexions, and God's mercies, make in some well-temper'd minds a kind of translation before Death, and Men do differ from themselves as well as from other Persons.

SIR THOMAS BROWNE

The sinner of to-day is the saint of to-morrow. Wherefore, unmindful of the sins and shortcomings of our neighbours, let us look to our own imperfections, surely forgetting what God has forgotten: sins truly repented, which God has forgotten, 'tis no business of ours to remember.

MEISTER ECKHART

Thou canst begin a new life! See but things afresh as thou usedst to see them; for in this consists the new life.

MARCUS AURELIUS

Do not feel qualms or despondency or discomfiture if thou dost not invariably succeed in acting from right principles; but when thou art foiled, come back again to them, and rejoice if on the whole thy conduct is worthy of a man, and love the course to which thou returnest.

MARCUS AURELIUS

If any one has committed a serious sin, let him beware thinking of it. For where our thoughts are, there we also are with our soul. Let not your soul sink into the mire of sin; it may not be able to extricate itself and repent.

And even if a man has committed a minor offence, why should he think of it? Why should he place his soul in the mire? Turn mire hither and thither, and it remains mire. What good can come to Heaven from disturbing your sin in your mind? During the time thus consumed you may perform a good deed which will truly be like presenting God with a pearl.

Turn away from evil; hold it not in remembrance; do good. If you have sinned much, balance it by doing much good. Resolve to-day, from the depth of your heart and in a joyful mood, to abstain from sin and to do good. Hurry over the prayer: "For the Sin," and meditate preferably on the prayer: "And Thou, O Lord, shalt reign."

RABBI YITZHAK MEIR OF GER

It is a great grace of God to practise self-examination; but too much is as bad as too little, as they say; believe me, by God's help, we shall advance more by contemplating the Divinity than by keeping our eyes fixed on ourselves.

ST. TERESA

When thou fallest into a fault, in what matter soever it be, do not trouble nor afflict thyself for it. . . . The common enemy will make thee believe, as soon as thou fallest into any fault, that thou walkest in error, and therefore art out of God and his favour, and herewith would he make thee distrust of the divine Grace, telling thee of thy misery, and making a giant of it; and putting it into thy head that every day thy soul grows worse instead of better, whilst it so often repeats these failings. O blessed Soul, open thine eyes; and shut the gate against these diabolical suggestions, knowing thy misery, and trusting in the mercy divine. Would not he be a mere fool who, running at tournament with others, and falling in the best of the career, should lie weeping on the ground and afflicting himself with discourses upon his fall? Man (they would tell him), lose no time, get up and take the course again, for he that rises again quickly and continues his race is as if he had never fallen. If thou seest thyself fallen once and a thousand times, thou oughtest to make use of the remedy which I have given thee, that is, a loving confidence in the divine mercy. These are the weapons with which thou must fight and conquer cowardice and vain thoughts. This is the means thou oughtest to use—not to lose time, not to disturb thyself, and reap no good.

MOLINOS (abridged)

The wretch who constantly says, "I am bound, I am bound," only succeeds in being bound. He who says day and night, "I am a sinner, I am a sinner," verily becomes a sinner.

One must have such burning faith in God that one can say: "What? I have repeated God's name and can sin still cling to me? How can I be a sinner any more? How can I be in bondage any more?"

If a man repeats God's name, his body, mind, and everything becomes pure. Why should one talk only about sin and hell and such things? Say but once, "O Lord, I have undoubtedly done wicked things, but I won't repeat them." And have faith in His name.

SRI RAMAKRISHNA

When I was a youth, newly married, I lived with my father-in-law, a watchmaker. I desired greatly to visit a famous Rabbi, but had no money for the journey. I said to my father-in-law: "If you will give me a few gulden, I will repair the little watch with which you have had no patience to bother." He agreed, and I took apart the watch to discover the cause of the difficulty. I soon saw that nothing was lacking, but that a tiny hairspring was twisted. This I soon made straight, placed everything together and the watch began to keep time once more. Does this not teach that a slight twist of the heart often halts the normal moral feeling? A little adjustment and the heart beats properly again.

RABBI YERAHMIEL OF PZHYSHA

Vain e'en for God to say "Forever die!"
I live, unless I sin eternally.

ANGELUS SILESIUS

O Vala, what is Sin! that thou shudderest and weepest
At sight of thy once lov'd Jerusalem? What is Sin but a little
Error and fault that is soon forgiven? but mercy is not a Sin,
Nor pity nor love nor kind forgiveness. O! if I have Sinned,
Forgive and pity me! O unfold thy Veil in mercy and love!

BLAKE (from *Jerusalem*)

And there was heard a great lamenting in Beulah; all the Regions
Of Beulah were moved as the tender bowels are moved; and
they said:—

Why did you take Vengeance, O ye Sons of the mighty Albion?
Planting these Oaken Groves; Erecting these Dragon Temples.
Injury the Lord heals, but Vengeance cannot be healed:
As the Sons of Albion have done to Luvah, so they have in him
Done to the Divine Lord and Saviour, who suffers with those
that suffer,
For not one sparrow can suffer, and the whole Universe not
suffer also

In all its Regions, and its Father and Saviour not pity and weep.
But Vengeance is the destroyer of Grace and Repentance in
the bosom
Of the Injurer, in which the Divine Lamb is cruelly slain.

BLAKE (from *Jerusalem*)

Man must and will have Some Religion; if he has not the Religion of Jesus, he will have the Religion of Satan, and will erect the synagogue of Satan, calling the Prince of this World, God; and destroying all who do not worship Satan under the Name of God. Will any one say: Where are those who worship Satan under the Name of God? Where are they? Listen! Every Religion that Preaches Vengeance for Sin is the Religion of the Enemy and Avenger, and not of the Forgiver of Sin, and their God is Satan, Named by the Divine Name. . . .

BLAKE (from *Jerusalem*)

REDEMPTION

Having been tenant long to a rich Lord,
Not thriving, I resolved to be bold,
And make a suit unto him, to afford
A new small-rented lease, and cancell th' old.

In heaven at his manour I him sought:
They told me there, that he was lately gone
About some land, which he had dearly bought
Long since on earth, to take possession.

I straight return'd, and knowing his great birth,
Sought him accordingly in great resorts;
In cities, theatres, gardens, parks, and courts:
At length I heard a ragged noise and mirth

Of theeves and murderers: there I him espied,
Who straight, *Your suit is granted*, said, and died.

GEORGE HERBERT

Thee, God, I come from, to thee go,
All day long I like fountain flow
From thy hand out, swayed about
Mote-like in thy mighty glow.

What I know of thee I bless,
As acknowledging thy stress
On my being and as seeing
Something of thy holiness.

Once I turned from thee and hid,
Bound on what thou hadst forbid;
Sow the wind I would; I sinned:
I repent of what I did.

Bad I am, but yet thy child.
Father, be thou reconciled,
Spare thou me, since I see
With thy might that thou art mild.

I have life before me still
And thy purpose to fulfil;
Yea a debt to pay thee yet:
Help me, sir, and so I will.

But thou bidst, and just thou art,
Me shew mercy from my heart
Towards my brother, every other
Man my mate and counterpart.

GERARD MANLEY HOPKINS
(unfinished)

SECOND PART

III. MAN, FELLOW-WORKER WITH GOD

Un poco sostenuto.

In every age I come back
To deliver the holy,
To destroy the sin of the sinner,
To establish righteousness.

THE BHAGAVAD-GITA

God can no more do without us than we can do without him.

MEISTER ECKHART

No little worm can God make without me:
It bursts, unless I help both ceaselessly.

ANGELUS SILESIUS

And Moses said unto the Lord, O my Lord, I am not eloquent, neither heretofore, nor since thou hast spoken unto thy servant: but I am slow of speech, and of a slow tongue.

And the Lord said unto him, Who hath made man's mouth? or who maketh the dumb, or deaf, or the seeing, or the blind? have not I the Lord?

Now therefore go, and I will be with thy mouth, and teach thee what thou shalt say.

EXODUS

Then answered Amos, and said to Amaziah, I was no prophet, neither was I a prophet's son; but I was an herdman, and a gatherer of sycomore fruit:

And the Lord took me as I followed the flock, and the Lord said unto me, Go, prophesy unto my people Israel.

AMOS

In the year that king Uzziah died I saw also the Lord sitting upon a throne, high and lifted up, and his train filled the temple.

Above it stood the seraphims: each one had six wings; with

twain he covered his face, and with twain he covered his feet, and with twain he did fly.

And one cried unto another, and said, Holy, holy, holy, is the Lord of hosts: the whole earth is full of his glory.

And the posts of the door moved at the voice of him that cried, and the house was filled with smoke.

Then said I, Woe is me! for I am undone; because I am a man of unclean lips, and I dwell in the midst of a people of unclean lips: for mine eyes have seen the King, the Lord of hosts.

Then flew one of the seraphims unto me, having a live coal in his hand, which he had taken with the tongs from off the altar:

And he laid it upon my mouth, and said, Lo, this hath touched thy lips; and thine iniquity is taken away, and thy sin purged.

Also I heard the voice of the Lord, saying, Whom shall I send, and who will go for us? Then said I, Here am I; send me.

ISAIAH

And ye shall be brought before governors and kings for my sake, for a testimony against them and the Gentiles.

But when they deliver you up, take no thought how or what ye shall speak: for it shall be given you in that same hour what ye shall speak.

For it is not ye that speak, but the Spirit of your Father which speaketh in you.

ST. MATTHEW

The very best and utmost of attainment in this life is to remain still and let God act and speak in thee.

MEISTER ECKHART

And Isaac asked the Eternal: "King of the World, when Thou didst make the light, Thou didst say in Thy Torah that the light was good; when Thou didst make the extent of the firmament and the extent of the earth, Thou didst say in Thy Torah that they were good; and every herb Thou hast made, and every beast, Thou hast said that they were good; but when Thou hadst made man in Thine image, Thou didst not say in Thy Torah that man was good. Wherefore, Lord?" And God answered him: "Because man I have not yet perfected, and because through the Torah man is to perfect himself, and to perfect the world."

EDMOND FLEG (from a Midrashic source)

THE EXILE OF THE SHEKHINA

God is divided into two, through the created world and its actions. He is divided into the ultimate being of God, Elohut, which is remote and apart from the creatures, and the Presence of God, his Glory, the Shekhina, which dwells in the world, wandering astray and scattered. Redemption alone will unite both for Eternity. But it is the property of the soul of man, by means of service, to bring the Shekhina nearer to its source, and to let it re-enter into it. In this instant of homecoming, before it must again descend into the being of the world, the whirlpool which howls in the life of the stars is hushed, the torches of the great desolation are extinguished, the lash in the hand of fate is lowered, and the pain of the world is stilled and listens: the grace of graces has appeared, and blessing pours down into space, till the powers of entanglement begin to drag down the Glory again, and all is as before.

This is the meaning of Service. That prayer alone truly endures which is made for the sake of the Shekhina. "Through his own need and want man knows how to pray that the want of the Shekhina may be satisfied, and that through him who prays union of God with His Glory may take place." Man must recognise that his suffering comes through the suffering of the Shekhina; "he is one of its limbs," and in the appeasing of its privation is alone his own true appeasement. "He ought not to think about his own liberation from higher or lower needs, or be like one who hews down the eternal growth, and so creates separation. But he should do all for the sake of the want of the Shekhina, and thus all will be redeemed of itself, and his own suffering is calmed in the calming of the roots above. For all, above and below, is one Unity." "I am prayer," says the Shekhina. A Master said: "Mankind thinks it prays to God; it is not so, for prayer itself is the Divine."

MARTIN BUBER

When man is at one, God is One.

THE ZOHAR

The effort of the Middle Ages, which worked amid the ruins of the pagan world and on a mass of barbarian peoples who were beginning to be civilised, was to raise up to heaven a Terrestrial City that should be the Throne of the King of Glory. . . . In our own time those who are at work in the heart of a civilisation that was once Christian and that is now in dissolution and declining again towards barbarism have to prepare for a new world less pretentious dwellings that shall afford a shelter to men and where God whom Love always inclines to our weakness may also come and find a shelter for His goodness and His humanity. If such a work is essentially divine, it demands of the creature none the less a very full consciousness of the human factors that are set in motion. . . .

JACQUES MARITAIN

God himself . . . awaits man's help and contribution towards Creation. But we, instead of turning towards him his own image in ourselves and offering him freely the fruits of our creative strength, have wasted and squandered that strength in superficial self-affirmation.

NICHOLAS BERDYAEV

God's Self complains of thirst: but ah! the grief
That thou, who couldest, givest no relief!

ANGELUS SILESIUS

You, neighbour God, if sometimes in the night
I rouse you with loud knocking, I do so
only because I seldom hear you breathe;
I know: you are alone.
And should you need a drink, no one is there
to reach it to you, groping in the dark.
Always I hearken. Give but a small sign.
I am quite near.

Between us there is but a narrow wall,
and by sheer chance; for it would take
merely a call from your lips or from mine
to break it down,
and that all noiselessly.

The wall is builded of your images.

They stand before you hiding you like names,
And when the light within me blazes high
that in my inmost soul I know you by,
the radiance is squandered on their frames.

And then my senses, which too soon grow lame,
exiled from you, must go their homeless ways.

RAINER MARIA RILKE

When Moses threw the wand into the Red Sea, the sea, quite contrary to the expected miracle, did not divide itself to leave a dry passage for the Jews. Not until the first man had jumped into the sea did the promised miracle happen and the waves recede.

JEWISH LEGEND

So God when He wishes to perform in us, through us, and with us some act of great charity, first proposes it to us by His inspiration, secondly we favour it, thirdly we consent to it.

ST. FRANCIS DE SALES

The compassion that you see in the kindhearted is God's compassion: He has given it to them to protect the helpless.

SRI RAMAKRISHNA

God made no tools for himself, he needs none; he created for himself a partner in the dialogue of time, and one who is capable of holding converse.

MARTIN BUBER

It is senseless to ask how far my action reaches, and where God's grace begins; there is no common border-line; what concerns me alone, before I bring something about, is my action, and what concerns me alone, when the action is successfully done, is God's grace. The one is no less real than the other, and neither is a part-cause. God and man do not divide the government of the world between them; man's action is enclosed in God's action, but it is still real action.

MARTIN BUBER

Accordingly, in its relation to conduct, religion does not so much command us to perform our duties with the consciousness that they are the commands of God, as rather it is religion to do our duty with the consciousness of helping to create his deity.

SAMUEL ALEXANDER

We are all workmen: prentice, journeyman,
or master, building you—you towering nave.
And sometimes there will come to us a grave
wayfarer, who like a radiance thrills
the souls of all the hundred artisans,
as tremblingly he shows us a new skill.

We climb up on the rocking scaffolding,
the hammers in our hands swing heavily,
until our foreheads feel the caressing wing
of a bright hour that knows everything,
and hails from you as wind hails from the sea.

Then hammerstrokes sound, multitudinous,
and through the mountains echoes blast on blast.
Only at dusk we yield you up at last:
and slow your shaping contours dawn on us.

God, you are vast.

RAINER MARIA RILKE

Power is what is mighty. "Mighty" is related to "make," and to what "might be," what is possible. The future is what is possible. Power has to do with the future. External power holds future events in its hands. In this sense, too, the gods have been considered powerful. But more important, they are internal powers. We must remember that the gods have human shape. The rationalistic explanation quickly comes to mind that man has made god in his own image. The Bible has it the other way: God created man in His image, as His image He created him. This, I believe, is the profounder truth. In non-mythical terms: the image in which God appears to man does not show what man is but what he might be. It is the image of man's potentiality of being, that which determines his life. This potentiality is for man a power, not a concept. Concepts we have of things past, things we have mastered. But this potentiality is what we have not yet mastered. Man is not master over it, it is master over him. It may be up to us to fulfil this potentiality, or to fail it—but to choose it is not up to us. How it happens that the potentiality reveals itself to us, that remains hidden from us. It challenges us, and our life is obedience to it, or flight from it.

I do not say that this image of the objective potentiality exhausts the idea of divinity. The metaphysics behind the fact that the divine reveals itself to us in this fashion, that is something I do not dare touch upon. But I believe that this image is the form in which we can best manage to grasp in thought what we know of the divine.

C. F. VON WEIZSÄCKER

I confess that I do not see why the very existence of an invisible world may not in part depend on the personal response which any one of us may make to the religious appeal. God himself, in short, may draw vital strength and increase of very being from our fidelity. For my own part, I do not know what the sweat and blood and tragedy of this life mean, if they mean anything short of this. If this life be not a real fight, in which something is eternally gained for the universe by success, it is no better than a game of private theatricals from which one may withdraw at will. But it *feels* like a real fight,—as if there were something really wild in the universe which we, with all our idealities and faithfulnesses, are needed to redeem; and first of all to redeem our own hearts from atheisms and fears. For such a half-wild half-saved universe our nature is adapted. The deepest thing in our nature is this dumb region of the heart in which we dwell alone with our willingnesses and our unwillingnesses, our faiths and our fears. As through the cracks and crannies of caverns those waters exude from the earth's bosom which then form the fountain-heads of springs, so in these crepuscular depths of personality the sources of all our outer deeds and decisions take their rise. Here is our deepest organ of communication with the nature of things; and compared with these concrete movements of our soul all abstract statements and scientific arguments—the veto, for example, which the strict positivist pronounces upon our faith—sound to us like mere chatterings of the teeth. . . .

These then are my last words to you: Be not afraid of life. Believe that life *is* worth living, and your belief will help create the fact. The "scientific" proof that you are right may not be clear before the day of judgment (or some stage of being which that expression may serve to symbolise) is reached. But the faithful fighters of this hour, or the beings that then and there will represent them, may turn to the faint-hearted, who here decline to go on, with words like those with which Henry IV greeted the tardy Crillon after a great battle had been gained: "Hang yourself, brave Crillon! We fought at Arques, and you were not there!"

WILLIAM JAMES

THIRD PART

THE RELATION OF MAN TO MAN

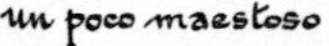
un poco maestoso

es
sucht der Bruder seine Brü... der und kann er helfen hilft er gern.
p dolce
cresc:

I

We cannot know whether we love God, although there may be strong reasons for thinking so, but there can be no doubt about whether we love our neighbour or no. Be sure that in proportion as you advance in fraternal charity, you are increasing in your love of God, for His Majesty bears so tender an affection for us, that I cannot doubt He will repay our love for others by augmenting, in a thousand different ways, that which we bear for Him.

ST. TERESA

Everything begins in mysticism and ends in politics.

CHARLES PÉGUY

Are not Religion and Politics the Same Thing? Brotherhood is Religion!

BLAKE (from *Jerusalem*)

He who would do good to another, must do it in minute particulars.
General good is the plea of the scoundrel, hypocrite, and flatterer.

BLAKE (from *Jerusalem*)

When thou cuttest down thine harvest in thy field, and hast forgot a sheaf in the field, thou shalt not go again to fetch it: it shall be for the stranger, for the fatherless, and for the widow: that the Lord thy God may bless thee in all the work of thine hands.

When thou beatest thine olive tree, thou shalt not go over the boughs again: it shall be for the stranger, for the fatherless, and for the widow.

When thou gatherest the grapes of thy vineyard, thou shalt not glean it afterward: it shall be for the stranger, for the fatherless, and for the widow.

And thou shalt remember that thou wast a bondman in the land of Egypt: therefore I command thee to do this thing.

DEUTERONOMY

And six years thou shalt sow thy land, and shalt gather in the fruits thereof:

But the seventh year thou shalt let it rest and lie still; that the poor of thy people may eat: and what they leave the beasts of the field shall eat. In like manner thou shalt deal with thy vineyard, and with thy oliveyard.

EXODUS

At the end of every seven years thou shalt make a release.

And this is the manner of the release; Every creditor that lendeth ought unto his neighbour shall release it: he shall not exact it of his neighbour, or of his brother; because it is called the Lord's release.

DEUTERONOMY

And ye shall hallow the fiftieth year, and proclaim liberty throughout all the land unto all the inhabitants thereof: it shall be a jubile unto you; and ye shall return every man unto his possession, and ye shall return every man unto his family.

A jubile shall that fiftieth year be unto you: ye shall not sow, neither reap that which groweth of itself in it, nor gather the grapes in it of thy vine undressed.

For it is the jubile; it shall be holy unto you: ye shall eat the increase thereof out of the field.

In the year of this jubile ye shall return every man unto his possession.

And if thou sell ought unto thy neighbour, or buyest ought of thy neighbour's hand, ye shall not oppress one another:

According to the number of years after the jubile thou shalt buy of thy neighbour, and according unto the number of years of the fruits he shall sell unto thee:

According to the multitude of years thou shalt increase the price thereof, and according to the fewness of years thou shalt diminish the price of it: for according to the number of the years of the fruits doth he sell unto thee.

Ye shall not therefore oppress one another; but thou shalt fear thy God: for I am the Lord your God.

LEVITICUS

If there be among you a poor man of one of thy brethren within any of thy gates in thy land which the Lord thy God giveth thee, thou shalt not harden thine heart, nor shut thine hand from thy poor brother:

But thou shalt open thine hand wide unto him, and shalt surely lend him sufficient for his need, in that which he wanteth.

Beware that there be not a thought in thy wicked heart, saying, The seventh year, the year of release, is at hand; and thine eye be evil against thy poor brother, and thou givest him nought; and he cry unto the Lord against thee, and it be sin unto thee.

Thou shalt surely give him, and thine heart shall not be grieved when thou givest unto him: because that for this thing the Lord thy God shall bless thee in all thy works, and in all that thou puttest thine hand unto.

For the poor shall never cease out of the land: therefore I command thee, saying, Thou shalt open thine hand wide unto thy brother, to thy poor, and to thy needy, in thy land.

And if thy brother, an Hebrew man, or an Hebrew woman, be sold unto thee, and serve thee six years; then in the seventh year thou shalt let him go free from thee.

And when thou sendest him out free from thee, thou shalt not let him go away empty:

Thou shalt furnish him liberally out of thy flock, and out of thy floor, and out of thy winepress: of that wherewith the Lord thy God hath blessed thee thou shalt give unto him.

And thou shalt remember that thou wast a bondman in the land of Egypt, and the Lord thy God redeemed thee: therefore I command thee this thing to day.

DEUTERONOMY

No man shall take the nether or the upper millstone to pledge: for he taketh a man's life to pledge.

DEUTERONOMY

When thou dost lend thy brother any thing, thou shalt not go into his house to fetch his pledge.

Thou shalt stand abroad, and the man to whom thou dost lend shall bring out the pledge abroad unto thee.

DEUTERONOMY

If thou at all take thy neighbour's raiment to pledge, thou shalt deliver it unto him by that the sun goeth down:

For that is his covering only, it is his raiment for his skin: wherein shall he sleep? and it shall come to pass, when he crieth unto me, that I will hear; for I am gracious.

EXODUS

Thou shalt not lend upon usury to thy brother; usury of money, usury of victuals, usury of any thing that is lent upon usury.

DEUTERONOMY

Thou shalt not see thy brother's ox or his sheep go astray, and hide thyself from them: thou shalt in any case bring them again unto thy brother.

And if thy brother be not nigh unto thee, or if thou know him not, then thou shalt bring it unto thine own house, and it shall be with thee until thy brother seek after it, and thou shalt restore it to him again.

In like manner shalt thou do with his ass; and so shalt thou do with his raiment; and with all lost thing of thy brother's, which he hath lost, and thou hast found, shalt thou do likewise: thou mayest not hide thyself.

DEUTERONOMY

If thou meet thine enemy's ox or his ass going astray, thou shalt surely bring it back to him again.

If thou see the ass of him that hateth thee lying under his burden, and wouldest forbear to help him, thou shalt surely help with him.

EXODUS

Thou shalt not wrest the judgment of thy poor in his cause.

EXODUS

Thou shalt not deliver unto his master the servant which is escaped from his master unto thee:

He shall dwell with thee, even among you, in that place which he shall choose in one of thy gates, where it liketh him best: thou shalt not oppress him.

DEUTERONOMY

Thou shalt not oppress an hired servant that is poor and needy, whether he be of thy brethren, or of thy strangers that are in thy land within thy gates:

At his day thou shalt give him his hire, neither shall the sun go down upon it; for he is poor, and setteth his heart upon it: lest he cry against thee unto the Lord, and it be sin unto thee.

DEUTERONOMY

Ye shall not afflict any widow, or fatherless child.

If thou afflict them in any wise, and they cry at all unto me, I will surely hear their cry. . . .

EXODUS

Thou shalt not avenge, nor bear any grudge against the children of thy people, but thou shalt love thy neighbour as thyself: I am the Lord.

LEVITICUS

But the stranger that dwelleth with you shall be unto you as one born among you, and thou shalt love him as thyself; for ye were strangers in the land of Egypt: I am the Lord your God.

LEVITICUS

II

And it came to pass, when David had made an end of speaking these words unto Saul, that Saul said, Is this thy voice, my son David? And Saul lifted up his voice, and wept.

And he said to David, Thou art more righteous than I: for thou hast rewarded me good, whereas I have rewarded thee evil.

And thou hast shewed this day how that thou hast dealt well with me: forasmuch as when the Lord had delivered me into thine hand, thou killedst me not.

For if a man find his enemy, will he let him go well away? wherefore the Lord reward thee good for that thou hast done unto me this day.

And now, behold, I know well that thou shalt surely be king, and that the kingdom of Israel shall be established in thine hand.

I SAMUEL

Wherefore have we fasted, say they, and thou seest not? wherefore have we afflicted our soul, and thou takest no knowledge? Behold, in the day of your fast ye find pleasure, and exact all your labours.

Behold, ye fast for strife and debate, and to smite with the fist of wickedness: ye shall not fast as ye do this day, to make your voice to be heard on high.

Is it such a fast that I have chosen? a day for a man to afflict his soul? is it to bow down his head as a bulrush, and to spread sackcloth and ashes under him? wilt thou call this a fast, and an acceptable day to the Lord?

Is not this the fast that I have chosen? to loose the bands of wickedness, to undo the heavy burdens, and to let the oppressed go free, and that ye break every yoke?

Is it not to deal thy bread to the hungry, and that thou bring the poor that are cast out to thy house? when thou seest the naked, that thou cover him; and that thou hide not thyself from thine own flesh?

Then shall thy light break forth as the morning, and thine health shall spring forth speedily: and thy righteousness shall go before thee; the glory of the Lord shall be thy reward.

Then shalt thou call, and the Lord shall answer; thou shalt cry, and he shall say, Here I am. If thou take away from the midst of thee the yoke, the putting forth of the finger, and speaking vanity;

And if thou draw out thy soul to the hungry, and satisfy the afflicted soul; then shall thy light rise in obscurity, and thy darkness be as the noon day:

And the Lord shall guide thee continually, and satisfy thy soul in drought, and make fat thy bones: and thou shalt be like a watered garden, and like a spring of water, whose waters fail not.

ISAIAH

Wherewith shall I come before the Lord, and bow myself before the high God? shall I come before him with burnt offerings, with calves of a year old?

Will the Lord be pleased with thousands of rams, or with ten thousands of rivers of oil? shall I give my firstborn for my transgression, the fruit of my body for the sin of my soul?

He hath shewed thee, O man, what is good; and what doth the Lord require of thee, but to do justly, and to love mercy, and to walk humbly with thy God?

MICAH

Then one of them, which was a lawyer, asked him a question, tempting him, and saying,

Master, which is the great commandment in the law?

Jesus said unto him, Thou shalt love the Lord thy God with all thy heart, and with all thy soul, and with all thy mind.

This is the first and great commandment.

And the second is like unto it, Thou shalt love thy neighbour as thyself.

On these two commandments hang all the law and the prophets.

ST. MATTHEW

Then came Peter to him, and said, Lord, how oft shall my brother sin against me, and I forgive him? till seven times?

Jesus saith unto him, I say not unto thee, Until seven times: but, Until seventy times seven.

ST. MATTHEW

And, behold, a certain lawyer stood up, and tempted him, saying, Master, what shall I do to inherit eternal life?

He said unto him, What is written in the law? how readest thou?

And he answering said, Thou shalt love the Lord thy God with all thy heart, and with all thy soul, and with all thy strength, and with all thy mind; and thy neighbour as thyself.

And he said unto him, Thou hast answered right: this do, and thou shalt live.

But he, willing to justify himself, said unto Jesus, And who is my neighbour?

And Jesus answering said, A certain man went down from Jerusalem to Jericho, and fell among thieves, which stripped him of his raiment, and wounded him, and departed, leaving him half dead.

And by chance there came down a certain priest that way: and when he saw him, he passed by on the other side.

And likewise a Levite, when he was at the place, came and looked on him, and passed by on the other side.

But a certain Samaritan, as he journeyed, came where he was: and when he saw him, he had compassion on him,

And went to him, and bound up his wounds, pouring in oil

and wine, and set him on his own beast, and brought him to an inn, and took care of him.

And on the morrow when he departed, he took out two pence, and gave them to the host, and said unto him, Take care of him; and whatsoever thou spendest more, when I come again, I will repay thee.

Which now of these three, thinkest thou, was neighbour unto him that fell among the thieves?

And he said, He that shewed mercy on him. Then said Jesus unto him, Go, and do thou likewise.

ST. LUKE

Jesus went unto the mount of Olives.

And early in the morning he came again into the temple, and all the people came unto him; and he sat down, and taught them.

And the scribes and Pharisees brought unto him a woman taken in adultery; and when they had set her in the midst,

They say unto him, Master, this woman was taken in adultery, in the very act.

Now Moses in the law commanded us, that such should be stoned: but what sayest thou?

This they said, tempting him, that they might have to accuse him. But Jesus stooped down, and with his finger wrote on the ground, as though he heard them not.

So when they continued asking him, he lifted up himself, and said unto them, He that is without sin among you, let him first cast a stone at her.

And again he stooped down, and wrote on the ground.

And they which heard it, being convicted by their own conscience, went out one by one, beginning at the eldest, even unto the last: and Jesus was left alone, and the woman standing in the midst.

When Jesus had lifted up himself, and saw none but the woman, he said unto her, Woman, where are those thine accusers? hath no man condemned thee?

She said, No man, Lord. And Jesus said unto her, Neither do I condemn thee: go, and sin no more.

ST. JOHN

And one of the Pharisees desired him that he would eat with him. And he went into the Pharisee's house, and sat down to meat.

And, behold, a woman in the city, which was a sinner, when she knew that Jesus sat at meat in the Pharisee's house, brought an alabaster box of ointment.

And stood at his feet behind him weeping, and began to wash his feet with tears, and did wipe them with the hairs of her head, and kissed his feet, and anointed them with the ointment.

Now when the Pharisee which had bidden him saw it, he spake within himself, saying, This man, if he were a prophet, would have known who and what manner of woman this is that toucheth him: for she is a sinner.

And Jesus answering said unto him, Simon, I have somewhat to say unto thee. And he saith, Master, say on.

There was a certain creditor which had two debtors: the one owed five hundred pence, and the other fifty.

And when they had nothing to pay, he frankly forgave them both. Tell me therefore, which of them will love him most?

Simon answered and said, I suppose that he, to whom he forgave most. And he said unto him, Thou hast rightly judged.

And he turned to the woman, and said unto Simon, Seest thou this woman? I entered into thine house, thou gavest me no water for my feet: but she hath washed my feet with tears, and wiped them with the hairs of her head.

Thou gavest me no kiss: but this woman since the time I came in hath not ceased to kiss my feet.

My head with oil thou didst not anoint: but this woman hath anointed my feet with ointment.

Wherefore I say unto thee, Her sins, which are many, are

forgiven; for she loved much: but to whom little is forgiven, the same loveth little.

And he said unto her, Thy sins are forgiven.

ST. LUKE

Then shall the King say unto them on his right hand, Come, ye blessed of my Father, inherit the kingdom prepared for you from the foundation of the world:

For I was an hungred, and ye gave me meat: I was thirsty, and ye gave me drink: I was a stranger, and ye took me in:

Naked, and ye clothed me: I was sick, and ye visited me: I was in prison, and ye came unto me.

Then shall the righteous answer him, saying, Lord, when saw we thee an hungred, and fed thee? or thirsty, and gave thee drink?

When saw we thee a stranger, and took thee in? or naked, and clothed thee?

Or when saw we thee sick, or in prison, and came unto thee?

And the King shall answer and say unto them, Verily I say unto you, Inasmuch as ye have done it unto one of the least of these my brethren, ye have done it unto me.

ST. MATTHEW

He riseth from supper, and laid aside his garments; and took a towel, and girded himself.

After that he poureth water into a bason, and began to wash the disciples' feet, and to wipe them with the towel wherewith he was girded.

Then cometh he to Simon Peter: and Peter saith unto him, Lord, dost thou wash my feet?

Jesus answered and said unto him, What I do thou knowest not now; but thou shalt know hereafter.

Peter saith unto him, Thou shalt never wash my feet. Jesus answered him, If I wash thee not, thou hast no part with me.

Simon Peter saith unto him, Lord, not my feet only, but also my hands and my head.

Jesus saith to him, He that is washed needeth not save to wash his feet, but is clean every whit: and ye are clean, but not all.

For he knew who should betray him; therefore said he, Ye are not all clean.

So after he had washed their feet, and had taken his garments, and was set down again, he said unto them, Know ye what I have done to you?

Ye call me Master and Lord: and ye say well; for so I am.

If I then, your Lord and Master, have washed your feet; ye also ought to wash one another's feet.

ST. JOHN

And when they were come to the place, which is called Calvary, there they crucified him, and the malefactors, one on the right hand, and the other on the left.

Then said Jesus, Father, forgive them; for they know not what they do. And they parted his raiment, and cast lots.

ST. LUKE

Though I speak with the tongues of men and of angels, and have not charity, I am become as sounding brass, or a tinkling cymbal.

And though I have the gift of prophecy, and understand all mysteries, and all knowledge; and though I have all faith, so that I could remove mountains, and have not charity, I am nothing.

And though I bestow all my goods to feed the poor, and though I give my body to be burned, and have not charity, it profiteth me nothing.

Charity suffereth long, and is kind; charity envieth not; charity vaunteth not itself, is not puffed up.

Doth not behave itself unseemly, seeketh not her own, is not easily provoked, thinketh no evil;

Rejoiceth not in iniquity, but rejoiceth in the truth;

Beareth all things, believeth all things, hopeth all things, endureth all things.

Charity never faileth: but whether there be prophecies, they shall fail; whether there be tongues, they shall cease; whether there be knowledge, it shall vanish away.

For we know in part, and we prophesy in part.

But when that which is perfect is come, then that which is in part shall be done away.

When I was a child, I spake as a child, I understood as a child, I thought as a child: but when I became a man, I put away childish things.

For now we see through a glass, darkly; but then face to face: now I know in part; but then shall I know even as also I am known.

And now abideth faith, hope, charity, these three; but the greatest of these is charity.

I CORINTHIANS

Let love be without dissimulation. Abhor that which is evil; cleave to that which is good.

Be kindly affectioned one to another with brotherly love; in honour preferring one another;

Not slothful in business; fervent in spirit; serving the Lord;

Rejoicing in hope; patient in tribulation; continuing instant in prayer;

Distributing to the necessity of saints; given to hospitality.

Bless them which persecute you: bless, and curse not.

Rejoice with them that do rejoice, and weep with them that weep.

Be of the same mind one toward another. Mind not high things, but condescend to men of low estate. Be not wise in your own conceits.

Recompense to no man evil for evil. Provide things honest in the sight of all men.

If it be possible, as much as lieth in you, live peaceably with all men.

Dearly beloved, avenge not yourselves, but rather give place unto wrath: for it is written, Vengeance is mine; I will repay, saith the Lord.

Therefore if thine enemy hunger, feed him; if he thirst, give him drink: for in so doing thou shalt heap coals of fire on his head.

Be not overcome of evil, but overcome evil with good.

ROMANS

Owe no man any thing, but to love one another: for he that loveth another hath fulfilled the law.

For this, Thou shalt not commit adultery, Thou shalt not kill, Thou shalt not steal, Thou shalt not bear false witness, Thou shalt not covet; and if there be any other commandment, it is briefly comprehended in this saying, namely, Thou shalt love thy neighbour as thyself.

Love worketh no ill to his neighbour: therefore love is the fulfilling of the law.

ROMANS

Where there is neither Greek nor Jew, circumcision nor uncircumcision, Barbarian, Scythian, bond nor free: but Christ is all, and in all.

Put on therefore, as the elect of God, holy and beloved, bowels of mercies, kindness, humbleness of mind, meekness, longsuffering;

Forbearing one another, and forgiving one another, if any man have a quarrel against any: even as Christ forgave you, so also do ye.

And above all these things put on charity, which is the bond of perfectness.

COLOSSIANS

Whosoever hateth his brother is a murderer: and ye know that no murderer hath eternal life abiding in him.

I JOHN

If a man say, I love God, and hateth his brother, he is a liar: for he that loveth not his brother whom he hath seen, how can he love God whom he hath not seen?

I JOHN

There is no fear in love; but perfect love casteth out fear: because fear hath torment. He that feareth is not made perfect in love.

I JOHN

Even so the tongue is a little member, and boasteth great things. Behold, how great a matter a little fire kindleth!

And the tongue is a fire, a world of iniquity: so is the tongue among our members, that it defileth the whole body, and setteth on fire the course of nature; and it is set on fire of hell.

For every kind of beasts, and of birds, and of serpents, and of things in the sea, is tamed, and hath been tamed of mankind:

But the tongue can no man tame; it is an unruly evil, full of deadly poison.

Therewith bless we God, even the Father; and therewith curse we men, which are made after the similitude of God.

Out of the same mouth proceedeth blessing and cursing. My brethren, these things ought not so to be.

Doth a fountain send forth at the same place sweet water and bitter?

Can the fig tree, my brethren, bear olive berries? either a vine, figs? so can no fountain both yield salt water and fresh.

Who is a wise man and endued with knowledge among you? let him shew out of a good conversation his works with meekness of wisdom.

But if ye have bitter envying and strife in your hearts, glory not, and lie not against the truth.

This wisdom descendeth not from above, but is earthly, sensual, devilish.

For where envying and strife is, there is confusion and every evil work.

But the wisdom that is from above is first pure, then peaceable, gentle, and easy to be intreated, full of mercy and good fruits, without partiality, and without hypocrisy.

And the fruit of righteousness is sown in peace of them that make peace.

JAMES

Brethren, if a man be overtaken in a fault, ye which are spiritual, restore such an one in the spirit of meekness; considering thyself, lest thou also be tempted.

Bear ye one another's burdens, and so fulfil the law of Christ.

GALATIANS

For if there be first a willing mind, it is accepted according to that a man hath, and not according to that he hath not.

For I mean not that other men be eased, and ye burdened:

But by an equality, that now at this time your abundance may be a supply for their want, that their abundance also may be a supply for your want: that there may be equality:

As it is written, He that had gathered much had nothing over; and he that had gathered little had no lack.

II CORINTHIANS

Look not every man on his own things, but every man also on the things of others.

PHILIPPIANS

Pure religion and undefiled before God and the Father is this, To visit the fatherless and widows in their affliction, and to keep himself unspotted from the world.

JAMES

III

This only is charity, to do all, all that we can.

JOHN DONNE

Charity can have no excess till it contradicts that love which we are to have in Heaven, till it is more than that which would lay down its life even for an enemy, till it exceeds that which the first Christians practised, when they had all things common; till it exceeds that of St. John, who requires him that has two coats to give to him that has none, and he that has meat to do likewise; till it is loving our poor brethren more than Christ has loved us; till it goes beyond the command of loving our neighbour as we love ourselves; till it forgets that our own life is to be preserved.

WILLIAM LAW

He who withholds but a pennyworth of worldly goods from his neighbour, knowing him to be in need of it, is a robber in the sight of God. . . . Further I declare, who spares a penny for himself to put it by against a rainy day, thinking, I may need that for to-morrow, is a murderer before God.

MEISTER ECKHART

Moreover, brethren, though robbers, who are highwaymen, should with a two-handed saw carve you in pieces limb by limb, yet if the mind of any one of you should be offended thereat, such an one is no follower of my gospel.

THE BUDDHA

Proceeding onwards in our search of religious extravagance, we next come upon excesses of Tenderness and Charity. Here saintliness has to face the charge of preserving the unfit, and breeding parasites and beggars. "Resist not evil," "Love your enemies," these are saintly maxims of which men of this world find it hard to speak without impatience. Are the men of this world right, or are the saints in possession of the deeper range of truth?

No simple answer is possible. Here, if anywhere, one feels the complexity of the moral life, and the mysteriousness of the way in which facts and ideals are interwoven.

Perfect conduct is a relation between three terms: the actor, the objects for which he acts, and the recipients of the action. In order that conduct should be abstractly perfect, all three terms, intention, execution, and reception, should be suited to one another. The best intention will fail if it either work by false means or address itself to the wrong recipient. Thus no critic or estimator of the value of conduct can confine himself to the actor's animus alone, apart from the other elements of the performance. As there is no worse lie than a truth misunderstood by those who hear it, so reasonable arguments, challenges to magnanimity, and appeals to sympathy or justice, are folly when we are dealing with human crocodiles and boa-constrictors. The saint may simply give the universe into the hands of the enemy by his trustfulness. He may by non-resistance cut off his own survival.

Herbert Spencer tells us that the perfect man's conduct will appear perfect only when the environment is perfect: to no inferior environment is it suitably adapted. We may paraphrase this by cordially admitting that saintly conduct would be the most perfect conduct conceivable in an environment where all were saints already; but by adding that in an environment where few are saints, and many the exact reverse of saints, it must be ill adapted. We must frankly confess, then, using our empirical common sense and ordinary practical prejudices, that in the world that actually is, the virtues of sympathy, charity, and non-resistance may be, and often have been, manifested in excess. The powers of darkness have systematically taken advantage of them. The whole modern scientific organisation of charity is a consequence of the failure of simply giving alms. The whole history of constitutional government is a commentary on the excellence of resisting evil, and when one cheek is smitten, of smiting back and not turning the other cheek also.

You will agree to this in general, for in spite of the Gospel, in spite of Quakerism, in spite of Tolstoi, you believe in fighting fire with fire, in shooting down usurpers, locking up thieves, and freezing out vagabonds and swindlers.

And yet you are sure, as I am sure, that were the world confined to these hard-headed, hard-hearted, and hard-fisted methods exclusively, were there no one prompt to help a brother first, and find out afterwards whether he were worthy; no one willing to drown his private wrongs in pity for the wronger's person; no one ready to be duped many a time rather than live always on suspicion; no one glad to treat individuals passionately and impulsively rather than by general rules of prudence; the world would be an infinitely worse place than it is now to live in. The tender grace, not of a day that is dead, but of a day yet to be born somehow, with the golden rule grown natural, would be cut out from the perspective of our imaginations.

The saints, existing in this way, may, with their extravagances of human tenderness, be prophetic. Nay, innumerable times they have proved themselves prophetic. Treating those whom they met, in spite of the past, in spite of all appearances, as worthy, they have stimulated them to *be* worthy, miraculously transformed them by their radiant example and by the challenge of their expectation.

From this point of view we may admit the human charity which we find in all saints, and the great excess of it which we find in some saints, to be a genuinely creative social force, tending to make real a degree of virtue which it alone is ready to assume as possible. The saints are authors, *auctores*, increasers, of goodness. The potentialities of development in human souls are unfathomable. So many who seemed irretrievably hardened have in point of fact been softened, converted, regenerated, in ways that amazed the subjects even more than they surprised the spectators, that we never can be sure in advance of any man that his salvation by the way of love is hopeless. We have no right to speak of human crocodiles and boa-constrictors as of fixedly incurable beings. We know not the complexities of personality, the smouldering emotional fires, the other facets of the character-polyhedron, the resources of the subliminal region. St. Paul long ago made our ancestors familiar with the idea that every soul is virtually sacred. Since Christ died for us all without exception, St. Paul said, we must despair of no one. This belief in the essential sacredness of every one expresses itself to-day in all sorts of humane customs and reformatory institutions, and in a growing aversion to the death penalty and to brutality in punishment. The saints, with their extravagance of human tenderness, are the great torch-bearers of this belief, the tip of the wedge, the clearers of the darkness. Like the single drops which sparkle in the sun as they are flung far ahead of the advancing edge of a wave-crest or of a flood, they show the way and are forerunners. The world is not yet with them, so they often seem in the midst of the world's affairs to be preposterous. Yet they are impregnators of the world, vivifiers and animaters of potentialities of goodness which but for them would lie forever dormant. It is not possible to be quite as mean as we naturally are, when they have passed before us. One fire kindles another; and without that over-trust in human worth which they show, the rest of us would lie in spiritual stagnancy.

Momentarily considered, then, the saint may waste his tenderness and be the dupe and victim of his charitable fever, but the general function of his charity in social evolution is vital and essential. If things are ever to move upward, some one must be ready to take the first step, and assume the risk of it. No one who is not willing to try charity, to try non-resistance as the saint is always willing, can tell whether these methods will or will not succeed. When they do succeed, they are far more powerfully successful than force or worldly prudence.

Force destroys enemies; and the best that can be said of prudence is that it keeps what we already have in safety. But non-resistance, when successful, turns enemies into friends; and charity regenerates its objects. These saintly methods are, as I said, creative energies; and genuine saints find in the elevated excitement with which their faith endows them an authority and impressiveness which makes them irresistible in situations where men of shallower nature cannot get on at all without the use of worldly prudence. This practical proof that worldly wisdom may be safely transcended is the saint's magic gift to mankind. Not only does his vision of a better world console us for the generally prevailing prose and barrenness; but even when on the whole we have to confess him ill adapted, he makes some converts, and the environment gets better for his ministry. He is an effective ferment of goodness, a slow transmuter of the earthly into a more heavenly order.

WILLIAM JAMES

IV

A man may love evil by willing evil to his neighbours in three ways: For first, he may hope to be prosperous through his neighbour's degradation, and may therefore hope for that degradation; and again, he may himself fear to lose power, grace, honour, or reputation because of his neighbour's advancement, and may therefore be miserable at that advancement; and again, he may feel himself injured by his neighbour, and wish to be revenged, so that he sets himself to seek out the other's hurt.

DANTE

Lord, I perceive my soul deeply guilty of envy. . . . I had rather thy work were undone than done better by another than by myself! . . . Dispossess me, Lord, of this bad spirit, and turn my envy into holy emulation; . . . yea, make other men's gifts to be mine, by making me thankful to thee for them.

THOMAS FULLER

The flowers of the earth do no grudge at one another, though one be more beautiful and fuller of virtue than another; but they stand kindly one by another, and enjoy one another's virtue.

JAKOB BOEHME

Although I am far from Thee, may no one else be far from Thee.

HAFIZ

Lord of the world, I beg of you to redeem Israel. And if you do not want to do that, then redeem the Gentiles.

PRAYER OF RABBI ISRAEL OF KOZNITZ

But good Men's wishes extend beyond their lives, for the happiness of times to come, and never to be known unto them. And therefore while so many question prayers for the dead, they charitably pray for those who are not yet alive; they are not so enviously ambitious to go to Heaven by themselves; they cannot but humbly wish, that the little Flock might be greater, the narrow Gate wider, and that, as many are called, so not a few might be chosen.

SIR THOMAS BROWNE

To reflect that another human being, if at a distance of ten thousand years from the year 1883, would enjoy one hour's more life, in the sense of fulness of life, in consequence of anything I had done in my little span, would be to me a peace of soul.

RICHARD JEFFERIES

Now may every living thing, feeble or strong, omitting none, or tall or middle-sized or short, subtle or gross of form, seen or unseen, those dwelling near or far away,—whether they be born or yet unborn—may every living thing be full of bliss.

THE BUDDHA

What is a charitable heart? It is the heart of him who burns with pity for all creation—for every human being, every bird, every animal, every demon. He looks at the creatures or remembers them, and his eyes are filled with tears. His heart also is filled with deep compassion and limitless patience; it overflows with tenderness, and cannot bear to see or hear any evil or the least grief endured by the creature.

Therefore he offers his prayer constantly for the dumb creatures and for the enemies of truth and for those who do him harm, that they may be preserved and pardoned. And for the reptiles also he prays with great compassion, which rises without measure from the depths of his heart till he shines again and is glorious like God.

ST. ISAAK OF SYRIA

PROP. XLV. Hatred can never do good.

Proof: We endeavour to destroy the man whom we hate, that is, we endeavour to do something which is bad. Therefore, etc., *Q.e.d.* . . .

Corollary I: Envy, derision, contempt, rage, revenge, and the other emotions which have reference to hatred or arise from it, are bad . . .

PROP. XLVI. He who lives under the guidance of reason endeavours as much as possible to repay his fellow's hatred, rage, contempt, etc., with love and nobleness.

Proof: All emotions of hatred are bad: and therefore he who lives according to the precepts of reason will endeavour as much as possible to bring it to pass that he is not assailed by emotions of hatred, and consequently he will endeavour to prevent any one else from suffering those emotions. But hatred is increased by reciprocated hatred, and, on the contrary, can be demolished by love in such a way that hatred is transformed into love. Therefore he who lives under the guidance of reason will endeavour to repay another's hatred, etc., with love, that is nobleness. *Q.e.d.*

Note: He who wishes to revenge injuries by reciprocal hatred will live in misery. But he who endeavours to drive away hatred by means of love, fights with pleasure and confidence: he resists equally one or many men, and scarcely needs at all the help of fortune. Those whom he conquers yield joyfully, not from want of force but increase thereof. All these things follow so clearly from the definitions alone of love and intellect that there is no need for me to point them out.

SPINOZA

The best thing then we can bring to pass, as long as we have no perfect knowledge of our emotions, is to conceive some manner of living aright or certain rules of life, to commit them to memory, and to apply them continuously to the individual things which come in our way frequently in life, so that our imagination may be deeply affected with them and they may be always ready for us. E.g., we placed among the rules of life . . . that hatred must be overcome by love or nobleness, not requited by reciprocated hatred. But in order that this rule may be always ready for us when we need it, we must often think and meditate on the common injuries done to men, and in what manner and according to what method they may best be avoided by nobility of character. For if we unite the image of the injury to the image of this rule, it will always be ready for us . . . when an injury is done to us.

SPINOZA

"Who hates his neighbour has not the rights of a child." And not only has he no rights as a child, he has no "father." God is not my father in particular, or any man's father (horrible presumption and madness!), no, he is only father in the sense of father of all, and consequently only my father in so far as he is the father of all. When I hate some one or deny that God is his father—it is not he who loses, but me: for then I have no father.

KIERKEGAARD

The man who truly loves his neighbour, therefore loves also his enemy. This distinction, "friend or enemy," is a difference in the object of love, but love for one's neighbour truly has an object which is without discrimination; the neighbour is the absolutely indistinguishable difference between man and man, or it is the eternal resemblance before God—and the enemy also has this resemblance. We think that it is impossible for a man to love his enemy, alas! for enemies can hardly bear to look at each other. Oh, well, then close your eyes—then the enemy absolutely resembles your neighbour; close your eyes and remember the commandment that *thou shalt love*, then you love—your enemy? No, then you love your neighbour, for you do not see that he is your enemy.

KIERKEGAARD

The branches of ire and envy are these: hatred, evil suspicion, false and unreasonable deeming, melancholy rising of heart against them, despising, mis-saying, unreasonable blaming, unkindness, backbiting, misliking, angriness, and heaviness against them that despise thee or speak evil of thee or against thee, a gladness of their trouble, and a fury against sinful men, and other that will not do as thee thinketh they should do, with a great desire of thine heart under colour of charity and righteousness that they were well punished and chastised for their sin. This stirring seemeth good, nevertheless if thou ransack it well thou shalt find it more fleshly against the person than ghostly against the sin. Thou shalt love the man, be he never so sinful, and thou shalt hate sin in ilk a man what that he be. Many are beguiled in this, for they set the bitter instead of the sweet, and take darkness instead of light, as the prophet saith: Woe be to them that say evil is good and good is evil, and set light as darkness, and bitter instead of sweet. Those do all those that when they should hate the sin of their neighbour and love the person, they hate the person instead of the sin, and ween that they hate the sin.

WALTER HYLTON

Look and bethink thee how Christ loved Judas, that was both His deadly enemy, and a sinful caitiff. How goodly Christ was to him, how benign, how courteous, and how lowly to him that He knew damnable. And nevertheless He chose him to His

Apostle, and sent him for to preach with other Apostles. He gave him power to work miracles, He showed to him the same good cheer in word and in deed as He did to other Apostles, He washed his feet and fed him with His precious body, and preached to him as He did to other Apostles; He bewrayed him not openly nor mis-said him not, nor despised him nor spake never evil of him; and yet though he had done all these he had said but sooth. And over more, when Judas took him He kissed him and called him His friend. And all this charity showed Christ to Judas which he knew for damnable; in no manner feigning nor flattering, but in soothfastness of good love and clean charity.

WALTER HYLTON

[Christ has appeared on earth for a few moments during the terror of the Inquisition. The Grand Inquisitor has had Him flung into prison, that he may burn Him on the morrow. The Inquisitor reviles Christ bitterly, and now concludes:] "Know that I fear Thee not. Know that I too have been in the wilderness, I too have lived on roots and locusts, I too prized the freedom with which Thou hast blessed men, and I too was striving to stand among Thy elect. . . . But I awakened and would not serve madness. I turned back and joined the ranks of those *who have corrected Thy work*. . . . What I say to Thee will come to pass, and our dominion will be built up. I repeat, to-morrow Thou shalt see that obedient flock who at a sign from me will hasten to heap up the hot cinders about the pile on which I shall burn Thee for coming to hinder us. For if anyone ever deserved our fires, it is Thou. To-morrow I shall burn Thee. *Dixi*." . . .

When the Inquisitor ceased speaking he waited some time for his Prisoner to answer him. His silence weighed down upon him. He saw that the Prisoner had listened intently all the time, looking gently in his face and evidently not wishing to reply. The old man longed for Him to say something, however bitter and terrible. But He suddenly approached the old man in silence and softly kissed him on his bloodless aged lips. That was all his answer. The old man shuddered. His lips moved. He went to the door, opened it, and said to Him: "Go, and come no more . . . come not at all, never, never!" And he let Him out into the dark alleys of the town. The Prisoner went away.

DOSTOEVSKY

Never listen to accounts of the frailties of others; and if anyone should complain to you of another, humbly ask him not to speak about him at all.

ST. JOHN OF THE CROSS

No man can justly censure or condemn another, because indeed no man truly knows another. This I perceive in my self; for I am in the dark to all the world, and my nearest friends behold me but in a cloud. Those that know me but superficially, think less of me than I do of my self; those of my neer acquaintance think more; God, who truly knows me, knows that I am nothing; for he only beholds me and all the world, who looks not on us through a derived ray, or a trajection of a sensible species, but beholds the substance without the helps of accidents, and the forms of things as we their operations. Further, no man can judge another, because no man knows himself: for we censure others but as they disagree from that humour which we fancy laudable in our selves, and commend others but for that wherein they seem to quadrate and consent with us.

SIR THOMAS BROWNE

Everything that is unconscious in ourselves we discover in our neighbour, and we treat him accordingly. We no longer subject him to the test of drinking poison; we do not burn him or put screws on him; but we injure him by means of moral verdicts pronounced with the deepest conviction. What we combat in him is usually our own inferior side.

C. G. JUNG

One has only to grow older to become more tolerant. I see no fault that I might not have committed myself.

GOETHE

We all make mistakes, but everyone makes different mistakes.

THE DYING BEETHOVEN

Forgiving love is a possibility only for those who know they are not good, who feel themselves in need of divine mercy, who . . . know that the differences between the good man and the bad man are insignificant in [God's] sight.

REINHOLD NIEBUHR

Nothing spoils human Nature more than false Zeal. The *Good-nature* of an Heathen is more God-like than the furious *Zeal* of a Christian.

Our Fallibility and the Shortness of our Knowledge should make us peaceable and gentle: because I *may* be Mistaken, I *must* not be dogmatical and confident, peremptory and imperious. I *will* not break the certain Laws of Charity, for a doubtful Doctrine or of uncertain Truth.

BENJAMIN WHICHCOTE

Almighty God, have mercy on N and N and on all that bear me evil will, and would me harm, and their faults and mine together, by such easy, tender, merciful means as Thine infinite wisdom best can divine, vouchsafe to amend and redress, and make us saved souls in heaven together where we may ever live and love together with thee and thy blessed saints, O glorious Trinity, for the bitter passion of our sweet saviour Christ, amen.

ASCRIBED TO SIR THOMAS MORE

Most merciful and loving Father,
We beseech Thee most humbly, even with all our hearts,
To pour out upon our enemies with bountiful hands whatsoever things Thou knowest may do them good.
And chiefly a sound and uncorrupt mind,
Where-through they may know Thee and love Thee in true charity and with their whole heart,
And love us, Thy children, for Thy sake.
Let not their first hating of us turn to their harm,
Seeing that we cannot do them good for want of ability.
Lord, we desire their amendment and our own.
Separate them not from us by punishing them,
But join and knot them to us by Thy favourable dealing with them.
And, seeing we be all ordained to be citizens of the one everlasting city,
Let us begin to enter into that way here already by mutual love,
Which may bring us right forth thither.

AN ELIZABETHAN PRAYER FOR OUR ENEMIES

V

A brother asked Abbâ Poemen, saying, "Tell me, why it is that when I offer repentance to a brother who is wroth with me I do not see him pleased with me?" The old man said unto him, "Tell me truly: when thou offerest to him repentance, dost thou not think that thou art not doing it because thou hast sinned against him, but because of the commandment?" And the brother said unto him "It is even thus." The old man said unto him, "Because of this God doth not permit him to be pleased with thee, and because thou dost not offer repentance to him in fulfilment of thine own desire, but as if thou hadst not sinned against him, but he had sinned against thee."

THE PARADISE OF THE FATHERS

On one occasion three old men went to Abbâ Akîlâ, and on one of them rested some small suspicion of evil; and one of them said unto him, "Father, make me a net," and he replied, "I will not make thee a net." Then another said unto him, "Do us an act of grace, and make us a net, so that we may be able to keep thee in remembrance in our monastery"; and Akîlâ said again, "I am not at leisure to do so." Then the third brother, on whom rested the suspicion of evil, also said unto him, "Father, make me a net which I can possess direct from thy hands"; and Akîlâ answered straightway, and said unto this man, "I will make one for thee." And afterwards the other two brethren said unto him privately: "Consider how much we entreated thee, and yet thou wouldst not be persuaded to make a net for us, and thou didst say to this man, 'I will make thee one immediately!' " The old man said unto them, "I told you that I would not make one, and ye were not grieved, because I had not the leisure; but if I had not made one for this man, he would have said, 'It was because the old man had heard about my sins that he was unwilling to make a net for me.' "

THE PARADISE OF THE FATHERS

Two brethren went to the market to sell their wares, and whilst one of them had gone to perform the service, he who was left by himself fell into fornication; and the other brother came and said unto him, "My brother, let us go to the cell," but he said unto him, "I cannot go, for I have fallen into fornication." Now whilst he was seeking to do better, the brother began to swear to him, saying, "I also, when I was away from thee, fell in the same manner, nevertheless, come, and let us repent together, and it may happen that God will pardon us." And when they came to their cells they informed the old men about the temptation which had come to them, and whatsoever the old men told them to do the two brothers did, and the one brother repented with the other, just as if he had sinned with him. Now God saw the labour of his love, and in a few days He sent a revelation unto one of the old men concerning the matter, saying, "For the sake of the love of that brother who did not sin, forgive thou him that did commit sin." This is what is meant by the words, "A man should lay down his soul for his friend."

THE PARADISE OF THE FATHERS

An aged man, whom Abraham hospitably invited to his tent, refused to join him in prayer to the one spiritual God. Learning that he was a fire-worshipper, Abraham drove him from his door. That night God appeared to Abraham in a vision and said: "I have borne with that ignorant man for seventy years; could you not have patiently suffered him one night?"

THE TALMUD

I went up to Heaven in a dream and stood at the Gates of Paradise in order to observe the procedure of the Heavenly Tribunal. A learned Rabbi approached and wished to enter. "Day and night," he said, "I studied the Holy Torah." "Wait," said the Angel. "We will investigate whether your study was for its own sake or whether it was as a matter of profession or for the sake of honours."

A Zaddik[1] next approached. "I fasted much," he said. "I underwent many ablutions; I studied the Zohar."[2] "Wait," said the Angel, "until we have completed our investigation to learn whether your motives were pure."

Then a tavern-keeper drew near. "I kept an open door and fed without charge every poor man who came to my inn," he said.

The Heavenly Portals were opened to him. No investigation was required.

[1] Religious leader. [2] Mystical Treatise.

RABBI AARON LEIB OF PRIMISHLAN

A thief in his old age was unable to ply his "trade" and was starving. A wealthy man, hearing of his distress, sent him food. Both the rich man and the thief died on the same day. The trial of the magnate occurred first in the Heavenly Court; he was found wanting and sentenced to Purgatory. At the entrance, however, an Angel came hurrying to recall him. He was brought back to the Court and learned that his sentence had been reversed. The thief whom he had aided on earth had stolen the list of his iniquities.

THE YEHUDI

A Rabbi ordered his Warden to assemble ten men for a Minyan[1] to chant Psalms for the recovery of a sick man. When they entered, a friend of the Rabbi exclaimed: "I see among them notorious thieves."

"Excellent," retorted the Rabbi. "When all the Heavenly Gates of Mercy are closed, it requires experts to open them."

[1] Quorum for prayer.

HASIDIC STORY

A teamster sought the Rabbi of Berditchev's advice as to whether he should give up his occupation because it interfered with regular attendance at the synagogue.

"Do you carry poor travellers free of charge?" asked the Rabbi.

"Yes," answered the teamster.

"Then you serve the Lord in your occupation just as faithfully as you would by frequenting the synagogue."

HASIDIC STORY

The wife of the Rabbi of Roptchitz said to him: "Your prayer was lengthy to-day. Have you succeeded in bringing it about that the rich should be more generous in their gifts to the poor?"

The Rabbi replied: "Half of my prayer I have accomplished. The poor are willing to accept them."

HASIDIC STORY

When Rabbi Levi Yitzhak accepted the call to become Rabbi of Berditchev he stipulated that he should be invited to participate only in those meetings when new ordinances were to be decided. Once it was resolved to vote upon a prohibition against house-to-house begging by the poor. It was suggested that a public fund be substituted to aid them. The Rabbi was called, but he protested, saying: "Why do you summon me upon an old matter?" "But it is new," they said.

"You are mistaken," was his reply. "It is as old as Sodom and Gomorrah, where direct aid to the poor was forbidden. Perhaps they also had a public fund, the object of which was that the wealthy should be freed from the necessity of coming face to face with the poor."

HASIDIC STORY

Rabbi Mendel was accustomed to restrain an angry rebuke until he had investigated the *Shulchan Arukh*[1] to learn whether anger is permissible in the particular instance. But how much genuine anger could he feel after completing his search?

[1] An authoritative list of many hundreds of commands and prohibitions incumbent on Jews.

HASIDIC STORY

When you speak evil of another man, the Satan will compel you to be his witness against the object of your words. Would you become the Satan's assistant?

RABBI PINHAS OF KORETZ

He who gives a penny to a poor man receives six blessings: he who shows his sympathy with the poor man receives eleven blessings.

RABBI NAHMAN OF BRATZLAV

An opponent of Rabbi Shmelke wished to shame him in public. He sent him a flask of very old and strong wine on the day before the Day of Atonement in the hope that he would become drunk from it. The Rabbi tasted a little and perceived the sender's intention. When he was reciting Psalms after the Services, he repeated several times the verse: "By this I know that Thou delightest in me, that mine enemy doth not triumph over me," and translated it thus: "By this I shall know that Thou art pleased with me, that those who wished to disgrace me receive no harm because of me."

HASIDIC STORY

A father complained to the Baalshem that his son had forsaken God. "What, Rabbi, shall I do?"

"Love him more than ever," was the Baalshem's reply.

HASIDIC STORY

To sin against a fellow-man is worse than to sin against the Creator. The man you harmed may have gone to an unknown place, and you may lose the opportunity to beg his forgiveness. The Lord, however, is everywhere and you can always find Him when you seek Him.

A HASIDIC RABBI

Rabbi Shmelke once had no money to give to a beggar. He ransacked his wife's drawer, took from it a ring and gave it to the destitute man. His wife returned, saw that the drawer was open and that her ring was missing. She raised a hue and cry, and when her husband explained his action she asked him to run after the beggar, since the ring was worth fifty thalers.

The Rabbi ran swiftly in pursuit, and catching up with the beggar, said: "I have just learned that the ring is worth fifty thalers. Let no one cheat you by giving you less than its value."

HASIDIC STORY

It may sometimes happen that thine own hand inadvertently strikes thee. Wouldst thou take a stick and chastise thy hand for its heedlessness, and thus add to thy pain? It is the same when thy neighbour, whose soul is one with thine, because of insufficient understanding does thee harm: shouldst thou retaliate, it would be thou who wouldst suffer.

RABBI SHMELKE OF NIKOLSBURG

Rabbi Wolf of Zbarazh once saw thieves robbing his home. He remained still and murmured: "I do not wish to cause you to be guilty of a sin, and therefore I make you a gift of everything you take."

In a moment he noticed that they were taking a jar containing medicine. He then approached them and said: "Do not fear to take away whatever you can place in your bag, for I am presenting these things to you as gifts; but, I beg of you, do not consume the contents of the jar you have included. It is medicine and may harm you."

HASIDIC STORY

Love the wicked man. Why? Because he will then love you, and love will unite his soul and yours. As a consequence, inasmuch as you hate wickedness you will transfer your hate to him, thereby causing him to repent and turn from evil to good.

RABBI RAFAEL OF BERSHAD

Cherish no hate for thy brother who offends, because you have not offended like him. If your fellow-man possessed your nature, he might not have sinned. If you possessed his nature, you might have offended as he has done. A man's transgressions depend not entirely upon his free choice, but often upon many other circumstances.

A HASIDIC RABBI

I hate nobody. How could we hate men who believe that they control that which drives them, that driving fate which will hold us as long as this earth has breath?

Believe me, it is hard not to hate—only the realisation of the compulsion behind compulsion in men's lives gives us knowledge and makes us wise and understanding.

ERNST TOLLER

ABEL

My brother Cain, the wounded, liked to sit
Brushing my shoulder, by the staring water
Of life, or death, in cinemas half-lit
By scenes of peace that always turned to slaughter.

He liked to talk to me. His eager voice
Whispered the puzzle of his bleeding thirst,
Or prayed me not to make my final choice,
Unless we had a chat about it first.

And then he chose the final pain for me.
I do not blame his nature: he's my brother;
Nor what you call the times: our love was free,
Would be the same at any time; but rather

The ageless ambiguity of things
Which makes our life mean death, our love be hate.
My blood that streams across the bedroom sings:
"I am my brother opening the gate!"

DEMETRIOS CAPETANAKIS

ONE IN THE PUBLIC GALLERY

The Seraph scanned the murderer in the dock—
The motionless Judge, beneath the court-room clock,
The listening jury, warders, counsel, Clerk;
Ay, one and all who shared that deepening dark:
    And then, as I shunned to see,
He turned his burning eyes and looked at me.

WALTER DE LA MARE

VI

Him who destroys one human life, the Scripture regards as if he had destroyed the whole world.

THE TALMUD

The life and destiny of the least of human beings has an absolute meaning in respect of eternity; his life and his destiny are everlasting. For that reason one may not do away with a single human creature and escape punishment; we must consider the divine image and likeness in every one, from the most noble to the most despicable.

NICHOLAS BERDYAEV

The Scriptures relate that God bade Abraham offer his son as a burnt-offering, and Abraham prepared to obey. But an angel stopped him and instantly he heeded the angel's voice even though God had not himself revoked his command. What the Torah teaches us thereby is this: None but God can command us to destroy a man, and if the very smallest angel comes after the command has been given and cautions us: "Lay not thy hand upon . . ." we must obey him.

RABBI MENDEL OF KOSOV

The more attention one gives to the punishment of death, the more he will be inclined to adopt the opinion of Beccaria, —that it ought to be disused . . . Whence originated the prodigal fury with which the punishment of death has been inflicted? It is the effect of resentment which at first inclines to the greatest rigour; and of an imbecility of soul, which finds in the rapid destruction of convicts the great advantage of having no further occasion to concern oneself about them.

JEREMY BENTHAM

VII

Be like a tree. The tree gives shade even to him who cuts off its boughs.

SRI CHAITANYA

Say to thyself at daybreak: I shall come across the busy-body, the thankless, the overbearing, the treacherous, the envious, the unneighbourly. All this has befallen them because they know not good from evil. But I, in that I have comprehended the nature of the Good that it is beautiful, and the nature of Evil that it is ugly, and the nature of the wrong-doer himself that it is akin to me, not as partaker of the same blood and seed but of intelligence and a morsel of the Divine, can neither be injured by any of them—for no one can involve me in what is debasing—nor can I be wroth with my kinsman and hate him. For we have come into being for co-operation, as have the feet, the hands, the eyelids, the rows of upper and lower teeth. Therefore to thwart one another is against Nature; and we do thwart one another by showing resentment and aversion.

. . . .

If a man's armpits are unpleasant, art thou angry with him? If he has foul breath? What would be the use? The man has such a mouth, he has such armpits. Some such effluvium was bound to come from such a source. *But the man has sense*, quotha! *With a little attention he could see wherein he offends.* I congratulate thee! Well, thou too hast sense. By a rational attitude, then, in thyself evoke a rational attitude in him, enlighten him, admonish him. If he listen, thou shalt cure him, and have no need of anger.

. . . .

When thou wouldst cheer thine heart, think upon the good qualities of thy associates; as for instance, this one's energy, that one's modesty, the generosity of a third, and some other trait of a fourth. For nothing is so cheering as the images of the virtues mirrored in the characters of those who live with us, and presenting themselves in as great a throng as possible. Have these images then ever before thine eyes.

. . . .

It is a man's especial privilege to love even those who stumble. And this love follows as soon as thou reflectest that they are of kin to thee and that they do wrong involuntarily and through ignorance, and that within a little while both they and thou will be dead; and this, above all, that the man has done thee no hurt; for he has not made thy ruling Reason worse than it was before.

. . . .

Does a man do thee wrong? Go to and mark what notion of good and evil was his that did the wrong. Once perceive that and thou wilt feel compassion, not surprise or anger. For thou hast still thyself either the same notion of good and evil as he or another not unlike. Thou needst must forgive him then. But if thy notions of good and evil are no longer such, all the more easily shalt thou be gracious to him that sees awry.

. . . .

If he did wrong, with him lies the evil. But maybe he did no wrong.

. . . .

Enter into every man's ruling Reason, and give every one else an opportunity to enter into thine.

. . . .

If a man makes a slip, enlighten him with loving-kindness, and shew him wherein he hath seen amiss. Failing that, blame thyself or not even thyself.

. . . .

Does another's wrong-doing shock thee? Turn incontinently to thyself and bethink thee what analogous wrong-doing there is of thine own, such as deeming money to be a good or pleasure or a little cheap fame and the like. For by marking this thou wilt quickly forget thy wrath, with this reflection too to aid thee, that a man is under constraint; for what should he do? Or, if thou art able, remove the constraint.

. . . .

A branch cut off from its neighbour branch cannot but be cut off from the whole plant. In the very same way a man severed from one man has fallen away from the fellowship of all men. Now a branch is cut off by others, but a man separates himself from his neighbour by his own agency in hating him or turning his back upon him; and is unaware that he has thereby sundered himself from the whole civic community. But mark the gift of Zeus who established the law of fellowship. For it is in our power to grow again to the neighbour branch, and again become perfective of the whole. But such a schism constantly repeated makes it difficult for the seceding part to unite again and resume its former condition. And in general the branch that from the first has shared in the growth of the tree and lived with its life is not like that which has been cut off and afterwards grafted on to it, as the gardeners are apt to tell you. Be of one bush, but not of one mind.

As those who withstand thy progress along the path of right reason will never be able to turn thee aside from sound action, so let them not wrest thee from a kindly attitude towards them; but keep a watch over thyself in both directions alike, not only in steadfastness of judgment and action but also in gentleness towards those who endeavour to stand in thy path or be in some other way a thorn in thy side. For in fact it is a sign of weakness to be wroth with them, no less than to shrink from action and be terrified into surrender. For they that do the one or the other are alike deserters of their post, the one as a coward, the other as estranged from a natural kinsman and friend.

MARCUS AURELIUS

Christianity also speaks of suffering, but it speaks more of guilt. What is guilt? First, guilt is what produces suffering. Guilt is what we do to one another day by day in the fight for life. The individual kills in order to live. But there is more than killing. Theft, envy, calumny, indifference are guilt. Guilt is want of love.

But would not all nature then be guilty? Can I call the lion guilty that slays its prey? The lion would not be a lion if it did not kill. It cannot do otherwise. Can I call guilty the strong man who follows his heroic instincts?

But between lion and man runs the divide of freedom. The lion has the innocence of nature. Objectively, all nature is in the state which, in man, turns to guilt, but subjectively, nature is not guilty. Man is no longer bound to his instinctive actions. He has insight. The possibility of choice is before him. The man who treats his fellow as the lion treats its prey can do otherwise, and therefore he is guilty.

The story of man's fall expresses this in mythical terms. Man enters into guilt by eating from the tree of knowledge. That tree has been planted by God. "Adam has become like one of us and knows what is good and evil"—this is not only what the serpent had claimed, God Himself says it afterwards. Knowledge is indeed the objective potentiality for which man is meant. Yet by grasping knowledge against the will of God man becomes guilty. Against the will of God, that means against the *salutary*[1] objective potentiality of knowing. The *salutary*[1] potentiality of knowing is knowing in love. For man experiences God as love in the redemption from the fall that is revealed in Christ.

Seen with external objectivity, original suffering and original guilt are age-old biological facts. All beings fight the fight for life. All must suffer and die, all must cause suffering and must kill. Subjectively, however, their suffering is less than that of man in proportion to their lesser sensitivity and, above all, their lesser vision of past and future. Man is essentially the suffering

[1] Italics mine. V.G.

being. Man alone bears attributable guilt. But in man's suffering and in his guilt we grow aware of what objectively was there even before. It says in the story of man's fall: "And Adam and Eve saw that they were naked, and they were ashamed." Man is the being who shudders at his own naturalness.

The shudder would be senseless if man did not feel within himself the possibility of a goodness beyond that of instinct, the goodness of insight. And even as the shudder also reflects the desperate external state into which man has fallen by the decay of his instincts, so man's external existence is put in order only through the goodness of insight. One of the ways of ordering is the making of laws. Lawmakers in the olden days were rightly thought to be divine, or divine messengers. For the law orders the life of man by his objective potentiality, by the spirit.

But it turns out that every law that is made is only negative. It bars certain misdeeds, but not the attitude that becomes the source of ever new misdeeds. This is expressed in the Sermon on the Mount. "You have been told: Thou shalt not kill, and he who kills is guilty of judgment. But I say to you, he who is angry with his brother is guilty of judgment. You have been told: Thou shalt not commit adultery. But I say to you, he who looks at a woman to lust after her has already committed adultery with her in his heart." The external regulation of life is not enough. It shifts the guilt to a less visible and hence more dangerous sphere. The stirrings of instinct themselves must be changed.

But even good will cannot accomplish this. This is where the despair that lies in the Christian doctrine of original sin is rooted in experience. I see that I must change my instincts, yet I cannot change them. It has been asked, how can the God of Christianity be a god of love if he gives to his own creatures commandments they cannot keep? Objections of this sort avoid reality and escape into a metaphysical construction. They take at face value in the Christian concept of God what after all is no more than a mythical parable, and neglect that in it which is immediate experience. The conflict exists between two sets of facts both of which can be established objectively: on the one hand, the instinct to fight our fellows, an instinct that is there for better or worse; on the other hand, the conditions that have to be met if mankind is to go on living. We can change our faith, but we cannot thereby escape this conflict. The conflict expresses the simple fact that man is a being who cannot remain such as he is. He cannot go back to the innocence of the animal, he must go forward to a new innocence, or perish. And the one possibility open to him, surely, is expressed in the words: God is Love.

What is this love? It is a transformation of man down even into his unconsciousness. It is a fusion of his insight with his instincts, a fusion that makes possible an attitude toward his fellows which was impossible before. The stirrings of man's instincts are the raw material. From this material, love builds a new person. We speak of love even on the level of instincts. Love between man and woman, a mother's love for her child, are necessities of human nature. They are strong and beautiful, but at their source they are blind. Christian love is seeing. It is bound up with knowledge, and it is the attitude in which alone knowledge is good. Think of the parable of the good Samaritan. A man lies by the roadside, beaten half to death. Two others pass and do not help him. A third, a stranger, sees *this man needs help*, and helps. Everything is in this seeing. For once the stranger has seen in his heart the other's plight, the help comes almost of itself. Everyone knows full well that he would have to help if he were to see the distress, and looks the other way just for this reason. Love is an attitude of the soul which, in seeing, resolves the fight for life.

Is this love at all possible? Like every true, new possibility, it cannot be derived from what has gone before. Will, of its own power, can perform single good deeds, but it cannot endow itself with love. But once we have experienced the possibility of love, something remains behind in us called conscience. We know then that without love we are missing the essential. Love itself comes from the objective potentiality, from God, and if it comes to us we experience it as an act of grace. Love can be given to us—that is the whole substance of the Christian doctrine of salvation. It is rarely given to us before, in despair of ourselves, we have asked for it.

C. F. VON WEIZSÄCKER

VIII

FROM "JERUSALEM"

She looked and saw Joseph the Carpenter in Nazareth and Mary
His espoused Wife. And Mary said, If thou put me away from thee
Dost thou not murder me? Joseph spoke in anger and fury: Should I
Marry a Harlot and an Adulteress? Mary answer'd: Art thou more pure
Than thy Maker, who forgiveth Sins and calls again Her that is Lost?

. . . .

He who envies or calumniates, which is murder and cruelty,
Murders the Holy-one. Go tell them this and overthrow their cup,
Their bread, their altar-table, their incense, and their oath;
Their marriage and their baptism, their burial and consecration.
I have tried to make friends by corporeal gifts, but have only
Made enemies; I never made friends but by spiritual gifts,
By severe contentions of friendship and the burning fire of thought.
He who would see the Divinity must see him in his Children,
One first in friendship and love, then a Divine Family, and in the midst
Jesus will appear; so he who wishes to see a Vision, a perfect Whole,
Must see it in its Minute Particulars, Organised, and not as thou,
O Fiend of Righteousness, pretendest; thine is a Disorganised
And snowy cloud; brooder of tempests and destructive War,
You smile with pomp and rigor; you talk of benevolence and virtue;
I act with benevolence and virtue, and get murder'd time after time;
You accumulate Particulars, and murder by analysing, that you

May take the aggregate, and you call the aggregate Moral Law;
And you call that swell'd and bloated Form a Minute Particular.
But General Forms have their vitality in Particulars; and every
Particular is a Man, a Divine Member of the Divine Jesus.

. . . .

And he who takes vengeance alone is the criminal of Providence.
If I should dare to lay my finger on a grain of sand
In way of vengeance, I punish the already punish'd. O whom
Should I pity if I pity not the sinner who is gone astray?
O Albion, if thou takest vengeance, if thou revengest thy wrongs,
Thou art for ever lost! What can I do to hinder the sons
Of Albion from taking vengeance or how shall I them persuade?

BLAKE

I SAW A MONK OF CHARLEMAINE

I

I saw a Monk of Charlemaine
Arise before my sight:
I talk'd to the Grey Monk where he stood
In beams of infernal light.

II

Gibbon arose with a lash of steel,
And Voltaire with a wracking wheel:
The Schools, in clouds of learning roll'd,
Arose with War in iron and gold.

III

"Thou lazy monk," they said afar,
"In vain condemning glorious War,
And in thy cell thou shalt ever dwell.
Rise, War, and bind him in his cell!"

IV

The blood red ran from the Grey Monk's side,
His hands and feet were wounded wide,
His body bent, his arms and knees
Like to the roots of ancient trees.

V

"I see, I see," the Mother said,
"My children will die for lack of bread.
What more has the merciless tyrant said?"
The Monk sat down on her stony bed.

VI

His eye was dry, no tear could flow;
A hollow groan first spoke his woe.
He trembled and shudder'd upon the bed;
At length with a feeble cry he said:

VII

"When God commanded this hand to write
In the studious hours of deep midnight,
He told me that all I wrote should prove
The bane of all that on Earth I love.

VIII

"My brother starv'd between two walls;
Thy children's cry my soul appals:
I mock'd at the wrack and grinding chain;
My bent body mocks at their torturing pain.

IX

"Thy father drew his sword in the North;
With his thousands strong he is marchèd forth;
Thy brother has armèd himself in steel
To revenge the wrongs thy children feel.

X

"But vain the sword and vain the bow,
They never can work War's overthrow;
The hermit's prayer and the widow's tear
Alone can free the world from fear.

XI

"The hand of Vengeance sought the bed
To which the purple tyrant fled;
The iron hand crush'd the tyrant's head,
And became a tyrant in his stead.

XII

"Until the tyrant himself relent,
The tyrant who first the black bow bent,
Slaughter shall heap the bloody plain:
Resistance and War is the tyrant's gain.

XIII

"But the tear of love—and forgiveness sweet,
And submission to death beneath his feet—
The tear shall melt the sword of steel,
And every wound it has made shall heal.

XIV

"For the tear is an intellectual thing,
And a sigh is the sword of an Angel King,
And the bitter groan of the martyr's woe
Is an arrow from the Almighty's bow."

BLAKE

FROM "PROMETHEUS UNBOUND"

Panthea. Look, sister, where a troop of Spirits gather
Like flocks of clouds in Spring's delightful weather
Thronging in the blue air!
Ione. And see! more come,
Like fountain-vapours when the winds are dumb,
That climb up the ravine in scattered lines.
And hark! is it the music of the pines?
Is it the lake? is it the waterfall?
Panthea. 'Tis something sadder, sweeter far than all.

CHORUS OF SPIRITS OF THE MIND

From unremembered ages we
Gentle guides and guardians be
Of heaven-oppressed Mortality.
And we breathe, and sicken not,
The atmosphere of human thought:
Be it dim and dank and grey,
Like a storm-extinguished day
Travelled o'er by dying gleams;
  Be it bright as all between
Cloudless skies and windless streams,
  Silent, liquid, and serene.
As the birds within the wind,
  As the fish within the wave,
As the thoughts of man's own mind
  Float through all above the grave:
We make there our liquid lair,
Voyaging cloudlike and unpent
Through the boundless element.
Thence we bear the prophecy
Which begins and ends in thee!

Ione. More yet come, one by one: the air around them
Looks radiant as the air around a star.

FIRST SPIRIT

On a battle-trumpet's blast
I fled hither, fast, fast, fast,
Mid the darkness upward cast.
From the dust of creeds outworn,
From the tyrant's banner torn,
Gathering round me, onward borne,
There was mingled many a cry—
"Freedom! Hope! Death! Victory!"
Till they faded through the sky.
And one sound, above, around,
One sound, beneath, around, above,
Was moving; 'twas the soul of Love;
'Twas the hope, the prophecy,
Which begins and ends in thee.

SECOND SPIRIT

A rainbow's arch stood on the sea
Which rocked beneath, immovably;
And the triumphant storm did flee
(Like a conqueror, swift and proud)
Between,—with many a captive cloud,
A shapeless, dark, and rapid crowd,
Each by lightning riven in half.
I heard the thunder hoarsely laugh:
Mighty fleets were strewn like chaff,
And spread beneath, a hell of death,
O'er the white waters. I alit
On a great ship lightning-split;
And speeded hither on the sigh
Of one who gave an enemy
His plank, then plunged aside to die.

SHELLEY

The great secret of morals is love; or a going out of our own nature, and an identification of ourselves with the beautiful which exists in thought, action, or person, not our own. A man, to be greatly good, must imagine intensely and comprehensively; he must put himself in the place of another and of many others; the pains and pleasures of his species must become his own. The great instrument of moral good is the imagination.

SHELLEY

I think of every single person who has been kind to me in my prison life . . . down to the poor thief who, recognising me as we tramped round the yard at Wandsworth, whispered to me in the hoarse prison voice men get from long and compulsory silence: "I am sorry for you; it is harder for the likes of you than it is for the likes of us."

OSCAR WILDE

I was walking along the street . . . I was stopped by a decrepit old beggar.

Bloodshot, tearful eyes, blue lips, coarse rags, festering wounds. . . . Oh, how hideously poverty had eaten into this miserable creature!

He held out to me a red, swollen, filthy hand. He groaned, he mumbled of help.

I began feeling in all my pockets. . . . No purse, no watch, not even a handkerchief. . . . I had taken nothing with me. And the beggar was still waiting . . . and his outstretched hand feebly shook and trembled.

Confused, abashed, I warmly clasped the filthy, shaking hand. . . . "Don't be angry, brother; I have nothing, brother."

The beggar stared at me with his bloodshot eyes; his blue lips smiled; and he in his turn gripped my chilly fingers.

"What of it, brother?" he mumbled; "thanks for this, too. That is a gift too, brother."

I knew that I too had received a gift from my brother.

TURGENEV

IX

In that day shall there be a highway out of Egypt to Assyria, and the Assyrian shall come into Egypt, and the Egyptians shall serve with the Assyrians.

In that day shall Israel be the third with Egypt and with Assyria, even a blessing in the midst of the land:

Whom the Lord of hosts shall bless, saying, Blessed be Egypt my people, and Assyria the work of my hands, and Israel mine inheritance.

ISAIAH

"Thou shalt love thy neighbour as thyself." Rabbi Akiba said: That is the greatest principle in the Law. Ben Azzai said: The sentence, "This is the book of the generations of man" (Genesis v. 1) is even greater.

SIFRA

There is another offence unto Charity, which no Author hath ever written of, and few take notice of; and that's the reproach, not of whole professions, mysteries and conditions, but of whole Nations, wherein by opprobrious Epithets we miscall each other, and by an uncharitable Logick, from a disposition in a few, conclude a habit in all.

> Le mutin Anglois, et le bravache Escossois,
> Le bougre Italian, et le fol François,
> Le poultron Romain, le larron de Gascongne,
> L'Espagnol superbe, et l'Aleman yvrongne.

St. Paul, that calls the Cretians lyars, doth it but indirectly, and upon quotation of their own Poet. It is as bloody a thought in one way, as Nero's was in another; for by a word we wound a thousand, and at one blow assassine the honour of a Nation.

SIR THOMAS BROWNE

The words, "I am proud to be a German" or "I am proud to be a Jew" sounded ineffably stupid to me. As well say, "I am proud to have brown eyes."

Must I then join the ranks of the bigoted and glorify my Jewish blood now, not my German? Pride and love are not the same thing, and if I were asked where I belonged I should answer that a Jewish mother had borne me, that Germany had nourished me, Europe had formed me, my home was the earth, and the world my fatherland.

ERNST TOLLER

Christ showed me that the fifth temptation which deprives me of welfare is the separation we make of our own from other nations. I cannot but believe this, and therefore if in a moment of forgetfulness feelings of enmity towards a man of another nation may arise within me, yet in my calm moments I can no longer fail to acknowledge that feeling to be a false one, and I cannot justify myself, as I used to do, by claiming the superiority of my own people to others, basing this on the errors, cruelties, and barbarities of another nation, nor can I, at the first reminder of this, fail to try to be more friendly to a foreigner than to a compatriot.

But not only do I now know that my separation from other nations is an evil, ruining my welfare, but I also know the temptation that led me into that evil, and I can no longer, as I did formerly, consciously and quietly serve it. I know that that temptation lies in the delusion that my welfare is bound up only with that of the people of my own nation, and not with that of all the peoples of the earth. I now know that my union with other people cannot be severed by a line of frontier and by Government decrees about my belonging to this or that nation. I now know that all men everywhere are equals and brothers. Remembering now all the evil I have done, suffered, and seen, resulting from the enmity of nations, it is clear to me that the cause of it all lay in the gross fraud called patriotism and love of one's country. Remembering my education, I now see that a feeling of hostility to other nations, a feeling of separation from them, was never really natural to me, but that all these evil feelings were artificially inoculated into me by an insane education. I now understand the meaning of the words: Do good to your enemies; behave to them as to your own people. You are all children of one Father; so be like your Father, i.e. do not make distinctions between your own people and other peoples; be the same with them all. I now understand that my welfare is only possible if I acknowledge my unity with all the people of the world without exception. I believe this. And that belief has changed my whole valuation of what is good and evil, lofty and mean. What seemed to me good and lofty—love of fatherland, of one's own people, of one's State, and service of it to the detriment of the welfare of other peoples, the military achievements of men, all this now appears to me repulsive and pitiable. What seemed to me bad and shameful—rejection of fatherland, and cosmopolitanism—now appears to me, on the contrary, good and noble.

TOLSTOY

THE LITTLE BLACK BOY

My mother bore me in the southern wild,
  And I am black; but oh, my soul is white!
White as an angel is the English child,
  But I am black, as if bereaved of light.

My mother taught me underneath a tree,
  And, sitting down before the heat of day,
She took me on her lap and kissèd me,
  And, pointing to the East, began to say:

"Look on the rising sun: there God does live,
  And gives His light, and gives His heat away,
And flowers and trees and beasts and men receive
  Comfort in morning, joy in the noonday.

"And we are put on earth a little space,
  That we may learn to bear the beams of love,
And these black bodies and this sunburnt face
  Are but a cloud, and like a shady grove.

"For, when our souls have learned the heat to bear
  The cloud will vanish, we shall hear His voice,
Saying, 'Come out from the grove, My love and care,
  And round My golden tent like lambs rejoice.' "

Thus did my mother say, and kissèd me,
  And thus I say to little English boy.
When I from black, and he from white cloud free,
  And round the tent of God like lambs we joy,

I'll shade him from the heat till he can bear
  To lean in joy upon our Father's knee;
And then I'll stand and stroke his silver hair,
  And be like him, and he will then love me.

BLAKE

X

An Indian greeted a soldier who, at the time of the Indian Mutiny, was about to put a bayonet into his body, with the words, "And thou too art divine."

Quoted by REINHOLD NIEBUHR

The Grand Rabbin of Lyons was a Jewish chaplain to the French forces in the 1914–1918 war. One day a wounded man staggered into a trench and told the Rabbi that a Roman Catholic was on the point of death in no-man's-land, and was begging that his padre should come to him with a crucifix. The padre could not quickly be found. The Jew rapidly improvised a cross, ran out with it into no-man's-land, and was seen to hold it before the dying man's eyes. He was almost immediately shot by a sniper; the bodies of the Catholic and the Jew were found together.

FROM MEMORY

Pte. Clifford Elwood, of High Street, Nantyfyllon, Bridgend, Glamorganshire, and Bugler Robert Hunt, of King Street, Mansfield Woodhouse, Nottinghamshire, both stretcher-bearers, were returning to their lines on the Arakan front with a casualty when they heard a rustling in the bushes and the click of a rifle-bolt.

Out into their path stepped a 6-ft. Japanese with his rifle at the ready. He looked at the two men and the third man they carried on the stretcher, and then without a word or gesture dropped the muzzle of his rifle and stepped back into the jungle.

LEICESTER EVENING MAIL, May 19th, 1944

Mr. and Mrs. J. Gaines, of Fifteenth Avenue, Tong Road, Leeds, have received a letter from their son, Private Harry Gaines, who was wounded in the invasion and is in Worcester Royal Infirmary on this, his 19th birthday. He has wounds in both legs and the right arm.

He tells of the kindness of a German prisoner in a Red Cross hospital in Normandy in succouring him when he fell wounded: "He carried me for 70 yards to the beach, then looked down at me, smiled, put a cigarette in my mouth, lit it, and put his lighter in my pocket. Then he took off his white shirt, tore it into shreds and dressed my wounds. Having done this, he kissed me, with tears in his eyes, and then walked away to attend to other wounded."

YORKSHIRE EVENING POST, June 13th, 1944

The following is an extract from a letter received from an Austrian Jew now in the British Pioneer Corps in the B.L.A. He is attached to a hospital receiving German wounded. He had been for nine months in the concentration camps of Dachau and Buchenwald: he had been hung by the wrists to a tree and had once nearly died of gangrene, Jews at that time not being allowed medical attention in concentration camps. He also has reason to believe that his old mother was taken to Poland two years ago:

"This is being written in the solitude of a ward in which I am guarding wrecked members of the Herrenvolk. It is so strange a situation that I can hardly describe what I am feeling. Loneliness is perhaps the only word for it. These are men who set out to conquer the world, and they and their kind have done unspeakable things to me and my kind, and I am supposed to hate them with all my strength, and would be right to do so according to recognised standards of human behaviour. But I cannot hate, or is it that in the face of suffering hatred is silent? So it happens that the guard is turned into a nurse, and if a man, from losing too much blood, goes out of his mind and stammers incoherently, I have to talk him to sleep again. And it sometimes happens that men try to hold my hand when I have helped them. That makes me feel lonely.

"Only a few lines. It is midnight, and I am going off duty after having had a busy time with that man who lost so much blood that he went crackers. He had an operation and blood transfusion, and I was the only one able to talk to him. In the end he obeyed my orders instantly with 'Jawohl, Herr Doktor!' Once he said 'Sie sind so ein feiner Mensch'[1] and then 'Sie sind zu mir wie ein Vater.'[2] What shall I make of that? I can only draw one conclusion, which is that I am a terribly bad soldier and I am somehow glad about it.

. . . .

"The man I wrote about has died. The doctors fought for his life as if he were a celebrity."

[1] "You are a good man!" [2] "You are like a father to me."

LEFT NEWS, November 1944

Elizabeth Pilenko came from a wealthy land-owning family in the south of Russia. She went to the Women's University of St. Petersburg and began at the age of eighteen, while still a student, to teach in the evening courses at the great Putilov factory. She published two books of poems and was a close friend of some of the best-known younger Russian poets.

She became a keen socialist revolutionary, and during the years 1914–1917 her life was taken up with revolutionary activities. After the October Revolution she worked with extraordinary skill and audacity in rescuing victims from the Terror. Later she became Mayor of her own home town, working for justice between the Whites and the Reds, both of whom had resorted to violence against their opponents. She was denounced as a Bolshevist, tried and acquitted.

In 1923 she came to Paris. The excesses of the Revolution as it developed revolted her, though she remained to her death a staunch advocate of its principles. She found her way back to religious faith largely under the influence of Serge Bulgakov, who had been a Marxist. She presented herself to the authorities of the Russian Church in Paris and announced that she wished to become a religious, "beginning at once, to-day," and to found a monastery. She had her way, but she was not the traditional Russian Orthodox religious. She was accused by some of neglecting the long services and the traditional contemplation. "I must go my way," she said. "I am for the suffering people." In the early morning she was at the markets buying cheap food for the people she fed, bringing it back in a sack on her back. She was a familiar figure in the slum, in her poor black habit and her worn-out men's shoes.

The many Russian refugees in France in those days were stateless persons, many of them poverty-stricken, without privilege, without claim on any of the services which the country provided for the poor. Mother Maria worked among the poorest. She discovered that Russians who contracted tuberculosis were lying in a filthy hovel on the banks of the Seine into which the Paris police used to throw those syphilitic wrecks which they picked up along the riverside. With ten francs in her pocket she bought a château and opened a sanatorium.

Then she found that there were hundreds of Russians in lunatic asylums all over Europe. They had just "disappeared" into these institutions, where no questions were asked about them. She raised a public outcry and got many of them released. In those days the Russian congregations in and around Paris were living examples of what the early apostolic communities must have been. They were real homes for the poor and the unwanted. Russians living in tenements could find there comfort and friendship. The Churches had their own labour exchanges, clinics and many other services, and the convent, over which Mother Maria presided, was central to their life.

When the German occupation took place Mother Maria summoned her chaplain and told him that she felt that her particular duty was to render all possible assistance to persecuted Jews. She knew that this would mean imprisonment and probably death, and she gave him the option of leaving. He refused. For a month the convent was a haven for Jews. Women and children were hidden within its walls. Money poured in to enable them to escape from France and hundreds were got away. At the end of a month the Gestapo came. Mother Maria was arrested and sent to the concentration camp at Ravensbruck. Her chaplain was sent to Buchenwald, where he died of starvation and overwork.

The story of her life in the camp is only now being pieced together. She was known even to the guards as "that wonderful Russian nun," and it is doubtful whether they had any intention of killing her. She had been there two and a half years when a new block of buildings was erected in the camp, and the prisoners were told that these were to be hot baths. A day came when a few dozen prisoners from the women's quarters were lined up outside the buildings. One girl became hysterical. Mother Maria, who had not been selected, came up to her. "Don't be frightened," she said. "Look, I shall take your turn," and in line with the rest, she passed through the doors. It was Good Friday, 1945.

CHRISTIAN NEWS LETTER, April 17th, 1946

XI

In recent times a tendency has appeared in dogmatic religion which completely turns its back on thinking and at the same time declares that religion has nothing to do with the world and civilisation. It is not its business to realise the kingdom of God on earth. This extreme tendency is mainly represented by Karl Barth.

Karl Barth, who is the most modern theologian, because he lives most in the spirit of our age, more than any other has that contempt for thinking which is characteristic of our age. He dares to say that religion has nothing to do with thinking. He wants to give religion nothing to do with anything but God and man, the great antithesis. He says a religious person does not concern himself with what happens to the world. The idea of the kingdom of God plays no part with him. He mocks at what he calls "civilised Protestantism." The church must leave the world to itself. All that concerns the church is the preaching of revealed truth. Religion is turned aside from the world. . . .

It is something terrible to say that religion is not ethical. Karl Barth is a truly religious personality, and in his sermons there is much profound religion. But the terrible thing is that he dares to preach that religion is turned aside from the world and in so doing expresses what the spirit of the age is feeling.

ALBERT SCHWEITZER

Unfortunately, it is not enough to be a Catholic. One must still work in the temporal if one wishes to tear the future from temporal tyrannies.

CHARLES PÉGUY

It would be atrociously dishonest and wrong to wait for social improvement to follow man's moral perfecting; we must work actively for the reform of society.

NICHOLAS BERDYAEV

One must indeed think that there was nothing in common between the socialism of those days, our socialism, and that which we know to-day under that name. . . . By the restoration of industrial morality, by the purification of the industrial work-room, we hoped for no less, we sought no less than the temporal salvation of humanity. Only those will laugh who do not wish to realise that Christianity itself, which is the religion of eternal salvation, is stuck in this mire, in the mire of rotten economic, industrial morality; those who do not wish to realise that Christianity itself will not emerge from it, will not be drawn out of it, save through an economic industrial revolution; and lastly, that there is no place of perdition better made, better ordered, and better provided with tools, so to speak; that there is no more fitting tool of perdition than the modern work-room. . . .

The Church is nothing of what she was and she has become all that is most contrary to herself, all that is most contrary to her institution. And she will not reopen the door of the work-room and she will not be open once more to the people, unless she too, she like the rest of the world, unless she too pays the price of an economic revolution—a social revolution, an industrial revolution, in short, a temporal revolution for eternal salvation. Such is, eternally, temporally, the mysterious subjection of the eternal itself to the temporal. Such is properly the inscription of the eternal itself in the temporal. Economic expenses, social expenses, industrial expenses, temporal expenses must be met. Nothing can evade it, not even the eternal, not even the spiritual, not even the inner life.

CHARLES PÉGUY

It is undeniable that much of the true progress in social history is due to the open or indirect action of Christianity upon the human spirit: the abolition of slavery and serfdom, the recognition of freedom of conscience and of spiritual life are proofs of this. But instead of realising these social reforms themselves, Christians have often left them to the hands of others, they have often even done injustice and consented to adapting higher spiritual values in the interests of the ruling class and the established order. They have succeeded in producing a "bourgeois" Christianity. And now the most merciless judgment is being passed upon this "bourgeois" Christianity, on every adaptation of Christianity to human, selfish interests.

. . . .

Christian piety all too often has seemed to be the withdrawal from the world and from men, a sort of transcendent egoism, the unwillingness to share the suffering of the world and man. It was not sufficiently infused with Christian love and mercy. It lacked human warmth. And the world has risen in protest against this form of piety, as a refined form of egoism, as indifference to the world's sorrow. Against this protest only a reborn piety can stand. Care for the life of another, even material, bodily care, is spiritual in essence. Bread for myself is a material question: bread for my neighbour is a spiritual question.

. . . .

A new Christian piety must be revealed in our world. And upon this new Christian piety depends the fate of the world and that of man. It cannot be an abstract form, retirement from the world and mankind: it must be a form of spiritual effort exerted over man and the world, labour for man and the world. It cannot permit human slavery to cosmic or social and technical forces. It calls man to a kingly role, and to creative work in the world. The new Christian man does not curse the world, neither does he condemn and anathematise the possessed and the idolatrous. He shares the suffering of the world, bears in his body the tragedy of man. He strives to bring the liberating, spiritual element into all of human life. A personality which is strengthened and supported spiritually, cannot permit the powers of the world to divide its forces, can never permit itself to be possessed by demonic powers. Such a personality is not isolated and shut in upon itself, it is accessible to all universal meaning and open to all super-personal values.

This presents a very complex spiritual relationship between the personal and the super-personal, a problem of personality entering into communal relationships, which is something quite other than personality becoming non-personal. The new piety is the road not only from the world and man to God, but the reverse, from God to man, descent as well as ascent, that is, the realisation of the fulness of Divine-human truth, the truth of the God-man realised in life. In the old forms of Christian piety love of God often meant lack of love for man, repulsion from man, renunciation of the world as something accursed. The only possible escape from this is in a new piety in which love of God will be love for man as well, and where freedom from the powers of this world will at the same time mean love for all God's creation, a religion in which man's spiritual life will be not merely a process of attaining salvation, but creative in the world, as well. This does not mean a renunciation of asceticism, but only a new understanding of it, where the ascetic will be free from elements hostile to true life, and from what may be called religious nihilism.

Christianity is above all else a religion of love and liberty, but just because of this, the future is not determined by blind fate, either for good or for evil. Hence we move forward toward a tragic conflict. The new Christianity must rehumanise man and society, culture and the world. But for Christianity this process of humanisation is something not merely human; it is Divine-human, of the nature of the God-man. Only in Divine-humanity, in the Body of Christ, can man be saved. Otherwise he will be torn to pieces by demonic forces, by the demons of hatred and malice.

This problem of man takes precedence over that of society or of culture, and here man is to be considered, not in his inner spiritual life, not as an abstract spiritual being, but as an integral being, as a being social and cosmic, as well. A new day is dawning for Christianity in the world. Only a form of Socialism, which unites personality and the communal principle, can satisfy Christianity. The hour has struck when, after terrible struggle, after an unprecedented de-Christianisation of the world and its passage through all the results of that process, Christianity will be revealed in its pure form. Then it will be clear what Christianity stands for and what it stands against. Christianity will again become the only and the final refuge of man. And when the purifying process is finished, it will be seen that Christianity stands for man and for humanity, for the value and dignity of personality, for freedom, for social justice, for the brotherhood of men and of nations, for enlightenment, for the creation of a new life. And it will be clear that only Christianity stands for these things. The judgment upon Christianity is really judgment upon the betrayal of Christianity, upon its distortion and defilement, and the justice of this is that of judgment upon the fallen world and its sinful history. But the true and final renaissance will probably begin in the world only after the elementary, everyday problems of human existence are solved for all peoples and nations, after bitter human need and the economic slavery of man have been finally conquered. Only then may we expect a new and more powerful revelation of the Holy Spirit in the world.

NICHOLAS BERDYAEV

It follows that political society—if it has not the office (which belongs to a superior jurisdiction) of guiding human beings to their spiritual perfection and to their full freedom of autonomy, in other words to Eternal Life—is none the less essentially directed, even through the temporal end that gives the State its character, to the establishment of social conditions which will secure for the mass of men such a standard of material, intellectual, and moral life as will conduce to the well-being of the whole community; so that every citizen may find in it a positive help in the progressive achievement of his freedom of autonomy. . . .

We speak of freedom of autonomy in its pure and simple meaning and not in a relative sense only. This freedom of autonomy finds its highest type in the Saint. And by a paradox as wonderful as it is strange, this type of perfection which is one of supernatural exaltation makes an appeal to men of every condition, for it is achieved through the operation of a good will in the secret heart of man. A civilisation, then, the common good of which is referred to a type so transcendent, should necessarily aim at securing for the mass of its citizens conditions that are worthy of man and that will put each citizen thus equipped for the life of reason and of virtue in the way of advancing towards perfect freedom and of achieving his eternal destiny.

JACQUES MARITAIN

The spirit of Capitalism considered objectively is a spirit of exaltation of active and inventive power, of the dynamic energies of man and of individual enterprise; but it is a spirit of hatred of poverty and of contempt of the poor. The poor man is there as an instrument, not as a human personality; and if after abandoning him, in the very days that followed on the declaration of the Rights of Man, to be oppressed and degraded and reduced to the limit of human endurance, a movement was later started to raise and improve his condition, this movement sprang from the realisation that the instrument might otherwise become dangerous and also that it gives better results when it is clean and in good order, even in good moral order. In his turn again, the rich man exists only as consumer or paunch, not as a human personality; and the tragedy of such a civilisation is that to maintain and develop the monstrous economy of Usury or Moneylending, it is necessary to aim at making all men consumers or rich; but then if there are no more poor men to act as instruments the whole economy comes to an end and perishes. And it perishes also, as we have seen in our day, if there are not enough consumers to set the instruments to work.

The objective spirit of Capitalism is a spirit of bold and courageous conquest of the earth; but it is a spirit of the enslavement of all things to the endless increase of the sacred pile of material goods. Like all things in history it has elements of good and evil, of light and darkness, but it is its dark countenance that is now offered to the world. *Jam judicatus est.* Truth to tell, the Christian conscience has now only to take cognisance of this judgment. Let the dead body, the corpse of four centuries of labour and pain, of beauty, of heroism, and of crime, be buried by other dead, with speeches and conferences and wars and fireworks or red flags. The Christian is not without a sense of the sadness of this spectacle of death, but his face is set towards life.

JACQUES MARITAIN

If Christianity takes sides with the working class in the social struggle she does not do so in the name of that class; it is in the name of man, of the dignity of the workman, in the name of his human rights and of his soul which Capitalism so grievously grinds down.

NICHOLAS BERDYAEV

Materialistic Communism and Capitalism are equally liable to condemnation at the bar of the absolute values of Christianity, for they have a common principle. Marxian socialism sets class above personality and regards man solely as a function of society, nor do the bourgeois and capitalist ideologies see him differently; we find the same domination by an impersonal "collective" in both Capitalism and Communism.

NICHOLAS BERDYAEV

The social problem cannot be solved apart from the spiritual problem; unless there is a Christian renewal of souls, those of the workers above all, the sway of Socialism will become definitively a domination by the bourgeois spirit.

NICHOLAS BERDYAEV

Those who regard the decay of civilisation as something quite normal and natural console themselves with the thought that it is not civilisation, but *a* civilisation, which is falling a prey to dissolution; that there will be a new age and a new race in which there will blossom a new civilisation. But that is a mistake. The earth no longer has in reserve, as it had once, gifted peoples as yet unused, who can relieve us and take our place in some distant future as leaders of the spiritual life. We already know all those which the earth has to dispose of. There is not one among them which is not already taking such a part in our civilisation that its spiritual fate is determined by our own. All of them, the gifted and the ungifted, the distant and the near, have felt the influence of those forces of barbarism which are at work among us. All of them are, like ourselves, diseased, and only as we recover can they recover.

It is not the civilisation of a race, but that of mankind, present and future alike, that we must give up as lost, if belief in a rebirth of our civilisation is a vain thing.

But it need not be so given up. If the ethical is the essential element in civilisation, decadence changes into renaissance as soon as ethical activities are set to work again in our convictions and in the ideas which we undertake to stamp upon reality. The attempt to bring this about is well worth making, and it should be world-wide.

It is true that the difficulties that have to be reckoned with in this undertaking are so great that only the strongest faith in the power of the ethical spirit will let us venture on it.

. . . .

Again, the renewal of civilisation is hindered by the fact that it is so exclusively the individual personality which must be looked to as the agent in the new movement.

The renewal of civilisation has nothing to do with movements which bear the character of experiences of the crowd; these are never anything but reactions to external happenings. But civilisation can only revive when there shall come into being in a number of individuals a new tone of mind independent of the one prevalent among the crowd and in opposition to it, a tone of mind which will gradually win influence over the collective one, and in the end determine its character. It is only an ethical movement which can rescue us from the slough of barbarism, and the ethical comes into existence only in individuals.

The final decision as to what the future of a society shall be depends not on how near its organisation is to perfection, but on the degrees of worthiness in its individual members. The most important, and yet the least easily determinable, element in history is the series of unobtrusive general changes which take place in the individual dispositions of the many. These are what precede and cause the happenings, and this is why it is so difficult to understand thoroughly the men and the events of past times. The character and worth of individuals among the mass and the way they work themselves into membership of the whole body, receiving influences from it and giving others back, we can even to-day only partially and uncertainly understand.

One thing, however, is clear. Where the collective body works more strongly on the individual than the latter does upon it, the result is deterioration, because the noble element on which everything depends, viz., the spiritual and moral worthiness of the individual, is thereby necessarily constricted and hampered. Decay of the spiritual and moral life then sets in, which renders society incapable of understanding and solving the problems which it has to face. Therefore, sooner or later, it is involved in catastrophe.

That is the condition in which we are now, and that is why it is the duty of individuals to rise to a higher conception of their capabilities and undertake again the function which only the individual can perform, that of producing new spiritual-ethical ideas. If this does not come about in a multitude of cases nothing can save us.

A new public opinion must be created privately and unobtrusively. The existing one is maintained by the Press, by propaganda, by organisation, and by financial and other influences which are at its disposal. This unnatural way of spreading ideas must be opposed by the natural one, which goes from man to man and relies solely on the truth of the thoughts and the hearer's receptiveness for new truth. Unarmed, and following the human spirit's primitive and natural fighting method, it must attack the other, which faces it, as Goliath faced David, in the mighty armour of the age.

About the struggle which must needs ensue no historical analogy can tell us much. The past has, no doubt, seen the struggle of the free-thinking individual against the fettered spirit of a whole society, but the problem has never presented itself on the scale on which it does to-day, because the fettering of the collective spirit as it is fettered to-day by modern organisations, modern unreflectiveness, and modern popular passions, is a phenomenon without precedent in history.

Will the man of to-day have strength to carry out what the spirit demands from him, and what the age would like to make impossible?

In the over-organised societies which in a hundred ways have him in their power, he must somehow become once more an independent personality and so exert influence back upon them. They will use every means to keep him in that condition of impersonality which suits them. They fear personality because the spirit and the truth, which they would like to muzzle, find in it a means of expressing themselves. And their power is, unfortunately, as great as their fear.

There is a tragic alliance between society as a whole and its economic conditions. With a grim relentlessness those conditions tend to bring up the man of to-day as a being without freedom, without self-collectedness, without independence, in short as a human being so full of deficiencies that he lacks the qualities of humanity. And they are the last things that we can change. Even if it should be granted us that the spirit should begin its work, we shall only slowly and incompletely gain power over these forces. There is, in fact, being demanded from the will that which our conditions of life refuse to allow.

And how heavy the tasks that the spirit has to take in hand! It has to create the power of understanding the truth that is really true where at present nothing is current but propagandist truth. It has to depose ignoble patriotism, and enthrone the noble kind of patriotism which aims at ends that are worthy of the whole of mankind, in circles where the hopeless issues of past and present political activities keep nationalist passions aglow even among those who in their hearts would fain be free from them. It has to get the fact that civilisation is an interest of all men and of humanity as a whole recognised again in places where national civilisation is to-day worshipped as an idol, and the notion of a humanity with a common civilisation lies broken to fragments. It has to maintain our faith in the civilised State, even though our modern States, spiritually and economically ruined by the war, have no time to think about the tasks of civilisation, and dare not devote their attention to anything but how to use every possible means, even those which undermine the conception of justice, to collect money with which to prolong their own existence. It has to unite us by giving us a single ideal of civilised man, and this in a world where one nation has robbed its neighbour of all faith in humanity, idealism, righteousness, reasonableness, and truthfulness, and all alike have come under the domination of powers which are plunging us ever deeper into barbarism. It has to get attention concentrated on civilisation while the growing difficulty of making a living absorbs the masses more and more in material cares, and makes all other things seem to them to be mere shadows. It has to give us faith in the possibility of progress while the reaction of the economic on the spiritual becomes more pernicious every day and contributes to an ever growing demoralisation. It has to provide us with reasons for hope at a time when not only secular and religious institutions and associations, but the men, too, who are looked upon as leaders, continually fail us, when artists and men of learning show themselves as supporters of barbarism, and notabilities who pass for thinkers, and behave outwardly as such, are revealed, when crises come, as being nothing more than writers and members of academies.

All these hindrances stand in the path of the will to civilisation. A dull despair hovers about us. How well we now understand the men of the Greco-Roman decadence, who stood before events incapable of resistance, and, leaving the world to its fate, withdrew upon their inner selves! Like them, we are bewildered by our experience of life. Like them, we hear enticing voices which say to us that the one thing which can still make life tolerable is to live for the day. We must, we are told, renounce every wish to think or hope about anything beyond our own fate. We must find rest in resignation.

The recognition that civilisation is founded on some sort of theory of the universe, and can be restored only through a spiritual awakening and a will for ethical good in the mass of mankind, compels us to make clear to ourselves those difficulties in the way of a rebirth of civilisation which ordinary reflection would overlook. But at the same time it raises us above all considerations of possibility or impossibility. If the ethical spirit provides a sufficient standing ground in the sphere of events for making civilisation a reality, then we shall get back to civilisation, if we return to a suitable theory of the universe and the convictions to which this properly gives birth.

. . . .

But of what character must the theory be if ideas and convictions about civilisation are to be based on it?

It must be optimistic and ethical.

That theory of the universe is optimistic which gives existence the preference as against non-existence and thus affirms life as something possessing value in itself. From this attitude to the universe and to life results the impulse to raise existence, in so far as our influence can affect it, to its highest level of value. Thence originates activity directed to the improvement of the living conditions of individuals, of society, of nations and of humanity, and from it spring the external achievements of civilisation, the lordship of spirit over the powers of nature, and the higher social organisation.

Ethics is the activity of man directed to secure the inner perfection of his own personality. In itself it is quite independent of whether the theory of the universe is pessimistic or optimistic. But its sphere of action is contracted or widened according as it appears in connection with a theory of the first or the second type.

In the consistently pessimistic theory of the universe, as we have it in the thought of the Brāhmans or of Schopenhauer, ethics has nothing whatever to do with the objective world. It aims solely at securing the self-perfection of the individual as this comes to pass in inner freedom and disconnection from the world and the spirit of the world.

But the scope of ethics is extended in proportion as it develops and strengthens a connection with a theory of the universe which is affirmative toward the world and life. Its aim is now the inner perfection of the individual and at the same time the direction of his activity so as to take effect on other men and on the objective world. This freedom with its release from the world and its spirit ethics no longer holds up to man as an aim in itself. By its means man is to become capable of acting among men and in the world as a higher and purer force, and thus to do his part towards the actualisation of the ideal of general progress.

Thus the optimistic-ethical theory of the universe works in partnership with ethics to produce civilisation. Neither is capable of doing so by itself. Optimism supplies confidence that the world-process has somehow or other a spiritual and real aim, and that the improvement of the general relations of the world and of society promotes the spiritual-moral perfecting of the individual. From the ethical comes ability to develop the purposive state of mind necessary to produce action on the world and society and to cause the co-operation of all our achievements to secure the spiritual and moral perfection of the individual which is the final end of civilisation.

ALBERT SCHWEITZER

FOURTH PART

I. ACCEPTANCE

For Tiny
with great love

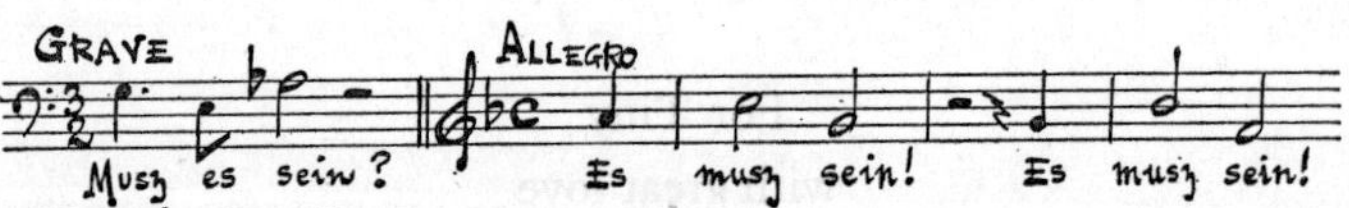
GRAVE
ALLEGRO
Musz es sein?
Es musz sein! Es musz sein!

Then Job arose, and rent his mantle, and shaved his head, and fell down upon the ground, and worshipped,

And said, Naked came I out of my mother's womb, and naked shall I return thither: the Lord gave, and the Lord hath taken away; blessed be the name of the Lord.

JOB

Then cometh Jesus with them unto a place called Gethsemane, and saith unto the disciples, Sit ye here, while I go and pray yonder.

And he took with him Peter and the two sons of Zebedee, and began to be sorrowful and very heavy.

Then saith he unto them, My soul is exceeding sorrowful, even unto death: tarry ye here, and watch with me.

And he went a little farther, and fell on his face, and prayed, saying, O my Father, if it be possible, let this cup pass from me; nevertheless not as I will, but as thou wilt.

And he cometh unto the disciples, and findeth them asleep, and saith unto Peter, What, could ye not watch with me one hour?

Watch and pray, that ye enter not into temptation: the spirit indeed is willing, but the flesh is weak.

He went away again the second time, and prayed, saying, O my Father, if this cup may not pass away from me, except I drink it, thy will be done.

And he came and found them asleep again: for their eyes were heavy.

And he left them, and went away again, and prayed the third time, saying the same words.

Then cometh he to his disciples, and saith unto them, Sleep on now, and take your rest: behold, the hour is at hand, and the Son of man is betrayed into the hands of sinners.

ST. MATTHEW

Rabbi Meir sat during the whole of the Sabbath-day in the School instructing the people. During his absence from the house his two sons died, both of them of uncommon beauty and enlightened in the Law. His wife bore them to her bed-chamber, and spread a white covering over their bodies. In the evening Rabbi Meir came home. "Where are my sons?" he asked. "I repeatedly looked round the School, and I did not see them there." She reached him a goblet. He praised the Lord at the going out of the Sabbath, drank, and again asked, "Where are my sons?" "They will not be afar off," she said, and placed food before him that he might eat. When he had said grace after the meal, she thus addressed him: "With thy permission, I would fain propose to thee one question." "Ask it then," he replied. "A few days ago a person entrusted some jewels into my custody, and now he demands them of me; should I give them back again?" "This is a question," said the Rabbi, "which my wife should not have thought it necessary to ask. What! wouldst thou hesitate to restore to every one his own?" "No," she replied; "but yet I thought it best not to restore them without acquainting you therewith." She then led him to the chamber, and took the white covering from the dead bodies. "Ah, my sons! my sons!" loudly lamented the father. "My sons! the light of my eyes!" The mother turned away and wept bitterly. At length she took her husband by the hand, and said: "Didst thou not teach me that we must not be reluctant to restore that which was entrusted to our keeping? See—the Lord gave, and the Lord hath taken away; blessed be the name of the Lord!"

THE TALMUD

My teacher, the Baalshem, realising the imminence of his death, exclaimed: "Lord of the Universe, I make Thee a gift of the remaining hours of my life."

RABBI PINHAS OF KORETZ

Rabbi Shmelke and his brother once petitioned their teacher, the Preacher of Mezeritz, to explain to them the words of the Mishnah:[1] "A man must bless God for the evil in the same way that he blesses Him for the good which befalls."

The Preacher replied: "Go to the House of Study, and you will find there a man smoking. He is Rabbi Zusya, and he will explain this to you."

When Rabbi Shmelke and his brother questioned Rabbi Zusya, he laughed and said: "I am surprised that the Rabbi sent you to me. You must go elsewhere, and make your inquiry from one who has suffered tribulations in his lifetime. As for me, I have never experienced anything but good all my days."

But Rabbi Shmelke and his brother knew full well that from his earliest hour to the present he had endured the most grievous sorrows. Thereupon they understood the meaning of the words of the Mishnah, and the reason their Rabbi had sent them to Rabbi Zusya.

[1] Rabbinic writings.

HASIDIC STORY

Let me not injure the felicity of others, if I say I am as happy as any: *Ruat caelum, fiat voluntas tua*, salveth all; so that whatsoever happens, it is but what our daily prayers desire. In brief, I am content; and what should Providence add more?

SIR THOMAS BROWNE

CHEERY BEGGAR

Beyond Mágdalen and by the Bridge, on a place called there
the Plain,
In Summer, in a burst of summertime
Following falls and falls of rain,
When the air was sweet-and-sour of the flown fineflower of
Those goldnails and their gaylinks that hang along a lime;

. . . .

The motion of that man's heart is fine
Whom want could not make píne, píne
That struggling should not sear him, a gift should cheer him
Like that poor pocket of pence, poor pence of mine.
. . . .

GERARD MANLEY HOPKINS (unfinished)

The children of Israel did not find in the manna all the sweetness and strength they might have found in it; not because the manna did not contain them, but because they longed for other meat.

ST. JOHN OF THE CROSS

He who is meek and contented, he who has an equal vision, whose mind is filled with the fullness of acceptance and of rest;
He who has seen Him and touched Him, he is freed from all fear and trouble.
To him the perpetual thought of God is like sandal paste smeared on the body, to him nothing else is delight:
His work and his rest are filled with music: he sheds abroad the radiance of love.
Kabir says: "Touch His feet, who is one and indivisible, immutable and peaceful; who fills all vessels to the brim with joy, and whose form is love."

KABIR

Dispose of me according to the wisdom of thy pleasure: thy will be done, though in my own undoing.

SIR THOMAS BROWNE

Things are greater than we, and will not comply with *us*; we, who are less than Things, must Comply with *them*.

BENJAMIN WHICHCOTE

I bowed as a leaf in rain;
As a tree when the leaf is shed
To winds in the season at wane:
And when from my soul I said,
May the worm be trampled: smite,
Sacred Reality! power
Filled me to front it aright.
I had come of my faith's ordeal.

GEORGE MEREDITH (from *A Faith on Trial*)

Sin is an Attempt to *controul* the immutable and unalterable Laws of everlasting Righteousness, Goodness and Truth, upon which the Universe depends.

BENJAMIN WHICHCOTE

In hell itself hell can your heaven be,
If there, says God, you give your will to me.

ANGELUS SILESIUS

It has been said, that there is of nothing so much in hell as of self-will. For hell is nothing but self-will, and if there were no self-will there would be no Devil and no hell. When it is said that Lucifer fell from Heaven, and turned away from God and the like, it means nothing else than that he would have his own will, and would not be of one will with the Eternal Will. So was it likewise with Adam in Paradise. And when we say self-will, we mean: To will otherwise than as the One and Eternal Will of God wills.

THEOLOGIA GERMANICA

LUCIFER IN STARLIGHT

On a starred night Prince Lucifer uprose.
Tired of his dark dominion swung the fiend
Above the rolling ball in cloud part screened,
Where sinners hugged their spectre of repose.
Poor prey to his hot fit of pride were those.
And now upon his western wing he leaned,
Now his huge bulk o'er Afric's sands careened,
Now the black planet shadowed Arctic snows.
Soaring through wider zones that pricked his scars
With memory of the old revolt from Awe,
He reached a middle height, and at the stars,
Which are the brain of heaven, he looked, and sank.
Around the ancient track marched, rank on rank,
The army of unalterable law.

GEORGE MEREDITH

Rabbi Bunam was once walking outside the city with some of his disciples. He bent, picked up a speck of sand, looked at it, and put it back exactly where he had found it. "He who does not believe," he said, "that God wants this bit of sand to lie in this particular place, does not believe at all."

HASIDIC STORY

He who is in a state of rebellion cannot receive grace, to use the phrase of which the Church is so fond—so rightly fond, I dare say—for in life as in art the mood of rebellion closes up the channels of the soul, and shuts out the airs of heaven.

OSCAR WILDE

Says the well-schooled and humble heart to Nature that gives and takes back all we have: *Give what thou wilt, take back what thou wilt.* But he says it without any bravado of fortitude, in simple obedience and good will to her.

MARCUS AURELIUS

Keep your heart in peace; let nothing in this world disturb it: all things have an end.

In all circumstances, however hard they may be, we should rejoice, rather than be cast down, that we may not lose the greatest good, the peace and tranquillity of our soul.

If the whole world and all that is in it were thrown into confusion, disquietude on that account would be vanity, because that disquietude would do more harm than good.

To endure all things with an equable and peaceful mind, not only brings with it many blessings to the soul, but also enables us, in the midst of our difficulties, to have a clear judgment about them, and to minister the fitting remedy for them.

ST. JOHN OF THE CROSS

When all looks fair about, and thou seest not a cloud so big as a Hand to threaten thee, forget not the Wheel of things: think of sullen vicissitudes, but beat not thy brains to foreknow them. Be armed against such obscurities rather by submission than fore-knowledge.

SIR THOMAS BROWNE

There lives no man on earth who may always have rest and peace without troubles and crosses, with whom things go always according to his will. There is always something to be suffered here, consider it as you will. And as soon as you are free of one adversity, perhaps two others come in its place. Therefore yield yourself willingly to them, and seek only that true peace of the heart, which none can take away from you, that you may overcome all adversity; the peace that breaks through all adversities and crosses, all oppression, suffering, misery, humiliation, and what more there may be of the like, so that a man may be joyful and patient therein, as were the beloved disciples and followers of Christ. Now if a man were lovingly to give his whole diligence and might thereto, he would very soon come to know that true eternal peace which is God Himself, as far as it is possible to a creature; insomuch that what was bitter to him before, would become sweet, and his heart would remain ever unmoved among all things.

THEOLOGIA GERMANICA

Disquietude is the greatest evil which happens to the soul except sin. For as the seditious and internal troubles of a State ruin it entirely and prevent it from being able to resist the foreigner, so our heart, being troubled and disquieted in itself, loses not only the force to maintain the virtues it has acquired, but more than this, even the means of resisting the temptations of the enemy, who thereupon makes all sorts of efforts to fish, as is said, in troubled waters.

Disquietude arises from an immoderate desire to be freed from an evil which we feel, or to gain the good which we hope for. And yet there is nothing which makes the evil worse and which removes the good to a greater distance than disquietude and worry. Birds are caught in nets and snares because when they find themselves entrapped they struggle and move immoderately to escape from it, and in doing so they entangle themselves so much the more. When, then, you are pressed with the desire of being freed from some evil, or of attaining some good, before all things place your spirit in a state of repose and tranquillity, calm your judgment and your will. And then, quite softly and gently, pursue the end of your desire, taking in order the means which will be suitable. And when I say quite softly, I do not wish to say negligently, but without worry, trouble, and disquietude. Otherwise, in place of giving effect to your desire, you will spoil everything, and will embarrass yourself very greatly.

ST. FRANCIS DE SALES

Nekhlyudov remembered how at Kuzminskoye he had meditated on his life and tried to solve the questions, what he ought to do, and how he ought to do it; and he remembered how he had become perplexed in these questions and had been unable to decide them, so many were the considerations involved in each. He now put to himself the same questions, and was astonished how simple it all was. It was simple because he now took no thought of what would happen to himself:—that no longer even interested him,—he was thinking only of what he ought to do. And strangely enough, while he was not considering his own needs, he knew without any doubt what he ought to do for others. . . .

The black cloud had moved on till it stood right above him: lightning lit up the whole courtyard and the thunder sounded directly overhead. The birds had all ceased singing, the leaves began to rustle, and the first flaws of the storm-wind reached the steps where he sat. . . . Nekhlyudov went into the house. "Yes, yes," he thought. "The work which is carried out by our life, the whole work, the whole meaning of this work is dark to me, and cannot be made intelligible. . . . Why should my friend die, and I be left alive? . . . Why was Katyusha born? . . . Why did this war come about? Of what use was my subsequent dissolute life? To understand all this, to understand the whole work of the Master is not in my power; but to do his will, written in my conscience, that is in my power, and that I know without a doubt. And when I do this, then undoubtedly I am at peace."

TOLSTOY (from *Resurrection*)

To regret one's own experiences is to arrest one's own development. To deny one's own experiences is to put a lie into the lips of one's own life. It is no less than a denial of the soul.

. . . .

The important thing, the thing that lies before me, the thing that I have to do, if the brief remainder of my days is not to be maimed, marred, and incomplete, is to absorb into my nature all that has been done to me, to make it part of me, to accept it without complaint, fear, or reluctance.

OSCAR WILDE

We can get in touch with another person only by an attitude of unprejudiced objectivity. This may sound like a scientific precept, and may be confused with a purely intellectual and detached attitude of mind. But what I mean to convey is something quite different. It is a human quality—a kind of deep respect for facts and events and for the person who suffers from them—a respect for the secret of such a human life. The truly religious person has this attitude. He knows that God has brought all sorts of strange and inconceivable things to pass, and seeks in the most curious ways to enter a man's heart. He therefore senses in everything the unseen presence of the divine will. This is what I mean by "unprejudiced objectivity." It is a moral achievement on the part of the doctor, who ought not to let himself be repelled by illness and corruption. We cannot change anything unless we accept it. Condemnation does not liberate, it oppresses. I am the oppressor of the person I condemn, not his friend and fellow-sufferer. I do not in the least mean to say that we must never pass judgment in the cases of persons whom we desire to help and improve. But if the doctor wishes to help a human being he must be able to accept him as he is. And he can do this in reality only when he has already seen and accepted himself as he is.

Perhaps this sounds very simple, but simple things are always the most difficult. In actual life it requires the greatest discipline to be simple, and the acceptance of oneself is the essence of the moral problem and the epitome of a whole outlook upon life. That I feed the hungry, that I forgive an insult, that I love my enemy in the name of Christ—all these are undoubtedly great virtues. What I do unto the least of my brethren, that I do unto Christ. But what if I should discover that the least amongst them all, the poorest of all the beggars, the most impudent of all the offenders, the very enemy himself—that these are within me, and that I myself stand in need of the alms of my own kindness—that I myself am the enemy who must be loved—what then? As a rule, the Christian's attitude is then reversed; there is no longer any question of love or long-suffering; we say to the brother within us "Raca," and condemn and rage against ourselves. We hide it from the world; we refuse to admit ever having met this least among the lowly in ourselves. Had it been God himself who drew near to us in this despicable form, we should have denied him a thousand times before a single cock had crowed. . . .

Neurosis is an inner cleavage—the state of being at war with oneself. Everything that accentuates this cleavage makes the patient worse, and everything that mitigates it tends to heal the patient. What drives people to war with themselves is the intuition or the knowledge that they consist of two persons in opposition to one another. The conflict may be between the sensual and the spiritual man, or between the ego and the shadow. It is what Faust means when he says: "Two souls, alas, dwell in my breast apart." A neurosis is a dissociation of personality.

Healing may be called a religious problem. In the sphere of social or national relations, the state of suffering may be civil war, and this state is to be cured by the Christian virtue of forgiveness for those who hate us. That which we try with the conviction of good Christians to apply to external situations, we must also apply to the inner state in the treatment of neurosis. This is why modern man has heard enough about guilt and sin. He is sorely enough beset by his own bad conscience, and wants rather to learn how he is to reconcile himself with his own nature—how he is to love the enemy in his own heart and call the wolf his brother. . . .

It is well known that Freudian psychoanalysis is limited to the task of making conscious the shadow-side and the evil within us. It simply brings into action the civil war that was latent, and lets it go at that. The patient must deal with it as best he can. Freud has unfortunately overlooked the fact that man has never yet been able single-handed to hold his own against the powers of darkness—that is, of the unconscious. Man has always stood in need of the spiritual help which each individual's own religion held out to him. The opening up of the unconscious always means the outbreak of intense spiritual suffering; it is as when a flourishing civilisation is abandoned to invading hordes of barbarians, or when fertile fields are exposed by the bursting of a dam to a raging torrent. . . .

To-day this eruption of destructive forces has already taken place, and man suffers from it in spirit. . . . We must first tread with the patient the path of his illness—the path of his mistake that sharpens his conflicts and increases his loneliness till it grows unbearable—hoping that from the psychic depths which cast up the powers of destruction the rescuing forces will come also. . . . It is as though, at the culmination of the illness, the destructive powers were converted into healing forces. . . . As the religious-minded person would say: guidance has come from God. . . . To the patient it is nothing less than a revelation when, from the hidden depths of the psyche, something arises to confront him—something strange that is not the "I" and is therefore beyond the reach of personal caprice. He has gained access to the sources of psychic life, and this marks the beginning of the cure. . . .

Such experiences reward the sufferer for the pains of the labyrinthine way. From this point forward a light shines through his confusion; he can reconcile himself with the warfare within and so come to bridge the morbid split in his nature upon a higher level.

C. G. JUNG

Out of evil, much good has come to me. By keeping quiet, repressing nothing, remaining attentive, and, hand in hand with that, by accepting reality—taking things as they are, and not as I wanted them to be—by doing all this, rare knowledge has come to me, and rare powers as well, such as I could never have imagined before. I always thought that, when we accept things, they overpower us in one way or another. Now this is not true at all, and it is only by accepting them that one can define an attitude toward them. So now I intend playing the game of life, being receptive to whatever comes to me, good and bad, sun and shadow that are for ever shifting, and, in this way, also accepting my own nature with its positive and negative sides. Thus everything becomes more alive to me. What a fool I was! How I tried to force everything to go according to my idea!

A PATIENT'S LETTER TO JUNG

To every man comes, sooner or later, the great renunciation. For the young, there is nothing unattainable; a good thing desired with the whole force of a passionate will, and yet impossible, is to them not credible. Yet, by death, by illness, by poverty, or by the voice of duty, we must learn, each one of us, that the world was not made for us, and that, however beautiful may be the things we crave, Fate may nevertheless forbid them. It is the part of courage, when misfortune comes, to bear without repining the ruin of our hopes, to turn away our thoughts from vain regrets. This degree of submission to Power is not only just and right: it is the very gate of wisdom.

But passive renunciation is not the whole of wisdom; for not by renunciation alone can we build a temple for the worship of our own ideals. Haunting foreshadowings of the temple appear in the realm of imagination, in music, in architecture, in the untroubled kingdom of reason, and in the golden sunset magic of lyrics, where beauty shines and glows, remote from the touch of sorrow, remote from the fear of change, remote from the failures and disenchantments of the world of fact. In the contemplation of these things the vision of heaven will shape itself in our hearts, giving at once a touchstone to judge the world about us, and an inspiration by which to fashion to our needs whatever is not incapable of serving as a stone in the sacred temple.

Except for those rare spirits that are born without sin, there is a cavern of darkness to be traversed before that temple can be entered. The gate of the cavern is despair, and its floor is paved with the gravestones of abandoned hopes. There Self must die; there the eagerness, the greed of untamed desire must be slain, for only so can the soul be freed from the empire of Fate. But out of the cavern the Gate of Renunciation leads again to the daylight of wisdom, by whose radiance a new insight, a new joy, a new tenderness, shine forth to gladden the pilgrim's heart.

BERTRAND RUSSELL

Renunciation does not take away. It gives. It gives the inexhaustible power of simple things.

MARTIN HEIDEGGER

FROM "MODERN LOVE"

[*The husband and wife, estranged, come together for a moment in acceptance of the eternal unity of the eternal "now."*]

We saw the swallows gathering in the sky,
And in the osier-isle we heard them noise.
We had not to look back on summer joys,
Or forward to a summer of bright dye:
But in the largeness of the evening earth
Our spirits grew as we went side by side.
The hour became her husband and my bride.
Love that had robbed us so, thus blessed our dearth!
The pilgrims of the year waxed very loud
In multitudinous chatterings, as the flood
Full brown came from the West, and like pale blood
Expanded to the upper crimson cloud.
Love that had robbed us of immortal things
This little moment mercifully gave,
Where I have seen across the twilight wave
The swan sail with her young beneath her wings.

[*But the wife, with mistaken chivalry, kills herself, to leave him free to go to his mistress; and the poet comments on their history.*]

Thus piteously love closed what he begat:
The union of this ever-diverse pair!
These two were rapid falcons in a snare,
Condemned to do the flitting of the bat.
Lovers beneath the singing sky of May
They wandered once; clear as the dew on flowers:
But they fed not on the advancing hours:
Their hearts held cravings for the buried day.
Then each applied to each that fatal knife,
Deep questioning, which probes to endless dole.
Ah, what a dusty answer gets the soul
When hot for certainties in this our life!—
In tragic hints here see what evermore
Moves dark as yonder midnight ocean's force,
Thundering like ramping hosts of warrior horse
To throw that faint thin line upon the shore!

GEORGE MEREDITH

THE DEAF BEETHOVEN CONDUCTS

Beethoven mounted the conductor's platform and the orchestra, knowing his weakness, found itself plunged into an anxious excitement, which was only too soon justified; for scarcely had the music begun before its creator offered a bewildering spectacle. At the *piano* passages he sank upon his knee, at the *forte* he leaped up; so that his figure, now shrinking into that of a dwarf, disappeared under the desk, and then stretched up far above it like a giant, his hands and arms working as though, with the beginning of the music, a thousand lives had entered every member. At first this happened without disturbance of the effect of the composition, for the disappearance and appearance of his body was synchronous with the dying away and swelling of the music; but, all at once, the genius ran ahead of the orchestra, and the composer disappeared at the *forte* passages and appeared again at the *piano*. Now danger was imminent, and, at the critical moment, Kapellmeister Umlauf took the commander's staff and indicated to the orchestra that he alone was to be followed. For a time Beethoven noticed nothing of the change. When he finally observed it a smile came to his lips which, if ever one which kind fate permitted me to see can be called so, deserved to be called "heavenly."

FRANZ WILD (who was present)

"I accept the universe," is reported to have been a favourite utterance of our New England transcendentalist, Margaret Fuller; and when someone repeated this phrase to Thomas Carlyle, his sardonic comment is said to have been: "Gad! she'd better!" At bottom the whole concern of both morality and religion is with the manner of our acceptance of the universe. Do we accept it only in part and grudgingly, or heartily and altogether? Shall our protests against certain things in it be radical and unforgiving, or shall we think that, even with evil, there are ways of living that must lead to good? If we accept the whole, shall we do so as if stunned into submission —as Carlyle would have us—"Gad! we'd better!"—or shall we do so with enthusiastic assent? Morality pure and simple accepts the law of the whole which it finds reigning, so far as to acknowledge and obey it, but it may obey it with the heaviest and coldest heart, and never cease to feel it as a yoke. But for religion, in its strong and fully developed manifestations, the service of the highest never is felt as a yoke. Dull submission is left far behind, and a mood of welcome, which may fill any place on the scale between cheerful serenity and enthusiastic gladness, has taken its place.

WILLIAM JAMES

The temper of acquiescence [in the existence of evil] is at the same time the temper which impels to amelioration without the fond expectation that the springs of pain will ever be sealed; and when it takes in the relation of God to the world, it prompts the recognition that this same attempt at betterment is at once implanted in us by the Space-Time out of which we are precipitated, and secures the deity to which the world is tending.

SAMUEL ALEXANDER

THE HOUND OF HEAVEN

I fled Him, down the nights and down the days;
  I fled Him down the arches of the years;
I fled Him, down the labyrinthine ways
  Of my own mind; and in the mist of tears
I hid from Him, and under running laughter.
      Up vistaed hopes I sped;
      And shot, precipitated,
Adown Titanic glooms of chasmèd fears,
  From those strong Feet that followed, followed after.
      But with unhurrying chase,
      And unperturbèd pace,
    Deliberate speed, majestic instancy,
      They beat—and a Voice beat
      More instant than the Feet—
  "All things betray thee, who betrayest Me."

      I pleaded, outlaw-wise,
By many a hearted casement, curtained red,
  Trellised with intertwining charities;
(For, though I knew His love Who followèd,
      Yet was I sore adread
Lest, having Him, I must have naught beside);
But, if one little casement parted wide,
  The gust of His approach would clash it to.
Fear wist not to evade, as Love wist to pursue.

Across the margent of the world I fled,
And troubled the gold gateways of the stars,
Smiting for shelter on their clangèd bars;
Fretted to dulcet jars
And silvern chatter the pale ports o' the moon.
I said to dawn, Be sudden; to eve, Be soon;
With thy young skiey blossoms heap me over
From this tremendous Lover!
Float thy vague veil about me, lest He see!
I tempted all His servitors, but to find
My own betrayal in their constancy,
In faith to Him their fickleness to me,
Their traitorous trueness, and their loyal deceit.
To all swift things for swiftness did I sue;
Clung to the whistling mane of every wind.
But whether they swept, smoothly fleet,
The long savannahs of the blue;
Or whether, Thunder-driven,
They clanged his chariot 'thwart a heaven
Plashy with flying lightnings round the spurn o' their feet:—
Fear wist not to evade as Love wist to pursue.
Still with unhurrying chase,
And unperturbèd pace,
Deliberate speed, majestic instancy,
Came on the following Feet,
And a Voice above their beat—
"Naught shelters thee, who wilt not shelter Me."

I sought no more that after which I strayed
In face of man or maid;
But still within the little children's eyes
Seems something, something that replies;
They at least are for me, surely for me!
I turned me to them very wistfully;
But, just as their young eyes grew sudden fair
With dawning answers there,
Their angel plucked them from me by the hair.

"Come then, ye other children, Nature's—share
With me" (said I) "your delicate fellowship;
    Let me greet you lip to lip,
    Let me twine with you caresses,
        Wantoning
    With our Lady-Mother's vagrant tresses,
        Banqueting
    With her in her wind-walled palace,
    Underneath her azured daïs,
    Quaffing, as your taintless way is,
        From a chalice
Lucent-weeping out of the dayspring."
        So it was done:
I in their delicate fellowship was one—
Drew the bolt of Nature's secrecies.
I knew all the swift importings
    On the wilful face of skies;
    I knew how the clouds arise
    Spumèd of the wild sea-snortings;
        All that's born or dies
    Rose and drooped with—made them shapers
Of mine own moods, or wailful or divine—
    With them joyed and was bereaven.
    I was heavy with the even,
    When she lit her glimmering tapers
    Round the day's dead sanctities.
    I laughed in the morning's eyes.
I triumphed and I saddened with all weather,
    Heaven and I wept together,
And its sweet tears were salt with mortal mine;
Against the red throb of its sunset-heart
        I laid my own to beat,
        And share commingling heat;
But not by that, by that, was eased my human smart.
In vain my tears were wet on Heaven's grey cheek.

For ah! we know not what each other says,
These things and I; in sound, *I* speak—
Their sound is but their stir, they speak by silences.
Nature, poor stepdame, cannot slake my drouth;
Let her, if she would owe me,
Drop yon blue bosom-veil of sky, and show me
The breasts o' her tenderness:
Never did any milk of hers once bless
My thirsting mouth.
Nigh and nigh draws the chase,
With unperturbèd pace,
Deliberate speed, majestic instancy;
And past those noisèd Feet
A voice comes yet more fleet—
"Lo! naught contents thee, who content'st not Me."

Naked I wait Thy love's uplifted stroke!
My harness piece by piece Thou hast hewn from me,
And smitten me to my knee;
I am defenceless utterly.
I slept, methinks, and woke,
And, slowly gazing, find me stripped in sleep.
In the rash lustihead of my young powers,
I shook the pillaring hours
And pulled my life upon me; grimed with smears,
I stand amid the dust o' the mounded years—
My mangled youth lies dead beneath the heap.
My days have crackled and gone up in smoke,
Have puffed and burst as sun-starts on a stream.
Yea, faileth now even dream
The dreamer, and the lute the lutanist;
Even the linked fantasies, in whose blossomy twist
I swung the earth a trinket at my wrist,
Are yielding; cords of all too weak account
For earth with heavy griefs so overplussed.

Ah! is Thy love indeed
A weed, albeit an amaranthine weed,
Suffering no flowers except its own to mount?
Ah! must—
Designer infinite!—
Ah! must Thou char the wood ere Thou canst limn with it?
My freshness spent its wavering shower i' the dust;
And now my heart is as a broken fount,
Wherein tear-drippings stagnate, spilt down ever
From the dank thoughts that shiver
Upon the sighful branches of my mind.
Such is; what is to be?
The pulp so bitter, how shall taste the rind?
I dimly guess what Time in mists confounds;
Yet ever and anon a trumpet sounds
From the hid battlements of Eternity;
Those shaken mists a space unsettle, then
Round the half-glimpsèd turrets slowly wash again.
But not ere him who summoneth
I first have seen, enwound
With glooming robes purpureal, cypress-crowned;
His name I know, and what his trumpet saith.
Whether man's heart or life it be which yields
Thee harvest, must Thy harvest fields
Be dunged with rotten death?

Now of that long pursuit
Comes on at hand the bruit;
That Voice is round me like a bursting sea:
"And is thy earth so marred,
Shattered in shard on shard?
Lo, all things fly thee, for thou fliest Me!
Strange, piteous, futile thing,
Wherefore should any set thee love apart?
Seeing none but I makes much of naught" (He said),
"And human love needs human meriting:

How hast thou merited—
Of all man's clotted clay the dingiest clot?
Alack, thou knowest not
How little worthy of any love thou art!
Whom wilt thou find to love ignoble thee
Save Me, save only Me?
All which I took from thee I did but take,
Not for thy harms,
But just that thou might'st seek it in My arms.
All which thy child's mistake
Fancies as lost, I have stored for thee at home:
Rise, clasp My hand, and come!"

Halts by me that footfall:
Is my gloom, after all,
Shade of His hand, outstretched caressingly?
"Ah, fondest, blindest, weakest,
I am He Whom thou seekest!
Thou dravest love from thee, who dravest Me."

FRANCIS THOMPSON

FOURTH PART

II. MAN'S DIGNITY AND RESPONSIBILITY

ANDTE
CON MOTO
ff

§ 1

Arise, then, freeman, stand forth in thy world. It is God's world. It is also thine.

JOSIAH ROYCE

For thou hast made him a little lower than the angels, and hast crowned him with glory and honour.

FROM PSALM 8

I have said, Ye are gods; and all of you are children of the most High.

FROM PSALM 82

When God made man the innermost heart of the Godhead was put into man.

MEISTER ECKHART

What is the worst thing the Evil Urge can achieve? To make man forget that he is the son of a king.

RABBI SHELOMO OF KARLIN

I am God's Other-Self: He finds in me
What is akin to Him eternally.

ANGELUS SILESIUS

I am the image of God: therefore if
God would see
Himself, He must look down, and see
Himself in me.

ANGELUS SILESIUS

I am as rich as God: no dust can be
(Believe me, man) he does not share with me.

ANGELUS SILESIUS

Came I to naught, then God's own death must be:
He would give up the ghost for lack of me.

ANGELUS SILESIUS

What will you do, God, when I die?
When I, your pitcher, broken, lie?
When I, your drink, go stale or dry?
I am your garb, the trade you ply,
you lose your meaning, losing me.

Homeless without me, you will be
robbed of your welcome, warm and sweet.
I am your sandals: your tired feet
will wander bare for want of me.

Your mighty cloak will fall away.
Your glance that on my cheek was laid
and pillowed warm, will seek, dismayed,
the comfort that I offered once—
to lie, as sunset colours fade
in the cold lap of alien stones.

What will you do, God? I am afraid.

RAINER MARIA RILKE

Kabir says: "Whether I be in the temple or the balcony, in the camp or in the flower garden, I tell you truly that every moment my Lord is taking His delight in me."

KABIR

I am more beautiful than aught you see,
For God, who's beauty, is in love with me.

ANGELUS SILESIUS

Are not two sparrows sold for a farthing? and one of them shall not fall on the ground without your Father.

But the very hairs of your head are all numbered.

Fear ye not therefore, ye are of more value than many sparrows.

ST. MATTHEW

Beloved, now are we the sons of God, and it doth not yet appear what we shall be: but we know that, when he shall appear, we shall be like him; for we shall see him as he is.

I JOHN

We carry with us the wonders we seek without us: there is all Africa and her prodigies in us; we are that bold and adventurous piece of Nature, which he that studies wisely learns in a *compendium* what others labour at in a divided piece and endless volume.

SIR THOMAS BROWNE

Now for my life, it is a miracle of thirty years, which to relate, were not a History, but a piece of Poetry, and would sound to common ears like a Fable. . . . Men that look upon my outside, perusing only my condition and Fortunes, do err in my Altitude; for I am above Atlas his shoulders. The earth is a point not only in respect of the Heavens above us, but of that heavenly and celestial part within us: that mass of Flesh that circumscribes me, limits not my mind: that surface that tells the Heavens it hath an end, cannot persuade me I have any: I take my circle to be above three hundred and sixty; though the number of the Ark do measure my body, it comprehendeth not my mind: whilst I study to find how I am a Microcosm, or little World, I find my self something more than the great. There is surely a piece of Divinity in us, something that was before the Elements, and owes no homage unto the Sun.

Nature tells me I am the Image of God, as well as Scripture: he that understands not thus much, hath not his introduction or first lesson, and is yet to begin the Alphabet of man.

SIR THOMAS BROWNE

Never are we so poor as men want to make us. Always we have the wealth which we are, the beauty which we live.

ERNST TOLLER

O my God, the soul which thou gavest me is pure.

THE HEBREW MORNING SERVICE

Thou, O my soul, hast told of my beginning; now I say to thee verily: I was made of love in that place; therefore, in the nobility of my nature, no creature can suffice me and none open me, save love alone.

MECHTHILD OF MAGDEBURG

Shall men, then, always walk in meekness? Not so, say the Masters. There are moments when haughtiness becomes a duty. When the Evil Inclination approaches, whispering in the ear: "You are unworthy to fulfil the Law," say: "I am worthy."

HASIDIC SAYING

Karl Barth . . . is the dehumanisation of Christianity. This mode of thought discovers in the creative world only sin and powerlessness. There remains a fervent faith in God, but in God absolutely transcendent, separated by an abyss from the world and from man. The image of God in man is shattered. The Word of God is the only connection between God and creation and for man there remains only the possibility of hearkening to God's word.

NICHOLAS BERDYAEV

I vow God is omnipotent, but he is impotent to thwart the humble soul with towering aspiration. And where I cannot master God and bend him to my will it is because I fail either in will or meekness. I say, and I would stake my life upon it, that by will a man might pierce a wall of steel, and accordingly we read about St. Peter that on catching sight of Jesus he walked upon the water in his eagerness to meet him.

MEISTER ECKHART

God is omnipotent—but powerless still
To stop my heart from wishing what it will.

ANGELUS SILESIUS

We classify these faculties thus, arranging them into a certain graduated order. We put in the first place posse, possibility; in the second, velle, volition; and in the third, esse, or being. The possibility we place in our nature; the volition in our will; and the being in the realisation by act. The first of these faculties expressed in the term posse is especially assigned to God, who has bestowed it on His creature; the other two, indicated in the terms velle and esse, must be referred to the human agent, because they flow forth from the fountain of his will. In his willing, therefore, and doing a good work consists man's praise; or rather this praise belongs both to the human being and to God, who has bestowed on him the "possibility" of exercising his actual will and work, and who evermore by the help of His grace assists this very possibility. That a man possesses this possibility of willing and effecting any good work comes from God alone. So that this one faculty may exist even where the other two have no being; but the converse is not true—that these latter can exist without that former one. It is, therefore, at my own option not to have a good inclination and not to do a good action; but it is by no means within my power not to have the possibility of good. This possibility is inherent in me whether I will or no; nor does nature at any time receive in this point an option for itself. Now the meaning of all this will be rendered clearer by an example or two. That we have the possibility of seeing with our eyes is no power of ours; but it is in our power that we make a good or a bad use of our eyes. So again that I may, by applying a general case in illustration, embrace all, the fact that we have the possibility of accomplishing every good thing by action, speech and thought come from Him who endowed us with this possibility, and also assists it. Accordingly—and this is a point which needs frequent repetition because of your calumniation of us—whenever we say that a man can live without sin, we also give praise to God by our acknowledgment of the possibility which we have received from Him, Who has bestowed such power upon us; and there is here no occasion for praising the human agent, since it is God's matter alone that is, for the moment, treated of: for the question is not about willing, or effecting, but simply and solely about that which may possibly be.

PELAGIUS

We contradict the Lord to His face when we say: It is hard, it is difficult; we cannot, we are men; we are encompassed with fragile flesh. O blind madness! O unholy audacity! We charge the God of all knowledge with a two-fold ignorance, that He does not seem to know what He has made nor what He has commanded, as though, forgetting the human weakness of which He is Himself the author, He imposed laws upon man which he cannot endure.

PELAGIUS

A sinfulness which is as much that of the race as of the individual, which depends on a freedom quite different from the power to choose between good and ill, which is "introduced into the human situation" and made inevitable by a "force of evil prior to any human action," is devoid of relevance to the conduct of individual lives; and for that reason alone it must stand discredited at the bar of ethics. . . .

The upshot of [the above] doctrine is the presentation of sin, as many are only too prone to regard it to-day, as some mysterious cosmic disaster, some vague blot upon the universe which we just cannot conjure away, something also on account of which we must all bow our heads in shame, and, in particular, something towards which we should adopt certain religious attitudes and about which theological doctrines have to be formed. The preacher must stand in his pulpit at appointed times to pronounce himself 'agin it,' and to announce the way of salvation. But none of this appears to touch the individual in the conduct of his life, and however much he may be induced to give formal assent to his own involvement in the sins of the world, he remains fundamentally serene in the assurance that it does not really concern him for the simple reason that there was nothing he could have done about it.

The Protestant Reformation was not in fact Protestant enough; for it conveyed its protest against the authoritarianism of the mediaeval Church too much within the assumptions about the individual upon which that Church proceeded and to which the abuses which the Reformers found most offensive were very directly due. In this way, while seeming to provide a remedy, and actually succeeding in large measure to cure the immediate and grosser manifestations of a great evil, it in fact lent a new and long lease of life to a view that strikes at the heart of true religion. That view, to put it bluntly, is the view that religion can be managed by proxy. . . . In some ways indeed the individual had much better standing in the teaching of the Roman Church than in the theology and practice of the Reformers. It was Luther who announced that "Free-will lies prostrate." . . .

An intangible cosmology has now to fill the role once ascribed to the Church as the vicarious bearer and trustee of the individual's religious interests. This isolates religion much more completely from life; it leaves the individual impotent and insignificant while the great cosmic forces run their play through to its appointed end. He is more a cipher than he could ever be if he left his soul in the keeping of an institution.

It need hardly be stressed how much the crisis of Western civilisation turns on a true estimate of the individual; neither need we detail here the factors that conspire to eclipse him or consider what adjustment of modern conditions will make for the truest development of persons. These are problems that will tax our energies to the utmost. But it will also be evident without elaboration how impossible of solution those problems will be, and how swiftly disaster will follow, if the very springs of individual responsibility are dried up in an apathetic surrender to oppressive doctrinal fictions.

. . . .

Either guilt has to be incurred deliberately or it has not. Sin cannot be in part the choice of the individual, in part the result of the fall or the "sin of man." The alternatives are quite exclusive, and the defiant paradoxes of the New Theology simply underline the inherent contradiction of attempts to retain the idea of freedom within a deterministic scheme. There can be no "partial determinism," although there can be various kinds of determinism, and although many factors may contribute to the situation within which a choice must be made. If, therefore, we speak of the "sin" of man or of some wickedness which infects the human situation as a whole and which cannot be identified with a sum total of the avoidable sins of individuals, the break with liberalism must be complete; for such notions have no room for individual freedom in any meaning we normally give to those terms. . . . But if, on the other hand, we are loth to surrender liberal principles, we must be equally uncompromising in rejecting ideas that are bound up with the traditionalist view.

. . . .

The more we are induced to think of one another in the light of Christ's revelation of the brotherhood of men, the more we shall find ourselves to be, *in this sense*, involved in the sins of others. No one who is morally sensitive could wish to dissociate himself from the moral attainment of others or wish to be spared the pain which is often the price of this supreme human relationship. But this, albeit crucial for a true view of divine and human relationships, is an entirely different matter from partaking of the guilt of another. We simply cannot in the latter way be wounded for the transgressions of others, we cannot at this point bear one another's burdens. . . . It is evident, as an immediate assurance of the moral consciousness, and thus independently of any kind of argument, that no person can be responsible for the action of another.

H. D. LEWIS

And Moses returned unto the Lord, and said, Oh, this people have sinned a great sin, and have made them gods of gold.

Yet now, if thou wilt forgive their sin—; and if not, blot me, I pray thee, out of thy book which thou hast written.

And the Lord said unto Moses, Whosoever hath sinned against me, him will I blot out of my book.

EXODUS

The son shall not bear the iniquity of the father, neither shall the father bear the iniquity of the son: the righteousness of the righteous shall be upon him, and the wickedness of the wicked shall be upon him.

EZEKIEL

Yea, and why even of yourselves judge ye not what is right?

ST. LUKE

Work out your own salvation with fear and trembling.

PHILIPPIANS

But you see that the mountain of Christian perfection is extremely high. Ah! my God, you say this; how then shall I be able to climb it? Courage, Philothea! When the little bees begin to take shape, they are called nymphs, and do not know yet how to fly over the flowers, or on the mountains, or on the neighbouring hills to gather honey. But little by little, nourishing themselves with the honey which their mothers have prepared, these little nymphs take wing and become strong, so that afterwards they fly to gather honey through the whole country. It is true that we are still little bees in devotion, we do not know how to climb as we would, which is nothing less than to attain the summit of Christian perfection. But if we begin to take shape by our desires and resolutions, our wings will begin to grow. We must therefore hope that one day we shall be spiritual bees, and shall fly. And meanwhile, let us live on the honey of the precepts which devout people of old have left us in so large quantity, and let us pray God that He will give us feathers like doves that not only shall we be able to fly in the time of the present life, but may also rest in the eternity of the future.

ST. FRANCIS DE SALES

As the appearance of the bow that is in the cloud in the day of rain, so was the appearance of the brightness round about. This was the appearance of the likeness of the glory of the Lord. And when I saw it, I fell upon my face, and I heard a voice of one that spake.

And he said unto me, Son of man, *stand upon thy feet*,[1] and I will speak unto thee.

[1] The emphasis is mine—V.G.

EZEKIEL

Live unto the Dignity of thy Nature, and leave it not disputable at last, whether thou hast been a Man. . . . Desert not thy title to a Divine particle and union with invisibles. Let true Knowledge and Virtue tell the lower World thou art a part of the higher. Let thy Thoughts be of things which have not entered into the Hearts of Beasts; think of things long past, and long to come; acquaint thy self with the *Choragium* of the Stars, and consider the vast expansion beyond them. Let intellectual Tubes give thee a glance of things, which visive Organs reach not. Have a glimpse of incomprehensibles, and Thoughts of things which Thoughts but tenderly touch. Lodge immaterials in thy Head; ascend unto invisibles; fill thy Spirit with Spirituals, with the mysteries of Faith, the magnalities of Religion, and thy Life with the Honour of God; without which, though Giants in Wealth and Dignity, we are but Dwarfs and Pygmies in Humanity, and may hold a pitiful rank in that triple division of mankind into Heroes, Men and Beasts. For though human Souls are said to be equal, yet is there no small inequality in their operations; some maintain the allowable Station of Men; many are far below it; and some have been so divine, as to approach the *Apogeum* of their Natures, and to be in the *Confinium* of Spirits.

SIR THOMAS BROWNE

A man who desires to help others by counsel or deed will refrain from dwelling on men's faults, and will speak but sparingly of human weaknesses. But he will speak at large of man's virtue and power, and the means of perfecting the same, that thus men may endeavour joyously to live, so far as in them lies, after the commandment of reason.

SPINOZA

There must be either a predestined Necessity and inviolable plan, or a gracious Providence, or a chaos without design or director. If then there be an inevitable Necessity, why kick against the pricks? If a Providence that is ready to be gracious, render thyself worthy of divine succour. But if a chaos without guide, congratulate thyself that amid such a surging sea thou hast in thyself a guiding Reason.

MARCUS AURELIUS

But as to the Whole, if God—all is well; if haphazard—be not thou also haphazard.

MARCUS AURELIUS

Moses has shown that we should all confess our gratitude for the powers we possess. The wise man should dedicate his sagacity, the eloquent man should devote his excellence of speech to the praise of God in prose and verse; and, in general, the natural philosopher should offer his physics, the moralist his ethics, the artist and the man of science the arts and sciences they know. So, too, the sailor and the pilot will dedicate their favourable voyage, the husbandman his fruitful harvest, the herdsman the increase of his cattle, the doctor the recovery of his patients, the general his victory in fight, and the statesman or the monarch his legal chieftaincy or kingly rule. In a word, he who is no lover of self will regard God as the true cause of all the powers of body and soul, and of all external goods. Let no one, therefore, however humble and insignificant he be, despairing of a better fortune, scruple to become a suppliant of God. Even if he can expect nothing more, let him give thanks to the best of his power for what he has already received. Infinite are the gifts he has: birth, life, nature, soul, sensation, imagination, desire, reason. Reason is a small word, but a most perfect thing, a fragment of the world-soul, or, as for the disciples of the Mosaic philosophy it is more pious to say, a true impression of the Divine Image.

PHILO

The feeling that man is not a mere casual visitor at the palace-gate of the world, but the invited guest whose presence is needed to give the royal banquet its sole meaning, is not confined to any particular sect in India. Let me quote here some poems from a mediaeval poet of Western India—Jnândâs—whose works are nearly forgotten, and have become scarce from the very exquisiteness of their excellence. In the following poem he is addressing God's messenger, who comes to us in the morning light of our childhood, in the dusk of our day's end, and in the night's darkness:

Messenger, morning brought you, habited in gold.
After sunset, your song wore a tune of ascetic grey, and
then came night.
Your message was written in bright letters across the black.
Why is such splendour about you, to lure the heart of one
who is nothing?

This is the answer of the messenger:

Great is the festival hall where you are to be the only guest.
Therefore the letter to you is written from sky to sky,
And I, the proud servant, bring the invitation with all
ceremony.

And thus the poet knows that the silent rows of stars carry God's own invitation to the individual soul.

The same poet sings:

What hast thou come to beg from the beggar, O King of
Kings?
My Kingdom is poor for want of him, my dear one, and
I wait for him in sorrow.

How long will you keep him waiting, O wretch,
who has waited for you for ages in silence and stillness?
Open your gate, and make this very moment fit for the
union.

It is the song of man's pride in the value given to him by Supreme Love and realised by his own love.

RABINDRANATH TAGORE

I say no man has ever yet been half devout enough,
None has ever yet adored or worship'd half enough,
None has begun to think how divine he himself is, and how
certain the future is.

WALT WHITMAN

I

Is there one in all the world who does not desire to be divinely beautiful?

To have the most perfect body—unerring skill, strength, limpid clearness of mind, as of the sunlight over the hills,

To radiate love wherever he goes, to move in and out, accepted?

The secret lies close to you, so close.

You are that person; it lies close to you, so close—deep down within—

But in Time it shall come forth and be revealed.

Not by accumulating riches, but by giving away what you have,

Shall you become beautiful;

You must undo the wrappings, not case yourself in fresh ones;

Not by multiplying clothes shall you make your body sound and healthy, but rather by discarding them;

Not by multiplying knowledge shall you beautify your mind;

It is not the food that you eat that has to vivify you, but you that have to vivify the food.

Always emergence, and the parting of veils for the hidden to appear;

The child emerges from its mother's body, and out of that body again in time another child.

When the body which thou now hast falls away, another body shall be already prepared beneath.

And beneath that again another.

Always that which appears last in time is first, and the cause of all—and not that which appears first.

2

Freedom has to be won afresh every morning,

Every morning thou must put forth thy strength afresh upon

the world, to create out of chaos the garden in which thou walkest.

(Behold! I love thee—I wait for thee in thine own garden, lingering till eventide among the bushes;

I tune the lute for thee; I prepare my body for thee, bathing unseen in the limpid waters.)

3

Wondrous is Man—the human body: to understand and possess this, to create it every day afresh, is to possess all things.

The tongue and all that proceeds from it: spoken and written words, languages, commands, controls, the electric telegraph girdling the earth;

The eyes ordaining, directing; the feet and all that they indicate—the path they travel for years and years;

The passions of the body, the belly and the cry for food, the heaving breast of love, and phallus, the fleshy thighs,

The erect proud head and neck, the sturdy back, and knees well-knit or wavering;

All the interminable attitudes and what they indicate;

Every relation of one man to another, every cringing, bullying, lustful, obscene, pure, honourable, chaste, just and merciful;

The fingers differently shaped according as they handle money for gain or for gift;

All the different ramifications and institutions of society which proceed from such one difference in the crook of a finger;

All that proceed from an arrogant or a slavish contour of the neck;

All the evil that goes forth from any part of a man's body which is not possessed by himself, all the devils let loose—from a twist of the tongue or a leer of the eye, or the unmanly act of any member—and swirling into society; all the good which gathers round a man who is clean and strong—the threads drawing from afar to the tips of his fingers, the interpretations in his eyes, all the love which passes through his limbs into heaven:

What it is to command and be Master of this wondrous body with all its passions and powers, to truly possess it—*that* it is to command and possess all things, that it is to create.

4

The art of creation, like every other art, has to be learnt:

Slowly slowly, through many years, thou buildest up thy body,

And the power that thou now hast (such as it is) to build up this present body, thou hast acquired in the past in other bodies;

So in the future shalt thou use again the power that thou now acquirest.

But the power to build up the body includes all powers.

Do not be dismayed because thou art yet a child of chance, and at the mercy greatly both of Nature and fate;

Because if thou wert not subject to chance, then wouldst thou be Master of thyself; but since thou art not yet Master of thine own passions and powers, in that degree must thou needs be at the mercy of some other power.

And if thou choosest to call that power "Chance," well and good. It is the angel with whom thou hast to wrestle.

5

Beware how thou seekest this for thyself and that for thyself. I do not say Seek not; but Beware how thou seekest.

For a soldier who is going a campaign does not seek what fresh furniture he can carry on his back, but rather what he can leave behind;

Knowing well that every additional thing which he cannot freely use and handle is an impediment to him.

So if thou seekest fame or ease or pleasure or aught for thyself, the image of that thing which thou seekest will come and cling to thee—and thou wilt have to carry it about;

And the images and powers which thou hast thus evoked will gather round and form for thee a new body—clamouring for sustenance and satisfaction;

And if thou art not able to discard this image now, thou wilt not be able to discard that body then: but wilt have to carry it about.

Beware then lest it become thy grave and thy prison—instead of thy winged abode, and palace of joy.

For (over and over again) there is nothing that is evil except because a man has not mastery over it; and there is no good thing that is not evil if it have mastery over a man;

And there is no passion or power, or pleasure or pain, or created thing whatsoever, which is not ultimately for man and for his use—or which he need be afraid of, or ashamed at.

The ascetics and the self-indulgent divide things into good and evil—as it were to throw away the evil;

But things cannot be divided into good and evil, but all are good so soon as they are brought into subjection.

And seest thou not that except for Death thou couldst never overcome Death—

For since by being a slave to things of sense thou hast clothed thyself with a body which thou art not master of, thou wert condemned to a living tomb were that body not to be destroyed.

But now through pain and suffering out of this tomb shalt thou come; and through the experience thou hast acquired shalt build thyself a new and better body;

And so on many times, till thou spreadest wings and hast all powers diabolic and angelic concentred in thy flesh.

6

And so at last I saw Satan appear before me—magnificent, fully formed.

Feet first, with shining limbs, he glanced down from above among the bushes,

And stood there erect, dark-skinned, with nostrils dilated with passion;

(In the burning intolerable sunlight he stood, and I in the shade of the bushes);

Fierce and scathing the effluence of his eyes, and scornful of dreams and dreamers (he touched a rock hard by and it split with a sound like thunder);

Fierce the magnetic influence of his dusky flesh; his great foot, well-formed, was planted firm in the sand—with spreading toes;

"Come out," he said with a taunt, "art thou afraid to meet me?"

And I answered not, but sprang upon him and smote him.

And he smote me a thousand times, and brashed and scorched and slew me as with hands of flame;

And I was glad, for my body lay there dead; and I sprang upon him again with another body;

And he turned upon me, and smote me a thousand times and slew that body;

And I was glad and sprang upon him again with another body—

And with another and another and again another;

And the bodies which I took on yielded before him, and were like cinctures of flame upon me, but I flung them aside;

And the pains which I endured in one body were powers which I wielded in the next; and I grew in strength, till at last I stood before him complete, with a body like his own and equal in might—exultant in pride and joy.

Then he ceased, and said, "I love thee."

And lo! his form changed, and he leaned backwards and drew me upon him,

And bore me up into the air, and floated me over the topmost trees and the ocean, and round the curve of the earth under the moon—

Till we stood again in Paradise.

EDWARD CARPENTER

All strength—all terror, single or in bands,
That ever was put forth in personal form—
Jehovah—with his thunder, and the choir
Of shouting Angels, and the empyreal thrones—
I pass them unalarmed. Not Chaos, not

The darkest pit of lowest Erebus,
Nor aught of blinder vacancy, scooped out
By help of dreams—can breed such fear and awe
As fall upon us often when we look
Into our Minds, into the Mind of Man—
My haunt, and the main region of my song.
—Beauty—a living Presence of the earth,
Surpassing the most fair ideal Forms
Which craft of delicate Spirits hath composed
From earth's materials—waits upon my steps;
Pitches her tents before me as I move,
An hourly neighbour. Paradise, and groves
Elysian, Fortunate Fields—like those of old
Sought in the Atlantic Main—why should they be
A history only of departed things,
Or a mere fiction of what never was?
For the discerning intellect of Man,
When wedded to this goodly universe
In love and holy passion, shall find these
A simple produce of the common day.
—I, long before the blissful hour arrives,
Would chant, in lonely peace, the spousal verse
Of this great consummation:—and, by words
Which speak of nothing more than what we are,
Would I arouse the sensual from their sleep
Of Death, and win the vacant and the vain
To noble raptures; while my voice proclaims
How exquisitely the individual Mind
(And the progressive powers perhaps no less
Of the whole species) to the external World
Is fitted:—and how exquisitely, too—
Theme this but little heard of among men—
The external World is fitted to the Mind;
And the creation (by no lower name
Can it be called) which they with blended might
Accomplish:—this is our high argument.

WORDSWORTH (from *The Excursion*)

What we have loved,
Others will love, and we will teach them how;
Instruct them how the mind of man becomes
A thousand times more beautiful than the earth
On which he dwells, above this frame of things
(Which, 'mid all revolution in the hopes
And fears of men, doth still remain unchanged)
In beauty exalted, as it is itself
Of quality and fabric more divine.

WORDSWORTH (from *The Prelude*)

FROM "PROMETHEUS UNBOUND"

DEMOGORGON

Man, who wert once a despot and a slave;
A dupe and a deceiver; a decay;
A traveller from the cradle to the grave
Through the dim night of this immortal day!

ALL

Speak: thy strong words may never pass away.

DEMOGORGON

This is the day which down the void abysm,
At the Earth-born's spell, yawns for Heaven's despotism,
And Conquest is dragged captive through the deep.
Love, from its awful throne of patient power
In the wise heart, from the last giddy hour
Of dread endurance, from the slippery, steep,
And narrow verge of crag-like agony, springs,
And folds over the world its healing wings.

Gentleness, Virtue, Wisdom, and Endurance—
These are the seals of that most firm assurance

Which bars the pit over Destruction's strength;
And, if with infirm hand Eternity,
Mother of many acts and hours, should free
The serpent that would clasp her with his length,
These are the spells by which to reassume
An empire o'er the disentangled doom.

To suffer woes which hope thinks infinite;
To forgive wrongs darker than death or night;
To defy power which seems omnipotent;
To love and bear; to hope till hope creates
From its own wreck the thing it contemplates;
Neither to change, nor falter, nor repent;
This, like thy glory, Titan, is to be
Good, great, and joyous, beautiful and free;
This is alone Life, Joy, Empire, and Victory!

SHELLEY

THE BIBLE

That! That! There I was told
That I *the Son of God* am made,
His Image. O Divine! And that fine Gold,
With all the Joys that here do fade,
Are but a Toy, compared to the Bliss
Which Hev'nly, God-like, and Eternal is.

That We on earth are Kings;
And, tho we're cloath'd with mortal Skin,
Are Inward Cherubins; hav Angels Wings;
Affections, Thoughts, and Minds within,
Can soar throu all the Coasts of Hev'n and Earth;
And shall be sated with Celestial Mirth.

THOMAS TRAHERNE

ADMIRATION

Can Human Shape so taking be,
That Angels com and sip
Ambrosia from a Mortal Lip!
Can Cherubims descend with Joy to see
God in his Works beneath!
Can Mortals breath
FELICITY!
Can Bodies fill the hev'nly Rooms
With welcom Odours and Perfumes!
Can Earth-bred Flow'rs adorn Celestial Bowers
Or yield such Fruits as pleas the hev'nly Powers!

Then may the Seas with Amber flow;
The Earth a Star appear;
Things be divine and hevenly here.
The Tree of Life in Paradise may grow
Among us now: the Sun
Be quite out-don
By Beams that shew
More bright than his: Celestial Mirth
May yet inhabit all this Earth.
It cannot be! Can Mortals be so blind?
Hav Joys so near them, which they never mind?

The Lilly and the Rosy-Train
Which, scatter'd on the ground,
Salute the Feet which they surround,
Grow for thy sake, O Man; that like a Chain
Or Garland they may be
To deck ev'n thee:
They all remain
Thy Gems; and bowing down their head
Their liquid Pearl they kindly shed
In Tears; as if they meant to wash thy Feet,
For Joy that they to serv thee are made meet.

The Sun doth smile, and looking down
From Hev'n doth blush to see
Himself excelled here by thee:
Yet frankly doth dispers his Beams to crown
A Creature so divine;
He lovs to shine,
Nor lets a Frown
Eclyps his Brow, becaus he givs
Light for the Use of one that livs
Abov himself. Lord! What is Man that he
Is thus admired like a Deity!

THOMAS TRAHERNE

THE SCRIBE

What lovely things
Thy hand hath made:
The smooth-plumed bird
In its emerald shade,
The seed of the grass,
The speck of stone
Which the wayfaring ant
Stirs—and hastes on!

Though I should sit
By some tarn in thy hills,
Using its ink
As the spirit wills
To write of Earth's wonders,
Its live, willed things,
Flit would the ages
On soundless wings
Ere unto Z
My pen drew nigh;
Leviathan told,
And the honey-fly:

And still would remain
My wit to try—
My worn reeds broken,
The dark tarn dry,
All words forgotten—
Thou, Lord, and I.

WALTER DE LA MARE

In a certain sense, every single human soul has more meaning and value than the whole of history with its empires, its wars and revolutions, its blossoming and fading civilisations.

NICHOLAS BERDYAEV

Human personality and individuality written and signed by God on each human countenance—in so extraordinary a way, sometimes, on the face of a great man—is something altogether sacred, something for the Resurrection, for eternal Life, for the beatific Union. Every human face is a very special door to Paradise, which cannot possibly be confused with any other, and through which there will never enter but one soul.

LÉON BLOY

The distorting power and the evil of egoism do not derive from man's unduly high opinion of himself, nor from his presumption to unconditional importance and immeasurable worth. Since every individual human being is a nucleus of living forces; since he is potentially capable of limitless perfecting and is actually capable of receiving absolute truth into his conscious mind and of introducing it into his life, he cannot be valued too highly. Seen rightly, every man has an absolute significance and value; he is irreplaceable; and therefore of immeasurable worth. (Is it not said in the Gospel: What shall a man give in exchange for his soul?) The failure of a man to recognise his own unconditional significance would be tantamount to his abdication from the dignity of man. Here is the root of all error, and the death of all faith. For how can a creature so poor and weak that it has lost faith even in itself, find the courage to believe in anything? No, the basic lie and evil do not come from the individual's self-awareness and self-esteem. They come from his disinclination to extend to others the recognition of an absolute worth rightly perceived by him in himself, but wrongly refused to others when, seeing himself exclusively as a central fact in life, he relegates all others to the periphery of his own existence, and ascribes to them only a fortuitous value dependent on himself.

It must of course be conceded that in theory—in the pursuit of theoretical thought—every sane man admits a perfect equality between himself and others; but in practice, in his feelings and dealings, he is ever affirming the immeasurable difference, the fundamental dissimilarity between himself and them: he himself is all-important, while they—when considered apart from their relation to him—are nothing at all. And yet it is exactly on every such occasion of exclusive self-affirmation that a man fails, and must fail, to attain the absolute worth which he claims for himself. The unconditional value which he rightly attributes to himself but wrongly refuses to recognise in others is only potentially his; it requires actualising. God *is* all; by which is meant that he contains, by virtue of the one absolute action of his being, the entirety of all positive content, the whole fullness of being. Man (the genus and the individual) is on the contrary only himself and nothing but himself to begin with; in order to become more—to become "all"—he must destroy the barriers of his isolation. And it is only in conjunction with others that he can actualise his own absolute worth, becoming irreplaceable as he becomes inseparable from all—a part of the all-in-one, a particularised organ of the absolute life. The truly individualised man is a particular and definite image (or aspect) of the all-in-one; and he establishes himself as a true individual through using his unique way of experiencing and appropriating the completeness of an "other." Therefore, when a man affirms himself to the exclusion of all else, he thereby deprives his own existence of all true sense, of all true content, and reduces his individuality to a hollow shell. And so egoism does not come of man's self-awareness or of the affirmation of his individuality; for it is, on the contrary, a negation of oneself and a way to self-destruction.

Our inherent egoism is constantly restrained and modified by the physical and metaphysical, historical and social conditions of human life. Powerful and varied hindrances prevent us from giving it full scope and incurring the terrible consequences to which our lack of restraint would lead. But nothing in the complex system of hindrances and correctives ordained by Providence and carried out by nature or history can affect the root of our egoism, which constantly pushes through the smooth surface of our personal and social ethics, and sometimes bursts forth into the open. Only one force can pull it up by the root. One force only can, and does, destroy it from within: the force of love, and above all of sexual love. The falsehood and evil of egoism are in the exclusive, absolute importance claimed by a man for himself, and refused to all others. Reason can show us how foolish and unjust any such claims are; but love actually annuls, destroys the claim, forcing us to recognise—no longer merely in abstract thought but in the deep of our emotions and living will—that another human being is of the greatest, the most absolute importance to us. Experiencing, when in love, the existential reality of another, and transposing the centre of our life beyond the limits of our own empirical selfhood, we thereby express and actualise our own reality, our own absolute significance: which consists in this very ability to step beyond the limits of our own factual, phenomenal being—in our capacity to live not only in ourselves but also in another.

VLADIMIR SOLOVIEV

RABBI AZRAEL'S DISCOURSE FROM "THE DYBBUK"

The world of God is great and holy. In all the world the holiest land is the Land of Israel. In the Land of Israel the holiest city is Jerusalem; in Jerusalem the holiest place was the Holy Temple, and the holiest spot in the Temple was the Holy of Holies. (*He pauses.*) In the world there are seventy nations, and of them the holiest is Israel. The holiest of the people of Israel is the tribe of the Levites. The holiest of the Levites are the priests, and amongst the priests, the holiest is the High Priest. (*Pause.*) The year has three hundred and fifty-four days. Of these the holidays are the holiest. Holier than the holidays are the Sabbaths and the holiest of the Sabbaths is the Day of Atonement, Sabbath of Sabbaths. (*Pause.*) There are in the world seventy tongues. The holiest of these is the holy tongue of Israel. The holiest of all things written in this tongue is the Holy Torah; of the Torah the holiest part is the Ten Commandments, and the holiest of all the words in the Ten Commandments is the Name of the Lord. (*Pause.*) At a certain hour, on a certain day of the year, all these four supreme holinesses met together. This took place on the Day of Atonement, at the hour when the High Priest entered the Holy of Holies and there revealed the Divine Name. And as this hour was holy and terrible beyond words, so also was it the hour of utmost peril for the High Priest, and for the entire commonweal of Israel. For if, in that hour (which God forbid), a sinful or a wayward thought had entered the mind of the High Priest, it would have brought the destruction of the world. (*Pause.*) Wherever a man stand to lift his eyes to heaven, that place is a Holy of Holies. Every human being created by God in His own image and likeness is a High Priest. Each day of a man's life is the Day of Atonement; and every word he speaks from his heart is the name of the Lord. Therefore the sin of any man, whether of commission or of omission, brings the ruin of a whole world in its train.

S. ANSKY

Every man who begets a free act projects his personality into the infinite. If he gives a poor man a penny grudgingly, that penny pierces the poor man's hand, falls, pierces the earth, bores holes in suns, crosses the firmament and compromises the universe. If he begets an impure act, he perhaps darkens thousands of hearts whom he does not know, who are mysteriously linked to him, and who need this man to be pure as a traveller dying of thirst needs the Gospel's draught of water. A charitable act, an impulse of real pity sings for him the divine praises, from the time of Adam to the end of the ages; it cures the sick, consoles those in despair, calms storms, ransoms prisoners, converts the infidel and protects mankind.

The whole of Christian philosophy lies in the unutterable importance of the free act and in the notion of an enveloping and indestructible mutual dependence. If God, in some eternal second of his power, willed to do what He has never done, annihilate even one man alone, it is altogether likely that creation would thereupon crumble into dust.

LÉON BLOY

It is written, "And he dreamed, and behold a ladder set up on the earth." That "he" is every man. Every man must know: I am clay, I am one of countless shards of clay, but "the top of it reached to Heaven"—my soul reaches to Heaven; "and behold the angels of God ascending and descending on it"—even the ascent and descent of the angels depend upon my deeds.

RABBI MOSHE OF KOBRYN

God therefore took man as a creature of indeterminate nature and, assigning him a place in the middle of the world, addressed him thus: "Neither a fixed abode nor a form that is thine alone nor any function peculiar to thyself have we given thee, Adam, to the end that according to thy longing and according to thy judgment thou mayest have and possess what abode, what form, and what functions thou thyself shalt desire. The nature of all other beings is limited and constrained within the bounds of laws prescribed by Us. Thou, constrained by no limits, in accordance with thine own free will, in whose hand We have placed thee, shalt ordain for thyself the limits of thy nature. We have set thee at the world's centre that thou mayest from thence more easily observe whatever is in the world. We have made thee neither of heaven nor of earth, neither mortal nor immortal, so that with freedom of choice and with honour, as though the maker and moulder of thyself, thou mayest fashion thyself in whatever shape thou shalt prefer. Thou shalt have the power to degenerate into the lower forms of life, which are brutish. Thou shalt have the power, out of thy soul's judgment, to be reborn into the higher forms, which are divine."

O supreme generosity of God the Father, O highest and most marvellous felicity of man! To him it is granted to have whatever he chooses, to be whatever he wills! Beasts as soon as they are born (so says Lucilius) bring with them from their mother's womb all they will ever possess. Spiritual beings, either from the beginning or soon thereafter, become what they are to be for ever and ever. On man when he came into life the Father conferred the seeds of all kinds and the germs of every way of life. Whatever seeds each man cultivates will grow to maturity and bear in him their own fruit. If they be vegetative, he will be like a plant. If sensitive, he will become brutish. If rational, he will grow into a heavenly being. If intellectual, he will be an angel and the son of God. And if, happy in the lot of no created thing, he withdraws into the centre of his own unity, his spirit, made one with God . . . shall surpass them all. Who would not admire this our chameleon? Or who could more greatly admire aught else whatever?

PICO DELLA MIRANDOLA

And now I seem to have come to the end of a long pilgrimage. I have made no discovery. Like a man waking out of sleep, I am once again looking at that to which I had for so long been blind.

I see now that in my civilisation it is Man who holds the power to bind into unity all the individual diversities. There is in Man, as in all beings, something more than the mere sum of the materials that went to his making. A cathedral is a good deal more than the sum of its stones. It is geometry and architecture. The cathedral is not to be defined by its stones, since those stones have no meaning apart from the cathedral, receive from it their sole significance. And how diverse the stones that have entered into this unity! The most grimacing of the gargoyles are easily absorbed into the canticle of the cathedral.

But the significance of Man, in whom my civilisation is summed up, is not self-evident: it is a thing to be taught. There is in mankind no natural predisposition to acknowledge the existence of Man, for Man is not made evident by the mere existence of men. It is because Man exists that we are men, not the other way round. My civilisation is founded upon the reverence for Man present in all men, in each individual. My civilisation has sought through the ages to reveal Man to men, as it might have taught us to perceive the cathedral in a mere heap of stones. This has been the text of its sermon—that Man is higher than the individual.

And this, the true significance of my civilisation, is what I had little by little forgotten. I had thought that it stood for a sum of men as stone stands for a sum of stones. I had mistaken the sum of stones for the cathedral, wherefore little by little my heritage, my civilisation, had vanished. It is Man who must be restored to his place among men. It is Man that is the essence of our culture. Man, the keystone in the arch of the community. Man, the seed whence springs our victory.

It is easy to establish a society upon the foundation of rigid rules. It is easy to shape the kind of man who submits blindly and without protest to a master, to the precepts of a Koran. The real task is to succeed in setting man free by making him master of himself.

But what do we mean by setting man free? You cannot free

a man who dwells in a desert and is an unfeeling brute. There is no liberty except the liberty of some one making his way towards something. Such a man can be set free if you will teach him the meaning of thirst, and how to trace a path to a well. Only then will he embark upon a course of action that will not be without significance. You could not liberate a stone if there were no law of gravity—for where will the stone go, once it is quarried?

My civilisation sought to found human relations upon the belief in Man above and beyond the individual, in order that the attitude of each person towards himself and towards others should not be one of blind conformity to the habits of the ant-hill, but the free expression of love. The invisible path of gravity liberates the stone. The invisible slope of love liberates man. My civilisation sought to make every man the ambassador of their common prince. It looked upon the individual as the path or the message of a thing greater than himself. It pointed the human compass towards magnetised directions in which man would ascend to attain his freedom.

I know how this field of energy came to be. For centuries my civilisation contemplated God in the person of man. Man was created in the image of God. God was revered in Man. Men were brothers in God. It was this reflection of God that conferred an inalienable dignity upon every man. The duties of each towards himself and towards his kind were evident from the fact of the relations between God and man. My civilisation was the inheritor of Christian values.

It was the contemplation of God that created men who were equal, for it was in God that they were equal. This equality possessed an unmistakable significance. For we cannot be equal except we be equal *in* something. The private and the captain are equal in the Nation. Equality is a word devoid of meaning if nothing exists in which it can be expressed.

This equality in the rights of God—rights that are inherent in the individual—forbade the putting of obstacles in the way of the ascension of the individual; and I understand why. God has chosen to adopt the individual as His path. But as this choice also implied the equality of the rights of God "over" the individual, it was clear that individuals were themselves subjected to common duties and to a common respect for law. As the manifestation of God, they were equal in their rights. As the servants of God, they were also equal in their duties.

I understand why an equality that was founded upon God involved neither contradiction nor disorder. Demagogy enters at the moment when, for want of a common denominator, the principle of equality degenerates into a principle of identity. At that moment the private refuses to salute the captain, for by saluting the captain he is no longer doing honour to the Nation, but to the individual.

As the inheritor of God, my civilisation made men equal in Man.

I understand the origin of the respect of men for one another. The scientist owed respect to the stoker, for what he respected in the stoker was God; and the stoker, no less than the scientist, was an ambassador of God. However great one man may be, however insignificant another, no man may claim the power to enslave another. One does not humble an ambassador. . . . Thus the love of God founded relations of dignity between men, relations between ambassadors and not between mere individuals.

As the inheritor of God, my civilisation founded the respect for Man present in every individual.

I understand the origin of brotherhood among men. Men were brothers in God. One can be a brother only *in* something. Where there is no tie that binds men, men are not united but merely lined up. One cannot be a brother to nobody. The pilots of Group 2–33 are brothers in the Group. Frenchmen are brothers in France.

As the inheritor of God, my civilisation made men to be brothers in Man.

I understand the meaning of the duties of charity which were preached to me. Charity was the service of God performed through the individual. It was a thing owed to God, however insignificant the individual who was its recipient. Charity never humiliated him who profited from it, nor ever bound him by the chains of gratitude, since it was not to him but to God that the gift was made. . . .

As the inheritor of God, my civilisation made charity to be a gift to Man present in the individual.

I understand the profound meaning of the humility exacted from the individual. Humility did not cast down the individual, it raised him up. It made clear to him his role as ambassador. As it obliged him to respect the presence of God in others, so it obliged him to respect the presence of God in himself, to make himself the messenger of God or the path taken by God. It forced him to forget himself in order that he might wax and grow; for if the individual exults in his own importance, the path is transformed into a sea.

As the inheritor of God, my civilisation preached self-respect, which is to say respect for Man present in oneself.

I understand, finally, why the love of God created men responsible for one another and gave them hope as a virtue. Since it made of each of them the ambassador of the same God, in the hands of each rested the salvation of all. No man had the right to despair, since each was the messenger of a thing greater than himself. Despair was the rejection of God within oneself. The duty of hope was translatable thus: "And dost thou think thyself important? But thy despair is self-conceit!"

As the inheritor of God, my civilisation made each responsible for all, and all responsible for each. The individual was to sacrifice himself in order that by his sacrifice the community be saved; but this was no matter of idiotic arithmetic. It was a matter of the respect for Man present in the individual. What made my civilisation grand was that a hundred miners were called upon to risk their lives in the rescue of a single miner entombed. And what they rescued in rescuing that miner was Man.

I understand by this bright light the meaning of liberty. It is liberty to grow as the tree grows in the field of energy of its seed. It is the climate permitting the ascension of Man. It is like a favourable wind. Only by the grace of the wind is the bark free on the waters.

A man built in this wise disposes of the power of the tree. What space may his roots not cover! What human pulp may he not absorb to grow and blossom in the sun!

ANTOINE DE SAINT-EXUPÉRY

§ 2

Men have two experiences—the experience of responsibility, and the experience of original sin.

The experience of responsibility is an experience of real responsibility. Men know themselves not merely as desiring goodness, but also as being capable of it. Without the capacity the responsibility would not be real; and the whole of our life—our spiritual life no less than our life in society—is based on an assurance that the capacity is there. If in fact we *cannot* relinquish selfishness and greed, then a resolution to do so, or a prayer for grace to do so, is wholly meaningless; and a law that even one sane individual *could not* obey would be the mark not of civilisation but of tyrannical cruelty. Yet we continue to resolve and pray and make laws, and shall never cease to do so.

But the experience of original sin is no less poignant. "For the good that I would I do not: but the evil that I would not, that I do. Now if I do that I would not, it is no more I that do it, but sin that dwelleth in me. I find then a law, that, when I would do good, evil is present with me. For I delight in the law of God after the inward man; but I see another law in my members, warring against the law of my mind, and bringing me with captivity to the law of sin which is in my members. O wretched man that I am! who shall deliver men from the body of this death?" Can there be a single spiritually adult person who has not risen from his bed time out of number to echo St. Paul's words with no less than St. Paul's agony?

Now men may be capable of goodness, or they may be "sold under sin." But they cannot, in any sense that the human mind can understand, simultaneously be both; and nothing could be more blasphemous than to force a reconciliation by means of metaphysical or theological constructions that are repugnant to reason, for reason is sacred. And the case is even worse when we assume, by way of explanation, a divine morality less exalted than man's.

What it comes to is this. Both experiences are real; and neither can they be reconciled by reason nor may they be reconciled against reason. But if both are real, both must correspond to one indivisible truth; and we must therefore dutifully accept both, and believe them reconciled in an ultimate reality to which, in our human nature, we have no access. Or perhaps, very obscurely, we have this access; for we live now and then in a fleeting realisation—without either ability or desire to explain—that compulsion to sin and power not to sin are somehow inextricably united.

Another word must be said. The rule for ourselves, in this regard, should not be the same as the rule for our neighbour. It is the responsibility, the ability to be and do good, that we must stress in our own case, albeit with great humility and with a proper forbearance when we fail. But in the case of our neighbour the emphasis must be different; here it is original sin, or heredity, or adverse circumstances, or the force of environment, that we must keep ever in our minds, while striving none the less to inspire him, in Spinoza's words, with a sense of "man's virtue and power." And the more we are aware of the compulsion to sin in ourselves, the more compassionately we shall sympathise with this compulsion in others.

X

FOURTH PART

III. ACTIVITY

tr
p
piu p
morendo
ppp

§ 1

What doth it profit, my brethren, though a man say he hath faith, and have not works? can faith save him?

If a brother or sister be naked, and destitute of daily food,

And one of you say unto them, Depart in peace, be ye warmed and filled; notwithstanding ye give them not those things which are needful to the body; what doth it profit?

Even so faith, if it hath not works, is dead, being alone.

Yea, a man may say, Thou hast faith, and I have works: shew me thy faith without thy works, and I will shew thee my faith by my works.

Thou believest that there is one God; thou doest well: the devils also believe, and tremble.

But wilt thou know, O vain man, that faith without works is dead?

Was not Abraham our father justified by works, when he had offered Isaac his son upon the altar?

Seest thou how faith wrought with his works, and by works was faith made perfect?

And the scripture was fulfilled which saith, Abraham believed God, and it was imputed unto him for righteousness: and he was called the Friend of God.

Ye see then how that by works a man is justified, and not by faith only.

Likewise also was not Rahab the harlot justified by works, when she had received the messengers, and had sent them out another way?

For as the body without the spirit is dead, so faith without works is dead also.

JAMES

All study of the Torah without work must in the end be futile and become the cause of sin.

RABBAN GAMALIEL III

I call heaven and earth to witness that whether it be Jew or heathen, man or woman, free or bondman—only according to their acts does the Divine spirit rest upon them.

TANNA DEBE ELIYAHU

Salvation is attained not by subscription to metaphysical dogmas, but solely by love of God that fulfils itself in action. This is a cardinal truth in Judaism.

CHASDAI CRESCAS

Let a man first do good deeds, and then ask God for [knowledge of] Torah: let a man first act as righteous and upright men act, and then let him ask God for wisdom: let a man first grasp the way of humility, and then ask God for understanding.

TANNA DEBE ELIYAHU

He whose wisdom exceeds his works, to what is he like? To a tree whose branches are many, but whose roots are few; and the wind comes and plucks it up and overturns it upon its face, as it is said, And he shall be like a lonely juniper tree in the desert, and shall not see when good cometh; but shall inhabit the parched places in the wilderness, a salt land and not inhabited. But he whose works exceed his wisdom, to what is he like? To a tree whose branches are few, but whose roots are many, so that even if all the winds in the world come and blow upon it, it cannot be stirred from its place, as it is said, And he shall be as a tree planted by the waters; and that spreadeth out its roots by the river, and shall not perceive when heat cometh, but his leaf shall be green; and shall not be troubled in the year of drought, neither shall cease from yielding fruit.

RABBI ELAEZER B. AZARIAH

Once I resolved to devote a whole day to the recitation of the entire Book of Psalms. When towards evening I was approaching the end, the Warden of my Rabbi came over to me, and said that the Rabbi wished to speak with me. I requested him to inform the Rabbi that I would see him as soon as I had finished.

But the Warden returned and bade me come immediately. The Rabbi asked me: "Why did you not obey my first summons?" I explained the reason.

The Rabbi replied: "I called you to make a collection for a poor Jew. Psalms can be chanted by the Angels as well, but mortal men are needed to aid the destitute. Charity is a greater duty than the chanting of Psalms, inasmuch as the Angels cannot perform charity."

A HASIDIC RABBI

There is no quality and there is no power of man that was created to no purpose. . . . But to what end can the denial of God have been created? This too can be uplifted through deeds of charity. For if someone comes to you and asks your help, you shall not turn him off with pious words, saying: "Have faith and take your troubles to God!" You shall act as if there were no God, as if there were only one person in all the world who could help this man—only yourself.

RABBI MOSHE LEIB OF SASOV

We should not go into holes, cloisters, cells and corners; for Christ saith: "Let your light shine before men, that your Father may have praise in your works."

JAKOB BOEHME

The more perfection anything has, the more active and the less passive it is; and contrariwise, the more active it is, the more perfect it becomes.

SPINOZA

The spirit is activity and creation and freedom.

NICHOLAS BERDYAEV

Christians are living in this sinful world and must bear its burden, they may not steal away from the battlefield.

NICHOLAS BERDYAEV

The worst of partialities is to withold oneself, the worst ignorance is not to act, the worst lie is to steal away.

CHARLES PÉGUY

Activity is better than inertia. Act, but with self-control. . . . The world is imprisoned in its own activity, except when actions are performed as worship of God. Therefore you must perform every action sacramentally.

THE BHAGAVAD-GITA

You have the right to work, but for the work's sake only. You have no right to the fruits of work. Desire for the fruits of work must never be your motive in working. Never give way to laziness, either.

Perform every action with your heart fixed on the Supreme Lord. Renounce attachment to the fruits. Be even-tempered in success and failure; for it is this evenness of temper which is meant by yoga. . . .

Devote yourself, therefore, to reaching union with Brahman. To unite the heart with Brahman and then to act: that is the secret of non-attached work. In the calm of self-surrender, the seers renounce the fruits of their actions, and so reach enlightenment.

THE BHAGAVAD-GITA

The just seeks nothing in his work; only thralls and hirelings ask anything for work, or work for any why. If thou wouldst be informed with, transformed into, righteousness, have no ulterior purpose in thy work; form no idea in thee in time or in eternity, not reward nor happiness nor this nor that, for verily all such works are dead.

MEISTER ECKHART

A man should orient his will and all his works to God and having only God in view go forward unafraid, not thinking, am I right or am I wrong? One who worked out all the chances ere starting his first fight would never fight at all. And if, going to some place, we must think how to set the front foot down we shall never get there. It is our duty to do the next thing: go straight on, that is the right way.

MEISTER ECKHART

Once when Rabbi Bunam honoured a man in his House of Prayer by asking him to blow the ram's horn, and the fellow began to make lengthy preparations to concentrate on the meaning of the sounds, the Rabbi cried out: "Fool, go ahead and blow!" [The ram's horn is blown during service on New Year and the Day of Atonement.]

HASIDIC STORY

Enoch was a cobbler; with each stitch of his awl that drew together the top and bottom leather, he joined God and His Shekhinah. [See The Exile of the Schekhina on p. 137.]

HASIDIC SAYING

I pray with the floor and the bench.

RABBI ZALMAN OF LADI

It is not only prayer that gives God glory but work. Smiting on an anvil, sawing a beam, whitewashing a wall, driving horses, sweeping, scouring, everything gives God some glory if being in his grace you do it as your duty. To go to communion worthily gives God great glory, but to take food in thankfulness and temperance gives him glory too. To lift up the hands in prayer gives God glory, but a man with a dungfork in his hand, a woman with a sloppail, give him glory too. He is so great that all things give him glory if you mean they should. So then, my brethren, live.

GERARD MANLEY HOPKINS

Duke Huan of Ch'i was reading a book at the upper end of the hall; the wheelwright was making a wheel at the lower end. Putting aside his mallet and chisel, he called to the Duke and asked him what book he was reading. "One that records the words of the Sages," answered the Duke. "Are those Sages alive?" asked the wheelwright. "Oh, no," said the Duke, "they are dead." "In that case," said the wheelwright, "what you are reading can be nothing but the lees and scum of bygone men." "How dare you, a wheelwright, find fault with the book I am reading? If you can explain your statement, I will let it pass. If not, you shall die." "Speaking as a wheelwright," he replied, "I look at the matter in this way; when I am making a wheel, if my stroke is too slow, then it bites deep but is not steady; if my stroke is too fast, then it is steady, but does not go deep. The right pace, neither slow nor fast, cannot get into the hand unless it comes from the heart. It is a thing that cannot be put into words; there is an art in it that I cannot explain to my son. That is why it is impossible for me to let him take over my work, and here I am at the age of seventy, still making wheels. In my opinion it must have been the same with the men of old. All that was worth handing on, died with them; the rest, they put into their books. That is why I said that what you were reading was the lees and scum of bygone men."

CHUANG TZU

"And men to-day—are they not always running about, to do something?

"But He says: *I have finished the work that Thou gavest Me to do.*"

Thus to me the stone-cutter, with chisel and mallet in hand all the while dishing out a sump-cover,

Standing out there in the Sun, in the light July breeze so cool,

Spoke the words of Christ—the old indestructible words—which all down the ages,

Whether in the mouth of stone-cutter or carpenter,

Emerge time after time from the heart of the people.

EDWARD CARPENTER

This preoccupation with immortality is for people of rank, and especially ladies, who have nothing to do. But an able man, who has something regular to do here, and must toil and struggle to produce day by day, leaves the future world to itself, and is active and useful in this.

GOETHE

If a man did only cast stones into the sea (if his brother be pleased with it, and that he get his living by it) then he is as acceptable to God as a preacher in a pulpit.

JAKOB BOEHME

Leave this chanting and singing and telling of beads! Whom dost thou worship in this lonely dark corner of a temple with doors all shut? Open thine eyes and see thy God is not before thee!

He is there where the tiller is tilling the hard ground and where the pathmaker is breaking stones. He is with them in sun and in shower, and his garment is covered with dust. Put off thy holy mantle and even like him come down on the dusty soil!

Deliverance? Where is this deliverance to be found? Our master himself has joyfully taken upon him the bonds of creation; he is bound with us all for ever.

Come out of thy meditations and leave aside thy flowers and incense! What harm is there if thy clothes become tattered and stained? Meet him and stand by him in toil and in sweat of thy brow.

RABINDRANATH TAGORE

He who thinks to reach God by running away from the world, when and where does he expect to meet him? How far can he fly—can he fly and fly, till he flies into nothingness itself? No, the coward who would fly can nowhere find him. We must be brave enough to be able to say: We are reaching him here in this very spot, now at this very moment. We must be able to assure ourselves that as in our actions we are realising ourselves, so in ourselves we are realising him who is the self of self. We must earn the right to say so unhesitatingly by clearing away with our own effort all obstruction, all disorder, all discords from our path of activity; we must be able to say, "In my work is my joy, and in that joy does the joy of my joy abide."

Whom does the Upanishad call *The chief among the knowers of Brahma*? He is defined as *He whose joy is in Brahma, whose play is in Brahma, the active one.* Joy without the play of joy is no joy at all—play without activity is no play. Activity is the play of joy. He whose joy is in Brahma, how can he live in inaction? For must he not by his activity provide that in which the joy of Brahma is to take form and manifest itself? That is why he who knows Brahma, who has his joy in Brahma, must also have all his activity in Brahma—his eating and drinking, his earning of livelihood and his beneficence. Just as the joy of the poet in his poem, of the artist in his art, of the brave man in the output of his courage, of the wise man in his discernment of truths, ever seeks expression in their several activities, so the joy of the knower of Brahma, in the whole of his everyday work, little and big, in truth, in beauty, in orderliness and in beneficence, seeks to give expression to the infinite.

Brahma himself gives expression to his joy in just the same way. *By his many-sided activity, which radiates in all directions, does he fulfil the inherent want of his different creatures.* That inherent want is he himself, and so he is in so many ways, in so many forms, giving himself. He works, for without working how could he give himself? His joy is ever dedicating itself in the dedication which is his creation.

In this very thing does our own true meaning lie, in this is our likeness to our father. We must also give up ourselves in many-sided variously aimed activity. In the Vedas he is called *the giver of himself, the giver of strength.* He is not content with giving us himself, but he gives us strength that we may likewise give ourselves. That is why the seer of the Upanishad prays to him who is thus fulfilling our wants, *May he grant us the beneficent mind,* may he fulfil that uttermost want of ours by granting us the beneficent mind. That is to say, it is not enough he alone should work to remove our want, but he should give us the desire and the strength to work with him in his activity and in the exercise of the good. Then, indeed, will our union with him alone be accomplished. The beneficent mind is that which shows us the want (*swārtha*) of another self to be the inherent want (*nihitārtha*) of our own self; that which shows that our joy consists in the varied aiming of our many-sided powers in the work of humanity. When we work under the guidance of this beneficent mind, then our activity is regulated, but does not become mechanical; it is action not goaded on by want, but stimulated by the satisfaction of the soul. Such activity ceases to be a blind imitation of that of the multitude, a cowardly following of the dictates of fashion. Therein we begin to see that *He is in the beginning and in the end of the universe*, and likewise see that of our own work is he the fount and the inspiration, and at the end thereof is he, and therefore that all our activity is pervaded by peace and good and joy.

The Upanishad says: *Knowledge, power, and action are of his nature.* It is because this naturalness has not yet been born in us that we tend to divide joy from work. Our day of work is not our day of joy—for that we require a holiday; for, miserable that we are, we cannot find our holiday in our work. The river finds its holiday in its onward flow, the fire in its outburst of flame, the scent of the flower in its permeation of the atmosphere; but in our everyday work there is no such holiday for us. It is because we do not let ourselves go, because we do not give ourselves joyously and entirely up to it, that our work overpowers us.

O giver of thyself! at the vision of thee as joy let our souls flame up to thee as the fire, flow on to thee as the river, permeate thy being as the fragrance of the flower. Give us strength to love, to love fully, our life in its joys and sorrows, in its gains and losses, in its rise and fall. Let us have strength enough fully to see and hear thy universe and to work with full vigour therein. Let us fully live the life thou hast given us, let us bravely take and bravely give. This is our prayer to thee. Let us once for all dislodge from our minds the feeble fancy that would make out thy joy to be a thing apart from action, thin, formless, and unsustained. Wherever the peasant tills the hard earth, there does thy joy gush out in the green of the corn, wherever man displaces the entangled forest, smooths the stony ground, and clears for himself a homestead, there does thy joy enfold it in orderliness and peace.

O worker of the universe! We would pray to thee to let the irresistible current of thy universal energy come like the impetuous south wind of spring, let it come rushing over the vast field of the life of man, let it bring the scent of many flowers, the murmurings of many woodlands, let it make sweet and vocal the lifelessness of our dried-up soul-life. Let our newly awakened powers cry out for unlimited fulfilment in leaf and flower and fruit.

RABINDRANATH TAGORE

§ 2

To give our Lord a perfect hospitality, Mary and Martha must combine.

ST. TERESA

FOURTH PART

IV. INTEGRITY

In memory of
Eleanor Rathbone

Andante
p dolce

§ 1

God wants the heart.

THE TALMUD

And the scribes which came down from Jerusalem said, He hath Beelzebub, and by the prince of the devils casteth he out devils.

And he called them unto him, and said unto them in parables, How can Satan cast out Satan?

And if a kingdom be divided against itself, that kingdom cannot stand.

And if a house be divided against itself, that house cannot stand.

And if Satan rise up against himself, and be divided, he cannot stand, but hath an end.

No man can enter into a strong man's house, and spoil his goods, except he will first bind the strong man; and then he will spoil his house.

ST. MARK

Lieh Tzu asked Kuan Yin, saying, " 'The Man of Extreme Power . . . can tread on fire without being burnt. Walk on the top of the whole world and not stagger.' May I ask how he attains to this?" "He is protected," said Kuan Yin, "by the purity of his breath. Knowledge and skill, determination and courage could never lead to this. . . . When a drunk man falls from his carriage, however fast it may be going, he is never killed. His bones and joints are not different from those of other men; but his susceptibility to injury is different from theirs. This is because his soul is intact.[1] He did not know that he was riding; he does not know that he has fallen out. Neither death nor life, astonishment nor fear can enter into his breast;

[1] Is impervious to disturbances from outside (*note by Arthur Waley*).

therefore when he bumps into things, he does not stiffen with fright. If such integrity of the spirit can be got from wine, how much greater must be the integrity that is got from Heaven?"

CHUANG TZU

[In reply to disciples who asked why he was watching a rope dancer so absorbedly.] This man is risking his life, and I cannot say why. But I am quite sure that while he is walking the rope he is not thinking of the fact that he is earning a hundred gulden by what he is doing, for if he did he would fall.

RABBI HAYYIM OF KROSNO

When he has no lust, no hatred,
A man walks safely among the things of lust and hatred.

THE BHAGAVAD-GITA

The centre of life is neither in thought nor in feeling nor in will, nor even in consciousness, so far as it thinks, feels, or wishes. For moral truth may have been penetrated and possessed in all these ways, and escape us still. Deeper even than consciousness, there is our being itself, our very substance, our nature. Only those truths which have entered into this last region, which have become ourselves, become spontaneous and involuntary, instinctive and unconscious, are really our life—that is to say, something more than our property. So long as we are able to distinguish any space whatever between the truth and us, we remain outside it. The thought, the feeling, the desire, the consciousness of life, are not yet quite life. But peace and repose can nowhere be found except in life and in eternal life, and the eternal life is the Divine life, is God. To become Divine is, then, the aim of life: then only can truth be said to be ours beyond the possibility of loss, because it is no longer outside of us, nor even in us, but we are it, and it is we; we ourselves are a truth, a will, a work of God. Liberty has become nature; the creature is one with its Creator—one through love.

HENRI FRÉDÉRIC AMIEL

After the death of Rabbi Uri of Strelisk, one of his Hasidim came to Rabbi Bunam. The latter welcomed him and asked him what particular trait of character it was Rabbi Uri's main purpose to instil in his Hasidim. The Hasid replied: "I believe Rabbi Uri sought to make his Hasidim very humble. The Rabbi would order a rich Hasid to draw water at the pump, and to bring in the pail on his shoulder—a thing the man would never have done at home."

Rabbi Bunam remarked: "My way is different; I will explain it to you by a parable: Three men were convicted of a crime, and were lodged in a dark dungeon. Two of them were men of intelligence, but the third was a witless person. When food was lowered in the dark, the witless one did not know how to take his share, and would break the plate, or cut himself with the knife. One of his fellow-prisoners sought to aid him by rehearsing with him the necessary behaviour, but the next day a different arrangement of the food would baffle him again. One of the prisoners then remarked: 'Why waste time teaching this fellow every time? Help me to bore a hole in the wall to admit light, and then he will know how to eat unaided.' Likewise, I attempt to admit into the soul of a man the fear and the love of God. This is a light whereby a man can learn wise conduct in its entirety, and not trait by trait."

HASIDIC STORY

Pleasing to God are all a good man's ways:
As pleasing when he drinks as when he prays.

ANGELUS SILESIUS

§ 2

EVENING ON CALAIS BEACH

It is a beauteous evening, calm and free,
  The holy time is quiet as a Nun
  Breathless with adoration; the broad sun
Is sinking down in its tranquillity;
The gentleness of heaven broods o'er the sea:
  Listen! the mighty Being is awake,
  And doth with his eternal motion make
A sound like thunder—everlastingly.
Dear Child! dear Girl! that walkest with me here,
  If thou appear untouch'd by solemn thought,
  Thy nature is not therefore less divine:
Thou liest in Abraham's bosom all the year;
  And worshipp'st at the Temple's inner shrine,
  God being with thee when we know it not.

WORDSWORTH

A villager, who year after year prayed in the Baalshem's House of Prayer on the Days of Awe,[1] had a son who was so dull-witted that he could not even grasp the shapes of the letters, let alone the meaning of the holy words. On the Days of Awe his father did not take him to town with him, because he did not understand anything. But when he was thirteen and of age according to the laws of God, his father took him along on the Day of Atonement, for fear the boy might eat on the fast-day simply because he did not know any better.

Now the boy had a small whistle which he always blew when he sat out in the fields to herd the sheep and the calves. He had taken this with him in the pocket of his smock and his father had not noticed it. Hour after hour, the boy sat in the House of Prayer and had nothing to say. But when the Additional Service

[1] The solemn period before the Day of Atonement.

commenced, he said: "Father, I have my little whistle with me. I want to sing on it." The father was greatly perturbed and told him to do no such thing, and the boy restrained himself. But when the Afternoon Service was begun, he said again: "Father, do let me blow my little whistle." The father became angry and said: "Where did you put it?" And when the boy told him, he laid his hand on his pocket so that the boy could not take it out. But now the Closing Prayer began. The boy snatched his pocket away from his father's hand, took out the whistle and blew a loud note. All were frightened and confused. But the Baalshem went on with the prayer, only more quickly and easily than usual. Later he said: "The boy made things easy for me."

HASIDIC STORY

A little farmer boy, having been left an orphan at an early age, was unable to read, but had inherited a large, heavy prayer book from his parents. On the Day of Atonement he brought it into the synagogue, laid it on the reading desk, and, weeping, cried out: "Lord of Creation! I do not know how to pray; I do not know what to say—I give Thee the entire prayer book."

HASIDIC STORY

An ignorant villager, having heard it is a good religious deed to eat and drink on the day before the Day of Atonement, drank himself into a stupor. He awoke late at night, too late for the opening service. Not knowing the prayers by heart, he devised a plan. He repeated the letters of the alphabet over and over, beseeching the Almighty to arrange them into the appropriate words of the prayers. The following day he attended the synagogue at Kotzk. After the closing service the Rabbi summoned him to inquire the cause of his absence the evening before. The villager confessed his transgression and asked whether his manner of reciting the prayers could be pardoned.

The Rabbi responded: "Your prayer was more acceptable than mine because you uttered it with the entire devotion of your heart."

HASIDIC STORY

Nothing is so beautiful as a child going to sleep while he is saying his prayers, says God.
I tell you nothing is so beautiful in the world. . . .
And yet I have seen beautiful sights in the world.
And I know something about it. My creation is overflowing with beauty.
My creation overflows with marvels.
There are so many that you don't know where to put them.
I have seen millions and millions of stars rolling under my feet like the sands of the sea.
I have seen days as scorching as flames,
Summer days of June and July and August.
I have seen winter evenings spread out like a cloak.
I have seen summer evenings as calm and soft as something shed by Paradise,
All studded with stars.
I have seen those slopes of the Meuse and those churches which are my own houses,
And Paris and Reims and Rouen and cathedrals which are my own palaces and my own castles,
So beautiful that I am going to keep them in heaven.
I have seen the capital of the kingdom and Rome the capital of Christendom.
I have heard mass sung and triumphant vespers.
And I have seen the plains and vales of France,
And they are more beautiful than anything.
I have seen the deep sea, and the deep forest, and the deep heart of man.
I have seen hearts devoured by love
During whole lifetimes
Lost in love

Burning like flames. . . .
I have seen martyrs blazing like torches,
Thus preparing for themselves palms everlastingly green.
And I have seen, beading under claws of iron,
Drops of blood which sparkled like diamonds.
And I have seen beading tears of love
Which will last longer than the stars in heaven.
And I have seen looks of prayer, looks of tenderness,
Lost in love,
Which will gleam for all eternity, nights and nights.
And I have seen whole lives from birth to death,
From baptism to viaticum,
Unrolling like a beautiful skein of wool.
But I tell you, says God, that I know of nothing so beautiful
    in the whole world
As a little child going to sleep while he is saying his prayers
Under the wing of his guardian angel
And laughs happily as he watches the angels and begins to go
    to sleep;
And is already mixing his prayers together and no longer knows
    what they are all about;
And sticks the words of *Our Father* among the words of *Hail,
    Mary*, all in a jumble,
While a veil is already coming down over his eyelids,
The veil of night over his gaze and over his voice.
I have seen the greatest saints, says God. But I tell you
I have never seen anything so funny and I therefore know of
    nothing so beautiful in the world
As that child going to sleep while he says his prayers
(As that little creature going to sleep in all confidence)
And getting his *Our Father* mixed up with his *Hail, Mary*.
Nothing is so beautiful and it is even one point
On which the Blessed Virgin agrees with me. . . .
And I can even say it is the only point on which we agree.
    Because as a rule we disagree,
She being for mercy,
Whereas I, of course, have to be for justice.

CHARLES PÉGUY

§ 3

I know thy works, that thou art neither cold nor hot: I would thou wert cold or hot.

So then because thou art lukewarm, and neither cold nor hot, I will spue thee out of my mouth.

REVELATION

He who can burn with enmity can also burn with love for God, but he who is coldly hostile will always find the way closed.

RABBI YAAKOV YITZHAK OF LUBLIN

'Tis Death my Soul to be Indifferent,
Set forth thy self unto thy whole Extent.

THOMAS TRAHERNE (from *Another*)

There is a story to the effect that a poor man asked his rich brother: "Why are you wealthy, and I am not?" The other answered: "Because I have no scruples against doing wrong." The poor brother began to misconduct himself, but he remained poor. He complained of this to his elder brother, who answered: "The reason your transgressions have not made you wealthy is that you did them not from conviction that it matters not whether we do good or evil, but solely because you desired riches."

How much more applicable is this to doing good with the proper intention!

THE BAALSHEM

If ye keep not Sabbath for the whole week, ye shall not see the Father.

ATTRIBUTED TO CHRIST (from the Oxyrhynchus Papyri)

The old-time rabbis used to teach that the kingdom of God would come if only the whole of Israel would really keep a single Sabbath simultaneously.

ALBERT SCHWEITZER

And a certain ruler asked him, saying, Good Master, what shall I do to inherit eternal life?

And Jesus said unto him, Why callest thou me good? none is good, save one, that is, God.

Thou knowest the commandments, Do not commit adultery, Do not kill, Do not steal, Do not bear false witness, Honour thy father and thy mother.

And he said, All these have I kept from my youth up.

Now when Jesus heard these things, he said unto him, Yet lackest thou one thing: sell all that thou hast, and distribute unto the poor, and thou shalt have treasure in heaven: and come, follow me.

And when he heard this, he was very sorrowful: for he was very rich.

ST. LUKE

§ 4

When Rabbi Baer's wife pressed her starving child to her bosom, the Rabbi heaved a rebellious sigh. Forthwith a voice from Heaven thundered into his ear: "Thou hast lost thy share in the World to Come."

"It matters not," said the Rabbi joyfully. "The thraldom of reward has gone; henceforth I will serve God as a freeman."

HASIDIC STORY

While absorbed in his devotions, the Rabbi of Ladi was heard to say: "My Lord and God. I do not desire Thy Paradise; I do not desire the bliss of the After World; I desire only Thee Thyself."

HASIDIC STORY

Spirit raves not for a goal.

GEORGE MEREDITH (from *A Faith on Trial*)

He who loves God cannot endeavour to bring it about that God should love him in return.

SPINOZA

This being so, we may, with reason, regard as a great absurdity what many, who are otherwise esteemed as great theologians, assert, namely, that if no eternal life resulted from the love of God, then they would seek what is best for themselves: as though they could discover anything better than God! This is just as silly as if a fish (for which, of course, it is impossible to live out of the water) were to say: if no eternal life is to follow this life in the water, then I will leave the water for the land.

SPINOZA

The general notion of the vulgar seems to be quite the contrary. For most seem to think that they are free in so far as they may give themselves up to lust, and that they lose their right in so far as they are obliged to live according to the divine laws. They therefore think that piety, religion, and all things which have reference to fortitude of mind are burdens which after death they will lay aside, and hope to receive a reward for their servitude, that is, their piety and religion. Not by this hope alone, but also, and even principally, by the fear of suffering dreadful punishments after death, are they induced to live, as far as their feebleness and weak-mindedness allows them, according to the divine laws; and if this hope or fear were not in men, but, on the other hand, if they thought that their minds were buried with their bodies, and that there did not remain for the wretches worn out with the burden of piety the hope of longer life, they would return to life according to their own ideas, and would direct everything according to their lust, and obey fortune rather than themselves. This seems no less absurd to me than if a man, when he discovered that he could not keep his body alive for ever with wholesome food, should straightway seek to glut himself with poison and deadly foods; or that a man, when he discovered that his mind was not eternal or immortal, should prefer to live without any mind at all: this all seems so absurd to me that it scarcely deserves to be refuted.

SPINOZA

[Suppose] that there is no reality other than the events which make up the life of man in the present world. Even the most devout should not find it very hard to make this supposition, for it is a belief that is actually held by many more persons than those who profess any profound religious convictions in Western countries to-day. There is nothing blatantly contradictory about it, no palpable absurdity. In that case we may suppose for a moment that the unbeliever is right. But would it not still be true that we ought to treat our neighbour in one way rather than another? Should we not still succour the needy, alleviate pain and avoid the infliction of it, seek a fair distribution of material goods, cultivate our talents, and generally so conduct ourselves that the fleeting spell of man's life on earth should be as full of richness and wonder and the glow of affection as it is possible for it to be? Admitting, as the present writer is most ready to admit, that life would be full of frustration and lack the only salve that will bring genuine easement to the mind of man, it would still be true, to limit ourselves to the obvious, that cruelty would merit condemnation and kindness praise. Indeed, these virtues and vices might reveal their nature all the more clearly in the glow of a purely secular light. And may not the understanding acquired in this way prove in the end a means of enrichment and sanity in the religious life itself?

H. D. LEWIS

Most of them place their greatest stress for salvation on a strict conformity to their foppish ceremonies, and a belief of their legendary traditions; wherein they fancy to have acquitted themselves with so much of supererogation, that one heaven can never be a condign reward for their meritorious life; little thinking that the Judge of all the earth at the last day shall put them off, with a who hath required these things at your hands; and call them to account only for the stewardship of his legacy, which was the precept of love and charity. It will be pretty to hear their pleas before the great tribunal: one will brag how he mortified his carnal appetite by feeding only upon fish: another will urge that he spent most of his time on earth in the divine exercise of singing psalms: a third will tell how many days he fasted, and what severe penance he imposed on himself for the bringing his body into subjection: another shall produce in his own behalf as many ceremonies as would load a fleet of merchant-men: a fifth shall plead, that in three-score years he never as much as touched a piece of money, except he fingered it through a thick pair of gloves: a sixth, to testify his former humility, shall bring along with him his sacred hood, so old and nasty, that any seaman had rather stand bare-headed on the deck, than put it on to defend his ears from the sharpest storms: the next that comes to answer for himself shall plead, that for fifty years together, he had lived like a sponge upon the same place, and was content never to change his homely habitation: another shall whisper softly, and tell the judge he has lost his voice by a continual singing of holy hymns and anthems: the next shall confess how he fell into a lethargy by a strict, reserved, and sedentary life: and the last shall intimate that he has forgot to speak, by having always kept silence, in obedience to the injunction of taking heed lest he should have offended with his tongue. But amidst all their fine excuses our Saviour shall interrupt them with this answer, Woe unto you, scribes and pharisees, hypocrites, verily I know you not; I left you but one precept, of loving one another, which I do not hear any one plead he has faithfully discharged: I told you plainly in my gospel, without any parable, that my father's kingdom was prepared, not for such as should lay claim to it by austerities, prayers, or fastings, but for those who should render themselves worthy of it by the exercise of faith, and the offices of charity: I cannot own such as depend on their own merits without a reliance on my mercy: as many of you therefore as trust to the broken reeds of your own deserts, may even go search out a new heaven, for you shall never enter into that, which from the foundations of the world was prepared only for such as are true of heart.

ERASMUS

Six hundred and thirteen commandments were given to Moses. . . . Then David came and reduced them to eleven. Then came Isaiah, and reduced them to six. Then came Micah, and reduced them to three. Then Isaiah came again, and reduced them to two, as it is said, "Keep ye judgment and do righteousness." Then came Amos, and reduced them to one, as it is said, "Seek ye me and live."

RABBI SIMLAI

To my Divine Mother I prayed only for pure love. I offered flowers at Her Lotus Feet and prayed: "Mother, here is Thy virtue, here is Thy vice. Take them both and grant me only pure love for Thee. Here is Thy knowledge, here is Thy ignorance. Take them both and grant me only pure love for Thee. Here is Thy purity, here is Thy impurity. Take them both, Mother, and grant me only pure love for Thee."

SRI RAMAKRISHNA

He who acts out of the pure love of God, not only does he not perform his actions to be seen of men, but does not do them even that God may know of them. Such an one, if he thought it possible that his good works might escape the eye of God, would still perform them with the same joy, and in the same pureness of love.

ST. JOHN OF THE CROSS

A master called Boethius says: "That we do not love the Best comes of our insufficiency." He has spoken the truth: The Best should be the dearest of all things to us! And in our love of it, neither helpfulness nor unhelpfulness, advantage not injury, gain nor loss, honour nor dishonour, praise nor blame, nor anything of the kind should be regarded; but what is in truth the Noblest and Best should be also the dearest of all things, and that for no other cause than that it is the Noblest and Best. Hereby should a man order his life, within and without!

THEOLOGIA GERMANICA

So long as a man seeks . . . his best as his, and for his own sake, he will never find it. For so long as he does this, he is not seeking his best, and how then should he find it? For so long as he does this, he seeks himself, and imagines that he is himself the Best; and seeing that he is not the Best, he seeks not the Best, so long as he seeks himself. But whosoever seeks, loves, and pursues the Good for the sake of the Good and for nothing but the love of the Good, not as from the Me, or as the I, Me, Mine, or for the sake of the Me, he will find it, for he seeks it aright. And they who seek it otherwise, err. Truly it is in this wise that the True and Perfect Good seeks and loves and pursues itself, and therefore it finds itself.

THEOLOGIA GERMANICA

Remember. If ye love right as God ye love not right as right, therefore ye neither take it nor love it as a whole but as divided. But God is right, so ye are not taking him nor loving him in his entirety. Take right as right and ye take it as God. Then where right is at work ye will be working too, seeing that ye do right all the time. Though hell stood in the way of right ye would still do right and that not as a hardship but a pleasure, because being right itself ye must do right.

MEISTER ECKHART

When I pray for aught my prayer goes for naught; when I pray for naught I pray as I ought. When I am one with that wherein are all things, past, present and to come, all the same distance and all just the same, then they are all in God and all in me. There is no thought of Henry or of Conrad. Praying for aught save God alone is idolatry and unrighteousness. They pray aright who pray in spirit and in truth.

MEISTER ECKHART

Ask God, O man, for neither that nor this:
Ask anything, and that thine idol is.

ANGELUS SILESIUS

We read in the gospel that our Lord went into the temple and cast out all them that sold and bought. . . . Now consider who they were that sold and bought therein and who they are still. Mark me well: I name none but the virtuous. Yet, even so, I can point out who the merchants were, and still are to this day, that thus buy and sell: those whom our Lord drove forth and cast out. He still does so to those that buy and sell in this temple: he would not leave a single one therein. Lo, they are merchants all who, while avoiding mortal sin and wishing to be virtuous, do good works to the glory of God, fasts, for example, vigils, prayers, etc., all of them excellent, but do them with a view to God's giving them somewhat, doing to them somewhat, they wish for in return. All such are merchants.

MEISTER ECKHART

Thus, in the soul of man there is a justice whose retributions are instant and entire. He who does a good deed is instantly ennobled. He who does a mean deed is by the action itself contracted. He who puts off impurity thereby puts on purity. If a man is at heart just, then in so far is he God; the safety of God, the immortality of God, the majesty of God, do enter into that man with justice. If a man dissemble, deceive, he deceives himself, and goes out of acquaintance with his own being. Character is always known. Thefts never enrich; alms never impoverish; murder will speak out of stone walls. The least admixture of a lie—for example, the taint of vanity, any attempt to make a good impression, a favourable appearance—will instantly vitiate the effect. But speak the truth, and all things alive or brute are vouchers, and the very roots of the grass underground there do seem to stir and move to bear your witness. For all things proceed out of the same spirit, which is differently named love, justice, temperance, in its different applications, just as the ocean receives different names on the several shores which it washes.

EMERSON (abridged by William James)

Blessedness is not the reward of virtue, but virtue itself: nor should we rejoice in it for that we restrain our lusts, but, on the contrary, because we rejoice therein we can restrain our lusts.

SPINOZA

Put an end once for all to this discussion of what a good man should be, and be one.

. . . .

How corrupt is the man, how counterfeit, who proclaims aloud: *I have elected to deal straightforwardly with thee!* Man, what art thou at? There is no need to give this out. The fact will instantly declare itself. It ought to be written on the forehead. There is a ring in the voice that betrays it at once, it flashes out at once from the eyes, just as the loved one can read at a glance every secret in his lover's looks. The simple and good man should in fact be like a man who has a strong smell about him, so that, as soon as ever he comes near, his neighbour is, will-he-nill-he, aware of it. A calculated simplicity is a stiletto. There is nothing more hateful than the friendship of the wolf for the lamb. Eschew that above all things. The good man, the kindly, the genuine, betrays these characteristics in his eyes and there is no hiding it.

. . . .

One man, when he has done another a kindness, is ready also to reckon on a return. A second is not ready to do this, but yet in his heart of hearts ranks the other as a debtor, and he is conscious of what he has done. But a third is in a manner not conscious of it, but is like the vine that has borne a cluster of grapes, and when it has once borne its due fruit looks for no reward beyond, as it is with a steed when it has run its course, a hound when it has singled out the trail, a bee when she hath made her comb. And so a man when he hath done one thing well, does not cry it abroad, but betakes himself to a second, as a vine to bear afresh her clusters in due season.

. . . .

Prize not anything as being to thine interest that shall ever force thee to break thy troth, to surrender thine honour, to hate, suspect, or curse anyone, to play the hypocrite, to lust after anything that needs walls and curtains. For he that has chosen before all else his own intelligence and good "genius," and to be a devotee of its supreme worth, does not strike a tragic attitude or whine, nor will he ask for either a wilderness or a concourse of men; above all he will live neither chasing anything not shunning it. And he recks not at all whether he is to have his soul overlaid with his body for a longer or a shorter span of time, for even if he must take his departure at once, he will go as willingly as if he were to discharge any other function that can be discharged with decency and orderliness, making sure through life of this one thing, that his thoughts should not in any case assume a character out of keeping with a rational and civic creature.

In the mind of the man that has been chastened and thoroughly cleansed thou wilt find no foul abscess or gangrene or hidden sore. Nor is his life cut short, when the day of destiny overtakes him, as we might say of a tragedian's part, who leaves the stage before finishing his speech and playing out the piece. Furthermore, there is nothing there slavish or affected, no dependence on others or severance from them, no sense of accountability, or skulking to avoid it.

. . . .

Never shalt thou cease murmuring until it be so with thee that the utilising, in a manner consistent with the constitution of man, of the material presented to thee and cast in thy way shall be to thee what indulgence is to the sensual. For everything must be accounted enjoyment that it is in a man's power to put into practice in accordance with his own nature; and it is everywhere in his power.

MARCUS AURELIUS

§ 5

Though the World be Histrionical, and most Men live Ironically, yet be thou what thou singly art, and personate only thy self. Swim smoothly in the stream of thy Nature, and live but one Man.

SIR THOMAS BROWNE

O ye gifted ones, follow your calling, for however various your talents may be, ye can have but one calling; . . . follow resolutely the one straight path before you, it is that of your good angel; let neither obstacles nor temptations induce you to leave it; bound along if you can; if not, on hands and knees follow it, perish in it, if needful; but ye need not fear that; no one ever yet died in the true path of his calling before he had attained the pinnacle. Turn into other paths, and for a momentary advantage or gratification ye have sold your inheritance, your immortality.

GEORGE BORROW

Being true to myself is not at all the same as fidelity to an object, or even to my past, but beyond all objects, and all the past, to a certain design that no object has been able to fulfil, and which opens before me always a new future.

LOUIS LAVELLE

Sincerity is the act whereby each of us at once knows and makes himself. . . .

It is the quality of sincerity to oblige me to be myself, that is to become, by my own agency, what I am. It is a search for my own essence, which begins to be adulterated as soon as I borrow from outside the motives of my actions. For this essence is never an object that I contemplate, but a work that I carry out, the bringing into play of certain powers that are within me, and which atrophy if I cease to exercise them. Sincerity consists in a certain tranquil courage by which we dare to enter existence, as we are.

LOUIS LAVELLE

RESOLUTION AND INDEPENDENCE

I

There was a roaring in the wind all night;
The rain came heavily and fell in floods;
But now the sun is rising calm and bright;
The birds are singing in the distant woods;
Over his own sweet voice the Stock-dove broods;
The Jay makes answer as the Magpie chatters;
And all the air is filled with pleasant noise of waters.

II

All things that love the sun are out of doors;
The sky rejoices in the morning's birth;
The grass is bright with rain-drops;—on the moors
The hare is running races in her mirth;
And with her feet she from the plashy earth
Raises a mist; that, glittering in the sun,
Runs with her all the way, wherever she doth run.

III

I was a Traveller then upon the moor;
I saw the hare that raced about with joy;
I heard the woods and distant waters roar;
Or heard them not, as happy as a boy:
The pleasant season did my heart employ:
My old remembrances went from me wholly;
And all the ways of men, so vain and melancholy.

IV

But, as it sometimes chanceth, from the might
Of joy in minds that can no further go,
As high as we have mounted in delight
In our dejection do we sink as low;
To me that morning did it happen so;
And fears and fancies thick upon me came;
Dim sadness—and blind thoughts, I knew not, nor could
name.

V

I heard the sky-lark warbling in the sky;
And I bethought me of the playful hare:
Even such a happy Child of earth am I;
Even as these blissful creatures do I fare;
Far from the world I walk, and from all care;
But there may come another day to me—
Solitude, pain of heart, distress, and poverty.

VI

My whole life I have lived in pleasant thought,
As if life's business were a summer mood;
As if all needful things would come unsought
To genial faith, still rich in genial good;
But how can He expect that others should
Build for him, sow for him, and at his call
Love him, who for himself will take no heed at all?

VII

I thought of Chatterton, the marvellous Boy,
The sleepless Soul that perished in his pride;
Of Him who walked in glory and in joy
Following his plough, along the mountain-side:
By our own spirits are we deified:
We Poets in our youth begin in gladness;
But thereof come in the end despondency and madness.

VIII

Now, whether it were by peculiar grace,
A leading from above, a something given,
Yet it befell that, in this lonely place,
When I with these untoward thoughts had striven,
Beside a pool bare to the eye of heaven
I saw a Man before me unawares:
The oldest man he seemed that ever wore grey hairs.

IX

As a huge stone is sometimes seen to lie
Couched on the bald top of an eminence;
Wonder to all who do the same espy,
By what means it could thither come, and whence;
So that it seems a thing endued with sense:
Like a sea-beast crawled forth, that on a shelf
Of rock or sand reposeth, there to sun itself;

X

Such seemed this Man, not all alive nor dead,
Nor all asleep—in his extreme old age:
His body was bent double, feet and head
Coming together in life's pilgrimage;
As if some dire constraint of pain, or rage
Of sickness felt by him in times long past,
A more than human weight upon his frame had cast.

XI

Himself he propped, limbs, body, and pale face,
Upon a long grey staff of shaven wood:
And, still as I drew near with gentle pace,
Upon the margin of that moorish flood
Motionless as a cloud the old Man stood,
That heareth not the loud winds when they call;
And moveth all together, if it move at all.

XII

At length, himself unsettling, he the pond
Stirred with his staff, and fixedly did look
Upon the muddy water, which he conned,
As if he had been reading in a book:
And now a stranger's privilege I took;
And, drawing to his side, to him did say,
"This morning gives us promise of a glorious day."

XIII

A gentle answer did the old Man make,
In courteous speech which forth he slowly drew:
And him with further words I thus bespake,
"What occupation do you there pursue?
This is a lonesome place for one like you."
Ere he replied, a flash of mild surprise
Broke from the sable orbs of his yet-vivid eyes.

XIV

His words came feebly, from a feeble chest,
But each in solemn order followed each,
With something of a lofty utterance drest—
Choice word and measured phrase, above the reach
Of ordinary men; a stately speech;
Such as grave Livers do in Scotland use,
Religious men, who give to God and man their dues.

XV

He told, that to these waters he had come
To gather leeches, being old and poor:
Employment hazardous and wearisome!
And he had many hardships to endure:
From pond to pond he roamed, from moor to moor;
Housing, with God's good help, by choice or chance;
And in this way he gained an honest maintenance.

XVI

The old Man still stood talking by my side;
But now his voice to me was like a stream
Scarce heard; nor word from word could I divide;
And the whole body of the Man did seem
Like one whom I had met with in a dream;
Or like a man from some far region sent,
To give me human strength, by apt admonishment.

XVII

My former thoughts returned: the fear that kills;
And hope that is unwilling to be fed;
Cold, pain, and labour, and all fleshly ills;
And mighty Poets in their misery dead.
—Perplexed, and longing to be comforted,
My question eagerly did I renew,
"How is it that you live, and what is it you do?"

XVIII

He with a smile did then his words repeat;
And said that, gathering leeches, far and wide
He travelled; stirring thus about his feet
The waters of the pools where they abide.
"Once I could meet with them on every side;
But they have dwindled long by slow decay;
Yet still I persevere, and find them where I may."

XIX

While he was talking thus, the lonely place,
The old Man's shape, and speech—all troubled me:
In my mind's eye I seemed to see him pace
About the weary moors continually,
Wandering about alone and silently.
While I these thoughts within myself pursued,
He, having made a pause, the same discourse renewed.

XX

And soon with this he other matter blended,
Cheerfully uttered, with demeanour kind,
But stately in the main; and, when he ended,
I could have laughed myself to scorn to find
In that decrepit Man so firm a mind.
"God," said I, "be my help and stay secure;
I'll think of the Leech-gatherer on the lonely moor!"

WORDSWORTH

THE SCARECROW

All winter through I bow my head
  Beneath the driving rain;
The North Wind powders me with snow
  And blows me black again;

At midnight in a maze of stars
I flame with glittering rime,
And stand, above the stubble, stiff
As mail at morning-prime.
But when that child, called Spring, and all
His host of children, come,
Scattering their buds and dew upon
These acres of my home,
Some rapture in my rags awakes;
I lift void eyes and scan
The skies for crows, those ravening foes,
Of my strange master, Man.
I watch him striding lank behind
His clashing team, and know
Soon will the wheat swish body high
Where once lay sterile snow;
Soon shall I gaze across a sea
Of sun-begotten grain,
Which my unflinching watch hath sealed
For harvest once again.

WALTER DE LA MARE

THE SERMON BY THE GRAVE

The Priest:

Now, when the soul has gone to meet its doom,
and here the dust lies, like an empty pod,—
now, my dear friends, we'll speak a word or two
about this dead man's pilgrimage on earth.
He was not wealthy, neither was he wise,
his voice was weak, his bearing was unmanly,
he spoke his mind abashed and faltering,
he scarce was master at his own fireside;
he sidled into church, as though appealing
for leave, like other men, to take his place.

It was from Gudbrandsdale, you know, he came.
When here he settled he was but a lad;—
and you remember how, to the very last,
he kept his right hand hidden in his pocket.
That right hand in the pocket was the feature
that chiefly stamped his image on the mind,—
and therewithal his writhing, his abashed
shrinking from notice wheresoe'er he went.
But, though he still pursued a path aloof,
and ever seemed a stranger in our midst,
you all know what he strove so hard to hide,—
the hand he muffled had four fingers only.—
I well remember, many years ago,
one morning; there were sessions held at Lundë.
'Twas war-time, and the talk in every mouth
turned on the country's sufferings and its fate.
I stood there watching. At the table sat
the Captain, 'twixt the Bailiff and the sergeants;
lad after lad was measured up and down,
passed, and enrolled, and taken for a soldier.
The room was full, and from the green outside,
where thronged the young folks, loud the laughter rang.
A name was called, and forth another stepped,
one pale as snow upon the glacier's edge.
They bade the youth advance; he reached the table;
we saw his right hand swaddled in a clout;—
he gasped, he swallowed, battling after words,—
but, though the Captain urged him, found no voice.
Ah yes, at last! Then with his cheek aflame,
his tongue now failing him, now stammering fast,
he mumbled something of a scythe that slipped
by chance, and shore his finger to the skin.
Straightway a silence fell upon the room.
Men bandied meaning glances; they made mouths;
they stoned the boy with looks of silent scorn.
He felt the hail-storm, but he saw it not.

Then up the Captain stood, the grey old man;
he spat, and pointed forth, and thundered "Go!"
  And the lad went. On both sides men fell back,
till through their midst he had to run the gauntlet.
He reached the door; from there he took to flight;—
up, up he went,—through wood and over hillside,
up through the stone-slips, rough, precipitous.
He had his home up there among the mountains.—
  It was some six months later he came here,
with mother, and betrothed, and little child.
He leased some ground upon the high hillside,
there where the waste lands trend away towards Lomb.
He married the first moment that he could;
he built a house; he broke the stubborn soil;
he throve, as many a cultivated patch
bore witness, bravely clad in waving gold.
At church he kept his right hand in his pocket,—
but sure I am at home his fingers nine
toiled every bit as hard as others' ten.—
One spring the torrent washed it all away.
  Their lives were spared. Ruined and stripped of all,
he set to work to make another clearing;
and, ere the autumn, smoke again arose
from a new, better-sheltered, mountain farm-house.
Sheltered? From torrent—not from avalanche;
two years, and all beneath the snow lay buried.
  But still the avalanche could not daunt his spirit.
He dug, and raked, and carted—cleared the ground—
and the next winter, ere the snow-blasts came,
a third time was his little homestead reared.
  Three sons he had, three bright and stirring boys;
they must to school, and school was far away;—
and they must clamber where the hill-track failed,
by narrow ledges through the headlong scaur.
What did he do? The eldest had to manage
as best he might, and, where the path was worst,

his father cast a rope round him to stay him;—
the others on his back and arms he bore.
  Thus he toiled, year by year, till they were men.
Now might he well have looked for some return.
In the New World, three prosperous gentlemen
their school-going and their father have forgotten.
  He was short-sighted. Out beyond the circle
of those most near to him he nothing saw.
To him seemed meaningless as cymbals' tinkling
those words that to the heart should ring like steel.
His race, his fatherland, all things high and shining,
stood ever, to his vision, veiled in mist.
  But he was humble, humble, was this man;
and since that sessions-day his doom oppressed him,
as surely as his cheeks were flushed with shame,
and his four fingers hidden in his pocket.—
Offender 'gainst his country's laws? Ay, true!
But there is one thing that the law outshineth
sure as the snow-white tent of Glittertind
has clouds, like higher rows of peaks, above it.
No patriot was he. Both for church and state
a fruitless tree. But there, on the upland ridge,
in the small circle where he saw his calling,
there he was great, because he was himself.
His inborn note rang true unto the end.
His days were as a lute with muted strings.
And therefore, peace be with thee, silent warrior,
that fought the peasant's little fight, and fell!
  It is not ours to search the heart and reins;—
that is no task for dust, but for its ruler;—
yet dare I freely, firmly, speak my hope:
he scarce stands crippled now before his God!

IBSEN (from *Peer Gynt*)

VERTUE

Sweet day, so cool, so calm, so bright,
The bridall of the earth and skie:
The dew shall weep thy fall to night;
For thou must die.

Sweet rose, whose hue angrie and brave
Bids the rash gazer wipe his eye:
Thy root is ever in its grave,
And thou must die.

Sweet spring, full of sweet dayes and roses,
A box where sweets compacted lie;
My musick shows ye have your closes,
And all must die.

Onely a sweet and vertuous soul,
Like season'd timber, never gives;
But though the whole world turn to coal,
Then chiefly lives.

GEORGE HERBERT

§ 6

If God were able to backslide from truth I would fain cling to truth and let God go.

MEISTER ECKHART

He who does not bellow the truth when he knows the truth makes himself the accomplice of liars and forgers.

CHARLES PÉGUY

I believe that in the history of the world one could easily find a very great number of examples of persons who, suddenly perceiving the truth, seize it. Or, having sought and found it, deliberately break with their interests, sacrifice their interests, break deliberately with their political friendships and even with their sentimental friendships. I do not believe that one finds many examples of men who, having accomplished this first sacrifice, have had the second courage to sacrifice their second interests, their second friendships. For it commonly happens that they find their new friends are worth no more than the old ones, that their second friends are worth no more than the first. *Woe to the lonely man*, and what they fear most is solitude. They are most willing, for the sake of the truth, to fall out with half of the world. All the more so when, by thus falling out with half of the world—not without a little repercussion—they usually make partisans among the second half of the world; partisans who ask nothing better than to be the antagonists of the first half. But if, for the love of this same truth, they foolishly go about breaking with this second half, who will become their partisans? . . .

A brave man—and so far, there are not many—for the sake of the truth breaks with his friends and his interests. Thus a new party is formed, originally and supposedly the party of justice and truth, which in less than no time becomes absolutely identical with the other parties. A party like the others; like all the others; as vulgar; as gross; as unjust; as false. Then for this second time, a superbrave man would have to be found to make a second break: but of these, there are hardly any left. . . .

And yet, the life of an honest man must be an apostasy and a perpetual desertion. The honest man must be a perpetual renegade, the life of an honest man must be a perpetual infidelity. For the man who wishes to remain faithful to truth must make himself continually unfaithful to all the continual, successive, indefatigable renascent errors. And the man who wishes to remain faithful to justice must make himself continually unfaithful to inexhaustibly triumphant injustices.

CHARLES PÉGUY

§ 7

If only they were to forsake me, and observe my teachings!

WORDS PUT INTO THE MOUTH OF GOD

(from the Talmud)

The least one can demand of people who judge any doctrine is that they should judge of it in the sense in which the teacher himself understood it. And he understood his teaching not as a distant ideal for humanity, obedience to which is impossible, nor as a mystical poetic fantasy wherewith he captivated the simple-minded inhabitants of Galilee. He understood his teaching as a real thing, and a thing which would save mankind. And he did not dream on the cross but died for his teaching, and many others are dying and will yet die. Of such a teaching one cannot say that it is a dream!

Every true doctrine is a dream to those in error. We have come to this, that there are many people (of whom I was one) who say that this teaching is visionary because it is not natural to man. It is not in accord, they say, with man's nature to turn the other cheek when one cheek is struck; it is not natural to give what is one's own to another; it is unnatural to work for others instead of for oneself. It is natural to man, they say, to defend his safety and the safety of his family and his property: in other words, it is natural for man to struggle for his own existence. The learned jurists prove scientifically that man's most sacred duty is to defend his rights, that is—to struggle.

But it is sufficient to free oneself for a moment from the thought that the order which exists and has been arranged by men is the best and is sacrosanct, for the objection that Christ's teaching is not accordant with man's nature to turn against the objector. Who will deny that to murder or torture, I will not say a man, but to torture a dog or kill a hen or calf is contrary and distressing to man's nature? (I know people who live by tilling the land, and who have given up eating meat merely because they had themselves to kill their own animals.) Yet the whole structure of our lives is such that each man's personal advantage is obtained by inflicting suffering on others, which is contrary to human nature. The whole order of our life and the whole complex mechanism of our institutions, designed for the infliction of violence, witness to the extent to which violence is contrary to human nature. Not a single judge would decide to strangle with a rope the man he condemns to death from the bench. Not a single magistrate would make up his mind himself to take a peasant from his weeping family and shut him up in prison. None of our generals or soldiers, were it not for discipline, oaths of allegiance, and declarations of war, would, I will not say kill hundreds of Turks and Germans and destroy their villages, but would even decline to wound a single man. All this is only done thanks to a very complex state and social machinery the purpose of which is so to distribute the responsibility for the evil deeds that are done that no one should feel the unnaturalness of those deeds. Some men write the laws; others apply them; a third set drill men and habituate them to discipline, that is to say, to senseless and implicit obedience; a fourth set —the people who are disciplined—commit all sorts of deeds of violence, even killing people, without knowing why or wherefore. But a man need only, even for a moment, free himself mentally from this net of worldly organisation in which he is involved to understand what is really unnatural to him.

TOLSTOY

FOURTH PART

V. HUMILITY

For Bone

Allegretto grazioso
Voy...... ez ce beau ta... pis d'her... be dou.... ce et fleu...ri...e
tr
Poco f
DIM:

§ 1

O Saviour, pour upon me thy Spirit of meekness and love,
Annihilate the Selfhood in me, be thou all my life,
Guide thou my hand which trembles exceedingly upon the rock
of ages.

BLAKE (from *Jerusalem*)

Lord, make me an instrument of Thy Peace. Where there is hatred, let me sow love; where there is injury, pardon; where there is doubt, faith; where there is despair, hope; where there is darkness, light; where there is sadness, joy.

O Divine Master, grant that I may not so much seek to be consoled, as to console; to be understood, as to understand; to be loved, as to love. For it is in giving that we receive, it is in pardoning that we are pardoned; it is in dying that we are born to eternal life.

ST. FRANCIS OF ASSISI

Moonless darkness stands between.
Past, O Past, no more be seen!
But the Bethlehem star may lead me
To the sight of Him who freed me
From the self that I have been.
Make me pure, Lord: Thou art holy;
Make me meek, Lord: Thou wert lowly;
Now beginning, and alway:
Now begin, on Christmas day.

GERARD MANLEY HOPKINS (fragment)

THE FLOWER

How fresh, O Lord, how sweet and clean
Are thy returns! ev'n as the flowers in Spring,
To which, besides their own demean,
The late-past frosts tributes of pleasure bring;
Grief melts away
Like snow in May,
As if there were no such cold thing.

Who would have thought my shrivel'd heart
Could have recover'd greennesse? It was gone
Quite under ground; as flow'rs depart
To see their mother-root, when they have blown;
Where they together
All the hard weather,
Dead to the world, keep house unknown.

These are thy wonders, Lord of power,
Killing and quickning, bringing down to hell
And up to heaven in an houre;
Making a chiming of a passing-bell.
We say amisse
This or that is;
Thy word is all, if we could spell.

O that I once past changing were,
Fast in thy Paradise, where no flower can wither!
Many a Spring I shoot up fair,
Offring at Heav'n, growing and groning thither;
Nor doth my flower
Want a spring-showre,
My sinnes and I joining together.

But while I grow in a straight line,
Still upwards bent, as if Heav'n were mine own,
Thy anger comes, and I decline:
What frost to that? what pole is not the zone,
Where all things burn,
When thou dost turn,
And the least frown of Thine is shown?

And now in age I bud again,
After so many deaths I live and write;
I once more smell the dew and rain,
And relish versing: O, my onely Light,
It cannot be
That I am he
On whom thy tempests fell all night.

These are thy wonders, Lord of love,
To make us see we are but flow'rs that glide;
Which when we once can finde and prove,
Thou hast a garden for us where to bide;
Who would be more,
Swelling through store,
Forfeit their Paradise by their pride.

GEORGE HERBERT

I am only the vessel in which the powers of life work, and create; and I dare not but be humble at the little I can manage to let come through.

ERNST TOLLER

Now mark: When the creature arrogates to itself anything good, such as Essence, Life, Knowledge, Wisdom, Power, and in short whatever we must call good, as if it were that or possessed that, or as if that pertained to it or proceeded from it,—as often as this comes to pass, the creature goes astray. What did the Devil do else? What was his going astray and his fall else, but that he presumed to be also somewhat, and would have it that somewhat was his, and somewhat was due to him? This presumption, and his I and Me and Mine, these were his going astray and his fall. And thus is he to this day. . . .

Now, that I arrogate anything good to myself, as if I were, or had done, or knew, or could perform any good thing, or that it were mine, that is all out of blindness and folly. For if the real truth were in me, I should understand that I am not that good thing, and that it is not mine, nor of me, and that it is not I who knows it, not I who is capable of it and can perform it, and the like. Yea, if this came to pass, presumption would needs cease of itself. . . . Then the man says: "Behold! I, poor fool that I was, thought it was I, but behold! it is, and was, of a truth, God!"

THEOLOGIA GERMANICA

It is my humility that gives God his divinity and the proof of it is this. God's peculiar property is giving. But God cannot give if he has nothing to receive his gifts. Now I make myself receptive to his gifts by my humility so I by my humility do make God giver and since giving is God's own peculiar property I do by my humility give God his property. The would-be giver must needs find a taker; without a taker he cannot be a giver for it is the taker by his taking that makes the man a giver. So God, to be the giver, must discover a receiver. Now none but the humble can receive the gift of God. So God, to use his godlike power of giving, will eke need my humility; without humility he cannot give me aught for I without humility cannot accept his gift. Thus it is true that I by my humility do give God his divinity.

MEISTER ECKHART

Thinking which keeps contact with reality must look up to the heavens, it must look over the earth, and dare to direct its gaze to the barred windows of a lunatic asylum. Look to the stars and understand how small our earth is in the universe. Look upon earth and know how minute man is upon it. The earth existed long before man came upon it. In the history of the universe, man is on the earth for but a second. Who knows but that the earth will circle round the sun once more without man upon it? Therefore we must not place man in the centre of the universe. And our gaze must be fixed on the barred windows of a lunatic asylum, in order that we may remember the terrible fact that the mental and spiritual are also liable to destruction.

Only when thinking thus becomes quite humble can it set its feet upon the way that leads to knowledge. The more profound a religion is, the more it realises this fact—that what it knows through belief is little compared with what it does not know. The first active deed of thinking is resignation—acquiescence in what happens. Becoming free, inwardly, from what happens, we pass through the gate of recognition on the way to ethics.

The deeper we look into nature, the more we recognise that it is full of life, and the more profoundly we know that all life is a secret and that we are united with all life that is in nature. Man can no longer live his life for himself alone. We realise that all life is valuable and that we are united to all this life. From this knowledge comes our spiritual relationship to the universe.

ALBERT SCHWEITZER

§ 2

He who has a humble mind is regarded as if he had offered all the sacrifices of the Law.

RABBI JOSHUA B. LEVI

There is a very high rung which only one man in a whole generation can reach: that of having learned all secret wisdom and then praying like a little child.

RABBI MENDEL OF RYMANOV

A king was told that a man of humility is endowed with long life. He attired himself in old garments, took up his residence in a small hut, and forbade anyone to show reverence before him. But when he honestly examined himself, the King found himself to be prouder of his seeming humility than ever before. A philosopher thereupon remarked to him: "Dress like a king; live like a king; allow the people to show due respect to you; but be humble in your inmost heart."

THE BAALSHEM

On one occasion they brought a man possessed of a devil to one of the old men of Thebes, and entreated him to cast the devil out, but the old man was unwilling to do so; but since they urged him strongly he was persuaded, and he had mercy on the man, and he said to the devil, "Get thee out from that which God hath fashioned." Then the devil answered and said, "I am going out, but I would ask thee to tell me one thing: What is the meaning of that which is written in the Gospel, Who are the goats and who are the sheep?" The old man answered and said, "I myself am one of the goats, but God knoweth who the sheep are"; and when the devil heard this, he cried out with a loud voice, saying, "Behold, I go forth because of thy humility," and straightway he left the man and departed.

THE PARADISE OF THE FATHERS

Rabbi Moshe Leib of Sasov once gave his last coin to a man of evil reputation. His students reproached him for it. Whereupon he replied: "Shall I be more particular than God, who gave the coin to me?"

HASIDIC STORY

Once the Rabbi of Apt came to a city in which two men competed for the privilege of giving him lodgings. Both houses were equally roomy and comfortable and in both households all the rules were observed with pious exactitude. But one of the men was in ill repute for his many love affairs and other sinful doings and he knew quite well that he was weak and thought little of himself. The other man, however, no one in the whole community could accuse of the slightest breach of conduct. With proud and stately steps he walked abroad, thoroughly aware of his spotless purity.

The rabbi selected the house of the man with a bad reputation. When he was asked for the reason for his choice, he answered: "Concerning the proud, God says: 'I and he cannot live together in this world.' And if God himself, blessed be he, cannot share a room with the proud, then how could I? We read in the Torah, on the other hand, '. . . who dwelleth with them in the midst of their uncleannesses.' And if God takes lodgings there, why shouldn't I?"

HASIDIC STORY

A man of piety complained to the Baalshem, saying: "I have laboured hard and long in the service of the Lord, and yet I have received no improvement. I am still an ordinary and ignorant person."

The Baalshem answered: "You have gained the realisation that you are ordinary and ignorant, and this in itself is a worthy accomplishment."

HASIDIC STORY

A young man was asked by Rabbi Yitzhak Meir of Ger if he had learned Torah. "Just a little," replied the youth.

"That is all anyone ever has learned of the Torah," was the Rabbi's answer.

HASIDIC STORY

It was the habit of Rabbi David Talner to spend half an hour early each morning reading his letters in his private room. An intimate asked why he did this before prayers the first thing of the day. The Rabbi answered: "I wish to commence the day aright. As you know, the more important a man is, the harder are his struggles against his evil thoughts, since the Satan strives hardest to tempt him. Hence when I look over my letters and read in the salutation that I am called a Zaddik, a Leader, a Holy Man, and the like, I pray to the Lord: 'You and I know that I do not merit these titles of honour. But since so many good men believe them in all sincerity, I beseech Thee to aid me to avoid the snares of Satan, so that these men may not feel shame.' "

HASIDIC STORY

When Rabbi Phineas Hurwitz came to Frankfurt to take up the post of Rabbi, he received an overpowering welcome. Thousands of people surrounded his carriage. A friend asked how he felt in this hour of triumph. The Rabbi replied: "I imagined that I was a corpse, being borne to the cemetery in the company of multitudes attending the funeral."

HASIDIC STORY

When Rabbi Shmelke came to Nikolsburg to assume his duties as Rabbi, he locked himself in a room and began to pace back and forth. One of the welcoming party overheard him repeating again and again the many forms of greeting he anticipated. When the welcome was concluded, the man confessed that he had overheard Rabbi Shmelke, and inquired if the Rabbi would explain his odd action.

Rabbi Shmelke said: "I dislike intensely honours which tend to self-pride; therefore I rehearsed to myself all the words of welcome. No one appreciates self-praise, and after becoming accustomed to these words of acclaim by frequent repetition, I no longer felt pride in hearing these very phrases uttered by the committee of welcome."

HASIDIC STORY

BONTZYE SHWEIG[1]

Down here, in *this* world, Bontzye Shweig's death made no impression at all. Ask anyone you like who Bontzye was, *how* he lived, and what he died of; whether of heart failure, or whether his strength gave out, or whether his back broke under a heavy load, and they won't know. Perhaps, after all, he died of hunger.

If a tram-car horse had fallen dead, there would have been more excitement. It would have been mentioned in the papers, and hundreds of people would have crowded round to look at the dead animal—even the spot where the accident took place.

But the tramway horse would receive less attention if there were as many horses as men—a thousand million.

Bontzye lived quietly and died quietly. He passed through *our* world like a shadow.

No wine was drunk at Bontzye's circumcision, no healths were proposed, and he made no beautiful speech when he was confirmed. He lived like a little dun-coloured grain of sand on the sea-shore, among millions of his kind; and when the wind lifted him and blew him over to the other side of the sea, nobody noticed it.

When he was alive, the mud in the street preserved no impression of his feet; after his death, the wind overturned the little board on his grave. The grave-digger's wife found it a long way off from the spot, and boiled a potful of potatoes over it. Three days after that, the grave-digger had forgotten where he had laid him.

If Bontzye had been given a tombstone, then, in a hundred years or so, an antiquarian might have found it, and the name "Bontzye Shweig" would have echoed once again in *our* air.

A shadow! His likeness remained photographed in nobody's brain, in nobody's heart; not a trace of him remained.

"No kith, no kin!" He lived and died alone!

Had it not been for the human commotion, someone might

[1] Bontzye = "mum."

have heard Bontzye's spine snap under its load; had the world been less busy, someone might have remarked that Bontzye (also a human being) went about with two extinguished eyes and fearfully hollow cheeks; that even when he had no load on his shoulders, his head drooped earthward as though, while yet alive, he were looking for his grave. Were there as few men as tramway horses, someone might perhaps have asked: What has happened to Bontzye?

When they carried Bontzye into the hospital, his corner in the underground lodging was soon filled—there were ten of his like waiting for it, and they put it up to auction among themselves. When they carried him from the hospital bed to the dead-house, there were twenty poor sick persons waiting for the bed. When he had been taken out of the dead-house, they brought in twenty bodies from under a building that had fallen in. Who knows how long he will rest in his grave? Who knows how many are waiting for the little plot of ground?

A quiet birth, a quiet life, a quiet death, and a quieter burial. But it was not so in the *other* world. *There* Bontzye's death made a great impression.

The blast of the great Messianic Shofar sounded through all the seven heavens: Bontzye Shweig has left the earth! The largest angels with the broadest wings flew about and told one another: Bontzye Shweig is to take his seat in the Heavenly Academy! In Paradise there was a noise and a joyful tumult: Bontzye Shweig! Just fancy! Bontzye Shweig!

Little child-angels with sparkling eyes, gold thread-work wings, and silver slippers, ran delightedly to meet him. The rustle of the wings, the tap-tap of the little slippers, and the merry laughter of the fresh, rosy mouths, filled all the heavens and reached to the Throne of Glory, and God Himself knew that Bontzye Shweig was coming.

Abraham, our father, stood in the gate, his right hand stretched out with a hearty greeting, and a sweet smile lit up his old face.

What are they wheeling through heaven?

Two angels are pushing a golden arm-chair into Paradise for Bontzye Shweig.

What flashed so brightly?

They were carrying past a gold crown set with precious stones —all for Bontzye Shweig.

"Before the decision of the Heavenly Court has been given?" ask the saints, not quite without jealousy.

"O," reply the angels, "that will be a mere formality. Even the prosecutor won't say a word against Bontzye Shweig. The case will not last five minutes."

Just consider: Bontzye Shweig!

When the little angels had met Bontzye in mid-air and played him a tune; when Abraham, our father, had shaken him by the hand like an old comrade; when he heard that a chair stood waiting for him in Paradise, that a crown lay ready for his head, and that not a word would be lost over his case before the Heavenly Court—Bontzye, just as in the other world, was too frightened to speak. His heart sank with terror. He is sure it is all a dream, or else simply a mistake.

He is used to both. He often dreamt, in the other world, that he was picking up money off the floor—there were whole heaps of it—and then he woke to find himself as poor as ever; and more than once people had smiled at him and given him a friendly word and then turned away and spit out.

"It is my luck," he used to think. And now he dared not raise his eyes, lest the dream should vanish, lest he should wake up in some cave full of snakes and lizards. He was afraid to speak, afraid to move, lest he should be recognised and flung into the pit.

He trembles and does not hear the angels' compliments, does not see how they dance round him, makes no answer to the greeting of Abraham, our father, and—when he is led into the presence of the Heavenly Court, he does not even wish it "good morning!"

He is beside himself with terror, and his fright increases when he happens to notice the floor of the Heavenly Courthouse; it is all alabaster set with diamonds. "And my feet standing on it!" He is paralysed. "Who knows what rich man, what rabbi, what saint they take me for—he will come—and that will be the end of me!"

His terror is such, he never even hears the president call out: "The case of Bontzye Shweig!", adding, as he hands the deeds to the advocate, "Read, but make haste!"

The whole hall goes round and round in Bontzye's eyes, there is a rushing in his ears. And through the rushing he hears more and more clearly the voice of the advocate, speaking sweetly as a violin.

"His name," he hears, "fitted him like the dress made for a slender figure by the hand of an artist-tailor."

"What is he talking about?" wondered Bontzye, and he heard an impatient voice break in with:

"No similes, please!"

"He never," continued the advocate, "was heard to complain of either God or man; there was never a flash of hatred in his eye; he never lifted it with a claim on heaven."

Still Bontzye does not understand, and once again the hard voice interrupts: "No rhetoric, please!"

"Job gave way—this one was more unfortunate——"

"Facts, dry facts!"

"When he was a week old, he was circumcised. . . ."

"We want no realism!"

"The Mohel who circumcised him did not know his work——"

"Come, come!"

"And he kept silent," the advocate went on, "even when his mother died, and he was given a stepmother at thirteen years old—a serpent, a vixen."

"Can they mean me after all?" thought Bontzye.

"No insinuations against a third party!" said the president, angrily.

"She grudged him every mouthful—stale, mouldy bread, tendons instead of meat—and *she* drank coffee with cream."

"Keep to the subject," ordered the president.

"She grudged him everything but her finger nails, and his black-and-blue body showed through the holes in his torn and fusty clothes. Winter time, in the hardest frost, he had to chop wood for her, barefoot, in the yard, and his hands were too young and too weak, the logs too thick, the hatchet too blunt. More than once he nearly dislocated his wrist; more than once his feet were nearly frost-bitten, but he kept silent, even to his father."

"To that drunkard?" laughs the accuser, and Bontzye feels cold in every limb.

"He never even complained to his father," finished up the advocate.

"And always alone," he continued, "no playmates, no school, nor teaching of any kind—never a whole garment—never a free moment."

"Facts, please!" reminded the president.

"He kept silent even later, when his father seized him by the hair in a fit of drunkenness, and flung him out into the street on a snowy winter's night. He quietly picked himself up out of the snow and ran whither his feet carried him.

"He kept silent all the way—however hungry he might be, he only begged with his eyes.

"It was a wild, wet night in spring time, when he reached the great town; he fell like a drop into the ocean, and yet he passed that same night under arrest. He kept silent and never asked why, for what. He was let out, and looked about for the hardest work. And he kept silent. Harder than the work itself was the finding of it—and he kept silent.

"Bathed in a cold sweat, crushed together under heavy loads, his empty stomach convulsed with hunger—he kept silent.

"Bespattered with mud, spat at, driven with his load off the pavement and into the street among the cabs, carts, and tramways, looking death in the eyes every moment—he kept silent.

"He never calculated how many pounds' burden go to a groschen, how many times he fell on an errand worth a dreier;

how many times he nearly panted out his soul going after his pay; he never calculated the difference between other people's lot and his—he kept silent.

"And he never insisted loudly on his pay; he stood in the doorway like a beggar, with a dog-like pleading in his eyes—'Come again later!' and he went like a shadow to come again later, and beg for his wage more humbly than before.

"He kept silent even when they cheated him of part, or threw in a false coin.

"He took everything in silence."

"They mean me after all," thought Bontzye.

"Once," continued the advocate, after a sip of water, "a change came into his life: there came flying along a carriage on rubber tyres drawn by two runaway horses. The driver already lay some distance off on the pavement with a cracked skull. The terrified horses foamed at the mouth, sparks shot from their hoofs, their eyes shone like fiery lamps on a winter's night—and in the carriage, more dead than alive, sat a man.

"And Bontzye stopped the horses. And the man he had saved was a charitable Jew, who was not ungrateful.

"He put the dead man's whip into Bontzye's hands, and Bontzye became a coachman. More than that—he was provided with a wife, and more still—with a child.

"And Bontzye kept silent!"

"Me, they mean me!" Bontzye assured himself again, and yet had not the courage to give a glance at the Heavenly Court.

He listens to the advocate further:

"He kept silent also when his protector became bankrupt and did not pay him his wages.

"He kept silent when his wife ran away from him, leaving him a child at the breast.

"He was silent also fifteen years later, when the child had grown up and was strong enough to throw him out of the house."

"Me, they mean me!" Now he is sure of it.

"He kept silent even," began the angelic advocate once more in a still softer and sadder voice, "when the same philanthropist paid all his creditors their due but him—and even when (riding once again in a carriage with rubber tyres and fiery horses) he knocked Bontzye down and drove over him.

"He kept silent. He did not even tell the police who had done for him."

"He kept silent even in the hospital, where one may cry out.

"He kept silent when the doctor would not come to his bedside without being paid fifteen kopeks, and when the attendant demanded another five—for changing his linen.

"He kept silent in the death-struggle—silent in death.

"Not a word against God; not a word against men!

"*Dixi!*"

Once more Bontzye trembled all over; he knew that after the advocate comes the prosecutor. Who knows what *he* will say?

Bontzye himself had remembered nothing of his life.

Even in the other world he forgot every moment what had happened in the one before. The advocate had recalled everything to his mind. Who knows what the prosecutor will not remind him of?

"Gentlemen," begins the prosecutor, in a voice biting and acid as vinegar—but he breaks off.

"Gentlemen," he begins again, but his voice is milder, and a second time he breaks off.

Then, from out the same throat, comes in a voice that is almost gentle:

"Gentlemen! *He* was silent! I will be silent, too!"

There is a hush—and there sounds in front a new, soft, trembling voice:

"Bontzye, my child," it speaks like a harp, "my dear child Bontzye!"

And Bontzye's heart melts within him. Now he would lift up his eyes, but they are blinded with tears; he never felt such sweet emotion before. "My child!" "My Bontzye!"—no one, since his mother died, had spoken to him with such words in such a voice.

"My child," continued the presiding judge, "you have suffered and kept silent; there is no whole limb, no whole bone in your body, without a scar, without a wound, not a fibre of your soul that has not bled—and you kept silent.

"There they did not understand. Perhaps you yourself did not know that you might have cried out, and that at your cry the walls of Jericho would have shaken and fallen. You yourself knew nothing of your hidden power.

"In the other world your silence was not understood, but *that* is the world of delusion; in the world of truth you will receive your reward.

"The Heavenly Court will not judge you; the Heavenly Court will not pass sentence on you; they will not apportion you a reward. Take what you will! Everything is yours!"

Bontzye looks up for the first time. He is dazzled; everything shines and flashes and streams with light.

"*Taki?*"[1] he asks shyly.

"Yes, really!" answers the presiding judge with decision; "really, I tell you, everything is yours; everything in heaven belongs to you. Because all that shines and sparkles is only the reflection of your hidden goodness, a reflection of your soul. You only take of what is yours."

"*Taki?*" asks Bontzye again, this time in a firmer voice.

"*Taki! taki! taki!*" they answer him from all sides.

"Well, if it is so," Bontzye smiles, "I would like to have every day, for breakfast, a hot roll with fresh butter."

The Court and the angels looked down, a little ashamed; the prosecutor laughed.

[1] Really?

ISAAC LOEB PEREZ

HUMILITY

Rabbi Nahman of Bratzlav says: "God does not do the same thing twice."

That which is, is single and for once. It plunges out of the flood of returns,[1] new and never having happened before; and having happened, it plunges back into the flood, unrecallable. Each thing reappears at some other time, but each thing is changed. And the turmoil which rules over the heavenly bodies, and the water and fire which build up the structure of the earth, and the mixing and unmixing which compose the life of the living, and the spirit of man, with all his mistaken attempts to seize the soft profusion of the possible—none of these can create one thing which is the same as another, or bring back again one of the things which are sealed up in what has already been. The happening-but-once is the eternity of the individual. For with his uniqueness he is engraved irrevocably in the heart of the universe, and he lies in the bosom of the timeless for ever as he who has been created in such and in no other manner.

Thus uniqueness is the essential property of man, and it is given to him in order that he may unfold it. This is just the intention of "the return," that the uniqueness should become ever purer and more perfect by means of it, and that he who returns should in each new life exist in less troubled and in less disturbed incomparability. For pure uniqueness and pure perfection are one, and he who has become so totally at one with himself that no otherness has power or place in him, has completed the journey, and is redeemed and rests in God.

"Every one should know and consider that his state is unique in the world, and that no one ever lived who is the same as he; for had there ever been any one the same as he, there would have been no need for him to exist. Each person is a new thing in the world, and he should make his quality perfect, for the coming of the Messiah is delayed through its not being perfect." He who strives can fulfil himself in his own way and in no

[1] A kind of metempsychosis is meant.—M.B.

other. "He who seizes the rung of his companion, and lets his own rung go, will make good neither his own nor the other's rung. Many copied in their actions Rabbi Simon ben Jochai, and they did not succeed, because they were not in his condition, and only acted as he did because they had seen him in his condition."

But just as a man seeks God in solitary fervour, and nevertheless there is a high service which the community alone can fulfil, and just as a man achieves something immense by his everyday actions, but not by himself alone, because he requires the world and things in order to perform those actions, thus the uniqueness of man is even so manifested by his life with others. For the more a man is truly unique, the more he can give to others and the more he will give to them. And his one trouble is that his power of giving is limited by those who receive. For "the giver is on the side of grace, and the receiver is on the side of justice. As when a man fills his goblet from out of a large vessel: the vessel pours from out of its fullness, but the goblet sets a limit to the gift."

The unique sees God and embraces him. The unique delivers fallen worlds. But the unique is not a whole but a part, and the purer and more perfect he is, the more intensely is he aware of being a part, and the feeling of the community of beings is the more awake in him. This is the mystery of humility.

"There is a light over every man, and when two souls meet, their lights come together, and a single light emerges from them. And this is termed to generate." To feel the universal generation as a sea, and oneself as a wave in it, this is the mystery of humility.

If anyone "abases himself too much and forgets that a man through his works and behaviour can call down an overflowing blessing on all the world," this is not humility. It is called impure humility: "The greatest evil is if thou dost forget that thou art a son of the king." He dwells in true humility who feels the others as he feels himself, and who feels himself in the others.

Pride is to contrast oneself with others. It is not he who knows himself who is proud-minded, but only he who compares himself with others. No man presumes if he rests in himself: all the heavens are open to him, and all the worlds devoted to him. He presumes who feels himself above others and regards himself as higher than the most insignificant of things—he who deals with weights and measures and gives judgment. A Zaddik says: "If the Messiah should come to-day, and should say: 'You are better than the others,' then I should say to him: 'You are not the Messiah.'"

The soul of the proud-minded lives inactive, and has no substance; it flutters and toils, but it is not blessed. Those thoughts are shadows which do not dwell upon their subjects, but only upon themselves and their glory. The act which has no regard to the goal, but aims only at prevailing, has no substance, only surface; no stability, only appearance. He who weighs and measures will be as empty and unreal as are weights and measures. "There is no room for God in him who is full of himself."

A story is told of a youth who went into seclusion and set himself free from the things of this world, in order to devote himself solely to learning and to service. He sat in solitude fasting from Sabbath to Sabbath, learning and praying, but his attention was centred on the pride of his action. It shone before his eyes, and his fingers burned to place it upon his brow as though it were the chaplet of the anointed, and so all his work fell over to "the other side," and the holy had no part in it. But his heart swelled only higher and higher, though the demons made sport of his actions, and he thought himself wholly possessed of God. Then it happened that once he got outside himself, and he perceived the things round about him, all of them silent and detached. Knowledge then took hold of him, and he saw his actions piled up at the feet of a gigantic idol, and he saw himself as in a dizzy void, given up to something that had no name. This, and nothing further, is told.

But the humble man has "the power to attract." There is

always a limit to a man while he considers himself above others, so "God cannot pour His holiness into him, for God is without limit." But if a man rests in himself as though in nothing, he is not limited by anything, and God can pour His glory into him.

The humility which is here meant is no willed and practised virtue, it is nothing but an inward state, feeling and expression. It is never forced, never a self-abasement, self-command, or self-determination. It is as without discord as a child's glance, and as simple as a child's speech.

The humble man lives in every being, and he knows the nature and the virtue of each. Because to him no one is "the other," he knows from within that no one is wanting in some hidden value; he knows that "no man exists who does not have his hour." The colours of the world do not merge for him in one another, but each soul stands in the splendour of its own existence. "In each man there is something precious that is in no other man. Therefore one should honour each man for that which is hidden within him, which only he and no one of his companions possesses."

"God does not look on the evil side," said a Zaddik; "how do I dare to do so?" He who, in his own life, lives according to the mystery of humility, can condemn no one. "He who gives judgment upon another man has given it upon himself."

He who separates himself from sinners walks in their guilt. But the saint is able to suffer for the sins of a man as though they were his own. To live in the life of others, this alone is righteousness.

To live with understanding of others is justice. To live in others as in oneself is love. For that feeling of nearness and that wish for nearness to a few, which among men is called love, is nothing but the remembrance of a heavenly life. "Those who in Paradise sat near each other and were neighbours and kinsmen, they are also near to each other in this world." But in reality love is something primally wide and upholding, and it extends to all the living, irrespective of choice or of separation.

A Zaddik said: "How can you say of me that I am a leader of my generation, when I still feel for those who are near to me or are of my own blood a love which is stronger than that which I feel for the sons of other men?" Or for beasts, as Rabbi Wolf would have said: he never shouted at a horse. Rabbi Moshe Loeb used to give drink to the neglected calves in the market, and of Rabbi Zusya it is told that he could not look at a cage without opening it, from thinking of "the birds' misfortune and their longing to fly in the open air as free wanderers, in accordance with their nature." But it is not only those beings on whom the short-sighted multitude bestows the name of living, who belong to the love of the lovers. "To thee there is nothing in which there is no life, and through its life each thing wears the form in which it stands before thine eyes. And look, this life is the life of God."

Thus it is meant: the love given to the living is the love of God, and it is higher than any other service. A master asked his disciple: "Thou knowest that two powers cannot take possession of the mind of man at the same time. When you rise from your couch in the morning there are two ways before you: love of God and love of man: which is the more important?" The other answered: "I know not." Then said the master: "In the prayer book which is in the hands of the people it is written: 'Before you pray, say the words, "Love thy neighbour as thyself."' Dost thou think that the venerable ones have commanded this without intention? If anyone says to you that he has love of God but no love of the living he speaks falsely, and pretends he has that which it is impossible to have."

Therefore, if anyone has departed from God his only salvation is in somebody loving him. When a father complained to the Baalshem: "My son has departed from God, what shall I do?" he answered: "Love him the more." One of the fundamental messages of the Hasidim is to love more. Its roots bury themselves deep and spread far. He who can understand this, understands Judaism afresh. There is great moving power within it. . . .

Rabbi Pinhas said, "When you see that someone hates you and does you harm, rally your spirit and love him more than ever." And he explains: The communion of the living is the chariot of the Divine Presence, and if there is a rift in the chariot it must be filled in, and where there is so little love on one side that the join falls apart, you must increase the love on your side in order to supply the want.

Once, before going on a journey, the favourite disciple of Rabbi Pinhas, Rabbi Raphael, called out to one of his pupils to sit beside him in the carriage. The other said: "I am afraid that it will give you too little room." The Rabbi said: "We will love each other more, and there will be room enough." Let these be our witnesses here—the symbol and the reality, so different from each other yet one and indivisible, the chariot of the Shekhina and the chariot of friends.

Love is a Being which lives in a realm larger than the realm of the individual, and speaks from a knowledge deeper than the knowledge of the individual. It dwells in truth *between* the creatures, that is, it dwells in God. Life covered and warranted by life, life flowing forth into life, not till you realise this can you perceive the soul of the world. What is wanting in one man is supplied by another. If one man loves too little, another will love the more.

Things help one another. But to help is to do spontaneously, with concentrated will, my own part of doing. He who loves more does not preach of love to the other, but only loves; as it were, he does not trouble about the other. And so he who helps does not, as it were, trouble himself about the other, but does his own part with the intention of helping. This means: what is essentially happening between one being and another, happens not through their intercourse but through everyone's apparently unconnected and purposeless act. This is told in a parable: "If someone would sing and cannot lift up his voice, and another comes and begins to sing, then the first is enabled to join in the song. This is the secret of union."

To help one another is not considered a task, but the

self-evident reality on which the companionship of the Hasidim is based. To help is not a virtue, but a pulse of existence. This is the new sense given to the old Jewish saying: "Charity delivers from death." It is commanded that he who helps should not think of the others who could help with him, of God or of men, nor should consider himself as part of a power, and as though he had merely to contribute; but that each man should stand, answerable and responsible, in integrity.

There is one thing more, and it is only another way of expressing the mystery of humility: to help, not out of pity, that is, from a sharp, quick pain which one wishes to expel, but out of love, which means to live with others. The man who merely pities does not feel in himself the suffering of the sufferer, he does not carry it in his heart, as one might share in the life of a tree, in its sucking-up of moisture and its putting forth of foliage, in the dream of its roots and the desire of its trunk and the thousand movements of its boughs; or as one might share in the life of an animal, with its movements and stretchings and clawings, and the joy of its sinews and limbs, and the dumb understanding of its brain. He who only pities receives from the mere outward manifestation of this sorrow, the sorrow of others, a sharp, quick pain, totally unlike the real sorrow of the sufferer.

He who helps must live with others, and it is only the help which springs from living with others that subsists in the sight of God. Thus it is told of the Zaddik Rabbi Bunam that when a poor man excited his pity he first provided for his pressing needs; then, when he felt the pangs of pity assuaged, he let himself be absorbed in the life and the needs of the other with deep, peaceful, devoted love, till he felt within himself the other's life and needs as though they were his own—and only then did he truly begin to help. He who in this way lives with others, in his own action realises the truth that all souls are one, for each is a spark of the primordial soul, and the whole of the primordial soul is in them.

Thus the humble man who is the righteous, the loving, and

the helper, lives: mixing with all and untouched by all, devoted to the multitude and collected in his uniqueness, establishing on the rocky heights of solitude the covenant with the eternal and in the valley of life the covenant with the earthly; blossoming out of profound dedication, and withdrawn from all the will of the wilful ones. He knows that all is in God, and greets his messengers as familiar friends. He fears not the before or the after, nor what is above or beneath, neither this world nor the world to come. He is at home, and can never be exiled. The earth cannot help being his cradle, and heaven cannot help being his mirror and his echo.

MARTIN BUBER
(interpreting the Hasidic doctrine of humility)

FOURTH PART

VI. FREEDOM

In memory of
Bernard Lewis Strauss

Allegro con moto.
Wir wol.... len mit Ver... traw... en auf
Got..... tes Hül - fe auf Gott.. es Hülfe bau - en.

§ 1

For if righteousness come by the law, then Christ is dead in vain.

GALATIANS

The grace of the Holy Ghost is not bound to any law.

ST. GREGORY THE GREAT

All creation is for [God] a communication of His very being, that is, He can only create free beings. He can only call into existence beings that He calls upon to make themselves.

LOUIS LAVELLE

Love—and do what you wish.

ST. AUGUSTINE

I am, in God's hands, my own master.

BOSSUET

Others gain authority over you if you possess a will distinct from God's will.

RABBI NAHMAN OF BRATZLAV

All those who allow themselves a wrong liberty make themselves their own aim and object.

HENRY SUSO

Christianity promises to make men free; it never promises to make them independent.

W. R. INGE

Therefore freedom for us means the nisus to the whole, the ἔρως or spirit of union, which is at once logic and love.

BERNARD BOSANQUET

It may now be very easily conceived what is human freedom, which I define to be this: it is, namely, a firm reality which our understanding acquires through direct union with God, so that it can bring forth ideas in itself, and effects outside itself, in complete harmony with its nature; without, however, its effects being subjected to any external causes, so as to be capable of being changed or transformed by them.

SPINOZA

And this brings us to the examination of . . . the distinction between autonomy and freedom. . . .

The more I enter into the whole of an activity with the whole of myself, the less legitimate is it to say that I am autonomous. In this sense, the philosopher is less autonomous than the scientist, and the scientist less autonomous than the technician. The man who is most autonomous is, in a certain sense, most fully involved. Only this non-autonomy of the philosopher or the great artist is not heteronomy any more than love is heterocentricity. It is rooted in Being, at a point either short of self or beyond self, and in a sphere which transcends all possible possession; the sphere, indeed, which I reach in contemplation or worship. And, in my view, this means that such non-autonomy is very freedom. . . . In the scale of sanctity and of artistic creation, where freedom glows with its fullest light, it is never autonomy. For the saint and the artist alike, autocentricity and the self are entirely swallowed up in love.

GABRIEL MARCEL

No Law, apart from a Lawgiver, is a proper object of reverence. It is mere brute fact; and every living thing, still more every person exercising intelligent choice, is its superior. The reverence of persons can be appropriately given only to that which itself is at least personal.

. . . .

Freedom is not absence of determination; it is spiritual determination, as distinct from mechanical or even organic determination. It is determination by what seems good as contrasted with determination by irresistible compulsion.

. . . .

The essential principle of spiritual authority is the evocation by Good of appreciation of itself; for only when this occurs is authority exercised over the spirit.

WILLIAM TEMPLE

Freedom, understood as something positive and joined with creativeness, becomes creative energy. Freedom means not only freedom of choice, but choice itself. Freedom cannot be simply a formal self-defence; it must lead to creative activity. The transition is inevitable from formal liberty, by which each protects and defends himself, to true freedom by means of which human society is creatively transformed. But the transition to true and creative liberty means, first of all, not the rights of the citizen, but of man as a concrete and integral being, a being rooted in the spiritual order.

NICHOLAS BERDYAEV

Christians have drawn false moral conclusions from the doctrine of original sin, have denied man's creative capacity, and given their support to those forms of social order which gave rise to pressure and suffering, because they considered this good for sinful man. One of the worst examples of this deformation of Christian truth we find in relation to the virtue of obedience and humility. How often has this been distorted into humility in the face of evil, obedience to evil itself, a denial of personal conscience! The religion of love and mercy has been transformed into a proclamation of cruel and relentless attitudes towards men. God's very idea of man as His image has been betrayed, as has that of the God-man and Divine-human life.

NICHOLAS BERDYAEV

What then is the meaning of freedom for modern man?

He has become free from the external bonds that would prevent him from doing and thinking as he sees fit. He would be free to act according to his own will, if he knew what he wanted, thought, and felt. But he does not know. He conforms to anonymous authorities and adopts a self which is not his. The more he does this, the more powerless he feels, the more is he forced to conform. . . . Both helplessness and doubt paralyse life, and in order to live, man tries to escape from freedom, negative freedom. He is driven into new bondage. This bondage is different from the primary bonds, from which, though dominated by authorities or the social group, he was not entirely separated. The escape does not restore his lost security, but only helps him to forget his self as a separate entity. He finds new and fragile security at the expense of sacrificing the integrity of his individual self. He chooses to lose his self since he cannot bear to be alone. Thus freedom—as freedom from—leads into new bondage.

Does our analysis lend itself to the conclusion that there is an inevitable circle that leads from freedom into new dependence? Does freedom from all primary ties make the individual so alone and isolated that inevitably he must escape into new bondage? Are *independence* and freedom identical with *isolation* and fear? Or is there a state of positive freedom in which the individual exists as an independent self and yet is not isolated but united with the world, with other men, and nature?

We believe that there is a positive answer, that the process of growing freedom does not constitute a vicious circle, and that man can be free and yet not alone, critical and yet not filled with doubts, independent and yet an integral part of mankind. This freedom man can attain by the realisation of his self, by being himself. What is realisation of the self? Idealistic philosophers have believed that self-realisation can be achieved by intellectual insight alone. They have insisted upon splitting human personality, so that man's nature may be suppressed and guarded by his reason. The result of this split, however, has been that not only the emotional life of man but also his intellectual faculties have been crippled. Reason, by becoming a guard set to watch its prisoner, nature, has become a prisoner itself; and thus both sides of human personality, reason and emotion, were crippled. We believe that the realisation of the self is accomplished not only by an act of thinking but also by the realisation of man's total personality, by the active expression of his emotional and intellectual potentialities. These potentialities are present in everybody; they become real only to the extent to which they are expressed. In other words, *positive freedom consists in the spontaneous activity of the total, integrated personality*. . . .

Spontaneous activity is not compulsive activity, to which the individual is driven by his isolation and powerlessness; it is not the activity of the automaton, which is the uncritical adoption of patterns suggested from the outside. Spontaneous activity is free activity of the self and implies, psychologically, what the Latin root of the word, *sponte*, means literally: of one's free will. By activity we do not mean "doing something," but the quality of creative activity that can operate in one's emotional, intellectual, and sensuous experiences and in one's will as well. One premise for this spontaneity is the acceptance of the total personality and the elimination of the split between "reason" and "nature"; for only if man does not repress essential parts of his self, only if he has become transparent to himself, and only if the different spheres of life have reached a fundamental integration, is spontaneous activity possible. . . .

Small children offer [an] instance of spontaneity. They have an ability to feel and think that which is really *theirs*; this spontaneity shows in what they say and think, in the feelings that are expressed in their faces. If one asks what makes for the attraction small children have for most people I believe that, apart from sentimental and conventional reasons, the answer must be that it is this very quality of spontaneity. . . .

Most of us can observe at least moments of our own spontaneity which are at the same time moments of genuine happiness. Whether it be the fresh and spontaneous perception of a landscape, or the dawning of some truth as the result of our thinking, or a sensuous pleasure that is not stereotyped, or the welling up of love for another person—in these moments we all know what a spontaneous act is and may have some vision of what human life could be if these experiences were not such rare and uncultivated occurrences.

Why is spontaneous activity the answer to the problem of freedom? We have said that negative freedom by itself makes the individual an isolated being, whose relationship to the world is distant and distrustful and whose self is weak and constantly threatened. Spontaneous activity is the one way in which man can overcome the terror of aloneness without sacrificing the integrity of his self; for in the spontaneous realisation of the self man unites himself anew with the world—with man, nature, and himself. Love is the foremost component of such spontaneity; not love as the dissolution of the self in another person, not love as the possession of another person, but love as spontaneous affirmation of others, as the union of the individual with others on the basis of the preservation of the individual self. The dynamic quality of love lies in this very polarity: that it springs from the need of overcoming separateness, that it leads to oneness—and yet that individuality is not eliminated. Work is the other component; not work as a compulsive activity in order to escape aloneness, not work as a relationship to nature which is partly one of dominating her, partly one of worship of and enslavement by the very products of man's hands, but work as creation in which man becomes one with nature in the act of creation. What holds true of love and work holds true of all spontaneous action, whether it be the realisation of sensuous pleasure or participation in the political life of the community. It affirms the individuality of the self and at the same time it unites the self with man and nature. The basic dichotomy that is inherent in freedom—the birth of individuality and the pain of aloneness—is dissolved on a higher plane by man's spontaneous action.

In all spontaneous activity the individual embraces the world. Not only does his individual self remain intact; it becomes stronger and more solidified. *For the self is as strong as it is active.* There is no genuine strength in possession as such, neither of material property nor of mental qualities like emotions or thoughts. There is also no strength in use and manipulation of objects; what we use is not ours simply because we use it. Ours is only that to which we are genuinely related by our creative activity, be it a person or an inanimate object. Only those qualities that result from our spontaneous activity give strength to the self and thereby form the basis of its integrity. . . .

This implies that what matters is the activity as such, the process and not the result. In our culture the emphasis is just the reverse. We produce not for a concrete satisfaction but for the abstract purpose of selling our commodity; we feel that we can acquire everything material or immaterial by buying it, and thus things become ours independently of any creative effort of our own in relation to them. In the same way we regard our personal qualities and the result of our efforts as commodities that can be sold for money, prestige, and power. The emphasis thus shifts from the present satisfaction of creative activity to the value of the finished product. Thereby man misses the only satisfaction that can give him real happiness—the experience of the activity of the present moment—and chases after a phantom that leaves him disappointed as soon as he believes he has caught it—the illusory happiness called success.

If the individual realises his self by spontaneous activity and thus relates himself to the world, he ceases to be an isolated atom; he and the world become part of one structuralised whole; he has his rightful place, and thereby his doubt concerning himself and the meaning of life disappears. This doubt sprang from his separateness and from the thwarting of life; when he can live, neither compulsively nor automatically but spontaneously, the doubt disappears. He is aware of himself as an active and creative individual and recognises that *there is only one meaning of life: the act of living itself*. . . .

Positive freedom as the realisation of the self implies the full affirmation of the uniqueness of the individual. Men are born equal, but they are also born different. The basis of this difference is the inherited equipment, physiological and mental, with which they start life, to which is added the particular constellation of circumstances and experiences that they meet with. This individual basis of the personality is as little identical with any other as two organisms are ever identical physically. The genuine growth of the self is always a growth on this particular basis; it is an organic growth, the unfolding of a nucleus that is peculiar for this one person and only for him. The development of the automaton, in contrast, is not an organic growth. The growth of the basis of the self is blocked and a pseudo self is superimposed upon this self, which is—as we have seen—essentially the incorporation of extraneous patterns of thinking and feeling. Organic growth is possible only under the condition of supreme respect for the peculiarity of the self of other persons as well as of our own self. This respect for and cultivation of the uniqueness of the self is the most valuable achievement of human culture, and it is this very achievement that is in danger to-day.

The uniqueness of the self in no way contradicts the principle of equality. The thesis that men are born equal implies that they all share the same fundamental human qualities, that they share the basic fate of human beings, that they all have the same inalienable claim on freedom and happiness. It furthermore means that their relationship is one of solidarity, not one of domination-submission. What the concept of equality does not mean is that all men are alike. Such a concept of equality is derived from the rôle that the individual plays in his economic activities to-day. In the relation between the man who buys and the one who sells, the concrete differences of personality are eliminated. In this situation only one thing matters, that the one has something to sell and the other has money to buy it. In economic life one man is not different from another; as real persons they are, and the cultivation of their uniqueness is the essence of individuality.

ERICH FROMM

§ 2

FROM "JERUSALEM"

I know of no other Christianity and of no other Gospel than the liberty both of body and mind to exercise the Divine Arts of Imagination. Imagination the real and eternal World of which this Vegetable Universe is but a faint shadow, and in which we shall live in our Eternal or Imaginative Bodies, when these Vegetable Mortal Bodies are no more. The Apostles knew of no other Gospel. What were all their spiritual gifts? What is the Divine Spirit? is the Holy Ghost any other than an Intellectual Fountain? What is the Harvest of the Gospel and its Labours? What is that Talent which it is a curse to hide? What are the Treasures of Heaven which we are to lay up for ourselves? are they any other than Mental Studies and Performances? What are all the Gifts of the Gospel? are they not all Mental Gifts? Is God a Spirit who must be worshipped in Spirit and in Truth? and are not the Gifts of the Spirit Everything to Man? O ye Religious, discountenance every one among you who shall pretend to despise Art and Science! I call upon you in the Name of Jesus! What is the Life of Man but Art and Science? is it Meat and Drink? is not the Body more than Raiment? What is Mortality but the things relating to the Body, which Dies? What is Immortality but the things relating to the

Spirit, which Lives Eternally? What is the Joy of Heaven but Improvement in the things of the Spirit? What are the Pains of Hell but Ignorance, Bodily Lust, Idleness, and devastation of the things of the Spirit? Answer this to yourselves, and expel from among you those who pretend to despise the labours of Art and Science, which alone are the labours of the Gospel. Is not this plain and manifest to the thought? Can you think at all and not pronounce heartily, That to Labour in Knowledge is to Build up Jerusalem; and to Despise Knowledge is to Despise Jerusalem and her Builders. And remember, He who despises and mocks a Mental Gift in another, calling it pride and selfishness and sin, mocks Jesus, the giver of every Mental Gift, which always appear to the ignorance-loving Hypocrite as Sins; but that which is a Sin in the sight of cruel Man, is not so in the sight of our kind God. Let every Christian, as much as in him lies, engage himself openly and publicly before all the World in some Mental pursuit for the Building up of Jerusalem.

I stood among my valleys of the south,
And saw a flame of fire, even as a Wheel
Of fire surrounding all the heavens; it went
From west to east against the current of
Creation, and devour'd all things in its loud
Fury and thundering course round heaven and earth.
By it the Sun was roll'd into an orb,
By it the Moon faded into a globe,
Travelling thro' the night; for from its dire
And restless fury, Man himself shrunk up
Into a little root a fathom long.
And I asked a Watcher and a Holy One
Its Name? He answer'd, It is the Wheel of Religion.
I wept and said: Is this the law of Jesus,
This terrible devouring sword turning every way?
He answer'd: Jesus died because he strove
Against the current of this Wheel; its Name

Is Caiaphas, the dark Preacher of Death,
Of sin, of sorrow, and of punishment;
Opposing Nature, it is Natural Religion.
But Jesus is the bright Preacher of Life,
Creating Nature from this fiery Law
By self-denial and forgiveness of Sin.
Go, therefore, cast out devils in Christ's name,
Heal thou the sick of spiritual disease,
Pity the evil, for thou art not sent
To smite with terror and with punishments
Those that are sick, like to the Pharisees,
Crucifying and encompassing sea and land,
For proselytes to tyranny and wrath.
But to the Publicans and Harlots go,
Teach them True Happiness, but let no curse
Go forth out of thy mouth to blight their peace,
For Hell is open'd to Heaven; thine eyes beheld
The dungeon burst, and the Prisoners set free.

England! awake! awake! awake!
Jerusalem thy Sister calls!
Why wilt thou sleep the sleep of death,
And close her from thy ancient walls?

Thy hills and valleys felt her feet
Gently upon their bosoms move;
Thy gates beheld sweet Zion's ways;
Then was a time of joy and love.

And now the time returns again;
Our souls exult, and London's towers
Receive the Lamb of God to dwell
In England's green and pleasant bowers.

BLAKE

FROM "AN ENEMY OF THE PEOPLE"

FROM ACT IV:

DR. STOCKMANN. . . . I am about to make great revelations, my fellow-citizens! I am going to announce to you a far more important discovery than the trifling fact that our water-works are poisoned, and that our health-resort is built on pestilential ground. . . .

For *this* is the great discovery I made yesterday! (*In a louder tone.*) The most dangerous foe to truth and freedom in our midst is the compact majority. . . .

The majority is never right. Never, I say! That's one of the social lies a free, thinking man is bound to rebel against. Who make up the majority in any given country? Is it the wise men or the fools? I think we must agree that the fools are in a terrible, overwhelming majority, all the wide world over. . . .

I have said that I won't waste a word on the little, narrow-chested, short-winded crew that lie in our wake. Pulsating life has nothing more to do with them. I will rather speak of the few individuals among us who have made all the new, germinating truths their own. These men stand, as it were, at the outposts, so far in the van that the compact majority has not yet reached them—and *there* they fight for truths that are too lately born into the world's consciousness to have won over the majority. . . .

What sort of truths do the majority rally round? Truths that are decrepit with age. When a truth is so old as that it's in a fair way to become a lie, gentlemen. (*Laughter and jeers.*) Yes, yes, you may believe me or not, as you please; but truths are by no means the wiry Methuselahs some people think them. A normally-constituted truth lives—let me say—as a rule, seventeen or eighteen years; at the outside twenty; seldom longer. And truths so stricken in years are always shockingly thin; yet it's not till then that the majority takes them up and recommends them to society as wholesome food. I can assure you there's not much nutriment in that sort of fare; you may take my word as a doctor for that. All these majority-truths are like last year's salt pork; they're like rancid, mouldy ham, producing all the moral scurvy that devastates society. . . .

The truths acknowledged by the masses, the multitude, were certain truths to the vanguard in our grandfathers' days. We, the vanguard of to-day, don't acknowledge them any longer; and I don't believe there's any other certain truth but this—that no society can live a healthy life upon such old, marrowless truths as these. . . .

ASLAKSEN. Both as a citizen of this town and as a man, I am deeply shocked at what I have here had to listen to. Dr. Stockmann has unmasked himself in a manner I should never have dreamt of. I am reluctantly forced to subscribe to the opinion just expressed by some worthy citizens; and I think we ought to formulate this opinion in a resolution. I therefore beg to move, "That this meeting declares the medical officer of the Baths, Dr. Thomas Stockmann, to be an enemy of the people."

FROM THE END OF THE PLAY:

DR. STOCKMANN. . . . Just come here, Katrine; see how bravely the sun shines to-day! And how the blessed fresh spring air blows in upon me!

MRS. STOCKMANN. Yes, if only we could live on sunshine and spring air, Thomas!

DR. STOCKMANN. Well, you'll have to pinch and save where you can—and we'll get on all right. That's my least concern. Now what *does* trouble me is, that I don't see any man with enough independence and nobility of character to dare to take up my work after me.

PETRA. Oh! don't bother about that, father; you have time before you.—Why, see, there are the boys already.

(EILIF *and* MORTEN *enter from the sitting-room.*)

MRS. STOCKMANN. Have you had a holiday to-day?

MORTEN. No; but we had a fight with the other fellows in play-time——

EILIF. That's not true; it was the other fellows that fought us.

MORTEN. Yes, and then Mr. Rörlund said we'd better stop at home for a few days.

DR. STOCKMANN (*snapping his fingers and springing down from the table*). Now I have it, now I have it, on my soul! You shall never set foot in school again!

THE BOYS. Never go to school!

MRS. STOCKMANN. Why, Thomas——

DR. STOCKMANN. Never, I say. I'll teach you myself—that's to say, I won't teach you any blessed thing——

MORTEN. Hurrah!

DR. STOCKMANN. —but I'll try to make free, noble-minded men of you.—Look here, you'll have to help me, Petra.

PETRA. Yes, father, you may be sure I will.

DR. STOCKMANN. And we'll have our school in the room where they reviled me as an enemy of the people. But we must have more pupils. I must have at least twelve boys to begin with.

MRS. STOCKMANN. You'll never get them in this town.

DR. STOCKMANN. We shall see! (*To the boys.*) Don't you know any street urchins—any regular ragamuffins——?

MORTEN. Yes, father, I know lots!

DR. STOCKMANN. That's all right; bring me a few of them. I want to experiment with the street-curs for once; there are sometimes excellent heads among them.

MORTEN. But what are we to do when we've become free and noble-minded men?

DR. STOCKMANN. Drive all the wolves out to the far west, boys.

(EILIF *looks rather doubtful;* MORTEN *jumps about, shouting "Hurrah!"*)

MRS. STOCKMANN. If only the wolves don't drive you out, Thomas.

DR. STOCKMANN. Are you quite mad, Katrine! Drive *me* out! now that I'm the strongest man in the town!

MRS. STOCKMANN. The strongest—now?

DR. STOCKMANN. Yes, I venture to say this: that now I'm one of the strongest men upon earth.

MORTEN. I say, father!

DR. STOCKMANN (*in a subdued voice*). Hush! you mustn't speak about it yet; but I've made a great discovery.

MRS. STOCKMANN. What, again?

DR. STOCKMANN. Yes, certainly. (*Gathers them about him, and speaks confidentially.*) This is what I've discovered, you see: the strongest man upon earth is he who stands most alone.

MRS. STOCKMANN (*shakes her head, smiling*). Ah! Thomas——!

PETRA (*grasping his hands encouragingly*). Father!

IBSEN

FROM "A MODERN SYMPOSIUM"

"May God forgive me," he cried, "that ever I have called myself a socialist, if this is what socialism means! But it does not! I will rescue the word! I will reclaim it for its ancient nobler sense—socialism the dream of the world, the light of the grail on the marsh, the mystic city of Sarras, the vale of Avalon! Socialism the soul of liberty, the bond of brotherhood, the seal of equality! Who is he that with sacrilegious hands would seize our Ariel and prison him in that tree of iniquity the State? Day is not farther from night, nor Good from Evil, than the socialism of the Revolution from this of the desk and the stool, from this enemy wearing our uniform and flaunting our coat of arms. For nigh upon a century we have fought for liberty; and now they would make us gaolers to bind our own souls. 1789, 1830, 1848—are these dates branded upon our hearts, only to stamp us as patient sheep in the flock of bureaucracy? No! They are the symbols of the spirit; and those whom they set apart, outcasts from the kingdoms of this world and citizens of the kingdom of God, wherever they wander are living flames to consume institutions and laws, and to light in the hearts of men the fires of pity and wrath and love. Our city is not built with blue books, nor cemented with office dust; nor is it bonds of red-tape that make and keep it one. No! it is the attraction, uncompelled, of spirits made free; the shadowing into outward form of the eternal joy of the soul!"

He paused and seemed to collect himself; and then in a quieter tone: "Socialism," he proceeded, "is one with anarchy! I know the terrors of that word; but they are the terrors of an evil conscience; for it is only an order founded on iniquity that dreads disorder. Why do you fear for your property and lives, you who fear anarchy? It is because you have stolen the one and misdevoted the other; because you have created by your laws the man you call the criminal; because you have bred hunger, and hunger has bred rage. For this I do not blame you, any more than I blame myself. You are yourselves victims of the system you maintain, and your enemy, no less than mine, if you knew it, is government. For government means compulsion, exclusion, distinction, separation; while anarchy is freedom, union and love. Government is based on egotism and fear, anarchy on fraternity. It is because we divide ourselves into nations that we endure the oppression of armaments; because we isolate ourselves as individuals that we invoke the protection of laws. If I did not take what my brother needs I should not fear that he would take it from me; if I did not shut myself off from his want, I should not deem it less urgent than my own. . . .

"Anarchy is not the absence of order, it is absence of force; it is the free outflowing of the spirit into the forms in which it delights; and in such forms alone, as they grow and change, can it find an expression which is not also a bondage. You will say this is chimerical. But look at history! Consider the great achievements of the Middle Age! Were they not the result of just such a movement as I describe? It was men voluntarily associating in communes and grouping themselves in guilds that built the towers and churches and adorned them with the glories of art that dazzles us still in Italy and France. The history of the growth of the state, of public authority and compulsion, is the history of the decline from Florence and Nuremberg to London and New York. As the power of the state grows the energy of the spirit dwindles; and if ever Allison's ideal should be realised, if ever the activity of the state should extend through and through to every department of life, the universal ease and comfort which may thus be disseminated throughout society will have been purchased dearly at the price of the soul. The denizens of that city will be fed, housed and clothed to perfection; only—and it is a serious drawback—only they will be dead. . . .

"To shatter material bonds that we may bind the closer the bonds of the soul, to slough dead husks that we may liberate living forms, to abolish institutions that we may evoke energies, to put off the material and put on the spiritual body, that, whether we fight with the tongue or the sword, is the inspiration of our movement, that, and that only, is the true and inner meaning of anarchy. . . .

"There are anarchists who never made a speech and never carried a rifle, whom we know as our brothers, though perhaps they know not us. Two I will name who live for ever, Shelley, the first of poets, were it not that there is one yet greater than he, the mystic William Blake. We are thought of as men of blood; we are hounded over the face of the globe. And who of our persecutors would believe that the song we bear in our hearts, some of us, I may speak at least for one, is the most inspired, the most spiritual challenge ever flung to your obtuse, flatulent, stertorous England:

'Bring me my bow of burning gold,
Bring me my arrows of desire,
Bring me my spear; O clouds unfold!
Bring me my chariot of fire!

'I will not cease from mental fight,
Nor shall my sword sleep in my hand,
Till I have built Jerusalem
In England's green and pleasant land.'

"England! No, not England, but Europe, America, the world! Where is Man, the new Man, there is our country. But the new Man is buried in the old; and wherever he struggles in his tomb, wherever he knocks we are there to help to deliver him. When the guards sleep, in the silence of the dawn, rises the crucified Christ. And the angel that sits at the grave is the angel of Anarchy."

G. LOWES DICKINSON

FROM "PROMETHEUS UNBOUND," ACT III

SCENE I.—*Heaven.* JUPITER *on his Throne;* THETIS *and the other Deities assembled.*

JUPITER. Ye congregated powers of heaven, who share
The glory and the strength of him ye serve,
Rejoice! henceforth I am omnipotent.
All else had been subdued to me; alone
The soul of man, like unextinguished fire,
Yet burns towards heaven with fierce reproach, and doubt,
And lamentation, and reluctant prayer,
Hurling up insurrection, which might make
Our antique empire insecure, though built
On eldest faith, and hell's coeval, fear;
And though my curses through the pendulous air,
Like snow on herbless peaks, fall flake by flake,
And cling to it; though under my wrath's night
It climbs the crags of life, step after step,
Which wound it, as ice wounds unsandalled feet,
It yet remains supreme o'er misery,

Aspiring, unrepressed, yet soon to fall:
Even now have I begotten a strange wonder,
That fatal child, the terror of the earth,
Who waits but till the destined hour arrive,
Bearing from Demogorgon's vacant throne
The dreadful might of ever-living limbs
Which clothed that awful spirit unbeheld,
To redescend, and trample out the spark.
Pour forth heaven's wine, Idæan Ganymede,
And let it fill the Dædal cups like fire,
And from the flower-inwoven soil divine
Ye all-triumphant harmonies arise,
As dew from earth under the twilight stars:
Drink! be the nectar circling through your veins
The soul of joy, ye ever-living Gods,
Till exultation burst in one wide voice
Like music from Elysian winds.
                                        And thou
Ascend beside me, veiled in the light
Of the desire which makes thee one with me,
Thetis, bright image of eternity!
When thou didst cry, "Insufferable might!
God! Spare me! I sustain not the quick flames,
The penetrating presence; all my being,
Like him whom the Numidian seps did thaw
Into a dew with poison, is dissolved,
Sinking through its foundations": even then
Two mighty spirits, mingling, made a third
Mightier than either, which, unbodied now,
Between us floats, felt, although unbeheld,
Waiting the incarnation, which ascends,
(Hear ye the thunder of the fiery wheels
Griding the winds?) from Demogorgon's throne.
Victory! victory! Feel'st thou not, O world,
The earthquake of his chariot thundering up
Olympus?

[*The Car of the* HOUR *arrives.* DEMOGORGON *descends, and moves towards the Throne of* JUPITER

Awful shape, what art thou? Speak!

DEMOGORGON. Eternity. Demand no direr name.
Descend, and follow me down the abyss.
I am thy child, as thou wert Saturn's child;
Mightier than thee: and we must dwell together
Henceforth in darkness. Lift thy lightnings not.
The tyranny of heaven none may retain,
Or reassume, or hold, succeeding thee:
Yet if thou wilt, as 'tis the destiny
Of trodden worms to writhe till they are dead,
Put forth thy might.

JUPITER. Detested prodigy!
Even thus beneath the deep Titanian prisons
I trample thee! thou lingerest?

Mercy! mercy!

No pity, no release, no respite! Oh,
That thou wouldst make mine enemy my judge,
Even where he hangs, seared by my long revenge,
On Caucasus! he would not doom me thus.
Gentle, and just, and dreadless, is he not
The monarch of the world? What then art thou?
No refuge! no appeal!

Sink with me then,

We two will sink on the wide waves of ruin,
Even as a vulture and a snake outspent
Drop, twisted in inextricable fight,
Into a shoreless sea. Let hell unlock
Its mounded oceans of tempestuous fire,
And whelm on them into the bottomless void
This desolated world, and thee, and me,
The conqueror and the conquered, and the wreck
Of that for which they combated.

Ai! Ai!

The elements obey me not. I sink
Dizzily down, ever, for ever, down.
And, like a cloud, mine enemy above
Darkens my fall with victory! Ai, Ai!

SCENE IV.—*A Forest. In the Background a Cave.* PROMETHEUS, ASIA, PANTHEA, IONE, *and the* SPIRIT OF THE EARTH
. . [*The* SPIRIT OF THE HOUR *enters.*

PROMETHEUS. We feel what thou hast heard and seen: yet speak.

SPIRIT OF THE HOUR. Soon as the sound had ceased whose thunder filled
The abysses of the sky and the wide earth,
There was a change: the impalpable thin air
And the all-circling sunlight were transformed,
As if the sense of love dissolved in them
Had folded itself round the spherèd world.
My vision then grew clear, and I could see
Into the mysteries of the universe:
Dizzy as with delight I floated down,
Winnowing the lightsome air with languid plumes,
My coursers sought their birthplace in the sun,
Where they henceforth will live exempt from toil,
Pasturing flowers of vegetable fire;
And where my moonlike car will stand within
A temple, gazed upon by Phidian forms
Of thee, and Asia, and the Earth, and me,
And you fair nymphs looking the love we feel,—
In memory of the tidings it has borne,—
Beneath a dome fretted with graven flowers,
Poised on twelve columns of resplendent stone,
And open to the bright and liquid sky.
Yoked to it by an amphisbænic snake
The likeness of those wingèd steeds will mock
The flight from which they find repose. Alas,

Whither has wandered now my partial tongue
When all remains untold which ye would hear?
As I have said, I floated to the earth:
It was, as it is still, the pain of bliss
To move, to breathe, to be; I wandering went
Among the haunts and dwellings of mankind,
And first was disappointed not to see
Such mighty change as I had felt within
Expressed in outward things; but soon I looked,
And behold, thrones were kingless, and men walked
One with the other even as spirits do,
None fawned, none trampled; hate, disdain, or fear,
Self-love or self-contempt, on human brows
No more inscribed, as o'er the gate of hell,
"All hope abandon ye who enter here";
None frowned, none trembled, none with eager fear
Gazed on another's eye of cold command,
Until the subject of a tyrant's will
Became, worse fate, the abject of his own,
Which spurred him, like an outspent horse, to death.
None wrought his lips in truth-entangling lines
Which smiled the lie his tongue disdained to speak;
None, with firm sneer, trod out in his own heart
The sparks of love and hope till there remained
Those bitter ashes, a soul self-consumed,
And the wretch crept a vampire among men,
Infecting all with his own hideous ill;
None talked that common, false, cold, hollow talk
Which makes the heart deny the *yes* it breathes,
Yet question that unmeant hypocrisy
With such a self-mistrust as has no name.
And women, too, frank, beautiful, and kind
As the free heaven which rains fresh light and dew
On the wide earth, past; gentle radiant forms,
From custom's evil taint exempt and pure;
Speaking the wisdom once they could not think,

Looking emotions once they feared to feel,
And changed to all which once they dared not be,
Yet being now, made earth like heaven; nor pride,
Nor jealousy, nor envy, nor ill shame,
The bitterest of those drops of treasured gall,
Spoilt the sweet taste of the nepenthe, love.

Thrones, altars, judgement-seats, and prisons; wherein,
And beside which, by wretched men were borne
Sceptres, tiaras, swords, and chains, and tomes
Of reasoned wrong, glozed on by ignorance,
Were like those monstrous and barbaric shapes,
The ghosts of a no-more-remembered fame,
Which, from their unworn obelisks, look forth
In triumph o'er the palaces and tombs
Of those who were their conquerors: mouldering round,
These imaged to the pride of kings and priests
A dark yet mighty faith, a power as wide
As is the world it wasted, and are now
But an astonishment; even so the tools
And emblems of its last captivity,
Amid the dwellings of the peopled earth,
Stand, not o'erthrown, but unregarded now.
And those foul shapes, abhorred by god and man,—
Which, under many a name and many a form
Strange, savage, ghastly, dark and execrable,
Were Jupiter, the tyrant of the world;
And which the nations, panic-stricken, served
With blood, and hearts broken by long hope, and love
Dragged to his altars soiled and garlandless,
And slain amid men's unreclaiming tears,
Flattering the thing they feared, which fear was hate,—
Frown, mouldering fast, o'er their abandoned shrines:
The painted veil, by those who were, called life,
Which mimicked, as with colours idly spread,
All men believed or hoped, is torn aside;

The loathsome mask has fallen, the man remains
Sceptreless, free, uncircumscribed, but man
Equal, unclassed, tribeless, and nationless,
Exempt from awe, worship, degree, the king
Over himself; just, gentle, wise: but man
Passionless?—no, yet free from guilt or pain,
Which were, for his will made or suffered them,
Nor yet exempt, though ruling them like slaves,
From chance, and death, and mutability,
The clogs of that which else might oversoar
The loftiest star of unascended heaven,
Pinnacled dim in the intense inane.

SHELLEY

§ 3

FREEDOM

God speaks:

When you love someone, you love him as he is.
I alone am perfect.
It is probably for that reason
That I know what perfection is
And that I demand less perfection of those poor people.
I know how difficult it is.
And how often, when they are struggling in their trials,
How often do I wish and am I tempted to put my hand under
  their stomachs
In order to hold them up with my big hand
Just like a father teaching his son how to swim
In the current of the river
And who is divided between two ways of thinking.
For on the one hand, if he holds him up all the time and if he
  holds him up too much,
The child will depend on this and will never learn how to swim.

But if he doesn't hold him up just at the right moment
That child is bound to swallow more water than is healthy for him.
In the same way, when I teach them how to swim amid their trials
I too am divided by two ways of thinking.
Because if I am always holding them up, if I hold them up too often,
They will never learn how to swim by themselves.
But if I don't hold them up just at the right moment,
Perhaps those poor children will swallow more water than is healthy for them.
Such is the difficulty, and it is a great one.
And such is the doubleness itself, the two faces of the problem.
On the one hand, they must work out their salvation for themselves. That is the rule.
It allows of no exception. Otherwise it would not be interesting. They would not be men.
Now I want them to be manly, to be men, and to win by themselves
Their spurs of knighthood.
On the other hand, they must not swallow more water than is healthy for them,
Having made a dive into the ingratitude of sin.
Such is the mystery of man's freedom, says God,
And the mystery of my government towards him and towards his freedom.
If I hold him up too much, he is no longer free
And if I don't hold him up sufficiently, I am endangering his salvation.
Two goods in a sense almost equally precious.
For salvation is of infinite price.
But what kind of salvation would a salvation be that was not free?
What would you call it?
We want that salvation to be acquired by himself,
Himself, man. To be procured by himself.

To come, in a sense, from himself. Such is the secret,
Such is the mystery of man's freedom.
Such is the price we set on man's freedom.
Because I myself am free, says God, and I have created man in my own image and likeness.
Such is the mystery, such the secret, such the price
Of all freedom.
That freedom of that creature is the most beautiful reflection in this world
Of the Creator's freedom. That is why we are so attached to it,
And set a proper price on it.
A salvation that was not free, that was not, that did not come from a free man could in no wise be attractive to us. What would it amount to?
What would it mean?
What interest would such a salvation have to offer?
A beatitude of slaves, a salvation of slaves, a slavish beatitude, how do you expect me to be interested in that kind of thing? Does one care to be loved by slaves?
If it were only a matter of proving my might, my might has no need of those slaves, my might is well enough known, it is sufficiently known that I am the Almighty.
My might is manifest enough in all matter and in all events.
My might is manifest enough in the sands of the sea and in the stars of heaven.
It is not questioned, it is known, it is manifest enough in inanimate creation.
It is manifest enough in the government,
In the very event that is man.
But in my creation which is endued with life, says God, I wanted something better, I wanted something more.
Infinitely better. Infinitely more. For I wanted that freedom.
I created that very freedom. There are several degrees to my throne.
When you once have known what it is to be loved freely, submission no longer has any taste.

All the prostrations in the world
Are not worth the beautiful upright attitude of a free man as
he kneels. All the submission, all the dejection in the world
Are not equal in value to the soaring up point,
The beautiful straight soaring up of one single invocation
From a love that is free.

CHARLES PÉGUY

My freedom to do within certain limits what I have resolved to do is an immediate experience. Whether or not to call on a friend to-night, that is something I have to think about precisely because I am free to do it or not to do it. I can be expected to obey traffic regulations because it is known that I can follow them if I want to. Throughout our thinking everywhere there are ideas that make sense only with reference to such freedom. It is the logical basis for the imperative mood in thought and speech. Demands can be made only on a will known to be free. In contrasting subject and object, we ascribe to the object not freedom but, at best, only some unpredictable behaviour, while the freedom to inquire and manipulate at will belongs logically among the defining characteristics of the subject endowed with understanding. The very concept of the law of nature requires that he who conducts the experiment be free to repeat at will the original conditions.

The subject itself, however, is often considered a special object that is merely one of the links in a chain of causation. If this is the case, then freedom of will is really only the freedom to do what I have decided to do. But it remains open why I decide to do this rather than that. Those who believe that every event is causally determined will then assume that my decision, too, has been determined by some cause, although the cause remains unknown to me. Thus, my will would "in reality" be unfree.

I do not know whether this theory is correct. I merely want to emphasise that it is a theory and not a matter of experience.

It represents a challenge for future empirical research. Let the determining factors of our actions be brought to light, and we shall believe in them. But the freedom which makes the subject what it is, that freedom is a matter of experience. I do not think that the admission of freedom as a matter of experience is in itself enough to refute determinism. For it has no reply to the assertion that the determining factors are merely unknown to us. But conversely, the revelation of some such unknown motives would not invalidate the admission in the sense in which it is intended. No science of psychology can take from me the burden of the decisions I must make in life. As long as the uncertainty of the future is not in fact removed, a being who says "I" must make his choices, whether he believes them to be predetermined or not.

There is an objective counterpart to this subjective experience of freedom, which can likewise be considered without reference to the theory of determinism. That is the freedom from the compulsion of instinct. The completely instinctive action is predetermined. If we subject an animal to a certain stimulus we can predict its reaction. We experience within ourselves the lack of freedom at those moments when we are at the mercy of our instincts. But rational action is free. Even in the case of an animal acting rationally, we are unable to predict which of several alternatives it will choose. For here a choice is made within the individual, and no heredity nor tradition relieves it of that choice. If there are any determining motives, they are at any rate essentially unknown at the moment the choice is made. It seems to me that all theories of indeterminism are based on this subjective experience of these objective facts.

Thus the idea of subjective freedom is threatened not by the theories of determinism, but rather by our own immediate experience of the absence of freedom, an experience we have, for instance, when we are acting under the compulsion of instinct. The most important experiences of this sort are made in the sphere of religion. I experience that I cannot do good even if I want to. I experience that if I do good, I do not do so out of my own power—I undergo it as an act of grace. These are the realities that lead beyond the idea of freedom. But they cannot be put into words unless the idea of freedom has first been presupposed.

C. F. VON WEIZSÄCKER

§ 4

The real slavery of Israel in Egypt was that they had learned to endure it.

RABBI HANOKH OF ALEXANDER

FIFTH PART

I. THE SELF

Adagio, ma non troppo e molto cantabile
pp
cresc:
p
tr

§ 1

For this commandment which I command thee this day, it is not hidden from thee, neither is it far off.

It is not in heaven, that thou shouldest say, Who shall go up for us to heaven, and bring it unto us, that we may hear it, and do it?

Neither is it beyond the sea, that thou shouldest say, Who shall go over the sea for us, and bring it unto us, that we may hear it, and do it?

But the word is very nigh unto thee, in thy mouth, and in thy heart, that thou mayest do it.

DEUTERONOMY

Behold, the days come, saith the Lord, that I will make a new covenant with the house of Israel, and with the house of Judah:

Not according to the covenant that I made with their fathers in the day that I took them by the hand to bring them out of the land of Egypt; which my covenant they brake, although I was an husband unto them, saith the Lord:

But this shall be the covenant that I will make with the house of Israel; After those days, saith the Lord, I will put my law in their inward parts, and write it in their hearts; and will be their God, and they shall be my people.

JEREMIAH

And when he was demanded of the Pharisees, when the kingdom of God should come, he answered them and said, The kingdom of God cometh not with observation:

Neither shall they say, Lo here! or, lo there! for, behold, the kingdom of God is within you.

ST. LUKE

We therefore conclude, finally, that, in order to make himself known to men, God can and need use neither words, nor miracles, not any other created thing, but only Himself.

SPINOZA

The World was more in me, then I in it.
The King of Glory in my Soul did sit.
And to Himself in me he always gave,
All that he takes Delight to see me have.
For so my Spirit was an Endless Sphere,
Like God himself, and Heaven and Earth was there.

THOMAS TRAHERNE (from *Silence*)

For heaven ghostly is as near down as up, and up as down, behind as before, before as behind, on one side as on other. Insomuch, that whoso had a true desire for to be at heaven, then that same time he were in heaven ghostly. For the high and the nearest way thither is run by desires, and not by paces of feet. And therefore saith Saint Paul of himself and many others thus: *Although our bodies be presently here on earth, nevertheless our living is in heaven.* He meant their love and their desire, the which ghostly is their life. And surely as verily is a soul there where it loveth, as in the body that liveth by it and to the which it giveth life. And therefore if we will go to heaven ghostly, we need not to strain our spirit neither up nor down, nor on one side nor on other.

THE CLOUD OF UNKNOWING

Comfort thee, comfort thee. Thy Father knows
  How wild man's ardent spirit, fainting, yearns
For mortal glimpse of death's immortal rose,
  The garden where the invisible blossom burns.
Humble thy trembling knees; confess thy pride;
  Be weary. Oh, whithersoever thy vaunting rove,
His deepest wisdom harbours in thy side,
  In thine own bosom hides His utmost love.

WALTER DE LA MARE
(from *The Imagination's Pride*)

Begin to search and dig in thine own field for this pearl of eternity that lies hidden in it; it cannot cost thee too much, nor canst thou buy it too dear, for it is *all*; and when thou hast found it thou wilt know that all which thou hast sold or given away for it is as mere a nothing as a bubble upon the water.

WILLIAM LAW

We are potentially all things; our personality is what we are able to realise of the infinite wealth which our divine-human nature contains hidden in its depths.

W. R. INGE (interpreting Plotinus)

Be ye lamps unto yourselves.
Be your own reliance.
Hold to the truth within yourselves
as to the only lamp.

THE BUDDHA

Folly, to drink from puddles by the way
When here at home the crystal fountains play!

ANGELUS SILESIUS

A young Rabbi complained to his Master: "During the hours when I am studying I feel filled with light and life, but as soon as I cease to study this mood disappears. What ought I do?"

Thereupon the Rabbi replied: "It is like a man who journeys through a forest on a dark night, and part of the way is accompanied by a companion who carries a lantern. At length they come to the point where their paths divide, and they must go on alone. If each carries his own lantern, he need fear no darkness."

HASIDIC STORY

I wish there be not among some such a light and poor esteem of *Heaven*, as makes them more to seek after *Assurance of Heaven* onely in the *Idea* of it as *a thing to come*, then after *Heaven it self*; which indeed we can never well be assured of, untill we find it rising up within our selves and glorifying our own Souls. When true *Assurance* comes, *Heaven* it self will appear upon the Horizon of our Souls, like a morning light chafing away all our dark and gloomy doubtings before it. We shall not need then to light up our Candles to seek for it in corners; no, it will display its own lustre and brightness so before us, that we may see it in its own light, and our selves the true possessours of it. We may be too nice and vain in seeking for *signes and tokens* of Christ's *Spiritual appearances* in the Souls of men, as well as the scribes and Pharisees were in seeking for them at his *First appearance* in the World. When he comes into us, let us expect till the works that he shall doe within us may testify of him; and be not over-credulous, till we find that he doth those works there which none other could doe. As for a true well-grounded *Assurance*, say not so much, *Who shall ascend up into heaven*, to fetch it down from thence? or *who shall descend into the deep*, to fetch it up from beneath? for in *the Growth* of true internal Goodness and in *the Progress* of true Religion it will freely unfold it self within us. Stay till the grain of Mustard-seed it self breaks forth from among the clods that buried it, till through the descent of the heavenly dew it sprouts up and discovers it self openly. This holy *Assurance* is indeed the budding and blossoming of Felicity in our own Souls; it is the inward sense and feeling of the true life, spirit, sweetness and beauty of Grace powerfully expressing its own Energy within us.

JOHN SMITH

Again, "Thou shalt love the Lord thy God with all thy heart, with all thy soul, and with all thy strength, and thy neighbour as thyself." Now these two precepts given by the written word of God are an absolute demonstration of the first original perfection of man, and also a full and invincible proof that the same original perfection is not quite annihilated, but lies in him as an hidden, suppressed seed of goodness capable of being raised up to its first perfection. For had not this divine unity, purity, and perfection of love towards God and man been man's first natural state of life, it could have nothing to do with his present state. For had any other nature or measure or kind of love begun in the first birth of his life, he could only have been called to that. For no creature has or can have a call to be above or act above its own nature. Therefore, as sure as man is called to this unity, purity, and perfection of love, so sure is it that it was at first his natural heavenly state and still has its seed or remains within him, as his only power and possibility of rising up to it again. And therefore all that man is called to, every degree of a new and perfect life, every future exaltation and glory he is to have from the mediation of Christ, is a full proof that the same perfection was originally his natural state and is still in him in such a seed or remains of existence as to admit of a perfect renewal.

And thus it is that you are to conceive of the holy Jesus or the Word of God as the hidden treasure of every human soul, born as a seed of the Word in the birth of the soul, immured under flesh and blood till as a day-star it arises in our hearts and changes the son of an earthly Adam into a son of God. And was not the Word and Spirit of God in us all, antecedent to any dispensation or written word of God, as a real seed of life in the birth of our own life, we could have no more fitness for the gospel-redemption than the animals of this world which have nothing of Heaven in them. And to call us to love God with all our hearts, to put on Christ, to walk according to the Spirit, if these things had not their real nature and root within us, would be as vain and useless as to make rules and orders how our eyes should smell and taste or our ears should see.

Now this mystery of an inward life hidden in man as his most precious treasure, as the ground of all that can be great or good in him, and hidden only since his fall, and which only can be opened and brought forth in its first glory by Him to whom all power in Heaven and on earth is given, is a truth to which almost every thing in nature bears full witness. Look where you will, nothing appears or works outwardly in any creature or in any effect of nature, but what is all done from its own inward invisible spirit, not a spirit brought into it but its own inward spirit, which is an inward invisible mystery, till made known or brought forth by outward appearances. . . .

What a miserable mistake is it therefore to place religious goodness in outward observances, in notions and opinions which good and bad men can equally receive and practise, and to treat the ready, real power and operation of an inward life of God in the birth of our souls as fanaticism and enthusiasm! when not only the whole letter and spirit of Scripture but every operation in nature and creature demonstrates that the Kingdom of Heaven must be all within us, or it never can possibly belong to us. Goodness, piety, and holiness can only be ours as thinking, willing, and desiring are ours, by being in us as a power of Heaven in the birth and growth of our own life.

WILLIAM LAW

MY SPIRIT

I

My Naked Simple Life was I.
That Act so Strongly Shind
Upon the Earth, the Sea, the Skie,
It was the Substance of My Mind.
The Sence it self was I.
I felt no Dross nor Matter in my Soul,
No Brims nor Borders, such as in a Bowl
We see, My Essence was Capacitie.
That felt all Things,
The Thought that Springs

Therfrom's it self. It hath no other Wings
To Spread abroad, nor Eys to see,
Nor Hands Distinct to feel,
Nor Knees to Kneel:
But being Simple like the Deitie
In its own Centre is a Sphere
Not shut up here, but evry Where.

2

It Acts not from a Centre to
Its Object as remote,
But present is, when it doth view,
Being with the Being it doth note.
Whatever it doth do,
It doth not by another Engine work,
But by it self; which in the Act doth lurk.
Its Essence is Transformed into a true
And perfect Act.
And so Exact
Hath God appeard in this Mysterious Fact,
That tis all Ey, all Act, all Sight,
And what it pleas can be,
Not only see,
Or do; for tis more Voluble then Light:
Which can put on ten thousand Forms,
Being clothd with what it self adorns.

3

This made me present evermore
With whatsoere I saw.
An Object, if it were before
My Ey, was by Dame Natures Law,
Within my Soul. Her Store
Was all at once within me; all her Treasures
Were my Immediat and Internal Pleasures,
Substantial Joys, which did inform my Mind.

With all she wrought,
My Soul was fraught,
And evry Object in my Heart a Thought
Begot, or was; I could not tell,
Whether the Things did there
Themselvs appear,
Which in my Spirit *truly* seemd to dwell;
Or whether my conforming Mind
Were not even all that therin shind.

4

But yet of this I was most sure,
That at the utmost Length,
(So Worthy was it to endure)
My Soul could best Express its Strength.
It was so Quick and Pure,
That all my Mind was wholy Every where
What ere it saw, twas ever wholy there;
The Sun ten thousand Legions off, was nigh:
The utmost Star,
Tho seen from far,
Was present in the Apple of my Eye.
There was my Sight, my Life, my Sence,
My Substance and my Mind
My Spirit Shind
Even there, not by a Transeunt Influence.
The Act was Immanent, yet there.
The Thing remote, yet felt even here.

5

O Joy! O Wonder, and Delight!
O Sacred Mysterie!
My Soul a Spirit infinit!
An Image of the Deitie!
A pure Substantiall Light!
That Being Greatest which doth Nothing seem!
Why twas my All, I nothing did esteem

But that alone. A Strange Mysterious Sphere!
A Deep Abyss
That sees and is
The only Proper Place of Heavenly Bliss.
To its Creator tis so near
In Lov and Excellence
In Life and Sence,
In Greatness Worth and Nature; And so Dear;
In it, without Hyperbole,
The Son and friend of God we see.

6

A Strange Extended Orb of Joy,
Proceeding from within,
Which did on evry side convey
It self, and being nigh of Kin
To God did evry Way
Dilate it self even in an Instant, and
Like an Indivisible Centre Stand
At once Surrounding all Eternitie.
Twas not a Sphere
Yet did appear
One infinit. Twas somwhat evry where.
And tho it had a Power to see
Far more, yet still it shind
And was a Mind
Exerted for it saw Infinitie
Twas not a Sphere, but twas a Might
Invisible, and gave Light.

7

O Wondrous Self! O Sphere of Light,
O Sphere of Joy most fair;
O Act, O Power infinit;
O Subtile, and unbounded Air!

O Living Orb of Sight!
Thou which within me art, yet Me! Thou Ey,
And Temple of his Whole Infinitie!
O what a World art Thou! a World within!
All Things appear,
All Objects are
Alive in thee! Supersubstancial, Rare,
Abov them selvs, and nigh of Kin
To those pure Things we find
In his Great Mind
Who made the World! tho now Ecclypsed by Sin.
There they are Usefull and Divine,
Exalted there they ought to Shine.

THOMAS TRAHERNE

§ 2

Become what thou art!

ORPHIC SAYING

It is the chiefest of Good Things for a Man to be *Himself*.

BENJAMIN WHICHCOTE

In the coming world they will not ask me: "Why were you not Moses?" They will ask me: "Why were you not Zusya?"

RABBI ZUSYA OF HANIPOL

Things cannot get out of their natures, or be or not be in despite of their constitutions. Rational existences in Heaven perish not at all, and but partially on Earth: that which is thus once will in some way be always: the first Living human Soul is still alive, and all Adam hath found no Period.

SIR THOMAS BROWNE

Now you shall hear how a man may become perfect, if he devotes himself to the work which is natural to him. A man will reach perfection if he does his duty as an act of worship to the Lord, who is the source of the universe, prompting all action, everywhere present.

A man's own natural duty, even if it seems imperfectly done, is better than work not naturally his own, even if this is well performed. When a man acts according to the law of his nature, he cannot be sinning. Therefore, no one should give up his natural work, even though he does it imperfectly. For all action is involved in imperfection, like fire in smoke.

THE BHAGAVAD-GITA

The apple tree never asks the beech how he shall grow; nor the lion, the horse, how he shall take his prey.

BLAKE (from *The Marriage of Heaven and Hell*)

It blooms because it blooms, the pretty rose:
Why, or who looks, it neither asks nor knows.

ANGELUS SILESIUS

Every man's leading propensity ought to be call'd his leading Virtue and his good Angel.

BLAKE (from comments on Lavater's *Aphorisms*)

If the fool could persist in his folly he would become wise.

BLAKE (from *The Marriage of Heaven and Hell*)

No bird soars too high, if he soars with his own wings.

BLAKE (from *The Marriage of Heaven and Hell*)

Even a slug is a star, if it dares to be its horned and slimy self.

JOHN HARGRAVE

The verse "From every man, whose heart stirs him, you shall take my offering" the Baalshem interpreted thus: It is by that which he longs for, that every man knows and apprehends the quality with which he has to serve God.

MARTIN BUBER

Every complexion of the inward man, when sanctified by humility, and suffering itself to be tuned and struck and moved by the Holy Spirit of God, according to its particular frame and turn, helps mightily to increase that harmony of divine praise, thanksgiving and adoration which must arise from different instruments, sounds and voices. To condemn this variety in the servants of God or to be angry at those who have not served Him in the way that we have chosen for ourselves is but too plain a sign that we have not enough renounced the elements of selfishness, pride and anger.

WILLIAM LAW

When I thus rest in the silence of contemplation, Thou, Lord, makest reply within my heart, saying: Be thou thine and I too will be thine. . . . Thou, Lord, canst not be mine if I be not mine own.

NICHOLAS OF CUSA

As kingfishers catch fire, dragonflies dráw fláme;
As tumbled over rim in roundy wells
Stones ring; like each tucked[1] string tells, each hung bell's
Bow swung finds tongue to fling out broad its name;
Each mortal thing does one thing and the same:
Deals out that being indoors each one dwells;
Selves[2]—goes itself; *myself* it speaks and spells;
Crying *Whát I dó is me: for that I came.*

[1] Plucked. [2] Fulfils its own individuality.

Í say móre: the just man justices;
Kéeps gráce: thát keeps all his goings graces;
Acts in God's eye what in God's eye he is—
Chríst—for Christ plays in ten thousand places,
Lovely in limbs, and lovely in eyes not his
To the Father through the features of men's faces.

GERARD MANLEY HOPKINS

§ 3

When Prince Mou of Wei was living as a hermit in Chung-shan, he said to the Taoist Chan Tzu, "My body is here amid lakes and streams; but my heart is in the palace of Wei. What am I to do?" "Care more for what you have in yourself," said Chan Tzu, "and less for what you can get from others." "I know I ought to," said the prince, "but I cannot get the better of my feelings." "If you cannot get the better of your feelings," replied Chan Tzu, "then give play to them. Nothing is worse for the soul than struggling not to give play to feelings that it cannot control. This is called the Double Injury, and of those that sustain it none live out their natural span."

CHUANG TZU

Nature will force her way, and if you try to stifle her by drowning, she comes up, not the fairest part of her uppermost.

GEORGE MEREDITH (from *Diana of the Crossways*)

Sooner murder an infant in its cradle than nurse unacted desires.

BLAKE (from *The Marriage of Heaven and Hell*)

Abstinence sows sand all over
The ruddy limbs and flaming hair;
But desire gratified
Plants fruits of life and beauty there.

BLAKE

All Bibles or sacred codes have been the causes of the following Errors:—

1. That Man has two real existing principles, viz. a Body and a Soul.

2. That Energy, called Evil, is alone from the Body; and that Reason, called Good, is alone from the Soul.

3. That God will torment Man in Eternity for following his Energies.

But the following Contraries to these are True:—

1. Man has no Body distinct from his Soul, for that called Body is a portion of Soul discerned by the five Senses, the chief inlets of Soul in this age.

2. Energy is the only life and is from the Body, and Reason is the bound or outward circumference of Energy.

3. Energy is Eternal Delight.

BLAKE (from *The Marriage of Heaven and Hell*)

Body and soul are not two substances but one. They are man becoming aware of himself in two different ways.

C. F. VON WEIZSÄCKER

Soul is in head and limbs and body whole:
Why then, be certain body is in soul!

ANGELUS SILESIUS

One shall not kill "the evil impulse," the passion, in oneself, but one shall serve God *with it*; it is the power which is destined to receive its direction from man.

MARTIN BUBER (interpreting Hasidism)

Blake, when he condemns abstinence, and Aldous Huxley, when he recommends inhibition [in the next extract], are emphasising different aspects of one truth.

X

There can be no non-attachment without inhibition. When the state of non-attachment has become "a second nature," inhibition will doubtless no longer be necessary; for impulses requiring inhibition will not arise. Those in whom non-attachment is a permanent state are few. For everyone else, such impulses requiring inhibition arise with a distressing frequency. The technique of inhibition needs to be learnt on all the planes of our being. On the intellectual plane—for we cannot hope to think intelligently or to practise the simplest form of "recollection" unless we learn to inhibit irrelevant thoughts. On the emotional plane—for we shall never reach even the lowest degree of non-attachment unless we can check as they arise the constant movements of malice and vanity, of lust and sloth, of avarice, anger and fear. On the physical plane—for if we are maladjusted (as most of us are in the circumstances of modern urban life), we cannot expect to achieve integration unless we inhibit our tendency to perform actions in the, to us, familiar, maladjusted way. Mind and body are organically one; and it is therefore inherently likely that, if we can learn the art of conscious inhibition on the physical level, it will help us to acquire and practise the same art on the emotional and intellectual levels. What is needed is a practical morality working at every level from the bodily to the intellectual.

ALDOUS HUXLEY

But this detachment (poverty, chastity, etc.) must not be mere amputation; everything which is shaken off must be simultaneously found again at a higher level.

GABRIEL MARCEL

[Too often in Christianity] asceticism was considered as an end, rather than a means, and so came to be anti-human, opposed to fullness of life and creativity.

NICHOLAS BERDYAEV

God wishes not to deprive us of pleasure; but He wishes to give us pleasure in its totality; that is to say, all pleasure. . . . What greater pleasure is there than to find myself the one thing that I ought to be, and the whole thing that I ought to be? . . .

There is nothing pleasurable save what is uniform with the most inmost depths of the divine nature.

HENRY SUSO

§ 4

Freedom is to be in possession of oneself.

HEGEL

Anything is free when it spontaneously expresses its own nature to the full in activity.

JOHN MACMURRAY

Thus freedom in general is the experience which each thing has of the working of its own nature; and a distinction parallel to ours of freedom and unfreedom exists for the plant and for the stone or the atom. The plant undergoes the wind which bends it, or the air which sets its respiration at work. But it enjoys its own free act of respiration. The stone is passive to the freezing water that splits it, but free in its resilience to deformation.

SAMUEL ALEXANDER

In our present form of human consciousness the true self of any individual man is not a datum, but an ideal.

JOSIAH ROYCE

That which it is the task of the person to create, is not a work in some way external to himself and capable of taking on an independent existence; in reality it is himself. . . . He realises himself not so much as a being [but rather] as a will to surpass the totality that he is and is not, an actuality in which he indeed feels himself "engaged," or implicated, but which does not satisfy him: which bears no relation to the aspiration with which he identifies himself. His desire is not *sum* but *sursum*. [It is God, explains Marcel, to whom the person aspires; and it is God, working within the person (who participates in Him) who is the ground of the aspiration.]

GABRIEL MARCEL

We can find no salvation for mind or soul unless we see the difference between our being and our life. The distinction may be in some ways a mysterious one, but the mystery itself is a source of light. To say "my being is not identical with my life" is to say two different things. First, that since I *am* not my life, my life must have been given to me; in a sense unfathomable to man, I am previous to it; *I am* comes before *I live*. Second, my being is something which is in jeopardy from the moment my life begins, and must be saved; my being is a stake, and therein perhaps lies the whole meaning of life. And from this second point of view, I am not *before* but *beyond* my life. This is the only possible way to explain the ordeal of human life (and if it is not an ordeal, I do not see what else it can be). And here again, I hope very much that these words will not stir up in our minds memories of stereotyped phrases drowsily heard in the torpor too often induced by a Sunday sermon. When Keats—certainly not a Christian in the strict meaning of the word—spoke of the world as a "vale of soul-making," and declared in the same letter of April 28th, 1819, that "as various as the Lives of Men are—so various become their souls, and thus does God make individual beings, Souls, Identical Souls, of the sparks of his own essence," he had the same idea as mine, though in his inimitable style it takes on far greater splendour and freshness.

GABRIEL MARCEL

Existence has no meaning for us except to permit us, not to realise an essence already posited, but to determine it by our choice, and to identify ourselves with it.

. . . .

To think is to be conscious of oneself, it is to possess oneself. But there is no difference between the act by which I know myself, and the act by which I create myself. In the same way as the fecundity of the Providential Act [i.e. God] unceasingly produces new beings in the world, I also unceasingly produce in myself new states by the act of my attention: thus, thanks to the operation of consciousness, I create myself as God creates the world. . . .

To know oneself is not, indeed, to discover and describe an object that is itself, it is to arouse in oneself a hidden life. Consciousness reveals to me powers that it sets in motion. For me it is at once an analysis and a bringing to light.

My nature, it may be said, is multiple, and made up of powers belonging to me before I am aware of them. But to know them is to exercise them; and before I exercise them, can I call them mine? In reality I cannot call *myself* that obscure treasure from which I endlessly draw, which offers me always new gifts and which ebbs out of me as soon as my attention is distracted, or my will fails.

. . . .

We do not in any sense create ideas. They are the elements of a universe of thought, as solid bodies are the elements of a material. They reveal themselves to us through an act of attention. . . . Thus it may be said that all the ideas come from God. But the order in which we arrange them is the work of man. It is only in our power to choose the course that our thought shall set out upon: whatever that course may be, an infinite amount of material is offered to us. It is for us to construct our own edifice.

. . . .

The object of life . . . is the discovery . . . by a deepening of the self, of the centre of the self that constitutes our unique and personal essence, and which we always run the risk of missing so long as we remain on the surface of things, and think only of self-aggrandisement.

. . . .

The self is not a reality which is given but a reality that seeks itself.

. . . .

We are not entirely present to ourselves until the day of our death.

LOUIS LAVELLE

Withdraw into yourself and look. And if you do not find yourself beautiful as yet, do as does the creator of a statue that is to be made beautiful; he cuts away here, he smooths there, he makes this line lighter, this other purer, until he has shown a beautiful face upon his statue. So do you also; cut away all that is excessive, straighten all that is crooked, bring light to all that is shadowed, labour to make all glow with beauty, and do not cease chiselling your statue until there shall shine out on you the godlike splendour of virtue, until you shall see the final goodness surely established in the stainless shrine.

And, when you have become this perfect work and see that it and you are one, when you are self-gathered in the purity of your being, nothing now remaining that can hinder your inner unity, nothing from without clinging to your inner self; when you find you are wholly yourself, wholly that Light which is the only true light—which is not measured by size, not narrowed by any circumscribed shape, nor again diffused as a thing void of term, but is wholly outside of measure as something greater than all measure and above all quantity—when you perceive that you have grown to this; you are now become very vision; now call up all your confidence, strike forward yet a step—you need a guide no longer—strain and see.

This is the only eye that sees the mighty Beauty. If the eye that undertakes the vision be dimmed by vice and unpurified, or weak and unable in its cowardly flinching to see the Uttermost Brightness, then it sees nothing, even though another point to what lies plain to see before it. To any vision must be brought an eye fitted to what is to be seen and having some likeness to it. Never did eye see the sun unless it had become sun-like, and never can soul see Beauty unless itself be beautiful.

Therefore, first let each become godlike and each beautiful who cares to see God and Beauty. Then, mounting, he will come on his upward way, first to Intelligence, and survey all the beautiful Ideas There, and will avow that this is Beauty, that the Ideas are Beauty, since all is beautiful by these, by the offspring and essence of Intelligence. And what he will see beyond this, we call the Nature of Good, that which carries Beauty as thrown out before It. So that, in the sum of the Intelligibles, the First is the Beautiful: if we discriminate among them, we call the Realm of Ideas the Intelligible Beauty, while the Good, that which lies beyond, is the Fountain at once and Principle of Beauty. Or we may make the Good and the Primal Beauty one and the same. And thus, always, Beauty's seat is There.

PLOTINUS

§ 5

Beloved Pan, and all ye other gods who haunt this place, give me beauty in the inward soul; and may the outward and inward man be at one. May I reckon the wise to be the wealthy, and may I have such a quantity of gold as a temperate man and he only can bear and carry.—Anything more? The prayer, I think, is enough for me.

SOCRATES' PRAYER (from Plato's *Phaedrus*)

Nothing can be more miserable than the man who goes through the whole round of things, and, as the poet says, *pries into the things beneath the earth*, and would fain guess the thoughts in his neighbour's heart, while having no conception that he needs but to associate himself with the divine 'genius' in his bosom, and to serve it truly.

. . . .

Men seek out retreats for themselves in the country, by the seaside, on the mountains, and thou too art wont to long above all for such things. But all this is unphilosophical to the last degree, when thou canst at a moment's notice retire into thyself. For nowhere can a man find a retreat more full of peace or more free from care than his own soul—above all if he have that within him, a steadfast look at which and he is at once in all good ease, and by good ease I mean nothing other than good order. Make use then of this retirement continually and regenerate thyself.

. . . .

Efface the opinion, *I am harmed*, and at once the feeling of being harmed disappears; efface the feeling, and the harm disappears at once.

That which does not make a man himself worse than before cannot make his life worse either, nor injure it whether from without or within.

. . . .

Be like a headland of rock on which the waves break incessantly; but it stands fast and around it the seething of the waters sinks to rest.

Ah, unlucky am I, that this has befallen me! Nay, but rather lucky am I that, though this has befallen me, yet am I still unhurt, neither crushed by the present nor dreading the future. For something of the kind could have befallen everyone, but everyone would not have remained unhurt in spite of it. Why then count that rather a misfortune than this a good fortune? And in any case dost thou reckon that a misfortune for a man which is not a miscarriage from his nature? And wouldst thou have that to be an aberration from a man's nature, which does not contravene the will of his nature? What then? This will thou hast learnt to know. Does what has befallen thee hinder thee one whit from being just, high-minded, chaste, sensible, deliberate, straightforward, modest, free, and from possessing all the other qualities, the presence of which enables a man's nature to come fully into its own? Forget not in future, when anything would lead thee to feel hurt, to take thy stand upon this axiom: *This is no misfortune, but to bear it nobly is good fortune.*

. . . .

Deem no word or deed that is in accord with Nature to be unworthy of thee, and be not plucked aside by the consequent censure of others or what they say, but if a thing is good to do or say, judge not thyself unworthy of it. For those others have their own ruling Reason and follow their own bent. Do not thou turn thine eyes aside, but keep to the straight path, following thy own and the universal Nature; and the path of these twain is one.

. . . .

Things of themselves cannot take the least hold of the Soul, nor have any access to her, nor deflect or move her; but the Soul alone deflects and moves herself, and whatever judgments she deems it right to form, in conformity with them she fashions for herself the things that submit themselves to her from without.

. . . .

When forced, as it seems, by thine environment to be utterly disquieted, return with all speed into thy self, staying in discord no longer than thou must. By constant recurrence to the harmony, thou wilt gain more command over it.

. . . .

Look within. Within is the fountain of Good, ready always to well forth if thou wilt alway delve.

. . . .

Pain is an evil either to the body—let the body then denounce it—or to the Soul; but the Soul can ensure her own fair weather and her own calm sea, and refuse to account it an evil. For every conviction and impulse and desire and aversion is from within, and nothing climbs in thither.

. . . .

They kill us, they cut us limb from limb, they hunt us with execrations! How does that prevent thy mind being still pure, sane, sober, just? Imagine a man to stand by a crystal-clear spring of sweet water, and to rail at it; yet it fails not to bubble up with wholesome water. Throw in mud or even filth and it will quickly winnow them away and purge itself of them and take never a stain. How then possess thyself of a living fountain and no mere well? By guiding thyself carefully every hour into freedom with kindliness, simplicity, and modesty.

. . . .

Observe what thy nature asks of thee, as one controlled by Nature alone, then do this and with a good grace, if thy nature as a living creature is not to be made worse thereby. Next must thou observe what thy nature as a living creature asks of thee. And this must thou wholly accept, if thy nature as a rational living creature be not made worse thereby. Now the rational is indisputably also the civic. Comply with these rules then and be not needlessly busy about anything.

. . . .

What if a man think scorn of me? That will be his affair. But it will be mine not to be found doing or saying anything worthy of scorn. What if he hate me? That will be his affair. But I will be kindly and good-natured to everyone, and ready to shew even my enemy where he has seen amiss, not by way of rebuke nor with a parade of forbearance, but genuinely and chivalrously like the famous Phocion, unless indeed he was speaking ironically. For such should be the inner springs of a man's heart that the Gods see him not wrathfully disposed at any thing or counting it a hardship. Why, what evil can happen to thee if thou thyself now doest what is congenial to thy nature, and welcomest what the Universal Nature now deems well-timed, thou who art a man intensely eager that what is for the common interest should by one means or another be brought about?

. . . .

Often have I marvelled how each one of us loves himself above all men, yet sets less store by his own opinion of himself than by that of everyone else. At any rate, if a God or some wise teacher should come to a man and charge him to admit no thought or design into his mind that he could not utter aloud as soon as conceived, he could not endure this ordinance for a single day. So it is clear that we pay more deference to the opinion our neighbours will have of us than to our own.

MARCUS AURELIUS

THE LAKE OF BEAUTY

Let your mind be quiet, realising the beauty of the world, and the immense the boundless treasures that it holds in store.
All that you have within you, all that your heart desires, all that your Nature so specially fits you for—that or the counterpart of it waits embedded in the great Whole, for you. It will surely come to you.
Yet equally surely not one moment before its appointed time will it come. All your crying and fever and reaching out of hands will make no difference.
Therefore do not begin that game at all.
Do not recklessly spill the waters of your mind in this direction and in that, lest you become like a spring lost and dissipated in the desert.
But draw them together into a little compass, and hold them still, so still;

And let them become clear, so clear—so limpid, so mirror-like;
At last the mountains and the sky shall glass themselves in
peaceful beauty,
And the antelope shall descend to drink, and to gaze at his
reflected image, and the lion to quench his thirst,
And Love himself shall come and bend over, and catch his
own likeness in you.

EDWARD CARPENTER

§ 6

Who will justify him that sinneth against his own soul? and who will glorify him that dishonoureth his own life?

ECCLESIASTICUS

The soul is its own witness; yea, the soul
Itself is its own refuge; grieve thou not,
O man, thy soul, the great internal Witness.

THE CODE OF MANU

This was the commandment, "Thou shalt love thy neighbour as thyself," but when the commandment is rightly understood, it also says the converse, "*Thou shalt love thyself in the right way*." If anyone, therefore, will not learn from Christianity to love *himself* in the right way, then neither can he love his neighbour; he may perhaps, as we say, "for life and death"—cling to one or several other human beings, but this is by no means loving one's neighbour. To love one's self in the right way and to love one's neighbour are absolutely analogous concepts, are at bottom one and the same. When the "as thyself" of the commandment has taken from you the selfishness which Christianity, sad to say, must presuppose as existing in every human being, then you have rightly learned to love yourself. Hence the law is: "You shall love yourself as you love your neighbour when you love him as yourself." Whoever has some knowledge of men will certainly admit that as he has often wished to be able to influence men to give up their self-love, so he has also often wished that it were possible to teach them to love themselves. When the busy man wastes his time and energy on vain and unimportant projects, is this not because he has not rightly learned to love himself? When the frivolous man abandons himself, almost as a mere nothing, to the folly of the moment, is not this because he does not rightly understand how to love himself?

When the melancholy man wishes to be done with life, aye, with himself, is this not because he will not learn strictly and earnestly to love himself? When a man, because the world or another man faithlessly betrayed him, yields himself up to despair, how was he to blame (for we are not here speaking of his innocent suffering), except for not having loved himself in the right way? When a man in self-torment thinks to do God a service by torturing himself, what is his sin except this, of not willing to love himself in the right way? Ah, and when a man presumptuously lays his hand upon himself, does not his sin precisely consist in not loving himself in the way in which a man *ought* to love himself? Oh, there is so much said in the world about treachery and faithlessness, and, God help us! this is unfortunately only too true, but let us still never forget that the most dangerous traitor of all is the one every man has in his own breast. This treachery, whether it consists in a man's selfishly loving himself, or in the fact that he selfishly does not wish to love himself in the right way, this treachery is certainly a mystery because there is no outcry about it, as is usual in cases of treachery and faithlessness. But is it not therefore all the more important that we should repeatedly be reminded about the Christian teaching: that a man should love his neighbour as himself, that is, as he ought to love himself?

KIERKEGAARD

Piety towards one's self is the great law of love, which we apprehend in the depths of our nature, because each of us is *this* creature who has been given *this* shape and has occupied *this* place in the order of creation; the moment we have apprehended this law, it is incumbent upon us to assert it with all our might. And the bliss of our soul lies in never resisting that silent appeal which mounts up from the depths of our being. . . .

[Piety's] particular aim is to maintain religious awe in the self towards the metaphysical deeps of its own reality, that mysterious reality with which God has endowed it. For our self is a holy temple of the Spirit, built by God's own hands, a wonderful inner universe with its own laws of gravity, still more marvellous than those we can see in the full vitality of the external universe with its infinity of mechanisms. It is a sanctuary, a Holy of Holies into which we may not enter, though it is ours, without a hidden and holy fear. We *may* not, I said. But also we *cannot*, in this Holy of Holies, enter the place of the altar with the eternal lamp of the most sacred mysteries burning before it. There is indeed a sense in which we are given to ourselves; and this is the meaning of our relative *aseitas*. But we are only entrusted to ourselves as works of art from the studio of an eternal Master. We are not our *own* masterpieces. That is why we are only left to ourselves as infinitely precious heirlooms, which we must treat as we would treat the treasure of our bliss.

PETER WUST

The assumption underlying the thinking of Luther and Calvin and also that of Kant and Freud, is: Selfishness is identical with self-love. To love others is a virtue, to love oneself is a sin. Furthermore, love for others and love for oneself are mutually exclusive.

Theoretically we meet here with a fallacy concerning the nature of love. Love is not primarily "caused" by a specific object, but is a lingering quality in a person which is only actualised by a certain "object" . . . The kind of love which can only be experienced with regard to one person demonstrates by this very fact that it is not love but a sado-masochistic attachment. The basic affirmation contained in love is directed towards the beloved person as an incarnation of essentially human qualities. Love for one person implies love for man as such. Love for man as such is not, as it is frequently supposed to be, an abstraction coming "after" the love for a specific person, or an enlargement of the experience with a specific "object"; it is its premise, although, genetically, it is acquired in the contact with concrete individuals.

From this it follows that my own self, in principle, is as much an object of my love as another person. The affirmation of my own life, happiness, growth, freedom, is rooted in the presence of the basic readiness of and ability for such an affirmation. If an individual has this readiness, he has it also towards himself; if he can only "love" others, he cannot love at all.

Selfishness is not identical with self-love but with its very opposite. Selfishness is one kind of greediness. Like all greediness, it contains an insatiability, as a consequence of which there is never any real satisfaction. Greed is a bottomless pit which exhausts the person in an endless effort to satisfy the need without ever reaching satisfaction. Close observation shows that while the selfish person is always anxiously concerned with himself, he is never satisfied, is always restless, always driven by the fear of not getting enough, of missing something, of being deprived of something. He is filled with burning envy of anyone who might have more. If we observe still closer, especially the unconscious dynamics, we find that this type of person is basically not fond of himself, but deeply dislikes himself.

The puzzle in this seeming contradiction is easy to solve. Selfishness is rooted in this very lack of fondness for oneself. The person who is not fond of himself, who does not approve of himself, is in constant anxiety concerning his own self. He has not the inner security which can exist only on the basis of genuine fondness and affirmation. He must be concerned about himself, greedy to get everything for himself, since basically he lacks security and satisfaction. The same holds true with the so-called narcissistic person, who is not so much concerned with getting things for himself as with admiring himself. While on the surface it seems that these persons are very much in love with themselves, they actually are not fond of themselves, and their narcissism—like selfishness—is an overcompensation for the basic lack of self-love. Freud has pointed out that the narcissistic person has withdrawn his love from others and turned it towards his own person. Although the first part of this statement is true, the second is a fallacy. He loves neither others nor himself.

ERICH FROMM

I love my life supremely because Thou art my life's sweetness.

NICHOLAS OF CUSA

For if I ought to love myself in Thee who art my likeness, I am most especially constrained thereto when I see that Thou lovest me as Thy creature and Thine image.

NICHOLAS OF CUSA

§ 7

From the reality of the man who moulds his own life into completeness, it is only one step to egocentric isolation from the world.

KARL JASPERS

It is sufficiently obvious that the systematic cultivation of self-awareness may as easily produce undesirable as desirable results. The development of personality may be regarded as an end in itself or, alternatively, as a means towards an ulterior end—the transcendence of personality through immediate cognition of ultimate reality and through moral action towards fellow individuals, action that is inspired and directed by this immediate cognition. Where personality is developed for its own sake, and not in order that it may be transcended, there tends to be a raising of the barriers of separateness and an increase of egotism.

ALDOUS HUXLEY

Self-expression is only possible through the object. This is due to the objectivity of the personal. Our personality *is* our objectivity. Our reality is a going out of ourselves to a reality beyond us and independent of us. Shut me up within the limits of my own organism, rob me of my capacity to pass beyond the limitations of my subjectivity, to enter into and enjoy that which is not me—then I become a mere animal, conscious not of things but merely of the excitements and images which they stimulate in me. The self is personal; and the expression of the self is personal. Self-expression is the expression of that capacity to enter into the life of the other and to be absorbed in it. It is because the artist loses himself in the reality of that which he describes or depicts or reveals, because of his individual self-effacement, that his work is a spontaneous expression of himself. That is one meaning of the penetrating saying of Jesus: "He that saveth his life shall lose it, and he that loseth his life shall keep it unto life eternal." Personal spontaneity is always objective, always in terms of the independent reality of an object which absorbs us. There is no other self-expression possible. If we block the avenues of the outpouring of self, if we withdraw from the reality of the world, if we allow our actions to be subjectively determined by mere instincts and habits, following our inclinations, we do not express ourselves, we frustrate our own self-expression, surrender our freedom and suffocate all creative spontaneity. The artist does not act by impulse, still less by the compulsion of rules, but by the nature of the reality which he apprehends. By doing this he becomes free and his action becomes a self-expression. In no other way can self-expression be achieved.

JOHN MACMURRAY

Love moves on a ground which is neither that of the self, nor that of the other *qua* other; I call it the Thou. I should think a more philosophical designation would be better, if it could be found; but at the same time I do think that abstract terms here might betray us, and land us once more in the region of the *other*, the *He*.

Love, in so far as distinct from desire or as opposed to desire, love treated as the subordination of the self to a superior reality, a reality at my deepest level more truly me than I am myself—love as the breaking of the tension between the self and the other, appears to me to be what one might call the essential ontological datum.

GABRIEL MARCEL

The paradox of the finite mind is its subjection to the continued polarity brought to bear upon a man by the *I* and the *Thou*. He tries to vanquish it in his compulsion to become a pure *I*, but he can only become a pure *I* by gravitating, with ever-increasing intensity, round the universal *Thou* of being and of all ontological community.

PETER WUST

The idea of the perfect unity of all can finally be realised, or incarnated, only through the fullness of perfect individualities. Therefore the ultimate goal is inseparably twofold: namely the highest development of every individuality, and every individuality's fullest union with all. The individual goal—the purpose of every individual life—is, of necessity, included here, for there is no need, nor is there a possibility, to subtract it or tear it away from the common goal. The world needs us as much as we need it. The universe is concerned, from the beginning of time, with the preservation, the development, and the raising into eternity of all that is really necessary and desirable for us, and of everything that is positive and worthwhile in every human individuality. It only rests with us to participate most actively and most consciously in the common historical progression—for our own sake and that of all others inseparably.

VLADIMIR SOLOVIEV

In the profoundest form of world- and life-affirmation, in which man lives his life on the loftiest spiritual and ethical plane, he attains to inner freedom from the world and becomes capable of sacrificing his life for some end. This profoundest world- and life-affirmation can assume the appearance of world- and life-negation. But that does not make it world- and life-negation: it remains what it is—the loftiest form of world- and life-affirmation. He who sacrifices his life to achieve any purpose for an individual or for humanity is practising life-affirmation. He is taking an interest in the things of this world and by offering his own life wants to bring about in the world something which he regards as necessary. The sacrifice of life for a purpose is not life-negation, but the profoundest form of life-affirmation placing itself at the service of world-affirmation.

ALBERT SCHWEITZER

In feeling, as in all else, the increase and deepening of individuality is a progress towards unity with the whole. Self-distinction, no doubt, becomes more marked; but true self-distinction is hostile to self-absorption. It is a distinction in identity, and is the reverse of exclusiveness, or of brooding over a blank indeterminate content.

BERNARD BOSANQUET

When we are told that it is a fatal dualism in the good to have two divergent paths of attainment, self-sacrifice and self-affirmation, that we approve of both, and cannot in principle determine ourselves to the preference of either, the answer is prepared by what has just been said. In principle every action combines the two; it is a single consequence of finiteness. The cost at which we achieve our ends varies in every instance, and in very many cases it would be impossible to say whether the element of self-affirmation or of self-sacrifice is predominant. Formally there are always both, and though they may seem to diverge as the one side or the other is more prominent, yet they both spring from the single principle we are tracing. And in as far as the self can come, in the highest experience, to surrender itself without loss, a convergence between self-sacrifice and self-affirmation begins within finite life which in principle, we can see, must be completed beyond it.

BERNARD BOSANQUET

God's life . . . sees the one plan fulfilled through all the manifold lives, the single consciousness winning its purpose by virtue of all the ideas, of all the individual selves, and of all the lives. No finite view is wholly illusory. Every finite intent taken precisely in its wholeness is fulfilled in the Absolute. The least life is not neglected, the most fleeting act is a recognised part of the world's meaning. You are for the divine view all that you now know yourself at this instant to be. But you are also infinitely more. The preciousness of your present purposes to yourself is only a hint of that preciousness which in the end links their meaning to the entire realm of Being.

And despite the vastness, the variety, the thrilling complexity of the life of the finite world, the ultimate unity is not far from any one of us. All variety of idea and object is subject, as we have seen, to the unity of the purpose wherein we alone live. Even at this moment, yes, even if we transiently forget the fact, we mean the Absolute. We win the presence of God when most we flee. We have no other dwelling-place but the single unity of the divine consciousness. In the light of the eternal we are manifest, and even this very passing instant pulsates with a life that all the worlds are needed to express. In vain would we wander in the darkness; we are eternally at home in God.

JOSIAH ROYCE

FIFTH PART

II. INTIMATIONS

ADAGIO
ff

§ 1

And the Lord said unto Moses, I will do this thing also that thou hast spoken: for thou hast found grace in my sight, and I know thee by name.

And he said, I beseech thee, shew me thy glory.

And he said, I will make all my goodness pass before thee, and I will proclaim the name of the Lord before thee; and will be gracious to whom I will be gracious, and will shew mercy on whom I will shew mercy.

And he said, Thou canst not see my face: for there shall no man see me, and live.

And the Lord said, Behold, there is a place by me, and thou shalt stand upon a rock:

And it shall come to pass, while my glory passeth by, that I will put thee in a clift of the rock, and will cover thee with my hand while I pass by:

And I will take away mine hand, and thou shalt see my back parts: but my face shall not be seen.

EXODUS

Wherefore at certain times when the soul is least thinking of it and least desiring it, God is wont to give it these Divine touches, by causing it certain recollections of Himself.

ST. JOHN OF THE CROSS

Suppose a man in hiding and he stirs, he shows his whereabouts thereby; and God does the same. No one could ever have found God; he gave himself away.

MEISTER ECKHART

What is that which shines through me, and strikes upon my heart without hurting it? And I shudder and kindle: shudder, in as much as I am unlike it; kindle, in as much as I am like it. It is Wisdom, Wisdom's self which thus shines into me . . .

ST. AUGUSTINE

Beauty, no other thing is, then a Beame
Flasht out between the Middle and Extreame.

ROBERT HERRICK

Nature is a world of symbolism, a rich hieroglyphic book: everything visible conceals an invisible mystery, and the last mystery of all is God.

CHRISTOPHE ERNST LUTHARDT

I still remember walking down the Notting Hill main road and observing the (extremely sordid) landscape with joy and astonishment. Even the movement of the traffic had something universal and sublime in it.

EVELYN UNDERHILL

For now the unborn God in the human heart
Knows for a moment all sublimities . . .
Old people at evening sitting in the doorways
See in a broken window of the slum
The Burning Bush reflected, and the crumb
For the starving bird is part of the broken Body
Of Christ Who forgives us—He with the bright Hair
—The Sun Whose Body was spilt on our fields to bring us
harvest.

EDITH SITWELL (from *Holiday*)

And so we stand with mirrors: someone here,
and someone there, with no agreement reached;
but catching, though, and passing the reflection
we've singled out from far, this pure reflection,
on to another from the gleaming mirror.
Ball-game for gods! A play of light, in which
three balls, perhaps, perhaps even nine, will cross,
not one of which, since first the world grew conscious,

ever fell wide. Catchers, that's what we are!
It comes invisibly through the air, and yet
how absolutely the mirror meets it!—this
(only then fully advent), this reflection,
that only gives us time to estimate
with how much force it will go on to where.

Just this. And our long childhood lasted for it;
necessity, affection, long farewells
were all endured for this. But this repays.

RAINER MARIA RILKE

THE KINGDOM OF GOD

"IN NO STRANGE LAND"

O World invisible, we view thee,
O World intangible, we touch thee,
O World unknowable, we know thee,
Inapprehensible, we clutch thee!

Does the fish soar to find the ocean,
The eagle plunge to find the air—
That we ask of the stars in motion
If they have rumour of thee there?

Not where the wheeling systems darken,
And our benumbed conceiving soars!—
The drift of pinions, would we hearken,
Beats at our own clay-shuttered doors.

The angels keep their ancient places;—
Turn but a stone, and start a wing!
'Tis ye, 'tis your estrangèd faces,
That miss the many-splendoured thing.

But (when so sad thou canst not sadder)
Cry;—and upon thy so sore loss
Shall shine the traffic of Jacob's ladder
Pitched betwixt Heaven and Charing Cross.

Yea, in the night, my Soul, my daughter,
Cry,—clinging Heaven by the hems;
And lo, Christ walking on the water,
Not of Gennesareth, but Thames!

FRANCIS THOMPSON

SCOFFERS

Mock on, mock on, Voltaire, Rousseau,
  Mock on, mock on; 'tis all in vain;
You throw the sand against the wind,
  And the wind blows it back again.

And every sand becomes a gem,
  Reflected in the beams divine;
Blown back, they blind the mocking eye,
  But still in Israel's paths they shine.

The atoms of Democritus
  And Newton's particles of light,
Are sands upon the Red Sea shore
  Where Israel's tents do shine so bright.

BLAKE

Thus far I have been speaking of the fourth and last kind of madness, which is imputed to him who, when he sees the beauty of earth, is transported with the recollection of the true beauty; he would like to fly away, but he cannot; he is like a bird fluttering and looking upward and careless of the world below; and he is therefore thought to be mad. And I have shown this of all inspirations to be the noblest and highest and the offspring of the highest to him who has or shares in it, and that he who loves the beautiful is called a lover because he partakes of it. For, as has been already said, every soul of man has in the way of nature beheld true being; this was the condition of her passing into the form of man. But all souls do not easily recall the things of the other world; they may have seen them for a short time only, or they may have been unfortunate in their earthly lot, and, having had their hearts turned to unrighteousness through some corrupting influence, they may have lost the memory of the holy things which once they saw. Few only retain an adequate remembrance of them; and they, when they behold here any image of that other world, are rapt in amazement; but they are ignorant of what this rapture means, because they do not clearly perceive. For there is no light of justice or temperance or any of the higher ideas which are precious to souls in the earthly copies of them: they are seen through a glass dimly; and there are few who, going to the images, behold in them the realities, and these only with difficulty. There was a time when with the rest of the happy band they saw beauty shining in brightness,—we philosophers following in the train of Zeus, others in company with other gods; and then we beheld the beatific vision and were initiated into a mystery which may be truly called most blessed, celebrated by us in our state of innocence, before we had any experience of evils to come, when we were admitted to the sight of apparitions innocent and simple and calm and happy, which we beheld shining in pure light, pure ourselves and not yet enshrined in that living tomb which we carry about, now that we are imprisoned in the body, like an oyster in his shell. Let me linger over the memory of scenes which have passed away.

But of beauty, I repeat again that we saw her there shining in company with the celestial forms; and coming to earth we find her here too, shining in clearness through the clearest aperture of sense. For sight is the most piercing of our bodily senses; though not by that is wisdom seen; her loveliness would have been transporting if there had been a visible image of her, and the other ideas, if they had visible counterparts, would be equally lovely. But this is the privilege of beauty, that being the loveliest she is also the most palpable to sight. Now he who is not newly initiated or who has become corrupted, does not easily rise out of this world to the sight of true beauty in the other; he looks only at her earthly namesake, and instead of being awed at the sight of her, he is given over to pleasure, and like a brutish beast he rushes on to enjoy and beget; he consorts with wantonness, and is not afraid or ashamed of pursuing pleasure in violation of nature. But he whose initiation is recent, and who has been the spectator of many glories in the other world, is amazed when he sees any one having a godlike face or form, which is the expression of divine beauty; and at first a shudder runs through him, and again the old awe steals over him; then looking upon the face of his beloved as of a god he reverences him, and if he were not afraid of being thought a downright madman, he would sacrifice to his beloved as to the image of a god.

PLATO (from the *Phaedrus*)

THE ECSTASY

Where, like a pillow on a bed,
  A pregnant bank swell'd up, to rest
The violet's reclining head,
  Sat we two, one another's best.
Our hands were firmly cèmented
  By a fast balm which thence did spring;
Our eye-beams twisted, and did thread
  Our eyes upon one double string.
So to engraft our hands, as yet
  Was all the means to make us one;
And pictures in our eyes to get
  Was all our propagation.
As 'twixt two equal armies Fate
  Suspends uncertain victory,
Our souls—which to advance their state
  Were gone out—hung 'twixt her and me.
And whilst our souls negotiate there,
  We like sepulchral statues lay;
All day the same our postures were,
  And we said nothing, all the day.

If any, so by love refined,
  That the soul's language understood,
And by good love were grown all mind,
  Within convenient distance stood,
He (though he knew not which soul spake,
  Because both meant, both spake the same)
Might thence a new concoction take,
  And part far purer than he came.
This Ecstasy doth unperplex
  (We said) and tell us what we love,
We see by this, it was not sex,
  We see, we saw not what did move:
But as all several souls contain
  Mixture of things, they know not what,
Love, these mixed souls doth mix again,
  And makes both one, each this and that.
A single violet transplant,
  The strength, the colour, and the size
(All which before was poor and scant)
  Redoubles still, and multiplies.
When love, with one another so
  Interinanimates two souls,
That abler soul, which thence doth flow,
  Defects of loneliness controls.
We then, who are this new soul, know,
  Of what we are composed and made,
For th' Atomies of which we grow,
  Are souls, whom no change can invade.
But O alas, so long, so far
  Our bodies why do we forbear?
They are ours, though they are not we, We are
  The intelligences, they the sphere.
We owe them thanks, because they thus,
  Did us, to us, at first convey,
Yielded their forces, sense, to us,
  Nor are dross to us, but allay.

On man heaven's influence works not so,
  But that it first imprints the air,
So soul into the soul may flow,
  Though it to body first repair.
As our blood labours to beget
  Spirits, as like souls as it can,
Because such fingers need to knit
  That subtle knot, which makes us man:
So must pure lovers' souls descend
  T' affections, and to faculties,
Which sense may reach and apprehend,
  Else a great Prince in prison lies.
To our bodies turn we then, that so
  Weak men on love revealed may look;
Love's mysteries in souls do grow,
  But yet the body is his book.
And if some lover, such as we,
  Have heard this dialogue of one,
Let him still mark us, he shall see
  Small change, when we are to bodies gone.

JOHN DONNE

§ 2

SWANN'S PHRASE

So Swann was not mistaken in believing that the phrase of the sonata did, really, exist. Human as it was from this point of view, it belonged, none the less, to an order of supernatural creatures whom we have never seen, but whom, in spite of that, we recognise and acclaim with rapture when some explorer of the unseen contrives to coax one forth, to bring it down from that divine world to which he has access to shine for a brief moment in the firmament of ours. This was what Vinteuil had done for the little phrase. Swann felt that the composer had been content (with the musical instruments at his disposal) to draw aside its veil, to make it visible, following and respecting its outlines with a hand so loving, so prudent, so delicate and so sure, that the sound altered at every moment, blunting itself to indicate a shadow, springing back into life when it must follow the curve of some more bold projection. And one proof that Swann was not mistaken when he believed in the real existence of this phrase, was that anyone with an ear at all delicate for music would at once have detected the imposture had Vinteuil, endowed with less power to see and to render its forms, sought to dissemble (by adding a line, here and there, of his own invention) the dimness of his vision or the feebleness of his hand.

The phrase had disappeared. Swann knew that it would come again at the end of the last movement, after a long passage which Mme. Verdurin's pianist always "skipped." There were in this passage some admirable ideas which Swann had not distinguished on first hearing the sonata, and which he now perceived, as if they had, in the cloak-room of his memory, divested themselves of their uniform disguise of novelty. Swann listened to all the scattered themes which entered into the composition of the phrase, as its premisses enter into the inevitable conclusion of a syllogism; he was assisting at the mystery of its birth. "Audacity," he exclaimed to himself, "as inspired, perhaps, as a Lavoisier's or an Ampère's, the audacity of a Vinteuil making experiment, discovering the secret laws that govern an unknown force, driving across a region unexplored towards the one possible goal the invisible team in which he has placed his trust and which he never may discern!" How charming the dialogue which Swann now heard between piano and violin, at the beginning of the last passage. The suppression of human speech, so far from letting fancy reign there uncontrolled (as one might have thought), had eliminated it altogether. Never was spoken language of such inflexible necessity, never had it known questions so pertinent, such obvious replies. At first the piano complained alone, like a bird deserted by its mate; the violin heard and answered it, as from a neighbouring tree. It was as at the first beginning of the world, as if there were not yet but these twain upon the earth, or rather in this world closed against all the rest, so fashioned by the logic of its creator that in it there should never be any but themselves; the world of this sonata. Was it a bird, was it the soul, not yet made perfect, of the little phrase, was it a fairy, invisibly somewhere lamenting, whose plaint the piano heard and tenderly repeated? Its cries were so sudden that the violinist must snatch up his bow and race to catch them as they came. Marvellous bird! The violinist seemed to wish to charm, to tame, to woo, to win it. Already it had passed into his soul, already the little phrase which it evoked shook like a medium's the body of the violinist, "possessed" indeed. Swann knew that the phrase was going to speak to him once again. And his personality was now so divided that the strain of waiting for the imminent moment when he would find himself face to face, once more, with the phrase, convulsed him in one of those sobs which a fine line of poetry or a piece of alarming news will wring from us, not when we are alone, but when we repeat one or the other to a friend, in whom we see ourselves reflected, like a third person, whose probable emotion softens him. It reappeared, but this time to remain poised in the air, and to sport there for a moment only, as though immobile, and shortly to expire. And so Swann lost nothing of the precious time for which it lingered. It was still there, like an iridescent bubble that floats for a while unbroken. As a rainbow, when its brightness fades, seems to subside, then soars again and, before it is extinguished, is glorified with greater splendour than it has ever shewn; so to the two colours which the phrase had hitherto allowed to appear it added others now, chords shot with every hue in the prism, and made them sing. Swann dared not move, and would have liked to compel all the other people in the room to remain still also, as if the slightest movement might embarrass the magic presence, supernatural, delicious, frail, that would so easily vanish. But no one, as it happened, dreamed of speaking. The ineffable utterance of one solitary man, absent, perhaps dead (Swann did not know whether Vinteuil were still alive), breathed out above the rites of those two hierophants, sufficed to arrest the attention of three hundred minds, and made of that stage on which a soul was thus called into being one of the noblest altars on which a supernatural ceremony could be performed.

MARCEL PROUST

THE COMING OF THE BUTTERFLIES

They ceased speaking, and remained leaning on the gate in silence. Anthony's eyes, passing over the garden, remained fixed where, two nights before, he had thought he saw the form of a lion. It seemed to him now, as he gazed, that a change had taken place. The smooth grass of the lawn was far less green than it had been, and the flowers in the beds by the house walls, on either side of the door, were either dying or already withered. Certainly he had not been in a state to notice much, but there had been left with him a general impression of growth and colour. Neither growth nor colour were now there: all seemed parched. Of course, it was hot, but still. . . .

There was a sudden upward sweep of green and orange through the air in front of him: he blinked and moved. As he recovered himself he saw, with startled amazement, that in the centre of the garden, almost directly above the place where he had seen the lion, there floated a butterfly. But—a butterfly! It was a terrific, a colossal butterfly, it looked as if it were two feet or more across from wing-tip to wing-tip. It was tinted and coloured with every conceivable brightness; green and orange predominating. It was moving upward in spiral flutterings, upward to a certain point, from which it seemed directly to fall close to the ground, then again it began its upward sweep, and again hovered and fell. Of the two men it seemed to be unaware; lovely and self-sufficient it went on with its complex manœuvres in the air. Anthony, after a few astonished minutes, took his eyes from it, and looked about him, first with a general gaze at all his surroundings, then more particularly at Mr. Tighe. The little man was pressed against the gate, his mouth slightly open, his eyes full of plenary adoration, his whole being concentrated on the perfect symbol of his daily concern. Anthony saw that it was no good speaking to him. He looked back at the marvel in time to see, from somewhere above his own head, another brilliancy—but much smaller—flash through the air, almost as if some ordinary butterfly had hurled itself towards its more gigantic image. And another followed it, and another, and as Anthony, now thoroughly roused, sprang up and aside, to see the better, he beheld the air full of them. Those of which he had caught sight were but the scattered first comers of a streaming host. Away across the fields they came, here in thick masses, there in thinner lines, white and yellow, green and red, purple and blue and dusky black. They were sweeping round, in great curving flights; mass following after mass, he saw them driving forward from far away, but not directly, taking wide distances in their sweep, now on one side, now on another, but always and all of them speeding forward towards the gate and the garden beyond. Even as a sudden new rush of aerial loveliness reached that border he turned his head, and saw a cloud of them hanging high above the butterfly of the garden, which rushed up towards them, and then, carrying a whirl of lesser iridescent fragilities with it, precipitated itself down its steep descent; and as it swept, and hovered, and again mounted, silent and unresting, it was alone. Alone it went soaring up, alone to meet another congregation of its hastening visitors, and then again multitudinously fell, and hovered; and again alone went upward to the tryst.

Bewildered and distracted, Anthony caught his companion's arm. Mr. Tighe was by now almost hanging to the gate, his hands clutching frenziedly the topmost bar, his jaws working. Noises were coming from his mouth; the sweat stood in the creases of his face. He gobbled at the soft-glowing vision; he uttered little cries and pressed himself against the bars; his knees were wedged between them, and his feet drawn from the ground in the intensity of his apprehension. And over him faster and thicker the great incursion passed, and the air over the garden was filled with butterflies, streaming, rising, sinking, hovering, towards their centre, and faster now than Anthony's eyes could see the single host of all that visitation rose and fell, only whenever he saw it towards the ground, it turned upwards in a solitary magnificence and whenever, having risen, it dropped again, it went encircled by innumerable tiny bodies and wings.

Credulous, breathless, he gazed, until after times unreckoned had passed, there seemed to be a stay. Lesser grew the clouds above; smaller the flights that joined them. Now there were but a score and now but twelve or ten—now only three tardy dancers waited above for the flight of their vision; and as again it rose, but one—coming faster than all the rest, reaching its strange assignation as it were at the last permitted moment, joining its summoning lord as it rose for the last time, and falling with it; and then the great butterfly of the garden floated idly in the empty air, and the whole army of others had altogether vanished from sight, and from knowledge. It also after a short while rose, curvetting, passed upward towards the roof of the house, settled there for a moment, a glowing splendour upon the red tiles, swept beyond it, and disappeared.

Anthony moved and blinked, took a step or two away, looked round him, blinked again, and turned back to Mr. Tighe. He was about to speak, but, seeing the other man's face, he paused abruptly. The tears were running down it; as his hands released the bars Anthony saw that he was trembling all over; he stumbled and could not get his footing upon the road. Anthony caught and steadied him.

"O glory, glory," Mr. Tighe said. "O glory everlasting!"

CHARLES WILLIAMS (from *The Place of the Lion*)

§ 3

This is my delight, thus to wait and watch at the wayside where shadow chases light and the rain comes in the wake of the summer.

Messengers, with tidings from unknown skies, greet me and speed along the road. My heart is glad within, and the breath of the passing breeze is sweet.

From dawn till dusk I sit here before my door, and I know that of a sudden the happy moment will arrive when I shall see.

In the meanwhile I smile and I sing all alone. In the meanwhile the air is filling with the perfume of promise.

RABINDRANATH TAGORE

We are aware of evanescent visitations of thought and feeling, sometimes associated with place or person, sometimes regarding our own mind alone, and always arising unforeseen and departing unbidden, but elevating and delightful beyond all expression: so that even in the desire and the regret they leave, there cannot but be pleasure, participating as it does in the nature of its object. It is as it were the interpenetration of a diviner nature through our own; but its footsteps are like those of a wind over the sea, which the coming calm erases, and whose traces remain only, as on the wrinkled sand which paves it. These and corresponding conditions of being are experienced principally by those of the most delicate sensibility and the most enlarged imagination; and the state of mind produced by them is at war with every base desire. The enthusiasm of virtue, love, patriotism, and friendship, is essentially linked with such emotions; and whilst they last, self appears as what it is, an atom to a universe. Poets are not only subject to these experiences as spirits of the most refined organisation, but they can colour all that they combine with the evanescent hues of this ethereal world; a word, a trait in the representation of a scene or a passion, will touch the enchanted chord, and reanimate, in those who have ever experienced those emotions, the sleeping, the cold, the buried image of the past. Poetry thus makes immortal all that is best and most beautiful in the world; it arrests the vanishing apparitions which haunt the interlunations of life, and veiling them, or in language or in form, sends them forth among mankind, bearing sweet news of kindred joy to those with whom their sisters abide—abide, because there is no portal of expression from the caverns of the spirit which they inhabit into the universe of things. Poetry redeems from decay the visitations of the divinity in man.

Poetry turns all things to loveliness; it exalts the beauty of that which is most beautiful, and it adds beauty to that which is most deformed; it marries exultation and horror, grief and pleasure, eternity and change; it subdues to union, under its light yoke, all irreconcilable things. It transmutes all that it touches, and every form moving within the radiance of its presence is changed by wondrous sympathy to an incarnation of the spirit which it breathes: its secret alchemy turns to potable gold the poisonous waters which flow from death through life; it strips the veil of familiarity from the world, and lays bare the naked and sleeping beauty, which is the spirit of its forms.

All things exist as they are perceived; at least in relation to the percipient. "The mind is its own place, and of itself can make a heaven of hell, a hell of heaven." But poetry defeats the curse which binds us to be subjected to the accident of surrounding impressions. And whether it spreads its own figured curtain, or withdraws life's dark veil from before the scene of things, it equally creates for us a being within our being. It makes us the inhabitant of a world to which the familiar world is a chaos. It reproduces the common universe of which we are portions and percipients, and it purges from our inward sight the film of familiarity which obscures from us the wonder of our being. It compels us to feel that which we perceive, and to imagine that which we know. It creates anew the universe, after it has been annihilated in our minds by the recurrence of impressions blunted by reiteration. It justifies the bold and true world of Tasso: *Non merita nome di creatore, se non Iddio ed il Poeta.*

SHELLEY

There was a Being whom my spirit oft
Met on its visioned wanderings, far aloft,
In the clear golden prime of my youth's dawn,
Upon the fairy isles of sunny lawn,
Amid the enchanted mountains, and the caves
Of divine sleep, and on the air-like waves
Of wonder-level dream, whose tremulous floor
Paved her light steps. On an imagined shore,
Under the grey beak of some promontory,
She met me, robed in such exceeding glory
That I beheld her not. In solitudes
Her voice came to me through the whispering woods,
And from the fountains, and the odours deep
Of flowers, which, like lips murmuring in their sleep
Of the sweet kisses which had lulled them there,
Breathed but of her to the enamoured air;
And from the breezes whether low or loud,
And from the rain of every passing cloud,
And from the singing of the summer birds,
And from all sounds, all silence. In the words
Of antique verse and high romance—in form,
Sound, colour—in whatever checks that storm
Which with the shattered present chokes the past—
And in that best philosophy whose taste
Makes this cold common hell, our life, a doom
As glorious as a fiery martyrdom—
Her Spirit was the harmony of truth.

Then from the caverns of my dreamy youth
I sprang, as one sandaled with plumes of fire,
And towards the lodestar of my one desire

I flitted, like a dizzy moth whose flight
Is as a dead leaf's in the owlet light,
When it would seek in Hesper's setting sphere
A radiant death, a fiery sepulchre,
As if it were a lamp of earthly flame.
But she, whom prayers or tears then could not tame,
Passed, like a God throned on a wingèd planet,
Whose burning plumes to tenfold swiftness fan it,
Into the dreary cone of our life's shade.
And, as a man with mighty loss dismayed,
I would have followed, though the grave between
Yawned like a gulf whose spectres are unseen:
When a voice said, "O thou of hearts the weakest,
The phantom is beside thee whom thou seekest."

SHELLEY (from *Epipsychidion*)

THE QUESTION

I

I dreamed that, as I wandered by the way,
  Bare Winter suddenly was changed to Spring;
And gentle odours led my steps astray,
  Mixed with a sound of waters murmuring
Along a shelving bank of turf, which lay
  Under a copse, and hardly dared to fling
Its green arms round the bosom of the stream,
But kissed it and then fled, as thou mightest in dream.

II

There grew pied wind-flowers and violets;
  Daisies, those pearled Arcturi of the earth,
The constellated flower that never sets;
  Faint oxlips; tender bluebells, at whose birth
The sod scarce heaved; and that tall flower that wets—
  Like a child, half in tenderness and mirth—

Its mother's face with Heaven's collected tears
When the low wind its playmate's voice it hears.

III

And in the warm hedge grew lush eglantine,
  Green cow-bind and the moonlight-coloured may,
And cherry-blossoms, and white cups whose wine
  Was the bright dew yet drained not by the Day;
And wild roses, and ivy serpentine,
  With its dark buds and leaves wandering astray;
And flowers, azure, black, and streaked with gold,
Fairer than any wakened eyes behold.

IV

And nearer to the river's trembling edge
  There grew broad flag-flowers, purple pranked with
    white,
And starry river-buds among the sedge,
  And floating water-lilies, broad and bright,
Which lit the oak that overhung the hedge
  With moonlight beams of their own watery light;
And bulrushes, and reeds of such deep green
As soothed the dazzled eye with sober sheen.

V

Methought that of these visionary flowers
  I made a nosegay, bound in such a way
That the same hues which in their natural bowers
  Were mingled or opposed, the like array
Kept these imprisoned children of the Hours
  Within my hand;—and then, elate and gay,
I hastened to the spot whence I had come,
That I might there present it—oh to whom?

SHELLEY

MONT BLANC

LINES WRITTEN IN THE VALE OF CHAMOUNI

I

The everlasting universe of Things
Flows through the Mind, and rolls its rapid waves
Now dark—now glittering—now reflecting gloom—
Now lending splendour, where from secret springs
The source of human thought its tribute brings
Of waters,—with a sound but half its own,
Such as a feeble brook will oft assume
In the wild woods, among the mountains lone,
Where waterfalls around it leap for ever,
Where woods and winds contend, and a vast river
Over its rocks ceaselessly bursts and raves.

II

Thus thou, Ravine of Arve—dark, deep Ravine—
Thou many-coloured many-voiced vale,
Over whose pines and crags and caverns sail
Fast cloud-shadows and sunbeams; awful scene,
Where Power in likeness of the Arve comes down
From the ice-gulfs that gird his secret throne,
Bursting through these dark mountains like the flame
Of lightning through the tempest;—thou dost lie,—
Thy giant brood of pines around thee clinging,
Children of elder time, in whose devotion
The chainless winds still come and ever came
To drink their odours, and their mighty swinging
To hear, an old and solemn harmony;
Thine earthly rainbows stretched across the sweep
Of the etherial waterfall, whose veil

Robes some unsculptured image; the strange sleep
Which, when the voices of the desert fail,
Wraps all in its own deep eternity;
Thy caverns echoing to the Arve's commotion
A loud lone sound no other sound can tame.
Thou art pervaded with that ceaseless motion,
Thou art the path of that unresting sound,
Dizzy Ravine! And, when I gaze on thee,
I seem, as in a trance sublime and strange,
To muse on my own separate fantasy,
My own, my human Mind, which passively
Now renders and receives fast influencings,
Holding an unremitting interchange
With the clear universe of Things around;
One legion of wild thoughts, whose wandering wings
Now float above thy darkness, and now rest
Where that or thou art no unbidden guest,
In the still cave of the witch Poesy,—
Seeking—among the shadows that pass by,
Ghosts of all things that are—some shade of thee,
Some phantom, some faint image. Till the breast
From which they fled recalls them, thou art there!

III

Some say that gleams of a remoter world
Visit the soul in sleep,—that death is slumber,
And that its shapes the busy thoughts outnumber
Of those who wake and live. I look on high;
Has some unknown omnipotence unfurled
The veil of life and death? Or do I lie
In dream, and does the mightier world of sleep
Spread far around and inaccessibly
Its circles? for the very spirit fails,
Driven like a homeless cloud from steep to steep

That vanishes among the viewless gales!
Far, far above, piercing the infinite sky,
Mont Blanc appears—still, snowy, and serene.
Its subject mountains their unearthly forms
Pile around it, ice and rock; broad vales between
Of frozen floods, unfathomable deeps,
Blue as the overhanging heaven, that spread
And wind among the accumulated steeps;
A desert peopled by the storms alone,
Save when the eagle brings some hunter's bone,
And the wolf tracks her there. How hideously
Its shapes are heaped around—rude, bare, and high,
Ghastly and scarred and riven!—Is this the scene
Where the old Earthquake-dæmon taught her young
Ruin? were these their toys? or did a sea
Of fire envelop once this silent snow?
None can reply—all seems eternal now.
The wilderness has a mysterious tongue
Which teaches awful doubt,—or faith so mild,
So solemn, so serene, that Man may be,
But for such faith, with Nature reconciled.
Thou hast a voice, great Mountain, to repeal
Large codes of fraud and woe; not understood
By all, but which the wise and great and good
Interpret, or make felt, or deeply feel.

IV

The fields, the lakes, the forests, and the streams,
Ocean, and all the living things that dwell
Within the dædal earth, lightning and rain,
Earthquake and fiery flood and hurricane,
The torpor of the year when feeble dreams
Visit the hidden buds, or dreamless sleep
Holds every future leaf and flower, the bound

With which from that detested trance they leap,
The works and ways of man, their death and birth,
And that of him, and all that his may be,
All things that move and breathe, with toil and sound
Are born and die, revolve, subside, and swell.
Power dwells apart in its tranquillity,
Remote, serene, and inaccessible:
And *this* the naked countenance of earth
On which I gaze, even these primæval mountains,
Teach the adverting mind. The glaciers creep,
Like snakes that watch their prey, from their far fountains,
Slow rolling on; there, many a precipice
Frost and the sun in scorn of mortal power
Have piled—dome, pyramid, and pinnacle,
A city of death, distinct with many a tower
And wall impregnable of beaming ice.
Yet not a city, but a flood of ruin,
Is there, that from the boundary of the skies
Rolls its perpetual stream; vast pines are strewing
Its destined path, or in the mangled soil
Branchless and shattered stand; the rocks, drawn down
From yon remotest waste, have overthrown
The limits of the dead and living world,
Never to be reclaimed. The dwelling-place
Of insects, beasts, and birds, becomes its spoil;
Their food and their retreat for ever gone,
So much of life and joy is lost. The race
Of man flies far in dread; his work and dwelling
Vanish, like smoke before the tempest's stream,
And their place is not known. Below, vast caves
Shine in the rushing torrents' restless gleam,
Which, from those secret chasms in tumult welling,
Meet in the Vale; and one majestic River,
The breath and blood of distant lands, for ever
Rolls its loud waters to the ocean-waves,
Breathes its swift vapours to the circling air.

V

Mont Blanc yet gleams on high: the power is there,
The still and solemn power, of many sights
And many sounds, and much of life and death.
In the calm darkness of the moonless nights,
In the lone glare of day, the snows descend
Upon that Mountain; none beholds them there,
Nor when the flakes burn in the sinking sun,
Or the star-beams dart through them. Winds contend
Silently there, and heap the snow, with breath
Rapid and strong, but silently. Its home
The voiceless lightning in these solitudes
Keeps innocently, and like vapour broods
Over the snow. The secret Strength of Things,
Which governs thought, and to the infinite dome
Of heaven is as a law, inhabits thee.
And what were thou and earth and stars and sea,
If to the human Mind's imaginings
Silence and solitude were vacancy?

SHELLEY

HYMN TO INTELLECTUAL BEAUTY

I

The awful shadow of some unseen Power
Floats, though unseen, among us; visiting
This various world with as inconstant wing
As summer winds that creep from flower to flower.
Like moonbeams that behind some piny mountain shower,
It visits with inconstant glance
Each human heart and countenance;
Like hues and harmonies of evening,
Like clouds in starlight widely spread,
Like memory of music fled,
Like aught that for its grace may be
Dear, and yet dearer for its mystery.

II

Spirit of BEAUTY, that dost consecrate
With thine own hues all thou dost shine upon
Of human thought or form, where art thou gone?
Why dost thou pass away, and leave our state,
This dim vast vale of tears, vacant and desolate?—
Ask why the sunlight not for ever
Weaves rainbows o'er yon mountain-river;
Why aught should fail and fade that once is shown;
Why fear and dream and death and birth
Cast on the daylight of this earth
Such gloom; why man has such a scope
For love and hate, despondency and hope!

III

No voice from some sublimer world hath ever
To sage or poet these responses given:
Therefore the names of Demon, Ghost, and Heaven,
Remain the records of their vain endeavour;
Frail spells, whose uttered charm might not avail to sever
From all we hear and all we see,
Doubt, chance, and mutability.
Thy light alone, like mist o'er mountains driven,
Or music by the night-wind sent
Through strings of some still instrument,
Or moonlight on a midnight stream,
Gives grace and truth to life's unquiet dream.

IV

Love, hope, and self-esteem, like clouds depart
And come, for some uncertain moments lent.
Man were immortal and omnipotent,
Didst thou, unknown and awful as thou art,
Keep with thy glorious train firm state within his heart.

Thou messenger of sympathies
That wax and wane in lovers' eyes!
Thou that to human thought art nourishment,
Like darkness to a dying flame!
Depart not as thy shadow came:
Depart not, lest the grave should be,
Like life and fear, a dark reality!

V

While yet a boy, I sought for ghosts, and sped
Through many a listening chamber, cave, and ruin,
And starlight wood, with fearful steps pursuing
Hopes of high talk with the departed dead.
I called on poisonous names with which our youth is fed.
I was not heard, I saw them not;
When, musing deeply on the lot
Of life, at that sweet time when winds are wooing
All vital things that wake to bring
News of birds and blossoming,
Sudden thy shadow fell on me:—
I shrieked, and clasped my hands in ecstasy!

VI

I vowed that I would dedicate my powers
To thee and thine: have I not kept the vow?
With beating heart and streaming eyes, even now
I call the phantoms of a thousand hours
Each from his voiceless grave. They have in visioned bowers
Of studious zeal or love's delight
Outwatched with me the envious night:
They know that never joy illumed my brow,
Unlinked with hope that thou wouldst free
This world from its dark slavery;
That thou, O awful Loveliness,
Wouldst give whate'er these words cannot express.

VII

The day becomes more solemn and serene
  When noon is past: there is a harmony
  In autumn, and a lustre in its sky,
Which through the summer is not heard or seen,
As if it could not be, as if it had not been.
    Thus let thy power, which like the truth
    Of Nature on my passive youth
  Descended, to my onward life supply
    Its calm,—to one who worships thee,
    And every form containing thee,
    Whom, Spirit fair, thy spells did bind
To fear himself, and love all humankind.

SHELLEY

FROM "THE PRELUDE"

Hastily rose our guide,
Leaving us at the board; awhile we lingered,
Then paced the beaten downward way that led
Right to a rough stream's edge, and there broke off;
The only track now visible was one
That from the torrent's further brink held forth
Conspicuous invitation to ascend
A lofty mountain. After brief delay
Crossing the unbridged stream, that road we took,
And clomb with eagerness, till anxious fears
Intruded, for we failed to overtake
Our comrades gone before. By fortunate chance,
While every moment added doubt to doubt,
A peasant met us, from whose mouth we learned
That to the spot which had perplexed us first
We must descend, and there should find the road,
Which in the stony channel of the stream
Lay a few steps, and then along its banks;
And, that our future course, all plain to sight,

Was downwards, with the current of that stream.
Loth to believe what we so grieved to hear,
For still we had hopes that pointed to the clouds,
We questioned him again, and yet again;
But every word that from the peasant's lips
Came in reply, translated by our feelings,
Ended in this,—*that we had crossed the Alps.*

Imagination—here the Power so called
Through sad incompetence of human speech,
That awful Power rose from the mind's abyss
Like an unfathered vapour that enwraps,
At once, some lonely traveller. I was lost;
Halted without an effort to break through;
But to my conscious soul I now can say—
"I recognise thy glory": in such strength
Of usurpation, when the light of sense
Goes out, but with a flash that has revealed
The invisible world, doth greatness make abode,
There harbours; whether we be young or old,
Our destiny, our being's heart and home,
Is with infinitude, and only there;
With hope it is, hope that can never die,
Effort, and expectation, and desire,
And something evermore about to be.
Under such banners militant, the soul
Seeks for no trophies, struggles for no spoils
That may attest her prowess, blest in thoughts
That are their own perfection and reward,
Strong in herself and in beatitude
That hides her, like the mighty flood of Nile
Poured from his fount of Abyssinian clouds
To fertilise the whole Egyptian plain.

The melancholy slackening that ensued
Upon those tidings by the peasant given
Was soon dislodged. Downwards we hurried fast,

And, with the half-shaped road which we had missed,
Entered a narrow chasm. The brook and road
Were fellow-travellers in this gloomy strait,
And with them did we journey several hours
At a slow pace. The immeasurable height
Of woods decaying, never to be decayed,
The stationary blasts of waterfalls,
And in the narrow rent at every turn
Winds thwarting winds, bewildered and forlorn,
The torrents shooting from the clear blue sky,
The rocks that muttered close upon our ears,
Black drizzling crags that spake by the way-side
As if a voice were in them, the sick sight
And giddy prospect of the raving stream,
The unfettered clouds and region of the Heavens,
Tumult and peace, the darkness and the light—
Were all like workings of one mind, the features
Of the same face, blossoms upon one tree;
Characters of the great Apocalypse,
The types and symbols of Eternity,
Of first, and last, and midst, and without end.

WORDSWORTH

FIFTH PART

III. THE MANY AND THE ONE

Adagio molto espressivo
cresc:
cresc
cresc:
p
cresc
cresc
cresc:
Cantabile
f
p cresc:
cresc:

espressivo
cresc:
cresc:
cresc:
cresc:
dim:
dim:
dim:
dim:
Tempo 1o.

cresc:
p
cresc:
cresc:
p
cresc:
p
cresc:
cresc:
p
Cantabile
cresc:
cresc:
cresc:
cresc:
p
p
cresc:
cresc:
p
cresc:

rinf
tr
p
cresc:
rf

rf
tr
cresc:
cresc:
cresc:

tr
Dim:
Dim:
Dim:
p

Sotto voce
tr
Sotto voce

Pizz:
Arco
cresc:
Pizz:
Arco
cresc:
cresc:
cresc:
p
cresc:
p
p
cresc:
p
cresc:
p
cresc:
p
p
cresc:
p
cresc:
cresc:

tr
p
cresc:
p
cresc:
p
cresc:
p
cresc:
p dolce
p
p
p
cresc:
p
cresc:
p
cresc:
p
cresc:
p

cresc:
cresc:
cresc:
cresc:
f
cresc:
f
p
cresc:
f
p
cresc:
f
p
Dim:
cresc:
Dim:
cresc:
pp
Dim:
cresc:
pp
Dim:
cresc:

tr
pp
Pizz:
pp

cresc:
cresc:
cresc:
p
p
pp
p
p

cresc:
p
p
pp
p
Arco
pp
p

ritard
ten
cresc:
p
pp
ten
cresc:
p
pp
ten
cresc:
p
pp
ten
cresc:
p
pp
ten

§ 1

And Moses said unto God, Behold, when I come unto the children of Israel, and shall say unto them, The God of your fathers hath sent me unto you; and they shall say to me, What is his name? what shall I say unto them?

And God said unto Moses, I AM THAT I AM: and he said, Thus shalt thou say unto the children of Israel, I AM hath sent me unto you.

EXODUS

Jesus said unto them, Verily, verily, I say unto you, Before Abraham was, I am.

ST. JOHN

Lift up the stone and there shalt thou find me: cleave the wood, and I am there.

ATTRIBUTED TO CHRIST
(from the Oxyrhynchus Papyri)

Nevertheless I live; yet not I, but Christ liveth in me.

GALATIANS

Behold, I stand at the door, and knock: if any man hear my voice, and open the door, I will come in to him, and will sup with him, and he with me.

REVELATION

It is evident that being can only appertain to the all, and that the being of every part is the being of the all present in it, and which sustains it together with all the other parts.

LOUIS LAVELLE

Things are all the same in God: they are God himself.

MEISTER ECKHART

Fully awakened souls . . . realise that it is God who does everything.

There was a monastery in a certain place. The monks residing there went out daily to beg their food. One day a monk, while out for his alms, saw a landlord beating a man mercilessly. The compassionate monk stepped in and asked the landlord to stop. But the landlord was filled with anger and turned his wrath against the innocent monk. He beat the monk till he fell unconscious on the ground. Someone reported the matter to the monastery. The monks ran to the spot and found their brother lying there. Four or five of them carried him back and laid him on a bed. He was still unconscious. The other monks sat around him sad at heart; some were fanning him. Finally someone suggested that he should be given a little milk to drink. When it was poured into his mouth he regained consciousness. He opened his eyes and looked around. One of the monks said, "Let us see whether he is fully conscious and can recognise us." Shouting into his ear, he said, "Revered sir, who is giving you milk?" "Brother," replied the holy man in a low voice, "he who beat me is now giving me milk."

SRI RAMAKRISHNA

He who has gotten the whole world plus God has gotten no more than God by himself.

MEISTER ECKHART

The highest Seraph has but a single image. He seizes as a unity all that his inferiors regard as manifold.

MEISTER ECKHART

It is told of a [Hasidic] Master, that in his hours of rapture he had to look at the clock in order to keep himself in this world, and of another, that when he wished to consider the separate phenomena of life, he had to put on spectacles in order to control his spiritual vision, "for otherwise he would have seen all the separate phenomena in the world as one."

But the highest grade which is recorded is that in which the man of ardour transcends his own enthusiasm. When a disciple once noticed and blamed a Master for his slackening of zeal, he was taught by another: "There is a very high grade of holiness; when a man reaches this, he is freed from a sense of his own existence and is no more capable of fervour." Thus fervour is fulfilled by its own annulment.

MARTIN BUBER

For them [beatified spirits] all things are transparent, and there is nothing dark or impenetrable, but everyone is manifest to everyone internally, and all things are manifest; for light is manifest to light. For everyone has all things in himself and sees all things in another; so that all things are everywhere and all is all and each is all, and the glory is infinite. Each of them is great, since the small also is great. In heaven the sun is all the stars, and again each and all are the sun. One thing in each is prominent above the rest; for it also shows forth all. There a pure movement reigns; but that which produces the movement, not being a stranger to it, does not trouble it. Rest is also perfect there, because no principle of agitation mingles with it.

PLOTINUS

In the City of the new Jerusalem there is neither Sun nor Moon; where glorifyed Eyes must see by the archetypal Sun, or the Light of God, able to illuminate Intellectual Eyes, and make unknown Visions. Intuitive perceptions in Spiritual beings may perhaps hold some Analogy unto Vision: but yet how they see us, or one another, what Eye, what Light, or what perception is required unto their intuition, is yet dark unto our apprehension; and even how they see God, or how unto our glorified

Eyes the Beatifical Vision will be celebrated, another World must tell us, when perceptions will be new, and we may hope to behold invisibles.

SIR THOMAS BROWNE

How all things weave themselves to one,
Working, living, each in other,
While up and down the angelic powers go,
Bearing the golden pitchers to and fro!
The splendour swings from hand to hand!
On wings of fragrance, on wings that bless
From heaven through all the world they press
Till all rings loud with their loveliness.

GOETHE (from *Faust*)

The ancient tradition that the world will be consumed in fire at the end of six thousand years is true, as I have heard from Hell.

For the cherub with his flaming sword is hereby commanded to leave his guard at tree of life, and when he does, the whole creation will be consumed and appear infinite and holy, whereas it now appears finite and corrupt.

This will come to pass by an improvement of sensual enjoyment.

But first the notion that man has a body distinct from his soul is to be expunged; this I shall do by printing in the infernal method, by corrosives, which in Hell are salutary and medicinal, melting apparent surfaces away, and displaying the infinite which was hid.

If the doors of perception were cleansed everything would appear to man as it is, infinite.

For man has closed himself up till he sees all things thro' narrow chinks of his cavern.

BLAKE (from *The Marriage of Heaven and Hell*)

The people think that they pray before God. But it is not so. For the prayer itself is the essence of the Godhead.

RABBI PINHAS OF KOREZ

Prayer is no other but the revelation of the will or mind of God.

JOHN SALTMARSH

He it is that desireth in thee, and He it is that is desired.

WALTER HYLTON

God in the depths of us receives God who comes to us: it is God contemplating God.

JAN VAN RUYSBROECK

What else, Lord, is Thy seeing, when Thou beholdest me with pitying eye, than that Thou art seen of me? In beholding me Thou givest Thyself to be seen of me, Thou who art a hidden God. None can see Thee save in so far as Thou grantest a sight of Thyself, nor is that sight aught else than Thy seeing him that seeth Thee.

NICHOLAS OF CUSA

God is the fire in me, I am the glow in Him.

ANGELUS SILESIUS

I am a single drop; how can it be
That God, the whole ocean, floweth into me?

ANGELUS SILESIUS

God in me, God without! Beyond compare!
A Being wholly here and wholly there!

ANGELUS SILESIUS

Put out my eyes, and I can see you still;
slam my ears to, and I can hear you yet;
and without any feet can go to you;
and tongueless, I can conjure you at will.
Break off my arms, I shall take hold of you
and grasp you with my heart as with a hand;
arrest my heart, my brain will beat as true;
and if you set this brain of mine afire,
then on my blood-stream I yet will carry you.

RAINER MARIA RILKE

Although, as from a prison walled with hate,
each from his own self labours to be free,
the world yet holds a wonder, and how great!
All life is LIVED: now this comes home to me.
But who, then, lives it? Things that patiently
stand there, like some unfingered melody
sleeping within a harp as day is going?
Is it the winds across the water blowing,
is it the branches beckoning each to each,
is it the flowers weaving fragrances,
the ageing alleys stretching endlessly?
Is it the warm beasts moving to and fro,
the birds in alien flight that sail from view?
This life—who lives it really? God, do you?

RAINER MARIA RILKE

The mental intellectual love towards God is the very love of God with which God loves himself, not in so far as he is infinite, but in so far as he can be expressed through the essence of the human mind considered under the species of eternity, that is, mental intellectual love towards God is part of the infinite love with which God loves himself. . . .

Hence it follows that God, in so far as he loves himself, loves men, and consequently that the love of God for men and the mind's intellectual love towards God is one and the same thing.

From this we clearly understand in what consists our salvation, blessedness, or liberty, namely, in the constant and eternal love for God, or in the love of God for men.

SPINOZA

There is therefore a sense in which we can say that the world of finite intelligence, though distinct from God, is still, in its ideal nature, one with Him. That which God creates, and by which He reveals the hidden treasures of His wisdom and love, is still not foreign to His own infinite life, but one with it. In the knowledge of the minds that know Him, in the self-surrender of the hearts that love Him, it is no paradox to affirm that He knows and loves Himself. As He is the origin and inspiration of every true thought and pure affection, of every experience in which we forget and rise above ourselves, so is He also of all these the end. If in one point of view religion is the work of man, in another it is the work of God. Its true significance is not apprehended till we pass beyond its origin in time and in the experience of a finite spirit, to see in it the revelation of the mind of God Himself. In the language of Scripture, "It is God that worketh in us to will and to do of His good pleasure: all things are of God, who hath reconciled us to Himself."

JOHN CAIRD

§ 2

The more we understand individual things, the more we understand God.

SPINOZA

The Infinite alone resides in Definite and Determinate Identity.

BLAKE (from *Jerusalem*)

Circle in point, blossom in seedling lies;
Those who seek God within the world are wise.

ANGELUS SILESIUS

It is only through the manifestations of Being, and only through those with which I enter into relations, that my being has any intercourse with infinite Being. The devotion of my being to infinite Being means devotion of my being to all the manifestations of being which need my devotion, and to which I am able to devote myself.

ALBERT SCHWEITZER

"That violence whereby sometimes a man doteth upon one creature is but a little spark of that love, even towards all, which lurketh in his nature. When we dote upon the perfections and beauties of some one creature, we do not love that too much, but other things too little. Never was anything in this world loved too much, but many things have been loved in a false way, and all in too short a measure." Traherne might have added (what many poets and novelists have remarked) that, when "we dote upon the perfections and beauties of some one creature," we frequently find ourselves moved to love other creatures. Moreover, to be in love is, in many cases, to have achieved a state of being, in which it becomes possible to have direct intuition of the essentially lovely nature of ultimate reality. "What a world would this be, were everything beloved as it ought to be!" For many people, everything is beloved as it ought to be, only when they are in love with "some one creature." The cynical wisdom of the folk affirms that love is blind. But in reality, perhaps, the blind are those who are not in love and who therefore fail to perceive how beautiful the world is and how adorable.

ALDOUS HUXLEY

In this light my spirit soon saw through all things; and in all creatures, in herb and grass, knew God—who He is, how He is, and what is His will.

JAKOB BOEHME

In all faces is seen the Face of faces, veiled, and in a riddle.

NICHOLAS OF CUSA

The rose that with your earthly eyes you see,
Has flowered in God from all eternity.

ANGELUS SILESIUS

THE SPARK

Calm was the evening, as if asleep,
But sickled on high with brooding storm,
Couched in invisible space. And, lo!
I saw in utter silence sweep
Out of that darkening starless vault
A gliding spark, as blanched as snow,
That burned into dust, and vanished in
A hay-cropped meadow, brightly green.

A meteor from the cold of space,
Lost in Earth's wilderness of air?—
Presage of lightnings soon to shine
In splendour on this lonely place?—
I cannot tell; but only how fair
It glowed within the crystalline
Pure heavens, and of its strangeness lit
My mind to joy at sight of it.

Yet what is common as lovely may be:
The petalled daisy, a honey bell,
A pebble, a branch of moss, a gem
Of dew, or fallen rain—if we
A moment in their beauty dwell;
Entranced, alone, see only them.
How blind to wait, till, merely unique,
Some omen thus the all bespeak!

WALTER DE LA MARE

THE SNOWDROP

Now—now, as low I stooped, thought I,
I will see what this snowdrop *is*;
So shall I put much argument by,
And solve a lifetime's mysteries.

A northern wind had frozen the grass;
Its blades were hoar with crystal rime,
Aglint like light-dissecting glass
At beam of morning-prime.

From hidden bulb the flower reared up
Its angled, slender, cold, dark stem,
Whence dangled an inverted cup
For tri-leaved diadem.

Beneath these ice-pure sepals lay
A triplet of green-pencilled snow,
Which in the chill-aired gloom of day
Stirred softly to and fro.

Mind fixed, but else made vacant, I,
Lost to my body, called my soul
To don that frail solemnity,
Its inmost self my goal.

And though in vain—no mortal mind
Across that threshold yet hath fared!—
In this collusion I divined
Some consciousness we shared.

Strange roads—while suns, a myriad, set—
Had led us through infinity;
And where they crossed, there then had met
Not two of us, but three.

WALTER DE LA MARE

I am the sacred smell of the earth,
The light of the fire,
Life of all lives,
Austerity of ascetics.

Know me, eternal seed
Of everything that grows:
The intelligence of those who understand,
The vigour of the active.
In the strong, I am strength
Unhindered by lust
And the objects of craving:
I am all that a man may desire
Without transgressing
The law of his nature.

THE BHAGAVAD-GITA

HOW MANY HEAVENS . . .

The emeralds are singing on the grasses
And in the trees the bells of the long cold are ringing,—
My blood seems changed to emeralds like the spears
Of grass beneath the earth piercing and singing.

The flame of the first blade
Is an angel piercing through the earth to sing
"God is everything!
The grass within the grass, the angel in the angel, flame
Within the flame, and He is the green shade that came
To be the heart of shade."

The grey-beard angel of the stone,
Who has grown wise with age, cried "Not alone
Am I within my silence,—God is the stone in the still stone,
the silence laid
In the heart of silence" . . . then, above the glade

The yellow straws of light
Whereof the sun has built his nest, cry "Bright
Is the world, the yellow straw
My brother,—God is the straw within the straw:—
All things are Light."

He is the sea of ripeness and the sweet apple's emerald lore.
So you, my flame of grass, my root of the world from which all Spring shall grow,
O you, my hawthorn bough of the stars, now leaning low
Through the day, for your flowers to kiss my lips, shall know
He is the core of the heart of love, and He, beyond labouring seas, our ultimate shore.

EDITH SITWELL

THE BEE-KEEPER

In the plain of the world's dust like a great Sea,
The golden thunders of the Lion and the Honey-Bee
In the Spirit, held with the Sun a Colloquy

Where an old woman stood—thick Earthiness—
Half Sun, half Clod,
A plant alive from the root, still blind with earth
And all the weight of Death and Birth.

She, in her primitive dress
Of clay, bent to her hives
And heard her sisters of the barren lives

Begin to stir . . . the Priestesses of the Gold Comb
Shaped by Darkness, and the Prophetesses
Who from a wingless pupa, spark of gold

In the Dark, rose with gold bodies bright as the Lion,
And the trace of the Hand of God on ephemeral wings
To sing the great Hymn of Being to the lost:

"This Earth is the honey of all Beings, and all Beings
Are the honey of this Earth . . . O bright immortal Lover
That is incarnate in the body's earth—
O bright immortal Lover Who is All!"

"This Water is the honey of all Beings, and all Beings
Are the honey of this Water . . . O the bright immortal Lover
That is in water and that is the seed
Of Life . . . O bright immortal Lover Who is All!"

"This Fire is the honey of all Beings, and all Beings
Are the honey of this Fire . . . O bright immortal Lover
That is in fire and shines in mortal speech—
O bright immortal Lover Who is All!"

"This Air is the honey of all Beings, and all Beings
Are the honey of this Air . . . O bright immortal Lover
That is in air and is our Being's breath—
O bright immortal Lover Who is all!"

"This Sun is the honey of all Beings, and all Beings
Are the honey of this Sun . . . O bright immortal Lover
That is in the sun and is our Being's sight—
O bright immortal Lover Who is all!"

"This Thunder is the honey of all Beings, and all Beings
Are the honey of this Thunder . . . O the bright immortal Lover,
That is in thunder and all voices—the beasts' roar—
Thunder of rising saps—the voice of Man!
O bright immortal Lover Who is All!"

This was the song that came from the small span
Of thin gold bodies shaped by the holy Dark. . . .

And the old woman in her mortal dress of clay
(That plant alive from the root, still thick with earth)
Felt all the saps of Day.

And in the plain of dust like a great Sea
The Lion in the Spirit cried, "Destroy—destroy
The old and wrinkled Darkness." But the Sun
—That great gold simpleton—laughed like a boy,
And kissed the old woman's cheek and blessed her clay.
The great Sun laughed, and dancing over Chaos,
Shouts to the dust "O mortal Lover! Think what wonders
May be born of our love—what golden heroes!"

The Bee in the Spirit said "The gold combs lay
In the cold rock and the slain Lion, amid spent golden
thunders."

EDITH SITWELL

"I am Brahma." Whoever knows this, "I am Brahma," knows all. Even the gods are unable to prevent his becoming Brahma.

THE UPANISHADS

Who sees his Lord
Within every creature,
Deathlessly dwelling
Amidst the mortal:
That man sees truly. . . .

Who sees the separate
Lives of all creatures
United in Brahman
Brought forth from Brahman,
Himself finds Brahman.

THE BHAGAVAD-GITA

Yes, we must become Brahma. We must not shrink from avowing this. Our existence is meaningless if we never can expect to realise the highest perfection that there is. If we have an aim and yet can never reach it, then it is no aim at all.

But can it then be said that there is no difference between Brahma and our individual soul? Of course the difference is obvious. Call it illusion or ignorance, or whatever name you may give it, it is there. You can offer explanations but you cannot explain it away. Even illusion is true as illusion.

Brahma is Brahma, he is the infinite ideal of perfection. But we are not what we truly are; we are ever to become true, ever to become Brahma. There is the eternal play of love in the relation between this being and the becoming; and in the depth of this mystery is the source of all truth and beauty that sustains the endless march of creation.

In the music of the rushing stream sounds the joyful assurance, "I shall become the sea." It is not a vain assumption; it is true humility, for it is the truth. The river has no other alternative. On both sides of its banks it has numerous fields and forests, villages and towns; it can serve them in various ways, cleanse them and feed them, carry their produce from place to place. But it can have only partial relations with these, and however long it may linger among them it remains separate; it never can become a town or a forest.

But it can and does become the sea. The lesser moving water has its affinity with the great motionless water of the ocean. It moves through the thousand objects on its onward course, and its motion finds its finality when it reaches the sea.

The river can become the sea, but she can never make the sea part and parcel of herself. If, by some chance, she has encircled some broad sheet of water and pretends that she has made the sea a part of herself, we at once know that it is not so, that her current is still seeking rest in the great ocean to which it can never set boundaries.

In the same manner, our soul can only become Brahma as the river can become the sea. Everything else she touches at one of her points, then leaves and moves on, but she never can leave Brahma and move beyond him. Once our soul realises her ultimate object of repose in Brahma, all her movements acquire a purpose. It is this ocean of infinite rest which gives significance to endless activities. It is this perfectness of being that lends to the imperfection of becoming that quality of beauty which finds its expression in all poetry, drama, and art.

RABINDRANATH TAGORE

It fills me with great joy and a high hope for the future of humanity when I realise that there was a time in the remote past when our poet-prophets stood under the lavish sunshine of an Indian sky and greeted the world with the glad recognition of kindred. It was not an anthropomorphic hallucination. It was not seeing man reflected everywhere in grotesquely exaggerated images, and witnessing the human drama acted on a gigantic scale in nature's arena of flitting lights and shadows. On the contrary, it meant crossing the limiting barriers of the individual, to become more than man, to become one with the All. It was not a mere play of the imagination, but it was the liberation of consciousness from all the mystifications and exaggerations of the self. These ancient seers felt in the serene depth of their mind that the same energy, which vibrates and passes into the endless forms of the world, manifests itself in our inner being as consciousness; and there is no break in unity. For these seers there was no gap in their luminous vision of perfection. They never acknowledged even death itself as creating a chasm in the field of reality. They said, *His reflection is death as well as immortality*. They did not recognise any essential opposition between life and death, and they said with absolute assurance, "It is life that is death." They saluted with the same serenity of gladness "life in its aspect of appearing and in its aspect of departure"—*That which is past is hidden in life, and that which is to come.* They knew that mere appearance and disappearance are on the surface like waves on the sea, but life which is permanent knows no decay or diminution.

Everything has sprung from immortal life and is vibrating with life, for *life is immense.*

This is the noble heritage from our forefathers waiting to

be claimed by us as our own, this ideal of the supreme freedom of consciousness. It is not merely intellectual or emotional, it has an ethical basis, and it must be translated into action. In the Upanishad it is said, *The supreme being is all-pervading, therefore he is the innate good in all.* To be truly united in knowledge, love, and service with all beings, and thus to realise one's self in the all-pervading God is the essence of goodness, and this is the keynote of the teachings of the Upanishads: *Life is immense!*

RABINDRANATH TAGORE

It costs me nothing to feel that I am; it is no burden to me. And yet if the mental, physical, chemical and other innumerable facts concerning all branches of knowledge which have united in myself could be broken up, they would prove endless. It is some untold mystery of unity in me, that has the simplicity of the infinite and reduces the immense mass of multitude to a single point.

This One in me knows the universe of the many. But, in whatever it knows, it knows the One in different aspects. It knows this room only because this room is One to it, in spite of the seeming contradiction of the endless facts contained in the single fact of the room. Its knowledge of a tree is the knowledge of a unity, which appears in the aspect of a tree.

This One in me is creative. Its creations are a pastime, through which it gives expression to an ideal of unity in its endless show of variety. Such are its pictures, poems, music, in which it finds joy only because they reveal the perfect forms of an inherent unity.

This One in me not only seeks unity in knowledge for its understanding and creates images of unity for its delight; it also seeks union in love for its fulfilment. It seeks itself in others. This is a fact, which would be absurd had there been no great medium of truth to give it reality. In love we find a joy which is ultimate because it is the ultimate truth. Therefore it is said in the Upanishads that the *advaitam* is *anantam*,—"the One is Infinite"; that the *advaitam* is *anandam*,—"the One is Love."

To give perfect expression to the One, the Infinite, through the harmony of the many; to the One, the Love, through the sacrifice of self, is the object alike of our individual life and our society.

RABINDRANATH TAGORE

One day, in a small village in Bengal, an ascetic woman from the neighbourhood came to see me. She had the name "Sarvakhepi" given to her by the village people, the meaning of which is "the woman who is mad about all things." She fixed her star-like eyes upon my face and startled me with the question, "When are you coming to meet me underneath the trees?" Evidently she pitied me who lived (according to her) prisoned behind walls, banished away from the great meeting-place of the All, where she had her dwelling. Just at that moment my gardener came with his basket, and when the woman understood that the flowers in the vase on my table were going to be thrown away, to make place for the fresh ones, she looked pained and said to me, "You are always engaged reading and writing; you do not see." Then she took the discarded flowers in her palms, kissed them and touched them with her forehead, and reverently murmured to herself, "Beloved of my heart." I felt that this woman, in her direct vision of the infinite personality in the heart of all things, truly represented the spirit of India.

RABINDRANATH TAGORE

At midnight the would-be ascetic announced:

"This is the time to give up my home and seek for God. Ah, who has held me so long in delusion here?"

God whispered, "I," but the ears of the man were stopped.

With a baby asleep at her breast lay his wife, peacefully sleeping on one side of the bed.

The man said, "Who are ye that have fooled me so long?"

The voice said again, "They are God," but he heard it not.

The baby cried out in its dream, nestling close to its mother.

God commanded, "Stop, fool, leave not thy home," but still he heard not.

God sighed and complained, "Why does my servant wander to seek me, forsaking me?"

RABINDRANATH TAGORE

There is a strange tree, which stands without roots and bears fruits without blossoming;
It has no branches and no leaves, it is lotus all over.
Two birds sing there; one is the Guru, and the other the disciple:
The disciple chooses the manifold fruits of life and tastes them, and the Guru beholds him in joy.
What Kabir says is hard to understand: "The bird is beyond seeking, yet it is most clearly visible. The Formless is in the midst of all forms. I sing the glory of forms."

KABIR

What then is man's true treasure? It is his Inward Vision (*ming*), a generalised perception that can come into play only when the distinction between "inside" and "outside," between "self" and "things," between "this" and "that" has been entirely obliterated. Chuang Tzu's symbol for this state of pure consciousness, which sees without looking, hears without listening, knows without thinking, is the god Hun-tun ("Chaos"): "Fuss, the god of the Southern Ocean, and Fret, the god of the Northern Ocean, happened once to meet in the realm of Chaos, the god of the centre. Chaos treated them very handsomely and they discussed together what they could do to repay his kindness. They had noticed that, whereas everyone else has seven apertures, for sight, hearing, eating, breathing and so on, Chaos had none. So they decided to make the experiment of boring holes in him. Every day they bored a hole, and on the seventh day Chaos died."

ARTHUR WALEY

In merely catching your own casting all's
mere cleverness and indecisive winning:—
only when all at once you're catching balls
an everlasting partner hurtles spinning
into your very centre, with trajecture
exactly calculated, curvingly
recalling God's stupendous pontifecture,—
only then catching's capability,
not yours, a world's. And if, not resting here,
you'd strength and will to throw them back again,—
no,—wonderfullier!—forgot such things, and then
found you'd already thrown . . . as, twice a year,
the flocking birds are thrown, the birds that wander,
thrown from an older to a younger, yonder,
ultramarine warmth,—in that mood of sheer
abandon you'd be equal to the game.
Both ease and difficulty would disappear:
you'd simply throw. A meteor would flame
out of your hands and tear through its own spaces.

RAINER MARIA RILKE

Everything beckons to us to perceive it,
murmurs at every turn, "Remember me!"
A day we passed, too busy to receive it,
will yet unlock us all its treasury.

Who shall compute our harvest? Who shall bar
us from the former years, the long-departed?
What have we learnt from living since we started,
except to find in others what we are?

Except to re-enkindle commonplace?
O house, O sloping field, O setting sun!
Your features form into a face, you run,
you cling to us, returning our embrace!
One space spreads through all creatures equally—
inner-world-space. Birds quietly flying go
flying through us. O, I that want to grow,
the tree I look outside at's growing in me!

I have a house within when I need care.
I have a guard within when I need rest.
The love that I have had!—Upon my breast
the beauty of the world clings, to weep there.

RAINER MARIA RILKE

. . . For even those that have only longed have related
themselves to the whole with webs too fine to observe;
round their refulgent hearts have rotated
worlds of night in a consummate curve.

RAINER MARIA RILKE

The desire of Man being Infinite, the possession is Infinite, and himself Infinite.

Application.

He who sees the Infinite in all things, sees God. He who sees the Ratio only, sees himself only.

Therefore

God becomes as we are that we may be as He is.

BLAKE

The only strength for me is to be found in the sense of a personal presence everywhere, it scarcely matters whether it be called human or divine; a presence which only makes itself felt at first in this and that particular form and feature. . . . Into this presence we come, not by leaving behind what are usually called earthly things, or by loving them less, but by living more intensely in them, and loving more what is really loveable in them; for it is literally true that this world *is* everything to us, if only we choose to make it so, if only we "live in the present" *because* it is eternity. . . .

R. L. NETTLESHIP

This increasing exploitation of life, is it not a result of the centuries-long disparagement of the here-and-now? What madness, to divert us towards a Beyond, when here, where we are, we are surrounded with tasks and expectations and futures! What imposture, to pilfer from us pictures of earthly delight in order to sell them to Heaven behind our backs! . . . And, since no vacuity can persist, is not everything that is taken away from here replaced by an illusion,—are not towns full of so much ugly artificial light and noise just because the true splendour in the song has been delivered over to some Jerusalem to be entered later?

RAINER MARIA RILKE

FAUST. The Spirit looks not forward, not behind,
Here in the Present,—
HELEN. Here our joy we find.

GOETHE

Both the first day and the last are happening at the present instant yonder.

MEISTER ECKHART

Everything in nature happens both mechanically and metaphysically, and the source of the mechanical is in the metaphysical.

LEIBNIZ (compressed)

THE HAPPY ENCOUNTER

I saw sweet Poetry turn troubled eyes
  On shaggy Science nosing on the grass,
  For by that way poor Poetry must pass
On her long pilgrimage to Paradise.
He snuffled, grunted, squealed; perplexed by flies,
  Parched, weatherworn, and near of sight, alas,
  From peering close where very little was
In dens secluded from the open skies.

But Poetry in bravery went down,
  And called his name, soft, clear, and fearlessly;
Stooped low, and stroked his muzzle overgrown;
  Refreshed his drought with dew; wiped pure and free
  His eyes: and lo! laughed loud for joy to see
In those grey deeps the azure of her own.

WALTER DE LA MARE

Cease not to think of the Universe as one living Being, possessed of a single Substance and a single Soul; and how all things trace back to its single sentience; and how it does all things by a single impulse; and how all existing things are joint causes of all things that come into existence; and how intertwined in the fabric is the thread and how closely woven the web.

MARCUS AURELIUS

All that is in tune with thee, O Universe, is in tune with me! Nothing that is in due time for thee is too early or too late for me! All that thy seasons bring, O Nature, is fruit for me! All things come from thee, subsist in thee, go back to thee. There is one who says *Dear City of Cecrops!* Wilt thou not say *O dear City of Zeus?*

MARCUS AURELIUS

§ 3

It is eternity now, I am in the midst of it. It is about me in the sunshine.

RICHARD JEFFERIES

ON THE BEACH AT NIGHT ALONE

On the beach at night alone,
As the old mother sways her to and fro singing her husky song,
As I watch the bright stars shining, I think a thought of the clef of the universes and of the future.

A vast similitude interlocks all,
All spheres, grown, ungrown, small, large, suns, moons, planets,
All distances of place however wide,
All distances of time, all inanimate forms,
All souls, all living bodies though they be ever so different, or in different worlds,
All gaseous, watery, vegetable, mineral processes, the fishes, the brutes,
All nations, colours, barbarisms, civilisations, languages,
All identities that have existed or may exist on this globe, or any globe,
All lives and deaths, all of the past, present, future,
This vast similitude spans them, and always has spann'd,
And shall forever span them and compactly hold and enclose them.

WALT WHITMAN

I lay among the ferns,
Where they lifted their fronds, innumerable, in the greenwood wilderness, like wings winnowing the air;
And their voices went past me continually.

And I listened, and lo! softly inaudibly raining I heard not the voices of the ferns only, but of all living creatures:
Voices of mountain and star,
Of cloud and forest and ocean,
And of the little rills tumbling amid the rocks,
And of the high tops where the moss-beds are and the springs arise.
As the wind at mid-day rains whitening over the grass,
As the night-bird glimmers a moment, fleeting between the lonely watcher and the moon,
So softly inaudibly they rained,
Where I sat silent.

And in the silence of the greenwood I knew the secret of the growth of the ferns;
I saw their delicate leaflets tremble breathing an undescribed and unuttered life;
And, below, the ocean lay sleeping;
And round them the mountains and the stars dawned in glad companionship for ever.

And a voice came to me, saying:
In every creature, in forest and ocean, in leaf and tree and bird and beast and man, there moves a spirit other than its mortal own,
Pure, fluid, as air—intense as fire,
Which looks abroad and passes along the spirits of all other creatures, drawing them close to itself,
Nor dreams of other law than that of perfect equality;
And this is the spirit of immortality and peace.

And whatsoever creature hath this spirit, to it no harm may befall:
No harm can befall, for wherever it goes it has its nested home, and to it every loss comes charged with an equal gain;
It gives—but to receive a thousand-fold;
It yields its life—but at the hands of love;
And death is the law of its eternal growth.

And I saw that was the law of every creature—that this spirit should enter in and take possession of it,
That it might have no more fear or doubt or be at war within itself any longer.
And lo! in the greenwood all around me it moved,
Where the sunlight floated fragrant under the boughs, and the fern-fronds winnowed the air;
In the oak-leaves dead of last year, and in the small shy things that rustled among them;
In the songs of the birds, and the broad shadowing leaves overhead;
In the fields sleeping below, and in the river and the high dreaming air;
Gleaming ecstatic it moved—with joy incarnate.
And it seemed to me, as I looked, that it penetrated all these things, suffusing them;
And wherever it penetrated, behold! there was nothing left down to the smallest atom which was not a winged spirit instinct with life.

EDWARD CARPENTER (from *Among the Ferns*)

CORRELATED GREATNESS

O nothing, in this corporal earth of man,
That to the imminent heaven of his high soul
Responds with colour and with shadow, can
Lack correlated greatness. If the scroll
Where thoughts lie fast in spell of hieroglyph

Be mighty through its mighty habitants;
If God be in His Name; grave potence if
The sounds unbind of hieratic chants;
All's vast that vastness means. Nay, I affirm
Nature is whole in her least things exprest.
Nor know we with what scope God builds the worm.
Our towns are copied fragments from our breast;
    And all man's Babylons strive but to impart
    The grandeurs of his Babylonian heart.

FRANCIS THOMPSON

Ah woe is me!
What have I dared? where am I lifted? how
Shall I descend, and perish not? I know
That love makes all things equal: I have heard
By mine own heart this joyous truth averred,—
The spirit of the worm beneath the sod,
In love and worship, blends itself with God.

SHELLEY (from *Epipsychidion*)

THE BOOK OF THEL

I

The daughters of the Seraphim led round their sunny flocks,
All but the youngest: she in paleness sought the secret air,
To fade away like morning beauty from her mortal day:
Down by the river of Adona her soft voice is heard,
And thus her gentle lamentation falls like morning dew:—

O life of this our spring! why fades the lotus of the water?
Why fade these children of the spring, born but to smile and fall?
Ah! Thel is like a wat'ry bow, and like a parting cloud;
Like a reflection in a glass; like shadows in the water;
Like dreams of infants, like a smile upon an infant's face;

Like the dove's voice; like transient day; like music in the air.
Ah! gentle may I lay me down and gentle rest my head,
And gentle sleep the sleep of death, and gently hear the voice
Of him that walketh in the garden in the evening time.

The Lilly of the valley breathing in the humble grass
Answered the lovely maid and said: I am a wat'ry weed,
And I am very small, and love to dwell in lowly vales,
So weak, the gilded butterfly scarce perches on my head.
Yet I am visited from heaven, and he that smiles on all
Walks in the valley, and each morn over me spreads his hand
Saying, Rejoice, thou humble grass, thou new-born lilly-flower,
Thou gentle maid of silent valleys and of modest brooks;
For thou shalt be clothed in light, and fed with morning manna,
Till summer's heat melts thee beside the fountains and the springs
To flourish in eternal vales: then why should Thel complain?
Why should the mistress of the vales of Har utter a sigh?
She ceas'd, and smil'd in tears, then sat down in her silver shrine.

Thel answered: O thou little virgin of the peaceful valley,
Giving to those that cannot crave, the voiceless, the o'ertired;
Thy breath doth nourish the innocent lamb, he smells thy milky garments,
He crops thy flowers while thou sittest smiling in his face,
Wiping his mild and meekin mouth from all contagious taints.
Thy wine doth purify the golden honey; thy perfume,
Which thou dost scatter on every little blade of grass that springs,
Revives the milked cow, and tames the fire-breathing steed.
But Thel is like a faint cloud kindled at the rising sun.
I vanish from my pearly throne, and who shall find my place?
Queen of the vales, the Lilly answered, ask the tender cloud,
And it shall tell thee why it glitters in the morning sky,
And why it scatters its bright beauty thro' the humid air.
Descend, O little cloud, and hover before the eyes of Thel.

The Cloud descended, and the Lilly bowed her modest head,
And went to mind her numerous charge among the verdant grass.

II

O little Cloud, the virgin said, I charge thee tell to me
Why thou complainest not when in one hour thou fade away;
Then we shall seek thee, but not find. Ah, Thel is like to Thee.
I pass away, yet I complain, and no one hears my voice.

The cloud then shew'd his golden head and his bright form emerg'd,
Hovering and glittering on the air before the face of Thel.
O virgin, know'st thou not our steeds drink of the golden springs
Where Luvah doth renew his horses? look'st thou on my youth,
And fearest thou because I vanish and am seen no more?
Nothing remains. O maid, I tell thee, when I pass away,
It is to tenfold life, to love, to peace, and raptures holy:
Unseen descending, weigh my light wings upon balmy flowers,
And court the fair-eyed dew, to take me to her shining tent.
The weeping virgin, trembling, kneels before the risen sun,
Till we arise link'd in a golden band and never part,
But walk united, bearing food to all our tender flowers.

Dost thou, O little Cloud? I fear that I am not like thee,
For I walk through the vales of Har, and smell the sweetest flowers;
But I feed not the little flowers. I hear the warbling birds,
But I feed not the warbling birds; they fly and seek their food:
But Thel delights in these no more, because I fade away,
And all shall say, without a use this shining woman liv'd,
Or did she only live to be at death the food of worms?

The Cloud reclin'd upon his airy throne, and answer'd thus:—

Then if thou art the food of worms, O virgin of the skies,
How great thy use, how great thy blessing; everything that lives
Lives not alone nor for itself: fear not, and I will call

The weak worm from its lowly bed, and thou shalt hear its voice.
Come forth, worm of the silent valley, to thy pensive queen.

The helpless worm arose, and sat upon the Lilly's leaf,
And the bright Cloud sail'd on, to find his partner in the vale.

III

Then Thel astonish'd view'd the Worm upon its dewy bed.

Art thou a Worm? Image of weakness, art thou but a Worm?
I see thee like an infant wrapped in the Lilly's leaf.
Ah weep not, little voice, thou canst not speak, but thou canst weep.
Is this a Worm? I see thee lay helpless and naked, weeping,
And none to answer, none to cherish thee with mother's smiles.
The Clod of Clay heard the Worm's voice and rais'd her pitying head;
She bow'd over the weeping infant, and her life exhal'd
In milky fondness, then on Thel she fix'd her humble eyes.

O beauty of the vales of Har, we live not for ourselves.
Thou seest me the meanest thing, and so I am indeed.
My bosom of itself is cold, and of itself is dark,
But he that loves the lowly, pours his oil upon my head
And kisses me, and binds his nuptial bands around my breast,
And says: Thou mother of my children, I have loved thee,
And I have given thee a crown that none can take away,
But how this is, sweet maid, I know not, and I cannot know.
I ponder, and I cannot ponder; yet I live and love.

The daughter of beauty wip'd her pitying tears with her white veil,
And said, Alas! I knew not this, and therefore did I weep;
That God would love a Worm I knew, and punish the evil foot
That wilful bruis'd its helpless form; but that He cherish'd it
With milk and oil I never knew, and therefore did I weep,

And I complain'd in the mild air, because I fade away,
And lay me down in thy cold bed, and leave my shining lot.

Queen of the vales, the matron Clay answered; I heard thy sighs,
And all thy moans flew o'er my roof, but I have call'd them down:
Wilt thou, O Queen, enter my house? 'tis given thee to enter
And to return: fear nothing, enter with thy virgin feet. . . .

BLAKE (the Motto and Part IV are omitted)

MELAMPUS

I

With love exceeding a simple love of the things
  That glide in grasses and rubble of woody wreck;
Or change their perch on a beat of quivering wings
  From branch to branch, only restful to pipe and peck;
Or, bristled, curl at a touch their snouts in a ball;
  Or cast their web between bramble and thorny hook;
The good physician Melampus, loving them all,
  Among them walked, as a scholar who reads a book.

II

For him the woods were a home and gave him the key
  Of knowledge, thirst for their treasures in herbs and flowers.
The secrets held by the creatures nearer than we
  To earth he sought, and the link of their life with ours:
And where alike we are, unlike where, and the veined
  Division, veined parallel, of a blood that flows
In them, in us, from the source by man unattained
  Save marks he well what the mystical woods disclose.

III

And this he deemed might be boon of love to a breast
  Embracing tenderly each little motive shape,
The prone, the flitting, who seek their food whither best
  Their wits direct, whither best from their foes escape:

For closer drawn to our mother's natural milk,
As babes they learn where her motherly help is great:
They know the juice for the honey, juice for the silk,
And need they medical antidotes find them straight.

IV

Of earth and sun they are wise, they nourish their broods,
Weave, build, hive, burrow and battle, take joy and pain
Like swimmers varying billows: never in woods
Runs white insanity fleeing itself: all sane
The woods revolve: as the tree its shadowing limns
To some resemblance in motion, the rooted life
Restrains disorder: you hear the primitive hymns
Of earth in woods issue wild of the web of strife.

V

Now sleeping once on a day of marvellous fire,
A brood of snakes he had cherished in grave regret
That death his people had dealt their dam and their sire,
Through savage dread of them, crept to his neck, and set
Their tongues to lick him: the swift affectionate tongue
Of each ran licking the slumberer: then his ears
A forked red tongue tickled shrewdly: sudden upsprung,
He heard a voice piping: Ay, for he has no fears!

VI

A bird said that, in the notes of birds, and the speech
Of men, it seemed: and another renewed: He moves
To learn and not to pursue, he gathers to teach;
He feeds his young as do we, and as we love loves.
No fears have I of a man who goes with his head
To earth, chance looking aloft at us, kind of hand:
I feel to him as to earth of whom we are fed;
I pipe him much for his good could he understand.

VII

Melampus touched at his ears, laid finger on wrist:
  He was not dreaming, he sensibly felt and heard.
Above, through leaves, where the tree-twigs thick intertwist,
  He spied the birds and the bill of the speaking bird.
His cushion mosses in shades of various green,
  The lumped, the antlered, he pressed, while the sunny snake
Slipped under: draughts he had drunk of clear Hippocrene,
  It seemed, and sat with a gift of the Gods awake.

VIII

Divinely thrilled was the man, exultingly full,
  As quick well-waters that come of the heart of earth,
Ere yet they dart in a brook are one bubble-pool
  To light and sound, wedding both at the leap of birth.
The soul of light vivid shone, a stream within stream;
  The soul of sound from a musical shell outflew;
Where others hear but a hum and see but a beam,
  The tongue and eye of the fountain of life he knew.

IX

He knew the Hours: they were round him, laden with seed
  Of hours bestrewn upon vapour, and one by one
They winged as ripened in fruit the burden decreed
  For each to scatter; they flushed like the buds in sun,
Bequeathing seed to successive similar rings,
  Their sisters, bearers to men of what men have earned:
He knew them, talked with the yet unreddened; the stings,
  The sweets, they warmed at their bosoms divined, discerned.

X

Not unsolicited, sought by diligent feet,
  By riddling fingers expanded, oft watched in growth
With brooding deep as the noon-ray's quickening wheat,
  Ere touch'd, the pendulous flower of the plants of sloth,

The plants of rigidness, answered question and squeeze,
  Revealing wherefore it bloomed uninviting, bent,
Yet making harmony breathe of life and disease,
  The deeper chord of a wonderful instrument.

XI

So passed he luminous-eyed for earth and the fates
  We arm to bruise or caress us: his ears were charged
With tones of love in a whirl of voluble hates,
  With music wrought of distraction his heart enlarged.
Celestial-shining, though mortal, singer, though mute,
  He drew the Master of harmonies, voiced or stilled,
To seek him; heard at the silent medicine-root
  A song, beheld in fulfilment the unfulfilled.

XII

Him Phoebus, lending to darkness colour and form
  Of light's excess, many lessons and counsels gave;
Showed Wisdom lord of the human intricate swarm,
  And whence prophetic it looks on the hives that rave;
And how acquired, of the zeal of love to acquire,
  And where it stands, in the centre of life a sphere;
And Measure, mood of the lyre, the rapturous lyre,
  He said was Wisdom, and struck him the notes to hear.

XIII

Sweet, sweet: 'twas glory of vision, honey, the breeze
  In heat, the run of the river on root and stone,
All senses joined, as the sister Pierides
  Are one, uplifting their chorus, the Nine, his own.
In stately order, evolved of sound into sight,
  From sight to sound intershifting, the man descried
The growths of earth, his adored, like day out of night,
  Ascend in song, seeing nature and song allied.

XIV

And there vitality, there, there solely in song,
Resides, where earth and her uses to men, their needs,
Their forceful cravings, the theme are: there is it strong,
The Master said: and the studious eye that reads
(Yea, even as earth to the crown of Gods on the mount)
In links divine with the lyrical tongue is bound.
Pursue thy craft: it is music drawn of a fount
To spring perennial; well-spring is common ground.

XV

Melampus dwelt among men: physician and sage,
He served them, loving them, healing them; sick or maimed
Or them that frenzied in some delirious rage
Outran the measure, his juice of the woods reclaimed.
He played on men, as his master, Phoebus, on strings
Melodious: as the God did he drive and check,
Through love exceeding a simple love of the things
That glide in grasses and rubble of woody wreck.

GEORGE MEREDITH

EARTH AND A WEDDED WOMAN

I

The shepherd, with his eye on hazy South,
Has told of rain upon the fall of day.
But promise is there none for Susan's drouth,
That he will come, who keeps in dry delay.
The freshest of the village three years gone,
She hangs as the white field-rose hangs short-lived;
And she and Earth are one
In withering unrevived.
Rain! O the glad refresher of the grain!
And welcome waterspouts, had we sweet rain!

II

Ah, what is Marriage, says each pouting maid,
When she who wedded with the soldier hides
At home as good as widowed in the shade,
A lighthouse to the girls that would be brides:
Nor dares to give a lad an ogle, nor
To dream of dancing, but must hang and moan,
        Her husband in the war,
        And she to lie alone.
Rain! O the glad refresher of the grain!
And welcome waterspouts, had we sweet rain!

III

They have not known; they are not in the stream;
Light as the flying seed-ball is their play,
The silly maids! and happy souls they seem;
Yet Grief would not change fates with such as they.
They have not struck the roots which meet the fires
Beneath, and bind us fast with Earth, to know
        The strength of her desires,
        The sternness of her woe.
Rain! O the glad refresher of the grain!
And welcome waterspouts, had we sweet rain!

IV

Now, shepherd, see thy word, where without shower
A borderless low blotting Westward spreads.
The hall-clock holds the valley on the hour;
Across an inner chamber thunder treads:
The dead leaf trips, the tree-top swings, the floor
Of dust whirls, dropping lumped: near thunder speaks,
        And drives the dames to door,
        Their kerchiefs flapped at cheeks.
Rain! O the glad refresher of the grain!
And welcome waterspouts of blessed rain!

V

Through night, with bedroom window wide for air,
Lay Susan tranced to hear all heaven descend:
And gurgling voices came of Earth, and rare,
Past flowerful, breathings, deeper than life's end,
From her heaved breast of sacred common mould;
Whereby this lone-laid wife was moved to feel
        Unworded things and old
        To her pained heart appeal.
Rain! O the glad refresher of the grain!
And down in deluges of blessed rain!

VI

At morn she stood to live for ear and sight,
Love sky or cloud, or rose or grasses drenched.
A lureful devil, that in glow-worm light
Set languor writhing all its folds, she quenched.
But she would muse when neighbours praised her face,
Her services, and staunchness to her mate:
        Knowing by some dim trace,
        The change might bear a date.
Rain! O the glad refresher of the grain!
Thrice beauteous is our sunshine after rain!

GEORGE MEREDITH

FROM "ADONAIS"

He has outsoared the shadow of our night.
  Envy and calumny and hate and pain,
And that unrest which men miscall delight,
  Can touch him not and torture not again.
  From the contagion of the world's slow stain
He is secure; and now can never mourn
  A heart grown cold, a head grown grey, in vain—
Nor, when the spirit's self has ceased to burn,
With sparkless ashes load an unlamented urn.

He lives, he wakes—'tis Death is dead, not he;
Mourn not for Adonais.—Thou young Dawn,
Turn all thy dew to splendour, for from thee
The spirit thou lamentest is not gone!
Ye caverns and ye forests, cease to moan!
Cease, ye faint flowers and fountains! and, thou Air,
Which like a mourning-veil thy scarf hadst thrown
O'er the abandoned Earth, now leave it bare
Even to the joyous stars which smile on its despair!

He is made one with Nature. There is heard
His voice in all her music, from the moan
Of thunder to the song of night's sweet bird.
He is a presence to be felt and known
In darkness and in light, from herb and stone,—
Spreading itself where'er that Power may move
Which has withdrawn his being to its own,
Which wields the world with never-wearied love,
Sustains it from beneath, and kindles it above.

He is a portion of the loveliness
Which once he made more lovely. He doth bear
His part, while the One Spirit's plastic stress
Sweeps through the dull sense world; compelling there
All new successions to the forms they wear;
Torturing the unwilling dross, that checks its flight,
To its own likeness, as each mass may bear;
And bursting in its beauty and its might
From trees and beasts and men into the heaven's light.

The splendours of the firmament of time
May be eclipsed, but are extinguished not;
Like stars to their appointed height they climb,
And death is a low mist which cannot blot
And brightness it may veil. When lofty thought
Lifts a young heart above its mortal lair,
And love and life contend in it for what
Shall be its earthly doom, the dead live there,
And move like winds of light on dark and stormy air.

The inheritors of unfulfilled renown
Rose from their thrones, built beyond mortal thought
Far in the unapparent. Chatterton
Rose pale, his solemn agony had not
Yet faded from him; Sidney, as he fought,
And as he fell, and as he lived and loved,
Sublimely mild, a spirit without spot,
Arose; and Lucan, by his death approved;—
Oblivion as they rose shrank like a thing reproved.

And many more, whose names on earth are dark,
But whose transmitted effluence cannot die
So long as fire outlives the parent spark,
Rose, robed in dazzling immortality.
"Thou art become as one of us," they cry;
"It was for thee yon kingless sphere has long
Swung blind in unascended majesty,
Silent alone amid an heaven of song.
Assume thy wingèd throne, thou Vesper of our throng!"

Who mourns for Adonais? Oh come forth,
Fond wretch, and know thyself and him aright.
Clasp with thy panting soul the pendulous earth;
As from a centre, dart thy spirit's light
Beyond all worlds, until its spacious might
Satiate the void circumference: then shrink
Even to a point within our day and night;
And keep thy heart light, lest it make thee sink,
When hope has kindled hope, and lured thee to the brink.

Or go to Rome, which is the sepulchre,
Oh not of him, but of our joy. 'Tis nought
That ages, empires, and religions, there
Lie buried in the ravage they have wrought;
For such as he can lend—they borrow not
Glory from those who made the world their prey;
And he is gathered to the kings of thought
Who waged contention with their time's decay,
And of the past are all that cannot pass away.

Go thou to Rome,—at once the paradise,
  The grave, the city, and the wilderness;
And where its wrecks like shattered mountains rise,
  And flowering weeds and fragrant copses dress
  The bones of Desolation's nakedness,
Pass, till the Spirit of the spot shall lead
  Thy footsteps to a slope of green access,
Where, like an infant's smile, over the dead
A light of laughing flowers along the grass is spread;

And grey walls moulder round, on which dull Time
  Feeds, like slow fire upon a hoary brand;
And one keen pyramid with wedge sublime,
  Pavilioning the dust of him who planned
  This refuge for his memory, doth stand
Like flame transformed to marble; and beneath
  A field is spread, on which a newer band
Have pitched in heaven's smile their camp of death,
Welcoming him we lose with scarce-extinguished breath.

Here pause. These graves are all too young as yet
  To have outgrown the sorrow which consigned
Its charge to each; and, if the seal is set
  Here on one fountain of a mourning mind,
  Break it not thou! too surely shalt thou find
Thine own well full, if thou returnest home,
  Of tears and gall. From the world's bitter wind
Seek shelter in the shadow of the tomb.
What Adonais is why fear we to become?

The One remains, the many change and pass;
  Heaven's light for ever shines, earth's shadows fly;
Life, like a dome of many-coloured glass,
  Stains the white radiance of eternity,
  Until Death tramples it to fragments.—Die,
If thou wouldst be with that which thou dost seek!
  Follow where all is fled!—Rome's azure sky,
Flowers, ruins, statues, music, words, are weak
The glory they transfuse with fitting truth to speak.

Why linger, why turn back, why shrink, my heart?
  Thy hopes are gone before: from all things here
They have departed; thou shouldst now depart.
  A light is past from the revolving year
  And man and woman; and what still is dear
Attracts to crush, repels to make thee wither.
  The soft sky smiles, the low wind whispers near:
'Tis Adonais calls! Oh hasten thither!
No more let life divide what death can join together.

That light whose smile kindles the universe,
  That beauty in which all things work and move,
That benediction which the eclipsing curse
  Of birth can quench not, that sustaining Love
  Which, through the web of being blindly wove
By man and beast and earth and air and sea,
  Burns bright or dim, as each are mirrors of
The fire for which all thirst, now beams on me,
Consuming the last clouds of cold mortality.

The breath whose might I have invoked in song
  Descends on me; my spirit's bark is driven
Far from the shore, far from the trembling throng
  Whose sails were never to the tempest given.
  The massy earth and spherèd skies are riven!
I am borne darkly, fearfully, afar!
  Whilst, burning through the inmost veil of heaven,
The soul of Adonais, like a star,
Beacons from the abode where the Eternal are.

SHELLEY

§ 4

FROM "THE SYMPOSIUM"

"These are the lesser mysteries of love, into which even you, Socrates, may enter; to the greater and more hidden ones which are the crown of these, and to which, if you pursue them in a right spirit, they will lead, I know not whether you will be able to attain. But I will do my utmost to inform you, and do you follow if you can. For he who would proceed aright in this matter should begin in youth to visit beautiful forms; and first, if he be guided by his instructor aright, to love one such form only—out of that he should create fair thoughts; and soon he will of himself perceive that the beauty of one form is akin to the beauty of another; and then if beauty of form in general is his pursuit, how foolish would he be not to recognise that the beauty in every form is one and the same! And when he perceives this he will abate his violent love of the one, which he will despise and deem a small thing, and will become a lover of all beautiful forms; in the next stage he will consider that the beauty of the mind is more honourable than the beauty of the outward form. So that if a virtuous soul have but a little comeliness, he will be content to love and tend him, and will search out and bring to the birth thoughts which may improve the young, until he is compelled to contemplate and see the beauty of institutions and laws, and to understand that the beauty of them all is of one family, and that personal beauty is a trifle; and after laws and institutions he will go on to the sciences, that he may see their beauty, being not like a servant in love with the beauty of one youth or man or institution, himself a slave mean and narrow-minded, but drawing towards and contemplating the vast sea of beauty, he will create many fair and noble thoughts and notions in boundless love of wisdom; until on that shore he grows and waxes strong, and at last the vision is revealed to him of a single science, which is the science of beauty everywhere. To this I will proceed; please to give me your very best attention:

"He who has been instructed thus far in the things of love, and who has learned to see the beautiful in due order and succession, when he comes toward the end will suddenly perceive a nature of wondrous beauty (and this, Socrates, is the final cause of all our former toils)—a nature which in the first place is everlasting, not growing and decaying, or waxing and waning; secondly, not fair in one point of view and foul in another, or at one time or in one relation or at one place fair, at another time or in another relation or at another place foul, as if fair to some and foul to others, or in the likeness of a face or hands or any other part of the bodily frame, or in any form of speech or knowledge, or existing in any other being, as for example, in an animal, or in heaven, or in earth, or in any other place; but beauty absolute, separate, simple, and everlasting, which without diminution and without increase, or any change, is imparted to the ever-growing and perishing beauties of all other things. He who from these ascending under the influence of true love, begins to perceive that beauty, is not far from the end. And the true order of going, or being led by another, to the things of love, is to begin from the beauties of earth and mount upwards for the sake of that other beauty, using these as steps only, and from one going on to two, and from two to all fair forms, and from fair forms to fair practices, and from fair practices to fair notions, until from fair notions he arrives at the notion of absolute beauty, and at last knows what the essence of beauty is. This, my dear Socrates," said the stranger of Mantineia, "is that life above all others which man should live, in the contemplation of beauty absolute; a beauty which if you once beheld, you would see not to be after the measure of gold, and garments, and fair boys and youths, whose presence now entrances you; and you and many a one would be content to live seeing them only and conversing with them without meat or drink, if that were possible—you only want to look at them and to be with them. But what if man had eyes to see the true beauty—the divine beauty, I mean, pure and clear and unalloyed, not clogged with the pollutions of mortality and all the colours and vanities of human life—thither looking, and holding converse with the true beauty simple and divine? Remember how in that communion only, beholding beauty with the eye of the mind, he will be enabled to bring forth, not images of beauty, but realities (for he has hold not of an image but of a reality), and bringing forth and nourishing true virtue to become the friend of God and be immortal, if mortal man may. Would that be an ignoble life?"

PLATO

"THIS IS THE GATE OF HEAVEN"

God made the universe and all the creatures contained therein as so many glasses wherein He might reflect His own glory. He hath copied forth Himself in the creation; and in this outward world we may read the lovely characters of the Divine goodness, power, and wisdom. . . . But how to find God here, and feelingly to converse with Him, and being affected with the sense of the Divine glory shining out upon the creation, how to pass out of the sensible world into the intellectual, is not so effectually taught by that philosophy which professed it most, as by true religion. That which knits and unites God and the soul together can best teach it how to ascend and descend upon those golden links that unite, as it were, the world to God. That Divine Wisdom, that contrived and beautified this glorious structure, can best explain her own art, and carry up the soul back again in these reflected beams to Him who is the Fountain of them. . . . Good men may easily find every creature pointing out to that Being whose image and superscription it bears, and climb up from those darker resemblances of the Divine wisdom and goodness, shining out in different degrees upon several creatures, till they sweetly repose themselves in the bosom of the Divinity; and while they are thus conversing with this lower world . . . they find God many times secretly flowing into their souls, and leading them silently out of the court of the temple into the Holy Place. . . . Thus religion, where it is in truth and power, renews the very spirit of our minds, and doth in a manner spiritualise this outward creation to us. . . . It is nothing but a thick mist of pride and self-love that hinders men's eyes from beholding that sun which enlightens them and all things else. . . . A good man is no more solicitous whether this or that good thing be mine, or whether my perfections exceed the measure of this or that particular creature; for whatsoever good he beholds anywhere, he enjoys and delights in it as much as if it were his own, and whatever he beholds in himself, he looks not upon it as his property, but as a common good; for all these beams come from one and the same Fountain and Ocean of light in whom he loves them all with an universal love. . . . Thus may a man walk up and down the world as in a garden of spices, and suck a Divine sweetness out of every flower. There is a twofold meaning in every creature, a literal and a mystical, and the one is but the ground of the other; and as the Jews say of their law, so a good man says of everything that his senses offer to him—it speaks to his lower part, but it points out something above to his mind and spirit. It is the drowsy and muddy spirit of superstition which is fain to set some idol at its elbow, something that may jog it and put it in mind of God. Whereas true religion never finds itself out of the infinite sphere of the Divinity . . . it beholds itself everywhere in the midst of that glorious unbounded Being who is indivisibly everywhere. A good man finds every place he treads upon holy ground; to him the world is God's temple; he is ready to say with Jacob, "How dreadful is this place! this is none other than the house of God, this is the gate of heaven."

JOHN SMITH

TO END

REVERENCE FOR LIFE

With Descartes, philosophy starts from the dogma: "I think, therefore I exist." With this poverty-stricken, arbitrarily chosen beginning, it is landed irretrievably on the road to the abstract. It never finds the entrance to ethics, and remains entangled in a dead world- and life-view. True philosophy must start from the most immediate and comprehensive fact of consciousness, which says: "I am life which wills to live, in the midst of life which wills to live." This is not a cleverly composed dogmatic formula. Day after day, hour after hour, I live and move in it. At every moment of reflexion it stands fresh before me. There bursts forth again and again from it as from roots that can never dry up, a living world- and life-view which can deal with all the facts of Being. A mysticism of ethical union with Being grows out of it.

As in my own will-to-live there is a longing for wider life and for the mysterious exaltation of the will-to-live which we call pleasure, with dread of annihilation and of the mysterious encroachment on the will-to-live which we call pain; so is it also in the will-to-live all around me, whether it can express itself before me, or remains dumb.

Ethics consist, therefore, in my experiencing the compulsion to show all will-to-live the same reverence as I do to my own. There we have given us that basic principle of the moral which is a necessity of thought: It is good to maintain and to promote life; it is bad to destroy life or to obstruct it.

As a matter of fact everything which in the ordinary ethical valuation of the relations of men to each other ranks as good, can be brought under the description of material and spiritual maintenance or promotion of human life, and of effort to bring it to its highest value. Conversely, everything which ranks as bad in human relations is in the last analysis material or spiritual destruction or obstruction of human life, and negligence in the effort to bring it to its highest value. Separate individual categories of good and evil which lie far apart and have apparently no connection at all with one another fit together like things which belong to each other, as soon as they are comprehended and deepened in this the most universal definition of good and evil.

The basic principle of the moral means, however, not only an ordering and deepening of the current views of good and evil, but also a widening of them. A man is truly ethical only when he obeys the compulsion to help all life which he is able to assist, and shrinks from injuring anything that lives. He does not ask how far this or that life deserves one's interest as being valuable, nor, beyond that, whether and how far it can appreciate such interest. Life as such is sacred to him. He tears no leaf from a tree, plucks no flower, and takes care to crush no insect. If in summer he is working by lamplight, he prefers to keep the window shut and breathe a stuffy atmosphere rather than see one insect after another fall with singed wings upon his table.

If he goes into the street after a shower and sees an earthworm which has strayed on to it, he bethinks himself that it must get dried up in the sun, if it does not get back soon enough to ground into which it can burrow, and so he lifts it from the deadly stone surface, and puts it on the grass. If he comes across an insect which has fallen into a puddle, he stops a moment in order to hold out a leaf or a stalk on which it can save itself.

He is not afraid of being laughed at as sentimental. It is the fate of every truth to be a subject for laughter until it is generally recognised. Once it was considered folly to assume that men of colour were really men and ought to be treated as such, but the folly has become an accepted truth. To-day it is thought to be going too far to declare that constant regard for everything that lives, down to the lowest manifestations of life, is a demand made by rational ethics. The time is coming, however, when people will be astonished that mankind needed so long a time to learn to regard thoughtless injury to life as incompatible with ethics.

Ethics are responsibility without limit towards all that lives.

The definition of ethics as a relation to things within a disposition to reverence for life, strikes one in its absolutely universal extent as cold. But it is the only complete one. Sympathy is too narrow to rank as the essence of the ethical. It denotes, of course, only interest in the suffering will-to-live. But ethics include also feeling as one's own all the circumstances and all the aspirations of the will-to-live, its pleasure, too, and its longing to live itself out to the full, as well as its urge to self-perfecting.

Love means more, since it includes fellowship in suffering, in joy, and in effort, but it shows the ethical only in a simile, although in a natural and deep one. It makes the solidarity produced by ethics analogous to that which nature calls forth on the physical side, for more or less temporary purposes between two beings which complete each other sexually, or between them and their offspring.

Thought must strive to bring to expression the nature of the ethical in itself. To effect this it comes inevitably to defining ethics as devotion to life which is inspired by reverence for life. Even if the word reverence for life sounds so general as to seem somewhat lifeless, what is signified by it is nevertheless something which the man into whose thought it has made its way can never get rid of. Sympathy, and love, and every kind of valuable emotion are given within it. With a restless living force reverence for life works upon the disposition into which it has entered, and throws it into the unrest of a feeling of responsibility which at no place and at no time ceases to affect it. Just as the screw which burrows through the water drives the ship along, so does reverence for life the man.

Arising, as it does, from an inner compulsion, the ethic of reverence for life is not dependent on the extent to which it is able to think itself out to a satisfying life-view. It need give no answer to the question of what significance the ethical man's work for the maintenance, promotion, and exalting of life can have in the total happenings of the course of nature. It does not let itself be misled by the calculation that the maintaining and completing of life which it practises is hardly worth consideration beside the tremendous, unceasing destruction of life which goes on through natural forces. Having the will to action, it can leave on one side all the problems of the success of its work. Full of significance for the world is the fact in itself that in the ethically developed man there has made its appearance in the world a will-to-live which is filled with reverence for life and devotion to life.

In my will-to-live the universal will-to-live experiences itself otherwise than in its other manifestations. In them it shows itself in a process of individualising which, so far as I can see from the outside, is bent merely on living itself out to the full, and in no way on union with any other will-to-live. The world is a ghastly drama of will-to-live divided against itself. One existence makes its way at the cost of another; one destroys the other. One will-to-live merely exerts its will against the other, and has no knowledge of it. But in me the will-to-live has come to know about other wills-to-live. There is in it a longing to arrive at unity with itself, to become universal.

Why does the will-to-live experience itself in this way in me alone? Is it because I have acquired the capacity of reflecting on the totality of Being? What is the goal of this evolution which has begun in me?

To these questions there is no answer. It remains a painful enigma for me that I must live with reverence for life in a world which is dominated by creative will which is also destructive will, and destructive will which is also creative.

I can do nothing but hold to the fact that the will-to-live in me manifests itself as will-to-live which desires to become one with other will-to-live. That is for me the light that shines in the darkness. The ignorance in which the world is wrapped has no existence for me; I have been saved from the world. I am thrown, indeed, by reverence for life into an unrest such as the world does not know, but I obtain from it a blessedness which the world cannot give. If in the tenderheartedness produced by being different from the world another person and I help each other in understanding and pardoning, when otherwise will would torment will, the division of the will-to-live is got rid of. If I save an insect from the puddle, life has devoted itself to life, and the division of life against itself is got rid of. Whenever my life devotes itself in any way to life, my finite will-to-live experiences its union with the infinite will in which all life is one, and I enjoy a feeling of refreshment which prevents me from pining away in the desert of life.

I therefore recognise it as the destiny of my existence to be obedient to this higher revelation of the will-to-live in me. I choose for my work the removal of this division of the will-to-live against itself, so far as the influence of my existence reaches. Knowing now the one thing needful, I leave on one side the enigma of the world and of my existence in it.

The surmisings and the longings of all deep religiousness are contained in the ethic of reverence for life. This religiousness, however, does not build up for itself a completed world-view, but resigns itself to the necessity of leaving its cathedral unfinished. It finishes the choir only, but in this choir piety maintains a living and never-ceasing divine service.

* * * * * *

The ethic of reverence for life shows its truth also in that it includes in itself the different elements of ethics in their natural connection. Hitherto no ethic has been able to present in their parallelism and their interaction the effort after self-perfecting, in which man acts upon himself from outside without deeds, and the activist ethic. The ethic of reverence for life can do this, and indeed in such a way that it not only answers academic questions, but also produces a deepening of ethical insight.

Ethics are reverence for the will-to-live within me and without me. From the former comes first the profound life-affirmation of resignation. I apprehend my will-to-live as not only something which can live itself out in happy occurrences, but also something which has experience of itself. If I refuse to let this self-experience disappear in thoughtlessness, and persist in feeling it to be valuable, I begin to learn the secret of spiritual self-assertion. I win an unsuspected freedom from the various destinies of life. At moments in which I had expected to find myself overwhelmed, I find myself exalted in an inexpressible and surprising happiness of freedom from the world, and I experience therein a clearing of my life-view. Resignation is the vestibule through which we enter ethics. Only he who in deepened devotion to his own will-to-live experiences inward freedom from outward occurrences, is capable of devoting himself in profound and steady fashion to the life of others.

Just as in the reverence for my own will-to-live I struggle for freedom from the destinies of life, so I struggle too for freedom from myself. Not only in face of what happens to me, but also with attention to the way in which I deal with the world, I practise the higher self-maintenance. Out of reverence for my own existence I place myself under the compulsion of veracity towards myself. Everything I acquired would be purchased too dearly by action in defiance of my convictions. I fear that if I were untrue to myself I should be wounding my will-to-live with a poisoned spear.

The fact that Kant makes, as he does, veracity towards oneself the centre point of his ethic, testifies to the depth of his ethical feeling. But because in his search for the essential nature of the ethical he fails to find his way through to reverence for life, he cannot comprehend the connection between veracity towards oneself and an activist ethic.

As a matter of fact the ethic of veracity towards oneself passes imperceptibly into that of devotion to others. Such veracity compels me to actions which manifest themselves as devotion in such a way that ordinary ethics derive them from devotion.

Why do I forgive anyone? Ordinary ethics say, because I feel sympathy with him. They allow men to seem to themselves, when they pardon others, frightfully good, and allow them to practise a style of pardoning which is not free from humiliation of the other. They thus make forgiveness a sweetened triumph of self-devotion.

The ethic of reverence for life does away with this unpurified view. All acts of forbearance and of pardon are for it acts forced from one by veracity towards oneself. I must practise unlimited forgiveness because, if I did not, I should be wanting in veracity to myself, for it would be acting as if I myself were not guilty in the same way as the other has been guilty towards me. Because my life is so liberally spotted with falsehood, I must forgive falsehood which has been practised upon me; because I myself have been in so many cases wanting in love, and guilty of hatred, slander, deceit, or arrogance, I must pardon any want of love, and all hatred, slander, deceit, or arrogance which have been directed against myself. I must forgive quietly and without drawing attention to it; in fact I do not really pardon at all, for I do not let things develop to any such act of judgment. Nor is this any eccentric proceeding; it is only a necessary widening and refinement of ordinary ethics.

The struggle against the evil that is in mankind we have to carry on not by judging others, but by judging ourselves. Struggle with oneself and veracity towards oneself are the means by which we work upon others. We quietly draw them into our efforts after the deep spiritual self-assertion which springs out of reverence for one's own life. Power makes no noise. It is there, and works. True ethics begin where the use of language ceases.

The innermost element then, in activist ethics, even if it appears as self-devotion, comes from the compulsion to veracity towards oneself, and obtains therein its true value. The whole ethic of being other than the world flows pure only when it comes from this source. It is not from kindness to others that I am tender-hearted, peaceable, forbearing, and friendly, but because by such behaviour I prove my own deepest self-assertion to be true. Reverence for life which I apply to my own existence, and reverence for life which keeps me in a temper of devotion to other existence than mine, interpenetrate each other.

* * * * * *

Ordinary ethics, because they are without any basic principle of the ethical, are obliged to engage at once in the discussion of conflicting duties. The ethic of reverence for life has no such need for hurry. It takes its own time to think out in all directions its own principle of the moral. Knowing itself to be firmly established, it then settles its position with regard to these conflicts.

It has to come to terms with three adversaries: these are thoughtlessness, egoistic self-assertion, and society.

To the first of these it pays usually insufficient attention, because no open conflicts arise between them. This adversary does, nevertheless, obstruct it imperceptibly.

There is, however, a wide field which our ethic can take possession of without any collision with the troops of egoism. Man can accomplish much that is good, without having to require of himself any sacrifice. And if there really goes with it a bit of his life, it is something so insignificant that he feels it no more than if he were losing a hair or a piece of dead skin.

Over wide stretches of conduct the inward liberation from the world, the being true to oneself, the being different from the world, yes, and even devotion to other life, is only a matter of giving attention to this particular relation. We fall short so much, because we do not keep ourselves up to it. We do not stand sufficiently under the pressure of any inward compulsion to be ethical. The steam hisses at all points out of the leaky boiler. The resulting losses of energy are as high as they are in ordinary ethics, because these ethics have at their disposal no single basic principle of the moral which works upon thought. They cannot repair the boiler; they do not, indeed, ever even examine it. Reverence for life, however, being something which is ever present to thought, penetrates unceasingly and in all directions men's observation, reflexion, and resolutions. A man can keep himself clear of it as little as the water can prevent itself from being coloured by the dye-stuff which is dropped into it. The struggle with thoughtlessness is started, and is always advancing.

But what is the relation between ethics and reverence for life in the conflicts which arise between inward compulsion to devotion, and necessary self-assertion?

I too am subject to division of my will-to-life against itself. In a thousand ways my existence stands in conflict with that of others. The necessity to destroy and to injure life is imposed upon me. If I walk along an unfrequented path, my foot brings destruction and pain upon the tiny creatures which populate it. In order to preserve my own existence, I must defend myself against the existence which injures it. I become a hunter of the mouse which inhabits my house, a murderer of the insect which wants to have its nest there, a mass-murderer of the bacteria which may endanger my life. I get my food by destroying plants and animals. My happiness is built upon injury done to my fellow-men.

How does our ethic assert itself in the tragic necessity to which I am subjected through the division of my will-to-live against itself?

Ordinary ethics seek compromises. They try to lay down how much of my existence and of my happiness I must sacrifice, and how much of them I may preserve at the cost of the existence and happiness of other lives. With this distinction they produce an experimental, relative ethic. They offer as ethical what is in reality not ethical but a mixture of non-ethical necessity and ethics. They thereby establish a huge confusion, and allow the starting of an ever-increasing obscuration of the conception of the ethical.

The ethic of reverence for life knows nothing of a relative ethic. It allows to rank as good only the maintenance and promotion of life. All destruction of and injury to life, under whatever circumstances they take place, it condemns as evil. It does not keep in store adjustments between ethics and necessity all ready for making up. It is always again and again and in ways that are always original coming to terms in men with reality. It does not abolish for man all ethical conflicts, but compels him to decide for himself in each case how far he can remain ethical and how far he must submit himself to the necessity for destruction of and injury to life, and therewith incur guilt. It is not by receiving instruction about agreement between ethical and necessary, that a man makes progress in ethics, but only by coming to hear more and more plainly the voice of the ethical, by becoming ruled more and more by the longing to preserve and promote life, and by becoming more and more obstinate in resistance to the necessity for destroying or injuring life.

In ethical conflicts man can arrive only at subjective decisions. No one can lay down for him at what point, on each occasion, lies the extreme limit of possibility for his persistence in the preservation and promotion of life. He alone has to decide, by letting himself be guided by a feeling of the highest possible responsibility towards other life.

We must never let ourselves become blunted and dull. We are living in truth, when our experience in these conflicts is ever deepening. The good conscience is an invention of the devil's.

* * * * * *

What does reverence for life say about the relations between men and the animal world?

Whenever I injure life of any sort, I must be quite clear whether it is necessary. Beyond the unavoidable, I must never go, not even with what seems insignificant. The farmer who has mown down a thousand flowers in his meadow to feed his cows, must be careful on his way home not to strike off in thoughtless pastime the head of a single flower by the roadside, for he thereby commits a wrong against life without being under the pressure of necessity.

Those who experiment with operations or the use of drugs upon animals, or inoculate them with diseases, so as to be able to bring help to mankind with the results gained, must never quiet any misgivings they feel with the general reflexion that their gruesome proceedings aim at a valuable result. They must first have considered in each individual case whether there is a real necessity to force upon any animal this sacrifice for the sake of mankind, and they must take the most careful pains to ensure that the pain inflicted is made as small as possible. How much wrong is committed in scientific institutions through neglect of anæsthetics, which to save time or trouble are not administered! How much, too, through animals being subjected to torture merely to give to students a demonstration of perfectly understood phenomena. By the very fact that animals have been subjected to experiments, and have by their pain won such valuable results for suffering men, a new and special relation of solidarity has been established between them and us. From that springs for each one of us a compulsion to do to every animal all the good we possibly can. By helping an insect when it is in difficulties I am thereby attempting to cancel part of man's ever new debt to the animal world. Whenever an animal is in any way forced into the service of man, every one of us must be concerned with the suffering which it has thereby to undergo. None of us must allow to take place any suffering for which he himself is not responsible, if he can hinder it in any way, at the same time quieting his conscience with the reflexion that he would be mixing himself up in something which does not concern him. No one must shut his eyes and regard as non-existent the sufferings of which he spares himself the sight. Let no one regard as light the burden of his responsibility. While so much ill-treatment of animals goes on, while the moans of thirsty animals in railway trucks sound unheard, while so much brutality prevails in our slaughter-houses, while animals have to suffer in our kitchens painful death from unskilled hands, while animals have to endure intolerable treatment from heartless men, or are left to the cruel play of children, we all share the guilt.

We are afraid of making ourselves conspicuous, if we let it be noticed how we feel for the sufferings which man brings upon the animals. We think at the same time that others have become more "rational" than we are, and that they take as being usual and as a matter of course, what we are excited about.

Yet suddenly they will let slip a word which shows us that they too have not yet learnt to acquiesce. And now, though they are strangers, they are quite near us. The mask in which we misled each other falls off. We know now, from one another, that we are alike in being unable to escape from the gruesome proceedings that are taking place unceasingly around us. What a happy making of a new acquaintance!

The ethic of respect for life guards us from letting each other believe through our silence that we no longer experience what, as thinking men, we must experience. It prompts us to keep each other sensitive to what distresses us, and to talk and to act together without any feeling of shyness, just as the responsibility we feel moves us to. It makes us keep on the look-out together for opportunities of bringing some sort of help to animals, to make up for the great misery which men inflict on them, and thus to step for a moment out of the incomprehensible horror of existence.

* * * * * *

In the matter also of our relation to other men, the ethic of reverence for life throws upon us a responsibility so unlimited as to be terrifying.

Here again it offers us no rules about the extent of the self-maintenance which is allowable; again, it bids us in each case come to terms with the absolute ethic of self-devotion. I have to decide in accordance with the responsibility of which I am conscious, how much of my life, my possessions, my rights, my happiness, my time, and my rest I must devote to others, and how much of them I may keep for myself.

In the question of possession, the ethic of reverence for life is outspokenly individualist, in the sense that wealth acquired or inherited must be placed at the service of the community, not through any measures taken by society, but through the absolutely free decision of the individual. It expects everything from a general increase in the feeling of responsibility. Wealth it regards as the property of society left in the sovereign control of the individual. One man serves society by carrying on a business in which a number of employees earn their living; another by giving away his wealth in order to help his fellows. Between these two extreme kinds of service let each decide according to the responsibility which he finds determined for him by the circumstances of his life. Let no one judge his neighbour. The one thing that matters is that each shall value what he possesses as means to action. Whether this is accomplished by his keeping and increasing his wealth, or by surrender of it, matters little. Wealth must reach the community in the most varied ways, if the latter is to profit by it in the best way.

Those who possess little wealth to call their own are most in danger of holding what they have in a purely selfish spirit. There is profound truth in the parable of Jesus which makes the servant who had received least the least loyal to his duty.

My rights too the ethic of reverence for life does not allow to belong to me. It forbids me to quiet my conscience with the reflexion that as the stronger, but by quite legitimate means, I am advancing myself at the cost of one who is weaker than I. In what the law and public opinion allow me it sets a problem before me. It bids me think of others, and makes me ponder whether I can allow myself the inward right to pluck all the fruit that my hand can reach. Thus it may happen that in obedience to consideration for the existence of others I do what seems to ordinary opinion to be folly. Yes, it may even show itself to be folly by the fact that my renunciation has not been of the slightest benefit to him for whom it was made. And yet I was right. Reverence for life is the highest court of appeal. What it commands has its own significance, even if it seems foolish or useless. We all look, of course, in one another, for the folly which indicates that we have higher responsibilities making themselves felt in ourselves. Yet it is only in proportion as we all become less rational, in the meaning given it by ordinary calculation, that the ethical disposition develops in us, and allows problems to become soluble which have hitherto been insoluble.

Nor will reverence for life grant me my happiness as my own. At the moments when I should like to enjoy myself without restraint, it wakes in me reflexion about misery that I see or suspect, and it does not allow me to drive away the uneasiness thereby caused to me. Just as the wave cannot exist for itself, but is ever a part of the heaving surface of ocean, so must I never live my life for itself, but always in the experience which is going on around me. It is an uncomfortable doctrine which the true ethic whispers into my ear. You are happy, it says; therefore you are called upon to give much. Whatever more than others you have received in health, natural gifts, working capacity, success, a beautiful childhood, harmonious family circumstances, you must not accept as being a matter of course. You must pay a price for them. You must show more than average devotion of life to life.

To the happy the voice of the true ethic is dangerous, if they venture to listen to it. When it calls to them, it never damps down the irrational which glows within it. It assails them to see whether it can get them out of their rut and turn them into adventurers of self-devotion, people of whom the world has too few. . . .

Reverence for life is an inexorable creditor! If it finds anyone with nothing to pledge but a little time and a little leisure, it lays an attachment on these. But its hardheartedness is good, and sees clearly. The many modern men who as industrial machines are engaged in callings in which they can in no way be active as men among men, are exposed to the danger of merely vegetating in an egoistic life. Many of them feel this danger, and suffer under the fact that their daily work has so little to do with spiritual and ideal aims and does not allow them to put into it anything of their human nature. Others acquiesce; the thought of having no duties outside their daily work suits them very well.

But that men should be so condemned or so favoured as to

be released from responsibility for devotion as men to men, the ethic of reverence for life will not allow to be legitimate. It demands that every one of us in some way and with some object shall be a man for men. To those who have no opportunity in their daily work of giving themselves as man to men, and have nothing else that they can give, it suggests their offering something of their time and leisure, even if these have been granted to them in scanty measure. Find for yourselves some secondary work (it says to them), an inconspicuous one, perhaps a secret one. Open your eyes and look for a human being or some work devoted to human welfare which needs from some one a little time or friendliness, a little sympathy, or sociability, or work. There may be a solitary or an embittered fellow-man, an invalid or an inefficient person to whom you can be something. Perhaps it is an old person or a child. Or some good work needs volunteers who can offer a free evening, or run errands. Who can enumerate the many ways in which that costly piece of fixed capital, a human being, can be employed! More of him is wanted everywhere! Hunt, then, for some situation for your humanity, and do not be frightened away if you have to wait, or to be taken on trial. And do not be disturbed by disappointments. Anyhow, do not be without some secondary work in which you give yourself as a man to men. There is one that is marked out for you, if you only truly will to have it. . . .

Thus does the true ethic speak of those who have only a little time and a little human nature to give. Well will it be with them if they listen to it, and are preserved from becoming stunted natures, because they have neglected this devotion of self to others.

But to everyone, in whatever state of life he finds himself, the ethic of respect for life does this: it forces him ever and again to be inwardly concerned with all the human destinies and all the other life-destinies which are going through their life-course around him, and to give himself, as man, to the man who needs a fellow-man. It will not allow the learned man to live only for his learning, even if his learning makes him very useful, nor the artist to live only for his art, even if by means of it he gives something to many. It does not allow the very busy man to think that with his professional activities he has fulfilled every demand upon him. It demands from all and every that they devote a portion of their life to their fellows. In what way and to what extent this is laid down for him the individual must gather from the thoughts which arise in him, and from the destinies in which his life moves. One man's sacrifice is outwardly unpretentious. He can accomplish it while continuing to live a normal life. Another is called to some conspicuous devotion, and must therefore put aside regard for his own progress. But let neither judge the other. The tasks of men have to be decided in a thousand ways to let the good become actual. What he has to bring as an offering is the secret of each individual. But one with another we have all to recognise that our existence reaches its true value only when we experience in ourselves something of the truth of the saying: "Whoever shall lose his life, the same shall find it" (St. Matt. x. 39).

* * * * * *

The ethical conflicts between society and the individual arise out of the fact that the latter has to bear not only a personal, but also a supra-personal responsibility. When my own person only is concerned, I can always be patient, always forgive, use all possible consideration, always be tenderhearted. But each of us comes into a situation when he is responsible not for himself only, but also for some undertaking, and then is forced into decisions which conflict with personal morality.

The industrialist who manages a business, however small, and the musician who undertakes public performances, cannot be men in the way they would like to be. The one has to dismiss a worker who is incapable or given to drink, in spite of any sympathy he has for him and his family; the other cannot let a singer whose voice is the worse for wear perform any longer, although he knows what distress he thus causes.

The more extensive a man's activities, the oftener he finds

himself in the situation of having to sacrifice something of his humanity to his supra-personal responsibility. Out of this conflict consideration brings the average person to the decision that the wider responsibility does, as a matter of principle, annul the personal. It is with this idea that society addresses the individual. For the quieting of consciences for which this decision is too categorical it perhaps lays down a few principles which undertake to determine in a way that is valid for everybody, how far in any case personal morality can have a say in the matter.

To the current ethic no course remains open but to sign this capitulation. It has no means of defending the fortress of personal morality, because it has not at its disposal any absolute notions of good and evil. Not so the ethic of reverence for life. That possesses, as we can see, what the other lacks. It therefore never surrenders the fortress, even if the latter is permanently invested. It feels itself in a position to persevere in holding it, and by continual sorties to keep the besiegers on the *qui vive*.

Only the most universal and absolute purposiveness in the maintenance and promotion of life, which is the objective aimed at by reverence for life, is ethical. All other necessity or expediency is not ethical, but only a more or less necessary necessity, or a more or less expedient expediency. In the conflict between the maintenance of my own existence and the destruction of, or injury to, another, I can never put the ethical and the necessary together to form a relative ethical; I must choose between ethical and necessary, and, if I choose the latter, must take it upon myself to be guilty through an act of injury to life. Similarly I am not at liberty to think that in the conflict between personal and supra-personal responsibility I can balance the ethical and the expedient to make a relative ethical, or even annul the ethical with the purposive; I must choose between the two. If under the pressure of the supra-personal responsibility I yield to the expedient, I become guilty in some way or other through failure in reverence for life.

The temptation to combine with the ethical into a relative

ethical the expedient which is commanded me by the supra-personal responsibility is especially strong, because it can be shown, in defence of it, that the person who complies with the demand of this supra-personal responsibility, acts unegoistically. It is not to his individual existence or his individual welfare that he sacrifices another existence or welfare, but he sacrifices an individual existence and welfare to what forces itself upon him as expedient in view of the existence or the welfare of a majority. But ethical is more than unegoistic. Ethical is nothing but the reverence felt by my will-to-live for every other will-to-live. Whenever I in any way sacrifice or injure life, I am not within the ethical, but I become guilty, whether it be egoistically guilty for the sake of maintaining my own existence or welfare, or unegoistically guilty for the sake of maintaining a greater number of other existences or their welfare.

This so easily made mistake of accepting as ethical a violation of reverence for life if it is based upon unegoistic considerations, is the bridge by crossing which ethics enter unintentionally the territory of the non-ethical. The bridge must be broken down.

Ethics go only so far as humanity does, humanity meaning respect for the existence and the happiness of individual human beings. Where humanity ends pseudo-ethics begin. The day on which this boundary is once for all universally recognised and marked out so as to be visible to everyone, will be one of the most important in the history of mankind. Thenceforward it can no longer happen that ethics which are not ethics at all are accepted as real ethics, and deceive and ruin individuals and peoples.

The ethics hitherto current have hindered us from becoming as earnest as we must be by the fact that they have utterly deceived us as to the many ways in which each one of us, whether through self-assertion, or by actions justified by supra-personal responsibility, become guilty again and again. True knowledge consists in being gripped by the secret that everything around us is will-to-live and seeing clearly how again and again we incur guilt against life.

Fooled by pseudo-ethics, man stumbles about in his guilt like a drunken man. If he becomes instructed and earnest he seeks the road which leads him least into guilt.

We are all exposed to the temptation of lessening the guilt of inhumanity which comes from our working under supra-personal responsibility, by withdrawing as far as possible into ourselves. But such freedom from guilt is not honestly obtained. Ethics start with world- and life-affirmation, and therefore will not allow us this flight into negation. They forbid us to be like the housewife who leaves the killing of the eels to her cook, and compels us to undertake all duties involving supra-personal responsibility which fall to us, even if we should be in a position to decline them for reasons more or less satisfactory.

Each one of us, then, has to engage, so far as he is brought to it by the circumstances of his life, in work which involves supra-personal responsibility, but we must do it not in the spirit of the collective body, but in that of the man who wishes to be ethical. In every individual case we struggle therefore to preserve as much humanity as is ever possible in such work, and in doubtful cases we venture to make a mistake on the side of humanity rather than on that of the object in view. When we have become instructed and earnest, we think of what is usually forgotten: that all public activity of whatever sort has to do not with facts only, but also with the creation of that spirit and temper which is desirable in the collective body. The creation of such a spirit and temper is more important than anything directly attained in the facts. Public work, in which the utmost possible effort is not made to preserve humanity, ruins the disposition. He who under the influence of supra-personal responsibility simply sacrifices men and human happiness when it seems commanded, accomplishes something. But he has not reached the highest level. He has only outward, not spiritual influence. We have spiritual influence only when others notice that we do not decide coldly in accordance with principles laid down once and for all, but in each individual case fight for humanity. There is too little among us of this kind of struggling.

From the smallest who is something in the smallest business, right up to the political ruler who holds in his hands the decision for peace or war, we act too much as men who in any given case can prepare without effort to be no longer men, but merely the executive of general interests. Hence there is no longer among us any trust in a righteousness lighted up with human feeling. Nor have we any longer any real respect for one another. We all feel ourselves in the power of a mentality of cold, impersonal, and usually unintelligent opportunism, which stiffens itself with appeals to principle, and in order to carry out small interests is capable of the greatest inhumanity and the greatest folly. We therefore see among us one temper of impersonal opportunism confronting another, and all problems are executed in a useless conflict of force against force because there is nowhere at hand such a spirit and temper as will make them soluble.

Only through our struggles for humanity can forces which work in the direction of the truly rational and expedient become powerful, while the present spirit and temper prevails. Hence the man who works under supra-personal responsibilities has to feel himself answerable not only for the successful result which is to be realised through him, but for the general spirit and temper which has to be created.

We therefore serve society without losing ourselves in it. We do not allow it to be our guardian in the matter of ethics. That would be as if the solo violinist allowed his bowing to be regulated by that of the double-bass player. Never for a moment do we lay aside our mistrust of the ideals established by society, and of the convictions which are kept by it in circulation. We always know that society is full of folly and will deceive us in the matter of humanity. It is an unreliable horse, and blind into the bargain. Woe to the driver if he falls asleep!

All this sounds too hard. Society serves ethics by giving legal sanction to its most elementary principles, and handing on the ethical principles of one generation to the next. That is much, and it claims our gratitude. But society is also something which checks the progress of ethics again and again, by arrogating to itself the dignity of the ethical teachers. To this, however, it has no right. The only ethical teacher is the man who thinks ethically, and struggles for an ethic. The conceptions of good and evil which are put in circulation by society are paper-money, the value of which is to be calculated not by the figures printed upon it, but by its relation to its exchange value in gold of the ethic of reverence for life. But so measured, its exchange value reveals itself as that of the paper-money of a half-bankrupt state.

The collapse of civilisation has come about through ethics being left to society. A renewal of it is possible only if ethics become once more the concern of thinking human beings, and if individuals seek to assert themselves in society as ethical personalities. In proportion as we secure this, society will become, instead of the purely natural entity, which it naturally is, an ethical one. Previous generations have made the terrible mistake of idealising society as ethical. We do our duty to it by judging it critically, and trying to make it, so far as is possible, more ethical. Being in possession of an absolute standard of the ethical, we no longer allow ourselves to make acceptable as ethics principles of expediency or even of the vulgarest opportunism. Nor do we remain any longer at the low level of allowing to be current as in any way ethical meaningless ideals, of power, of passion, or of nationalism, which are set up by miserable politicians and maintained in some degree of respect by bewildering propaganda. All the principles, dispositions, and ideals which make their appearance among us we measure, in their showy pedantry, with a rule on which the measures are given by the absolute ethic of reverence for life. We allow currency only to what is consistent with the claims of humanity. We bring into honour again regard for life and for the happiness of the individual. Sacred human rights we again hold high; not those which political rulers exalt at banquets and tread underfoot in their actions, but the true ones. We call once more for justice, not that which purblind authorities have elaborated in a legal scholasticism, nor that about which demagogues of all shades of colour shout themselves hoarse, but that which is filled to the full with the value of each single human existence. The foundation of law and right is humanity.

Thus we bring the principles, dispositions, and ideals of the collective body into agreement with humanity. At the same time we shape them in accordance with reason, for only what is ethical is truly rational. Only so far as the current disposition of men is animated by ethical convictions and ideals is it capable of truly purposive activity.

The ethic of reverence for life puts in our hands weapons for fighting false ethics and false ideals, but we have strength to use them only so far as we—each one in his own life—preserve our humanity. Only when those men are numerous who in thought and action bring humanity to terms with reality, will humanity cease to be current as a mere sentimental idea and become what it ought to be, a leaven in the spirit and temper of individuals and of society.

ALBERT SCHWEITZER

FROM THE CONVERSATIONS AND EXHORTATIONS OF FATHER ZOSSIMA

Young man, be not forgetful of prayer. Every time you pray, if your prayer is sincere, there will be new feeling and new meaning in it, which will give you fresh courage, and you will understand that prayer is an education. Remember, too, every day, and whenever you can, repeat to yourself, "Lord, have mercy on all who appear before Thee to-day." For every hour and every moment thousands of men leave life on this earth, and their souls appear before God. And how many of them depart in solitude, unknown, sad, dejected that no one mourns for them or even knows whether they have lived or not! And behold, from the other end of the earth perhaps, your prayer for their rest will rise up to God though you knew them not nor they you. How touching it must be to a soul standing in dread before the Lord to feel at that instant that, for him too, there is one to pray, that there is a fellow creature left on earth to love him too! And God will look on you both more graciously, for if you have had so much pity on him, how much will He have pity Who is infinitely more loving and merciful than you! And He will forgive him for your sake.

Brothers, have no fear of men's sin. Love a man even in his sin, for that is the semblance of Divine Love and is the highest love on earth. Love all God's creation, the whole and every grain of sand in it. Love every leaf, every ray of God's light. Love the animals, love the plants, love everything. If you love everything, you will perceive the divine mystery in things. Once you perceive it, you will begin to comprehend it better every day. And you will come at last to love the whole world with an all-embracing love. Love the animals: God has given them the rudiments of thought and joy untroubled. Do not trouble it, don't harass them, don't deprive them of their happiness, don't work against God's intent. Man, do not pride yourself on superiority to the animals; they are without sin, and you, with your greatness, defile the earth by your appearance on it, and leave the traces of your foulness after you—alas, it is true of almost every one of us! Love children especially, for they too are sinless like the angels; they live to soften and purify our hearts and as it were to guide us. Woe to him who offends a child! Father Anfim taught me to love children. The kind, silent man used often on our wanderings to spend the farthings given us on sweets and cakes for the children. He could not pass by a child without emotion. That's the nature of the man.

At some thoughts one stands perplexed, especially at the sight of men's sin, and wonders whether one should use force or humble love. Always decide to use humble love. If you resolve on that once for all, you may subdue the whole world. Loving humility is marvellously strong, the strongest of all things, and there is nothing else like it.

Every day and every hour, every minute, walk round yourself and watch yourself, and see that your image is a seemly one. You pass by a little child, you pass by, spiteful, with ugly words, with wrathful heart; you may not have noticed the child, but he has seen you, and your image, unseemly and ignoble, may remain in his defenceless heart. You don't know it, but you may have sown an evil seed in him and it may grow, and all because you were not careful before the child, because you did not foster in yourself a careful, actively benevolent love. Brothers, love is a teacher; but one must know how to acquire it, for it is hard to acquire, it is dearly bought, it is won slowly by long labour. For we must love not only occasionally, for a moment, but for ever. Everyone can love occasionally, even the wicked can.

My brother asked the birds to forgive him; that sounds senseless, but it is right; for all is like an ocean, all is flowing and blending; a touch in one place sets up movement at the other end of the earth. It may be senseless to beg forgiveness of the birds, but birds would be happier at your side—a little happier, anyway—and children and all animals, if you were nobler than you are now. It's all like an ocean, I tell you. Then you would pray to the birds too, consumed by an all-embracing love, in a sort of transport, and pray that they too will forgive you your sin. Treasure this ecstasy, however senseless it may seem to men.

My friends, pray to God for gladness. Be glad as children, as the birds of heaven. And let not the sin of men confound you in your doings. Fear not that it will wear away your work and hinder its being accomplished. Do not say, "Sin is mighty, wickedness is mighty, evil environment is mighty, and we are lonely and helpless, and evil environment is wearing us away and hindering our good work from being done." Fly from that dejection, children! There is only one means of salvation, then take yourself and make yourself responsible for all men's sins, that is the truth, you know, friends, for as soon as you sincerely make yourself responsible for everything and for all men, you will see at once that it is really so, and that you are to blame for everyone and for all things. But throwing your own indolence and impotence on others you will end by sharing the pride of Satan and murmuring against God.

Of the pride of Satan what I think is this: it is hard for us on earth to comprehend it, and therefore it is so easy to fall into error and to share it, even imagining that we are doing something grand and fine. Indeed, many of the strongest feelings and movements of our nature we cannot comprehend on earth. Let not that be a stumbling-block, and think not that it may serve as a justification to you for anything. For the Eternal Judge asks of you what you can comprehend and not what you cannot. You will know that yourself hereafter, for you will behold all things truly then and will not dispute them. On earth, indeed, we are as it were astray, and if it were not for the precious image of Christ before us, we should be undone and altogether lost, as was the human race before the flood. Much on earth is hidden from us, but to make up for that we have been given a precious mystic sense of our living bond with the other world, with the higher heavenly world, and the roots of our thoughts and feelings are not here but in other worlds. That is why the philosophers say that we cannot apprehend the reality of things on earth.

God took seeds from different worlds and sowed them on this earth, and His garden grew up and everything came up that could come up, but what grows lives and is alive only through the feeling of its contact with other mysterious worlds. If that feeling grows weak or is destroyed in you, the heavenly growth will die away in you. Then you will be indifferent to life and even grow to hate it. That's what I think. . . .

Remember particularly that you cannot be a judge of anyone. For no one can judge a criminal, until he recognises that he is just such a criminal as the man standing before him, and that he perhaps is more than all men to blame for that crime. When he understands that, he will be able to be a judge. Though that sounds absurd, it is true. If I had been righteous myself, perhaps there would have been no criminal standing before me. If you can take upon yourself the crime of the criminal your heart is judging, take it at once, suffer for him yourself, and let him go without reproach. And even if the law itself makes you his judge, act in the same spirit so far as possible, for he will go away and condemn himself more bitterly than you have done. If, after your kiss, he goes away untouched, mocking at you, do not let that be a stumbling-block to you. It shows his time has not yet come, but it will come in due course. And if it come not, no matter; if not he, then another in his place will understand and suffer, and judge and condemn himself, and the truth will be fulfilled. Believe that, believe it without doubt; for in that lies all the hope and faith of the saints.

Work without ceasing. If you remember in the night as you go to sleep, "I have not done what I ought to have done," rise up at once and do it. If the people around you are spiteful and callous and will not hear you, fall down before them and beg their forgiveness; for in truth you are to blame for their not wanting to hear you. And if you cannot speak to them in their bitterness, serve them in silence and in humility, never losing hope. If all men abandon you and even drive you away by force, then when you are left alone fall on the earth and kiss it, water it with your tears and it will bring forth fruit even though no one has seen or heard you in your solitude. Believe to the end, even if all men went astray and you were left the only one faithful; bring your offering even then and praise God in your loneliness. And if two of you are gathered together—then there is a whole world, a world of living love. Embrace each other tenderly and praise God, for if only in you two His truth has been fulfilled.

If you sin yourself and grieve even unto death for your sins or for your sudden sin, then rejoice for others, rejoice for the righteous man, rejoice that if you have sinned, he is righteous and has not sinned.

If the evil-doing of men moves you to indignation and overwhelming distress, even to a desire for vengeance on the evil-doers, shun above all things that feeling. Go at once and seek suffering for yourself, as though you were yourself guilty of that wrong. Accept that suffering and bear it and your heart will find comfort, and you will understand that you too are guilty, for you might have been a light to the evil-doers, even as the one man sinless, and you were not a light to them. If you had been a light, you would have lightened the path for others too, and the evil-doer might perhaps have been saved by your light from his sin. And even though your light was shining, yet you see men were not saved by it, hold firm and doubt not the power of the heavenly light. Believe that if they were not saved, they will be saved hereafter. And if they are not saved hereafter, then their sons will be saved, for your light will not die even when you are dead. The righteous man departs, but his light remains. Men are always saved after the death of the deliverer. Men reject their prophets and slay them, but they love their martyrs and honour those whom they have slain. You are working for the whole, you are acting for the future. Seek no reward, for great is your reward on this earth: the spiritual joy which is only vouchsafed to the righteous man. Fear not the great nor the mighty, but be wise and ever serene. Know the measure, know the times, study that. When you are left alone, pray. Love to throw yourself on the earth and kiss it. Kiss the earth and love it with an unceasing, consuming love. Love all men, love everything. . . .

DOSTOEVSKY

WISDOM

Wisdom is radiant and fadeth not away; and easily is she beheld of them that love her, and found of them that seek her. She forestalleth them that desire to know her, making herself first known. He that riseth up early to seek her shall have no toil, for he shall find her sitting at his gates. For to think upon her is perfectness of understanding, and he that watcheth for her sake shall quickly be free from care. Because she goeth about, herself seeking them that are worthy of her, and in their paths she appeareth unto them graciously, and in every purpose she meeteth them. For her true beginning is desire of discipline; and the care for discipline is love of her; and love of her is observance of her laws; and to give heed to her laws confirmeth incorruption; and incorruption bringeth near unto God; so then desire of wisdom promoteth to a kingdom. . . .

I myself also am mortal, like to all, and am sprung from one born of the earth, the man first formed, and in the womb of a mother was I moulded into flesh in the time of ten months, being compacted in blood of the seed of man and pleasure that came with sleep. And I also, when I was born, drew in the common air, and fell upon the kindred earth, uttering, like all, for my first voice, the selfsame wail: in swaddling clothes was I nursed, and with watchful cares. For no king had any other first beginning; but all men have one entrance into life, and a like departure. For this cause I prayed, and understanding was given me: I called upon God, and there came to me a spirit of wisdom. I preferred her before sceptres and thrones, and riches I esteemed nothing in comparison of her. Neither did I liken to her any priceless gem, because all the gold of the earth in her presence is a little sand, and silver shall be accounted as clay before her. Above health and comeliness I loved her, and I chose to have her rather than light, because her bright shining is never laid to sleep. But with her there came to me all good things together, and in her hands innumerable riches: and I rejoiced over them all because wisdom leadeth them; though

I knew not that she was the mother of them. As I learned without guile, I impart without grudging; I do not hide her riches. For she is unto men a treasure that faileth not, and they that use it obtain friendship with God, commended to him by the gifts which they through discipline present to him. . . .

For there is in her a spirit quick of understanding, holy, alone in kind, manifold, subtil, freely moving, clear in utterance, unpolluted, distinct, unharmed, loving what is good, keen, unhindered, beneficent, loving toward men, stedfast, sure, free from care, all powerful, all-surveying, and penetrating through all spirits that are quick of understanding, pure, most subtil: for wisdom is more mobile than any motion; yea, she pervadeth and penetrateth all things by reason of her pureness. For she is a breath of the power of God, and a clear effluence of the glory of the Almighty; therefore can nothing defiled find entrance into her. For she is an effulgence from everlasting light, and an unspotted mirror of the working of God, and an image of his goodness. And she, being one, hath power to do all things; and remaining in herself, reneweth all things: and from generation to generation passing into holy souls she maketh men friends of God and prophets. For nothing doth God love save him that dwelleth with wisdom. For she is fairer than the sun, and above all the constellations of the stars: being compared with light, she is found to be before it; for to the light of day succeedeth night, but against wisdom evil doth not prevail. . . .

Her I loved and sought out from my youth, and I sought to take her for my bride, and I became enamoured of her beauty. She glorifieth her noble birth in that it is given her to live with God, and the Sovereign Lord of all loved her. For she is initiated into the knowledge of God, and she chooseth out for him his works. But if riches are a desired possession in life, what is richer than wisdom, which worketh all things? And if understanding worketh, who more than wisdom is an artificer of the things that are? And if a man loveth righteousness, the fruits of wisdom's labour are virtues, for she teacheth soberness and understanding, righteousness and courage; and there is nothing in life for men more profitable than these. . . . When I am come into my house, I shall find rest with her; for converse with her hath no bitterness, and to live with her hath no pain, but gladness and joy. When I considered these things in myself, and took thought in my heart how that in kinship unto wisdom is immortality, and in her friendship is good delight, and in the labours of her hands is wealth that faileth not, and in assiduous communing with her is understanding, and great renown in having fellowship with her words, I went about seeking how to take her unto myself. Now I was a child of parts, and a good soul fell to my lot; nay rather, being good, I came into a body undefiled. But perceiving that I could not otherwise possess wisdom except God gave her me (yea and to know by whom the grace is given, this too came of understanding), I pleaded with the Lord and besought him, and with my whole heart I said,

O God of the fathers, and Lord who keepest thy mercy, who madest all things by thy word; and by thy wisdom thou formedst man, that he should have dominion over the creatures that were made by thee, and rule the world in holiness and righteousness, and execute judgement in uprightness of soul; give me wisdom, her that sitteth by thee on thy throne; and reject me not from among thy servants: because I am thy bondman and the son of thy handmaid, a man weak and short-lived, and of small power to understand judgement and laws. For even if a man be perfect among the sons of men, yet if the wisdom that cometh from thee be not with him, he shall be held in no account. Thou didst choose me before my brethren to be king of thy people, and to do judgement for thy sons and daughters. Thou gavest command to build a sanctuary in thy holy mountain, and an altar in the city of thy habitation, a copy of the holy tabernacle which thou preparedst aforehand from the beginning. And with thee is wisdom, which knoweth thy works, and was present when thou wast making the world, and which understandeth what is pleasing in thine eyes, and what is right according to thy commandments. Send her forth out of the holy heavens, and from the throne of thy glory bid her come, that being present with me she may toil with me, and that I may learn what is well-pleasing before thee. For she knoweth all things and hath understanding thereof, and in my doings she shall guide me in ways of soberness, and she shall guard me in her glory. And so shall my works be acceptable, and I shall judge thy people righteously, and I shall be worthy of my father's throne. For what man shall know the counsel of God? Or who shall conceive what the Lord willeth? For the thoughts of mortals are timorous, and our devices are prone to fail. For a corruptible body weigheth down the soul, and the earthy frame lieth heavy on a mind that is full of cares. And hardly do we divine the things that are on earth, and the things that are close at hand we find with labour; but the things that are in the heavens who ever yet traced out? And who ever gained knowledge of thy counsel, except thou gavest wisdom, and sentest thy holy spirit from on high? And it was thus that the ways of them which are on earth were corrected, and men were taught the things that are pleasing unto thee; and through wisdom were they saved.

THE WISDOM OF SOLOMON

The wolf also shall dwell with the lamb, and the leopard shall lie down with the kid; and the calf and the young lion and the fatling together; and a little child shall lead them.

And the cow and the bear shall feed; their young ones shall lie down together: and the lion shall eat straw like the ox.

And the sucking child shall play on the hole of the asp, and the weaned child shall put his hand on the cockatrice' den.

They shall not hurt nor destroy in all my holy mountain: for the earth shall be full of the knowledge of the Lord, as the waters cover the sea.

ISAIAH

THE END

Friend, let this be enough. If thou wouldst go on reading,
Go and thyself become the writing and the meaning.

ANGELUS SILESIUS

בָּרוּךְ אַתָּה יְיָ אֱלֹהֵינוּ מֶלֶךְ
הָעוֹלָם· שֶׁהֶחֱיָנוּ וְקִיְּמָנוּ
וְהִגִּיעָנוּ לַזְּמַן הַזֶּה·

NOTES ON WRITERS AND BOOKS, SOURCES AND ACKNOWLEDGMENTS, AND INDEX

NOTES ON WRITERS AND BOOKS

[I have written a note in the case of all writers who are dead—and of such books as the Zohar—except when it would clearly have been absurd to do so: and have preferred to err on the side of absurdity. I have written a note in the case of every living writer.]

Aaron Leib of Primishlan. Hasidic Rabbi, disciple of the Maggid of Zlotchov, who died about 1786.

Abélard, Peter. Scholastic philosopher. Held the Moral Theory of the Atonement, i.e. that Christ by his example moved men to love and repentance, and so effected their salvation. 1079–1142.

Alexander, Samuel. British philosopher, 1859–1938.

Amiel, Henri Frédéric. Swiss philosopher and critic, 1821–81.

Angelus Silesius. Pseudonym for Johann Scheffler, German physician and mystical poet, 1624–77.

Ansky, S. Jewish writer, 1863–1920.

Arika, Abba ("*Rab*"). Rabbi, A.D. 160–247.

Baalshem, The. Rabbi Israel ben Eliezer Baal Shem Tov ("Rabbi Israel, son of Eliezer, Master of the Good Name"), the leader of Hasidism, and one of the world's greatest religious geniuses. 1700–60.

Bentham, Jeremy. British philosopher and jurist, 1748–1832.

Berdyaev, Nicholas. Russian philosopher and theologian, 1874–1948.

Bhagavad-Gita, The. Perhaps the most famous book in Hindu religious literature, probably of some date between the fifth and second centuries B.C.

Bloy, Léon Marie. French writer and mystic, 1846–1917.

Boehme, Jakob. German mystic, 1575–1624.

Borrow, George Henry. British traveller and writer, 1803–81.

Bosanquet, Bernard. British philosopher, 1848–1923.

Bossuet, Jacques Bénigne. French divine, orator and writer, 1627–1704.

Bradley, Francis Herbert. British philosopher, 1846–1924.

Browne, Sir Thomas. British physician and writer, 1605–82.

Buber, Martin. Contemporary Israeli philosopher and theologian.

Bunam of Pzhysha. Hasidic Rabbi, d. 1827.

Caird, John. British divine and philosopher, 1820–98.

Capetanakis, Demetrios. Greek poet who wrote in English, and died in London during the war at the age of thirty-two.

Carpenter, Edward. British man of letters and social reformer, 1844–1929.

Chaitanya, Sri. Indian mystic, 1485–1533.

Chrysostom, St. John. Greek Father, 345–407.

Chuang Tzu. Chinese thinker of the fourth and third centuries B.C.

Clement of Alexandria. Christian philosopher, probably born about A.D. 150.

Cloud of Unknowing, The. A book by a British mystic of the fourteenth century.

Crescas, Chasdai. Jewish philosopher, 1340–1410.

Dickinson, G. Lowes. British man of letters, 1862–1932.

Dionysius the Areopagite. The "Pseudo-Dionysius", a Christian philosopher writing probably in the fifth century A.D. under the name of the Dionysius mentioned in Acts xvii. 34.

Donne, John. British poet and divine, 1573–1631.

Eckhart, Meister. German mystic, 1260?–1327.

Eleazer b. Azariah, Rabbi. Second century A.D.

Elimelekh of Lizhensk. Hasidic Rabbi, d. 1786.

Emerson, Ralph Waldo. American essayist, 1803–82.

Fénelon, François de Salignac de la Motte. French writer, Archbishop of Cambrai. 1651–1715.

Fleg, Edmond. Contemporary French writer on Jewish themes.

Fromm, Erich. Contemporary American psychologist.
Fuller, Thomas. British historian and divine, 1608–61.

Gamaliel III, Rabban. Third century A.D. Not to be confused with Gamaliel I of the Acts.
Gregory the Great, St. Pope. About 540–604.

Hafiz. Persian (Mohammedan) poet and mystic, d. 1388.
Hanokh of Alexander. Hasidic Rabbi, d. 1870.
Hargrave, John. Contemporary British writer.
Hasid, Hasidic, Hasidism. Hasid is a Hebrew word meaning "pious" or "devout." The word and its derivatives are used in this book with exclusive reference to the remarkable Jewish movement which originated in Podolia just before the middle of the eighteenth century under the inspiration of the Baalshem (*q.v.*), and which soon had millions of adherents, particularly in Eastern Europe. Martin Buber is its greatest contemporary interpreter. Louis I. Newman has well described the movement as follows: "Its chief emphasis has been upon a sense of mystical ecstasy in the communion of God and man; upon the joyful affirmation of life; upon compassion, charity and love; upon democracy and brotherhood between rich and poor; and upon the moral values of the religious system."
Hayyim of Krosno. Hasidic Rabbi, a disciple of the Baalshem (*q.v.*).
Hegel, Georg Wilhelm Friedrich. German philosopher, 1770–1831.
Heidegger, Martin. Contemporary German philosopher.
Herbert, George. British poet, 1593–1633.
Herrick, Robert. British poet, 1591–1674.
Hobhouse, Stephen. Contemporary British man of letters.
Hopkins, Gerard Manley. British poet, 1844–89.
Huxley, Aldous. Contemporary British novelist and man of letters.
Hylton, Walter. British mystic; probably d. 1396.

Ibsen, Henrik. Norwegian dramatist, 1828–1906.
Inge, W. R. Contemporary British philosopher and divine.

Isaak of Syria, St. Sixth-century Desert Father.
Israel of Koznitz. Hasidic Rabbi, d. 1814.
Israel of Rizhyn. Hasidic Rabbi, d. 1850.

Jalalu D-Din Rumi. Persian poet and mystic, 1207–73.
James, William. American psychologist and philosopher, 1842–1910.
Jaspers, Karl. Contemporary German philosopher.
Jefferies, Richard. British novelist and writer on the countryside, 1848–87.
Jerome, St. Christian scholar, about 340–420.
Johanan, Rabbi. Died A.D. 279.
John of the Cross, St. Spanish mystic, 1542–91.
Joshua b. Levi, Rabbi. Third century A.D.
Juliana of Norwich. British mystic, fourteenth and fifteenth centuries.
Jung, C. G. Contemporary Swiss psychologist and psychiatrist.

Kabir. Indian mystic, born probably about 1440.
Kierkegaard, Sören. Danish philosopher and theologian, 1813–55.

Lavelle, Louis. Contemporary French philosopher. Successor to Bergson and Le Roy at the Collège de France.
Law, William. British divine and mystic, greatly influenced by Jakob Boehme. 1686–1761.
Leibniz, Gottfried Wilhelm. German philosopher and mathematician, 1646–1716.
Lewis, H. D. Professor of Philosophy at University College, Bangor.
Luthardt, Christophe Ernst. Professor of Theology at the University of Leipzig, d. 1902.

Macmurray, John. Contemporary British philosopher.
Manu, The Code of. An ancient compilation of Hindu rules, moral teaching, etc.
Marcel, Gabriel. Contemporary French philosopher.

Marcus Aurelius Antoninus. Roman Emperor and Stoic philosopher. A.D. 121–180.

Mare, Walter de la. Contemporary British poet.

Maritain, Jacques. Contemporary French philosopher, theologian and sociologist.

Mechthild of Magdeburg. German poet and mystic, thirteenth century.

Meir, Rabbi. Second century A.D.

Mendel of Kosov. Hasidic Rabbi, d. 1825.

Mendel of Kotzk. Hasidic Rabbi, d. 1859.

Mendel of Rymanov. Hasidic Rabbi, d. 1815.

Meredith, George. British poet and novelist, 1828–1909.

Meynell, Alice. British poet, 1849–1922.

Midrash, The. Rabbinic homilies on the Bible, third to tenth centuries. Sifra and Tanhuma are Midrashic treatises.

Mirror of Perfection, The. Probably a Franciscan compilation of the fourteenth century.

Molinos, Miguel de. Spanish divine, 1640–97. Exponent of Quietism.

Moshe Leib of Sasov. Hasidic Rabbi, d. 1807.

Moshe of Kobryn. Hasidic Rabbi, d. 1858.

Nahman of Bratzlav. Hasidic Rabbi, d. 1810.

Nettleship, Richard Lewis. British philosopher, 1846–92.

Nicholas of Cusa. Philosopher and mystic, born at Cues on the Moselle in 1401. Became Cardinal.

Niebuhr, Reinhold. Contemporary American theologian and sociologist.

Origen. With Augustine, one of the two greatest theologians of the ancient church. About A.D. 185 to about A.D. 254.

Orphism. A Greek cult, of which Orpheus was the legendary founder.

Oxyrhynchus papyri. Two papyri found at Oxyrhynchus by Grenfell and Hunt in 1897 and 1903. Third century A.D.

Paracelsus, Theophrastus Bombast von Hohenheim. German physician and alchemist, about 1490–1541.

Paradise of the Fathers, The. "The Paradise or Garden of the Holy Fathers, being Histories of the Anchorites, Recluses, Monks, Coenobites and Ascetic Fathers of the Desert of Egypt between A.D. 250 and A.D. 400 *circiter*, compiled by Athanasius, Archbishop of Alexandria: Palladius, Bishop of Helenopolis: St. Jerome, and others."

Patmore, Coventry. British poet, 1823–96.

Péguy, Charles. French author, poet, Catholic, republican, socialist, patriot and Dreyfusard. 1873–1914.

Pelagius. British theologian, about A.D. 360 to about A.D. 420. His dispute with Augustine, which was of far-reaching importance, was a subtle and complicated affair, but came down to the following. Pelagius believed *simpliciter* that, by the grace of God, all men have freedom of will to choose good and reject evil. (The words "by the grace of God" are important.) Augustine believed that a man requires God's grace to use the freedom which God's grace has given.

Perez, Isaac Loeb. Jewish writer, 1851–1915.

Peter the Lombard. Bishop of Paris and pupil of Abélard (*q.v.*). Died 1160.

Philo. Jewish philosopher of Alexandria, born about the beginning of the Christian era.

Pico della Mirandola, Giovanni. Italian philosopher, theologian and cabalist, 1463–94.

Pinhas of Koretz. Hasidic Rabbi, died 1791.

Plotinus. Neoplatonic philosopher and mystic, born in Egypt A.D. 204 or 205, died 270.

Pringle-Pattison, A. S. British philosopher, 1856–1931.

Proust, Marcel. French novelist, 1871–1922.

Rafael of Bershad. Hasidic Rabbi, d. 1816.

Ramakrishna, Sri. Indian mystic, 1836–86.

Rashdall, Hastings. British philosopher and theologian. One of the greatest modern exponents of the Moral Theory of the Atonement. (See Abélard). 1858–1924.

Renan, Ernest. French philosopher and orientalist, 1823–92.

Rilke, Rainer Maria. German poet, 1875–1926.

Royce, Josiah. American philosopher, 1855–1916.

Russell, Bertrand. Contemporary British mathematician, philosopher and sociologist.

Ruskin, John. British writer and critic, 1819–1900.

Ruysbroeck, Jan van. Dutch mystic, 1293–1381.

Saint-Exupéry, Antoine de. French writer and aviator, 1900–45.

Sales, St. Francis de. Bishop of Geneva. 1567–1622.

Saltmarsh, John. "Preacher of the Gospel" and author of "Sparkles of Glory". Chaplain in Sir Thomas Fairfax's army.

Scholem, Gershom. Professor of Jewish Mysticism at the Hebrew University in Jerusalem.

Schweitzer, Albert. Contemporary German doctor, musician, theologian and servant of humanity.

Seraphim of Sarov, St. Russian monk, b. 1750–60, d. 1833.

Shelomo of Karlin. Hasidic Rabbi, d. 1792.

Shmelke of Nikolsburg. Hasidic Rabbi, d. 1778.

Sifra. See Midrash.

Simlai, Rabbi. Third century A.D.

Sitwell, Edith. Contemporary British poet.

Smith, John. Cambridge Platonist, 1618–52.

Soloviev, Vladimir. Russian philosopher and theologian, 1853–1900.

Spinoza, Baruch. Dutch philosopher, 1632–77.

Stawell, F. Melian. British classicist, 1869–1936.

Suso, Heinrich. German mystic, about 1300–66.

Suttie, Ian. British psychologist and psychiatrist, 1889–1935.

Symeon the New Theologian, St. Abbot of Saint-Mamas of Constantinople. ?949–1022.

Tagore, Rabindranath. Indian poet and writer, 1861–1941.

Tanhuma. See Midrash.

Tanna debe Eliyahu. Midrashic compilation of the second half of the tenth century, embodying much older material.
Temple, William. Archbishop of Canterbury. 1881–1944.
Teresa, St. Spanish mystic, 1515–82.
Theologia Germanica. One of the most beautiful works of German mysticism, written perhaps in the second half of the fourteenth century.
Thompson, Francis. British poet, 1859–1907.
Toller, Ernst. German playwright, poet, and fighter for human freedom, 1893–1939.
Traherne, Thomas. British poet, 1637?–74.

Underhill, Evelyn. British writer on mysticism, 1875–1941.
Upanishads, The. Hindu scriptures, 800–600 B.C.
Uri of Strelisk. Hasidic Rabbi, d. 1826.

Waley, Arthur. Contemporary British poet, writer and translator from the Chinese and Japanese.
Weizsäcker, Carl Friedrich von. Contemporary physicist.
Whichcote, Benjamin. British philosopher, 1609–83. Cambridge Platonist.
Whitehead, A. N. British mathematician and philosopher, 1861–1947.
Whitman, Walt. American poet, 1819–92.
Wild, Franz. Singer, contemporary with Beethoven.
Williams, Charles. British poet and novelist, 1886–1945.
Wust, Peter. German philosopher. Professor of Philosophy at the University of Cologne at the time of the first World War.

Yaakov Yitzhak of Lublin. Hasidic Rabbi, d. 1815.
Yehudi, The. Hasidic Rabbi, d. 1814.
Yerahmiel of Pzhysha. Hasidic Rabbi, son of the Yehudi (*q.v.*).
Yitzhak Meir of Ger. Hasidic Rabbi, d. 1866.

Zalman of Ladi. Hasidic Rabbi, d. 1813.
Zohar, The. A great work of Jewish mysticism. Perhaps 1290.
Zusya of Hanipol. Hasidic Rabbi, d. 1800.

SOURCES AND ACKNOWLEDGMENTS

My debt to my wife, in all the circumstances that produced this book, is one which (in the words, I think, of Oscar Wilde) "can happily never be repaid". My most loving thanks are due to Sheila Hodges, who has read the thing three or four times at various stages, and, apart from encouraging me, has suggested many valuable improvements. I am most grateful to Mrs. Namier for translating some Soloviev passages, to Madame Maria Kullman for translating some sentences of St. Isaak of Syria, to Professor Martin Buber for revising some translations of his work, and to Dr. W. A. M. Rose for preparing prose versions of some Angelus Silesius couplets—specially, in each case, for this book. I am indebted to Dr. Edith Sitwell for a particularly gracious courtesy. And I cordially thank Miss Rose Macaulay and Mr. H. F. Rubinstein for reading the manuscript at a very early stage, Mr. Geoffrey Watkins for the loan of some rare books, Mr. Colin Mason for preparing the versions of the music and Mr. W. Pecorini for copying them, and Mr. Arthur Penney, of the Camelot Press (the printers of the book), for exceptional kindness and care.

* * * * * *

I have sometimes given the source of a passage, as well as the name of the author, in the main text, but usually not; and I have sometimes retained the old spelling and sometimes not—according to whim.

* * * * * *

THE BIBLE. For the Old and New Testaments the Authorised Version has been used, except for the *Shema* (p.21), and except that chapter and verse numbers are not given, italics have been romanized, and the word 'Lord' is not printed in capitals. The Authorised Version is Crown Copyright, and is used by permission. For the *Shema*, I have used the Authorised Daily Prayer Book of the United Hebrew Congregations of the British Empire (which was translated by the late Rev. S. Singer). For the Apocrypha the Revised Version has been used, by permission of the University Presses of Oxford and Cambridge.

THE HEBREW PRAYER BOOK. The extracts are from the Authorised Daily Prayer Book (see above) and are printed by permission of the Singer Prayer Book Publication Committee.

* * * * * *

The citing of the names of authors, publishers and translators below will please be understood as acknowledging kind permission to reprint the relevant passages in the Anthology. The letter following a page number refers to the position of the passage on the page: thus 7a means the first passage that *begins* on page 7.

* * * * * *

ABÉLARD. The passage p. 45c is quoted by Hastings Rashdall in *The Idea of Atonement in Christian Theology* (Macmillan), and was no doubt translated by him. I thank the Executors as well as Messrs. Macmillan for permission. The passages p. 45d were translated by Dr. R. S. Franks (from Migne's *Patrologia*) and included in his *The Atonement* (Oxford University Press).

ALEXANDER, SAMUEL. From *Space, Time and Deity* (Macmillan). I thank the author's Executors for permission.

AMIEL, HENRI FRÉDÉRIC. From his *Journal* tr. by Mrs. Humphrey Ward (Macmillan).

ANGELUS SILESIUS. With a few exceptions, the verses have been rhymed by me from prose translations made by my friend Dr. W. A. M. Rose. The exceptions are pp. 57, 249, 477, which are from *The Spiritual Maxims of Angelus Silesius* tr. by Henry Bett (Epworth Press). The version of the couplet on p. 549 is from *The History of Nature* by C. F. von Weizsäcker tr. by Fred D. Wieck (University of Chicago Press).

ANSKY, S. From *The Dybbuk* tr. by Henry G. Alsberg and Winifred Katzin. I thank Messrs. Curtis Brown for permission on behalf of Messrs. Liveright, New York.

AQUINAS, ST. THOMAS. The passage is from the *Summa Theologica,* in a translation made by Fathers of the English Dominican Province (Burns Oates and Washbourne).

ARIKA, ABBA. Quoted in *A Short Survey of the Literature of Rabbinical and Mediaeval Judaism* by W. O. E. Oesterley and G. H. Box (S.P.C.K.)

AUGUSTINE, ST. From the *Confessions.*

BENTHAM, JEREMY. From *Theory of Legislation*.

BERDYAEV, NICHOLAS. From *Dostoevsky* tr. by Donald Attwater (Sheed and Ward)—pp. 51b, 94a, 99, 186b; *The End of Our Time* tr. by Donald Attwater (Sheed and Ward)—pp. 13c, 138c; *The Fate of Man in the Modern World* tr. by Donald A. Lowrie (S.C.M. Press)—pp. 9d, 10b, 38a, b, 211, 252, 272, 363, 407; and *Christianity and Class War* tr. by Donald Attwater (Sheed and Ward)—pp. 210, 216, 290.

BHAGAVAD-GITA. I have used the translation (published by Phoenix House under the title *The Song of God*) by Swami Prabhavananda and Christopher Isherwood.

BLOY, LÉON. From *Pilgrim of the Absolute, a Selection of his Writings edited by Raïssa Maritain* tr. by John Coleman and Harry Lorin Binsse (Eyre & Spottiswoode). I thank Pantheon Books (New York) for Canadian permission.

BOEHME. The passages on pp. 98, 169, 289 and 293 are from *The Threefold Life of Man* tr. by J. Sparrow, the translation having been corrected and amended (Watkins). The passage on p. 476 is translated by Willard Trask and quoted in Bernhart's Introduction to the *Theologica Germanica* (q.v.)

BORROW. From *Lavengro*.

BOSANQUET, BERNARD. From *The Value and Destiny of the Individual*. I thank Mrs. R. C. Bosanquet for permission.

BRADLEY, F. H. From *Appearance and Reality* (Clarendon Press).

BROWNE, SIR THOMAS. From *Religio Medici* and *Christian Morals*. I have used the text of the six-volume edition prepared by Geoffrey Keynes and published by Faber and Faber.

BUBER, MARTIN. From *Jewish Mysticism and the Legends of Baalshem* tr. by Lucy Cohen (Dent)—pp. 137, 351, 470; *Hasidism* (Philosophical Library, New York)—pp. 11, 96, 140d, 404, 406; and *Israel and the World* (Schocken Books, New York)—p. 140c. See also under "Hasidic Legends and Stories". Professor Buber has personally revised the translation of some passages from *Jewish Mysticism*.

THE BUDDHA. The passages on pp. 164, 170 are from *Some Sayings of the Buddha* tr. by F. L. Woodward (World's Classics, Oxford University Press).

CAIRD, JOHN. From *Introduction to the Philosophy of Religion*.

CAPETANAKIS, DEMETRIOS. From *Demetrios Capetanakis: a Greek Poet in England* (Lehmann).

CARPENTER, EDWARD. From *Towards Democracy* (Allen & Unwin).

CHESTERTON, G. K. Quoted in *Gilbert Keith Chesterton* by Maisie Ward (Sheed & Ward).

CHRISTIAN NEWS LETTER. I thank the Christian Frontier Council for permission.

CHRYSOSTOM, ST. JOHN. From the sermon *De Proditione Judae.*

CHUANG TZU. Translated by Arthur Waley in *Three Ways of Thought in Ancient China.* (Allen & Unwin).

CLEMENT OF ALEXANDRIA. From the *Protreptikos.*

CLOUD OF UNKNOWING. From the edition edited by Dom Justin McCann (Burns Oates and Washbourne).

CRESCAS, CHASDAI. Included in *A Book of Jewish Thoughts* by Dr. J. H. Hertz. I thank Mr. Samuel Hertz for permission.

DANTE. From the *Purgatorio.* I have used the version in Charles Williams' *The New Christian Year* (Oxford University Press).

DICKINSON, G. LOWES. From *A Modern Symposium* (Allen & Unwin).

DIONYSIUS THE AREOPAGITE. From *The Divine Names* tr. by C. E. Rolt (S.P.C.K.)

DONNE. The passage on p. 164 is from the Sermons.

DOSTOEVSKY. From *The Brothers Karamazov* tr. by Constance Garnett (Heinemann).

ECKHART, MEISTER. From the two-volume edition tr. by C. de B. Evans (Watkins).

ELEAZER b. AZARIAH. From *Ethics of the Fathers* in the Hebrew Prayer Book (q.v.)

EMERSON. Abridged by William James in *The Varieties of Religious Experience.*

ERASMUS. The passages on pp. 7, 9 are from the *De Libero Arbitrio;* that on p. 312 from the *Praise of Folly.*

FLEG, EDMOND. From *The Life of Moses* tr. by Stephen Haden Guest (Gollancz).

FROMM, ERICH. The passage on p. 11 is from *Man for Himself* (Kegan Paul). The other passages are from *The Fear of Freedom* (Kegan Paul).

FULLER, THOMAS. The passage on p. 126 is from *A Wounded Conscience;* that on p. 169 from *Good Thoughts in Bad Times.*

GAMALIEL III, RABBAN. From *Ethics of the Fathers* in the *Hebrew Prayer Book* (q.v.)

GOETHE. The following passages are from *Eckermann's Conversations* tr. by John Oxenford (Everyman's Library, Dent):

pp. 7, 293. The following passage is from W. H. van der Smissen's translation of *Faust* (Dent): 106b. The following passages are translated in *Goethe and Faust* by F. M. Stawell and G. Lowes Dickinson (Bell): 106a, c, 126 (from *Goethes Gespräche*, Biedermann), 176 (from *Maximen und Reflexionen* published by the Goethe-Gesellschaft, Weimar), 472, 490.

GREGORY THE GREAT, ST. From the *Dialogues*. I have used the translation in Charles Williams' *The New Christian Year* (Oxford University Press).

HAFIZ. From *Selection from the Rubaiyat and Odes of Hafiz* rendered into English Verse by a Member of the Persia Society of London (Watkins).

HASIDIC LEGENDS AND STORIES, AND SAYINGS OF HASIDIC RABBIS. The sources of these are *Tales of the Hasidim: the Early Masters* by Martin Buber tr. by Olga Marx (Schocken Books, New York); *Tales of the Hasidim: the Later Masters* (same author, translator and publisher); and the 800-page *The Hasidic Anthology*, translated, selected, compiled and arranged by Louis I. Newman, in collaboration with Samuel Spitz. From the Buber volumes come the following passages: pp. 8a, f, i, 11a, 57d, 95c, 125e, 169e, 186c, 230b, 249e, 276b, 289b, 291c, 302a, 304b, 308b, 340a, 341a, 389a (I have changed "exile" to "slavery"), 402c. From the Newman volume come the following passages: pp. 34f, 66, 125f, 126a, 128c, 130a, 179c, 180a, b, 181a, b, c, 182a, b, c, d, e, 183a, b, c, d, 184a, b, 226b, 227a, 252d, 289a, 303a, 305a, b, 308d, 309c, d, 340b, d, 341b, c, 342a, b, c, 361f, 395e. The following are from *Hasidism* by Martin Buber (Philosophical Library, New York); pp. 291d, e, 473a.

HEBREW MORNING SERVICE. From the Hebrew Prayer Book (q.v.)

HEIDEGGER, MARTIN. From an article *The Field Path* (World Review, Jan. 1950).

HOBHOUSE, STEPHEN. From *Selected Mystical Writings of William Law* ed. by Stephen Hobhouse (2nd ed., Rockliff).

HOPKINS, GERARD MANLEY. From *Poems of Gerard Manley Hopkins*, 3rd ed. (Oxford University Press). The prose passage on p. 292 is from *Note-books and Papers of Gerard Manley Hopkins* ed. by Humphry House (Oxford University Press).

HUXLEY, ALDOUS. From *Ends and Means* (Chatto & Windus).

HYLTON, WALTER. From *The Scale of Perfection, Newly Edited from MS. Sources by Evelyn Underhill* (Watkins).

IBSEN. The translation of *Peer Gynt* is by William and Charles Archer; that of *An Enemy of the People* by Mrs. E. Marx-Aveling. (Both Heinemann).

INGE, W. R. From *The Philosophy of Plotinus* (Longmans).

ISAAK OF SYRIA, ST. Translated by Maria Kullman.

JALALU D-DIN RUMI. The passage is my own adaptation of some sentences, put together in my own way, from the *Masnavi*. I have used as a basis (by kind permission of the publisher, Mr. Arthur Probsthain) Professor C. E. Wilson's version, but I alone am responsible for the adaptation.

JAMES, WILLIAM. The passages are from *The Varieties of Religious Experience*, except that on p. 142, which is from *The Will to Believe*. I thank Messrs. Paul R. Reynolds & Son of New York for permission.

JASPERS, KARL. From *Goethe and Our Future* (World Review, August 1949).

JEFFERIES, RICHARD. From *The Open Air*—p. 76; *The Life of the Fields*—p. 84; *The Story of My Heart*—p. 170.

JEROME, ST. From the *Dialogi contra pelagianos*.

JEWISH LEGENDS. That on p. 67 is from Fleg's (q.v.) *Life of Moses;* that on p. 139 is quoted in Erich Fromm's (q.v.) *Man for Himself*.

JOHANAN, RABBI. Included in *A Rabbinic Anthology* by C. G. Montefiore and H. Loewe (Macmillan).

JOHN OF THE CROSS, ST. The passages on pp. 175, 228, 231, 313 are from *The Living Flame of Love* tr. by David Lewis (Thomas Baker); that on p. 429 from *The Ascent of Mount Carmel*, in Professor Allison Peers' translation of the works (Burns Oates and Washbourne).

JOSHUA b. LEVI, RABBI. Included in *A Rabbinic Anthology* (See Johanan).

JULIANA OF NORWICH. From *Revelations of Divine Love*.

JUNG, C. G. The passages on pp. 95, 175, 234 are from *Modern Man in Search of a Soul* tr. by W. S. Dell and Cary F. Baynes (Kegan Paul). The passage on p. 236 is from *The Secret of the Golden Flower* tr. and explained by Richard Wilhelm with a European Commentary by C. G. Jung; tr. into English by Cary F. Baynes (Kegan Paul).

KABIR. From *One Hundred Poems of Kabir* tr. Rabindranath Tagore assisted by Evelyn Underhill (Macmillan). I thank the Trustees of Rabindranath Tagore as well as Messrs. Macmillan for permission.

KIERKEGAARD. The passages on pp. 8 and 172(a) are from the *Journals* tr. by Alexander Dru (Oxford University Press); those on pp. 172(b) and 417 from *Works of Love* tr. by David F. Swenson and Lillian Marvin Swenson (Oxford University Press and Princeton University Press).

LAVELLE, LOUIS. These passages are quoted in Paul Foulquié's *Existentialism* tr. by Kathleen Raine (Dennis Dobson).

LAW, WILLIAM. From *Selected Mystical Writings of William Law* ed. by Stephen Hobhouse (2nd ed., Rockliff).

LEWIS, H. D. From *Morals and the New Theology* (Gollancz).

MACMURRAY, JOHN. The passages on pp. 9, 408 are from *Freedom in the Modern World* (Faber and Faber); those on pp. 10 (e), 422 from *Reason and Emotion* (Faber and Faber); those on pp. 10 (f, g), 49 from *The Clue to History* (S.C.M. Press).

MANU, CODE OF. From *Indian Wisdom* by Sir Monier Monier-Williams (Luzac).

MARCEL, GABRIEL. The passage on p. 408 is quoted in Foulquié's *Existentialism* tr. by Kathleen Raine (Dennis Dobson). All other passages are from *Being and Having* tr. by Katharine Farrer (Dacre Press).

MARCUS AURELIUS. From the translation by C. R. Haines in the Loeb Classical Library, published by Heinemann.

MARE, WALTER DE LA. From the *Collected Poems* (Faber and Faber).

MARITAIN, JACQUES. From *Freedom in the Modern World* tr. by Richard O'Sullivan (Sheed & Ward).

MECHTHILD OF MAGDEBURG. Translated by Willard Trask and quoted in Bernhart's Introduction to the *Theologia Germanica* (q.v.)

MEIR, RABBI. The passage on p. 59 is quoted in Oesterley and Box (see Arika); that on p. 125 in Fleg's (q.v.) *Life of Moses.*

MEREDITH, GEORGE. I thank the Trustees as well as Messrs. Constable for permission. The extract on p. 7 is from *The Woods of Westermain.*

MEYNELL, ALICE. I thank Sir Francis Meynell for permission.

MIRROR OF PERFECTION. From "*The Little Flowers*" *and the Life of St. Francis with the* "*Mirror of Perfection*" (Everyman's Library, Dent). The *Mirror* is translated by Robert Steele.

MOLINOS. The abridgement is from *The Varieties of Religious Experience* by William James, q.v.

MORE, SIR THOMAS. Included in Charles Williams' *The New Christian Year* (Oxford University Press).

NETTLESHIP, R. L. From *Richard Lewis Nettleship, Lectures and Memories* (Macmillan). I thank Mr. David John for permission.

NICOLAS OF CUSA. From *The Vision of God* tr. by Emma Gurney Salter (Dent).

NIEBUHR, REINHOLD. The passage on p. 176 is from *An Interpretation of Christian Ethics* (S.C.M. Press). The story on p. 205 is quoted in *Moral Man and Immoral Society* from James B. Pratt's *India and its Faiths* (Constable).

ORIGEN. From the *Contra Celsum*.

OXYRHYNCHUS PAPYRI. From *The Apocryphal New Testament* tr. by M. R. James (Clarendon Press).

PARADISE OF THE FATHERS. Translated by Sir E. A. Wallis Budge (Chatto & Windus).

PÉGUY. From *Basic Verities* tr. by Ann and Julian Green (Kegan Paul).

PELAGIUS. The passage on p. 253 is from the *Pro Libero Arbitrio*, and is to be found in *The Anti-Pelagian Works of St. Augustine* tr. by Dr. Peter Holmes (T. & T. Clark). The passage on p. 254 is quoted by Niebuhr in *An Interpretation of Christian Ethics* (S.C.M. Press).

PEREZ, ISAAC LOEB. From *Stories and Pictures* tr. by Helena Frank (Jewish Publication Society of America).

PETER THE LOMBARD. From the *Sententiae*.

PHILO. Included in *A Book of Jewish Thoughts* (See Crescas)

PICO DELLA MIRANDOLA. From the *Oration on the Dignity of Man* tr. by Elizabeth Livermoore Forbes in *The Renaissance Philosophy of Man* ed. by Ernst Cassirer etc. (University of Chicago Press).

PLATO. The translations are by Benjamin Jowett.

PLOTINUS. The passage on p. 411 is from the first Ennead, tr. by Stephen MacKenna. I am grateful to Sir Ernest Debenham for permission. The passage on p. 471 is from the fifth Ennead, and is, I think, translated by Dean Inge, in whose *The Philosophy of Plotinus* (Longmans) it is cited.

PRINGLE-PATTISON, A. S. From *The Idea of God* (Clarendon Press).

PROUST. From *Swann's Way* tr. by C. K. Scott Moncrieff (Chatto & Windus).

RAMAKRISHNA. From *Ramakrishna: Prophet of New India* (the abridged *Gospel*) tr. by Swami Nikhilananda (Rider).

RASHDALL, HASTINGS. From *The Idea of Atonement in Christian Theology* (Macmillan). I am grateful to the Executors as well to Messrs. Macmillan for permission.

RENAN. From *The Life of Jesus* tr. by C. E. Wilbour (Everyman's Library, Dent).

RILKE. The following are from *Later Poems* tr. by J. B. Leishman (Hogarth Press): pp. 89, 430, 488, 489. The following is from imaginary letter "On God", quoted in *Later Poems:* p. 490. The following are from *Poems from the Book of Hours* tr. by Babette Deutsch (Vision Press): pp. 139, 141, 250, 474. The following is from a letter quoted in *Requiem and Other Poems* tr. by J. B. Leishman (Hogarth Press): p. 88.

ROYCE, JOSIAH. From *The World and the Individual* (Macmillan, New York). I am grateful to Mr. Stephen Royce for permission.

RUSKIN. From Modern Painters.

RUSSELL, BERTRAND. From *A Free Man's Worship* in *Mysticism and Logic* (Allen and Unwin).

SAINT-EXUPÉRY, ANTOINE DE. From *Flight to Arras* (Heinemann). I am grateful to Messrs. Harcourt, Brace of New York for Canadian permission.

SALES, ST. FRANCIS DE. From *Introduction to the Devout Life* tr. by the Rev. Thomas Barns (Methuen).

SALTMARSH, JOHN. From *Sparkles of Glory.*

SCHOLEM, GERSHOM. From *Major Trends in Jewish Mysticism* (Schocken Books, New York).

SCHWEITZER, ALBERT. The following are from *The Decay and Restoration of Civilization* tr. by C. T. Campion (Black): pp. 9, 217, 309. The following are from *Civilization and Ethics* tr. by C. T. Campion (Black): pp. 476, 517. The following is from *Indian Thought* tr. by Mrs. C. E. B. Russell (Hodder and Stoughton): p. 424. The following are from *Religion in Modern Civilization* (The Christian Century, Chicago): pp. 210, 339.

SERAPHIM OF SAROV, ST. From *St. Seraphim of Sarov* tr. by A. F. Dobbie-Bateman (S.P.C.K.)

SHELLEY. The prose passages are from *A Defence of Poetry.*

SIFRA. Included in *A Rabbinic Anthology* (See Johanan).

SIMLAI, RABBI. Included in *A Rabbinic Anthology* (See Johanan).

SITWELL, EDITH. From *The Canticle of the Rose* (Macmillan). The extract on p. 14 is from *Invocation.*

SMITH, JOHN. The passage on p. 396 is from *The Excellency and Nobleness of True Religion.* I am not sure of the provenance of the other passage, which is quoted in Inge's *Christian Mysticism* (Methuen).

SOLOVIEV. The passage on p. 9 is from *Lectures on Godmanhood,* with introduction by Peter Peter Zouboff (Dennis Dobson). The other passages are from *The Meaning of Love,* and have been translated by Julia de Beausobre (Mrs. Namier).

SPINOZA. The following are from the *Ethics* tr. by A. Boyle (Everyman's Library, Dent): pp. 93b, 127, 171, 172, 289, 310a, 310c, 316, 474, 475; the following from the *Short Treatise on God, Man, and his Well-Being* tr. by Dr. A. Wolf (Black): pp. 93d, 310b, 362, 393.

STAWELL, F. M., AND DICKINSON, G. LOWES. From *Goethe and Faust* (Bell).

SUSO, HEINRICH. From *The Life of Blessed Henry Suso by Himself* tr. by T. F. Knox (Methuen).

SUTTIE, IAN. From *The Origins of Love and Hate* (Kegan Paul).

TAGORE, RABINDRANATH. The following are from *Gitanjali* (Macmillan): pp. 87, 88a, 293, 442; the following from *Sādhanā* (Macmillan): pp. 88b, 109, 294, 482, 484; the following from *Creative Unity* (Macmillan): pp. 260, 485, 486a; and the following from *The Gardener* (Macmillan): p. 486b. I am grateful to the Trustees as well as to Messrs. Macmillan for permission.

TALMUD. The passages on pp. 34, 186, 301 are included in *A Rabbinic Anthology* (see Johanan); and those on pp. 179, 226 in *A Book of Jewish Thoughts* (see Crescas). That on p. 331 is quoted in *Israel and the World* by Martin Buber (q.v.)

TANHUMA. Included in *A Rabbinic Anthology* (see Johanan).

TANNA DEBE ELIYAHU. The passage on p. 228 (a) is included in *A Book of Jewish Thoughts* (see Crescas); that on p. 288 (c) in *A Rabbinic Anthology* (see Johanan).

TEMPLE, WILLIAM. From *Nature, Man and God* (Macmillan). I am grateful to Mrs. William Temple for permission.

TERESA, ST. From *The Interior Castle.* I am grateful to the Right Reverend the Lady Abbess of Stanbrook Abbey for permission to use the versions on pp. 128 and 147.

THEOLOGIA GERMANICA. From the edition with Susanna Winkworth's translation revised by Willard Trask to accord with Bernhart's version (Gollancz).

THOMPSON, FRANCIS. I am grateful to Sir Francis Meynell for permission.

TOLLER, ERNST. The passages on pp. 184, 252, 337 are from *Letters from Prison* tr. by R. Ellis Roberts (Bodley Head); that on p. 202 from *I was a German* (Bodley Head).

TOLSTOY. The passages on pp. 202, 331 are from *What I Believe* tr. by Aylmer Maude (World's Classics, Oxford University Press). The passage on p. 232 was "Englished" by Robert Bridges from a literal translation by Nevill Forbes, and is included in *The Spirit of Man* (Longmans).

TRAHERNE. From *The Poetical Works of Thomas Traherne* (P. J. and A. E. Dobell).

TURGENEV. From *Dream Tales and Prose Poems* tr. by Constance Garnett (Heinemann).

UNDERHILL, EVELYN. From *The Letters of Evelyn Underhill* (Longmans).

UPANISHADS. From *Indian Wisdom* by Sir Monier Monier-Williams (Luzac).

WALEY, ARTHUR. From *Three Ways of Thought in Ancient China* (Allen and Unwin). See also Chuang Tzu.

WEIZSÄCKER, C. F. VON. From *The History of Nature* tr. by Fred D. Wieck (University of Chicago Press).

WELLS, H. G. I am grateful to Mr. H. G. Wells' Executors for permission.

WHICHCOTE, BENJAMIN. From *Moral and Religious Aphorisms.*

WHITMAN. The passage on p. 261 is from *Starting from Paumanok.*

WILD, FRANZ. The story about Beethoven conducting is quoted in *Beethoven: the Search for Reality* by W. J. Turner (Dent) from Wild's autobiography. Spohr gives exactly the same account of this concert.

WILDE, OSCAR. From *De Profundis*—the complete version (Methuen). I am grateful to Mr. Vyvyan Holland for permission.

WILLIAMS, CHARLES. *The Place of the Lion* is shortly to be republished by Faber and Faber. I am grateful to Pearn, Pollinger and Higham, the late author's literary agents, for permission.

WUST, PETER. From *Peter Wust on the Nature of Piety* in *Being and Having* by Gabriel Marcel, tr. by Katherine Farrer (Dacre Press).

ZOHAR. The passage on p. 57 is included in *A Book of Jewish Thoughts* (see Crescas); that on p. 67 in *Zohar: Selected and Edited by Gershom Scholem* (Schocken Books, New York); that on p. 138 in Fleg's (q.v.) *Life of Moses*.

THE MUSIC

The sources are as follows: The first quotation on the title page, Stravinsky's *L'Oiseau de Feu* (reproduced by kind permission of J. and W. Chester, Ltd., London); the second, Berlioz' *L'Enfance du Christ;* the third, Mozart's *Magic Flute*. P. 30, Beethoven's Quartet in C sharp minor (opus 131); p. 42, Verdi's Requiem (by kind permission of G. Ricordi & Co., owners of the copyright); p. 56, Beethoven's Sixth Symphony; p. 92, Beethoven's Ninth Symphony; p. 124, Wagner's *Parsifal*; p. 134, Beethoven's *Fidelio*; p. 146, Beethoven's *Fidelio*; p. 224, Beethoven's Quartet in F (opus 135); p. 248, Beethoven's Fifth Symphony; p. 286, Beethoven's Quartet in C sharp minor (opus 131); p. 300, Gluck's *Orfeo*; p. 334, Berlioz' *L'Enfance du Christ*; p. 360, Beethoven's *Fidelio*; p. 392, Beethoven's Quartet in E flat (opus 127); p. 428, Mozart's *Magic Flute*; p. 459 sqq., Beethoven's Quartet in E flat (opus 127).

THE TITLE PAGE

The title page was designed and engraved by Reynolds Stone. The idea and the symbolism are taken from *Les Devises Heroiques* by Claude Paradin (Antwerp, 1562). Explaining the design, Paradin writes of "la grãde grace, que la bonté, benignité, & providence divine nous fait: nous envoyant annuellement une Revolution, coronnee de diversité de tous biens, s'entresuivans & tenans de prés, selõ leurs tems, & leurs saisons. Par le serpent, s'entend l'annee: en ensuivant l'Egiptienne antiquité."

INDEX